Europa Law Publishing, Groningen 2005

Fair Trading in EC Law

Fair Trading in EC Law

Information and Consumer Choice in the Internal Market

Dr. Malek Radeideh

Europa Law Publishing is a publishing company specializing in European Union Law and public international law.
For further information please contact Europa Law Publishing via email: info@europalawpublishing.com or visit our website at: www.europalawpublishing.com.

Typeset in Scala and Scala Sans, Graphic design by G2K Designers, Groningen/Amsterdam

NUR 828; ISBN 90-76871-40-x

British Library Cataloguing-in-Publication Data
A catalogue record for this book is available from the British Library

Preface

It is commonly understood that the evolution of EC trade law has been characterised by functional spillover. This means, in short, that the areas subjected to the influence of EC trade law range far more broadly than one might anticipate were one simply to read the text of the Treaty in a literal fashion, casting a particularly eager eye at the apparently reassuring declaration found in Article 5(1) EC that "The Community shall act within the limits of the powers conferred upon it by this Treaty and of the objectives assigned to it therein." Functional spillover might in part be attributable to a political and judicial environment that has been conducive to suppressing respect for the constitutionally fundamental principle of attributed competence. Article 5(1) EC rules out a self-authorisation by the EC of an expansion of its competence but on occasion one may readily suspect that the institutional momentum within the EC has brought about precisely such an expansionary self-authorisation. But it would mislead to adopt this as a complete narrative. There are perfectly good reasons why EC trade law has gained its remarkable depth and breadth. To make a market for Europe is not a narrow and technical exercise. Any national rule that impedes cross-border trade is put to the test of justification demanded by Articles 28 and 49 and consequently the European Court of Justice and its national judicial allies commonly have to consider the virtues of matters such as environmental or consumer protection, advanced through national regulatory devices, in the context of the competing claims to deregulation of the wider European market. So a judicial evaluation of the nature and purpose of environmental and consumer protection spills over from Treaty provisions ostensibly devoted to trade integration. And when the EC's political institutions develop a programme of legislative harmonisation pursuant to that famously functionally broad pair, Articles 94 and 95, they similarly engage in an exercise notionally aimed at improving the functioning of an integrated trading space for the EU but which must also involve an assessment of the quality of the regulatory environment. In short, whatever is subjected to the discipline of harmonisation becomes an EU regulatory responsibility. Trade law is built on an expansionist dynamic.

In this excellent and thought-provoking book Malek Radeideh uses this model as his springboard to examine what we may understand by the notion of "fair trading" in EC law. National rules that purport to promote fair trading may hinder cross-border trade and therefore it falls to courts to assess the nature and purpose of such rules. Diversity among national approaches to fair trading may generate a perceived need to harmonise regulatory intervention at European level, which obliges the EC legislature to make its own choices about the preferred regulatory techniques. The theme of Malek Radeideh's book holds that this material can and should be pieced together to provide a systematic understanding of what EC law envisages by notions of fair trading. It would undermine his quest were I to (ab)use this Preface by attempting a summary of his findings: suffice to conclude that I am sure that he has made a truly valuable contribution to the store of knowledge about how EC trade law brings about a re-shaping of patterns of market regulation in Europe. I am equally sure that anyone wishing to make a serious study of the likely effect of the proposed Directive on Unfair Commercial Practices will find this book simply invaluable, for it elucidates the constitutional and institutional rhythms that have shaped the EC's approach to fair trading hitherto. I am honoured to write this Preface and I have learned much from this book.

Stephen Weatherill
Oxford, November 2004

Acknowledgements

This book is a revised version of my PhD thesis, which I wrote during my employment at the Department of European and Economic Law at the Rijksuniversiteit Groningen, The Netherlands. Writing this book would not have been possible without the invaluable help of numerous people.

Laurence Gormley and Paul Nihoul were excellent thesis supervisors. They provided critical and constructive guidance, while leaving me at the same time the necessary freedom for developing my own ideas. I am very grateful for their experience and expertise, which I hope to have been able to incorporate into this book. Fabian Amtenbrink's amazing skill of combining professional criticism with amicable encouragement made him a brilliant co-supervisor. His constant readiness to discuss my ideas (or their absence) with me not only gave me vital mental support, but it also allowed me to complete the work on time. With Hans-W. Micklitz, Stephen Weatherill and Thomas Wilhelmsson as the external members of my reading committee I was moreover granted the great honour of having my thesis approved by three of the most distinguished experts in the field in Europe. I really appreciate this.

I would also like to thank the rest of my colleagues back in Groningen. Jochen Appeldoorn, Hans Borgesius, Gareth Davies, Barbara Hallebeek, Dimitry Kochenov, Hans Vedder, and Eveline Vonkeman provided an extraordinarily inspiring working environment. I am particularly happy about the bonds that have developed beyond the mere professional relationship.

I am heavily indebted to a lot of friends who backed and encouraged me in a multitude of different ways during the writing of this book. There are definitely too many of them to name them in an adequate way here. Fortunately, they are exactly the ones who know my sincere gratitude anyway. Yet, I would like to mention Tobias Schollak whose support in hard times was simply outstanding; it is to a considerable extent due to him that I have accomplished this book. Eleonora Rossi and Jaap van de Velden have not only become close friends, but they have proven to be the best paranymphs I could have had for the defence of my thesis. You and the unnamed – thank you all so much!

And yes, thanks also to the blessing of music. Listening to great music, going to fantastic concerts, and dancing to big beats have given me the ultimate drive to get this done.

Malek Radeideh
Berlin, November 2004

Contents

Notes to the Reader

- Articles without further indications refer to the Treaty establishing the European Community. Articles of the Treaty on European Union are followed by 'EU'. Articles without further indications in sections concerning a measure of secondary law refer to this measure.
- All references to Treaty Article numbers have tacitly been updated to reflect the numbering according to the Treaty of Amsterdam. Only Article numbers in direct quotations have not been altered, but they are followed by the current numbers in brackets.
- 'Court' or 'Court of Justice' refers to the European Court of Justice.
- 'At' in references to judgments refers to the paragraph number of the judgment. Where the paragraphs of the judgment are not numbered, 'at' refers to the page number in the European Court Reports.
- Cross-references in footnotes preceded by *supra* or *infra* concern sections of the same Chapter. Otherwise, the Chapter concerned is indicated.
- References to books in the footnotes usually feature a short title. It can unambiguously be related to the full title using the bibliography. The full titles to the abbreviations of journal titles will also be found in the bibliography.
- As a matter of principle, the analysis of Community documents is based on their English language version, except where indicated otherwise.
- Consumers have often been referred to in the plural in order to be gender neutral. Where the singular 'he' or 'his' is used, this is obviously to include the female gender and has been done so merely to facilitate the reading. Moreover, this approach follows that of the European Court of Justice.

Introduction

1 Fair trading – A deficiently analysed key area of Community law

Fair trading has played an important role in the national legal orders of the Member States since a long time before the existence of the European Community. Since the early days of the Community, the subject has moreover attracted much attention at EC level. In fact, the harmonisation of national fair trading laws has been on the Community's legislative agenda since the 1960s.[1] However, so far, the goal of introducing a general duty to trade fairly or a general duty not to trade unfairly has proven to be too ambitious. Several efforts towards comprehensive horizontal harmonisation have been made in this field, but, due to lack of political consensus, none of them has succeeded. Instead, a piecemeal approach has been pursued, resulting in the adoption of innumerable legislative instruments which, to greatly varying degrees, touch on the area of fair trading. Eventually, the idea of creating a general legislative framework for fair trading was reactivated and has resulted in a Commission proposal for a directive on unfair commercial practices and a Common Position by the Council thereon.[2] This new initiative constitutes compelling evidence that the issue of fair trading in EC law is as topical as ever.

While early efforts at horizontal harmonisation failed, Community fair trading law has not stood still at all. As indicated, the most obvious attempt to fill the gap has been the extensive adoption of sectoral legislation. Indeed, this has led to a respectable density of fair-trading rules at Community level, albeit limited in substance and field of application by their sectoral boundaries. At the same time, although perhaps somewhat more covertly, the Court of Justice has developed a general concept of fair trading on the basis of the Treaty's free movement provisions, when it was confronted with national fair trading rules which impede the free movement of goods and services within the Internal Market.

Community legislation relating to fair trading and the relevant case law of the Court of Justice have frequently been discussed individually, although the discussion clearly focuses on developments in secondary law, neglecting the binding framework provided by primary law as interpreted by the Court. What is lacking is a synthesising examination of the existing legal sources, which aims at establishing a homogenous concept of fair trading applicable in the current *acquis communautaire*, and which attaches the appropriate weight to the respective legal sources. It is suggested that Community Internal Market law provides such a homogenous concept of fair trading, that is to say a legal principle of fair trading. Identifying a principle of fair trading is not only enlightening as regards the ascertainment of presently valid Community law, but it is essential for the clarification of the normative background for future legislation.

---

1 See Chapter 2 at 2.1.

2 See Chapter 5 at 3.

2 The scope of this work

It is the aim of this work to identify a principle of fair trading in Community law, and to ascertain its content and the field of its application. Positively, the scope of the study is therefore determined by the notions 'fair trading', 'principle' and 'Community law', all of which have to be defined for the present purpose. On the negative side, national law, competition law, contract law and enforcement have been excluded from the scope.

2.1 Positive delimitation

2.1.1 Fair trading

It would be absurd to define the concept which is looked for before the quest has even begun. On the other hand, in order to find a particular concept, one must have an idea what one is looking for. This paradox can be resolved by not defining the principle of fair trading at the outset, but clarifying what it is to deal with for the present purposes.

Fair trading, as it is understood here, describes a market-behavioural standard in the pre-contractual or pre-transactional relationship between business and consumers. At the centre of fair trading is therefore any market conduct of business which aims at inducing the consumer to enter into a transaction, i.e. business conduct before a transactional decision has been made by the consumer. In most of the cases this decision is to buy or not to buy a good or service, that is to say to conclude or not to conclude a contract. However, since contract law is not within the scope of this study[3] and the definition of a 'contract' is disputable (and influenced by the national legal background), the term 'pre-contractual' is not meant technically, but involves any conceivable kind of factual transaction.[4]

'Trading' thus comprises the large variety of activities by which businesses attempt to sell their goods and services to consumers.[5] These activities are commonly described by terms as 'marketing practices', 'trade practices', 'commercial practices', 'sales promotion', 'advertising', or 'commercial communication'. The terms are used interchangeably in this study, as their meaning is considered to be within the presently proposed meaning of trading. However, the modern term 'commercial communication', as defined in Directive 2000/31 on electronic commerce, may illustrate best what 'trading' is about.[6] Article 2(f) of the Directive defines commercial communication as

---

3 See *infra* at 2.2.3.

4 For example, if the consumer is induced to give money to the trader although legally no contract has been concluded beforehand which put the consumer under such an obligation.

5 Cf. Howells/Wilhelmsson, *Consumer Law*, p. 165.

6 Directive 2000/31/EC on certain legal aspects of information society services, in particular electronic commerce, in the Internal Market (Directive on electronic commerce), OJ 2000 L 178/1.

> 'any form of communication designed to promote, directly or indirectly, the goods, services or image of a company, organisation or person pursuing a commercial, industrial or craft activity or exercising a regulated profession'.[7]

This definition indicates that communication is a necessity for any sales promotion and that 'trading' covers all kinds of marketing activities, given their communicative aspect. These activities may be product-related (e.g. packaging and labelling), price-related (e.g. price indications in general or special price offers), distribution-related (e.g. doorstep-selling or distance selling), or simply promotion-related (e.g. advertising on TV or cold-calling). Consequently, fair trading plays a role in the whole set of tools on which the successful marketing of a product from a business administrative point of view depends, the so-called 'marketing mix'.[8]

Fair trading, as it is discussed here, solely involves business-to-consumer relationships and not business-to-business relationships.[9] It thus concerns the economic interests of consumers in the sense of Article 153(1) of the Treaty. This approach is consistent with the current initiative for a directive on 'unfair commercial practices',[10] which likewise covers only business-to-consumer relations. As will be demonstrated, it matches furthermore the use of 'fair trading' by the Court as a mandatory requirement of public interest capable of justifying obstacles to free movement.[11] The understanding of fair trading as market conduct towards consumers does not mean that Community law concerning business-to-business commercial activities will be totally neglected. However,

---

7 In its Green Paper on Commercial Communications in the Internal Market, COM (96) 192 final, p. 1 the Commission pointed out that commercial communication was meant to include 'all forms of advertising, direct marketing, sponsorship, sales promotions and public relations promoting products and services'. See also the follow-up to the Green Paper COM (98) 121 final.

8 The commonly acknowledged elements of the marketing mix are: the product itself, its price, its promotion and its distribution, see Kotler/Armstrong/Saunders/Wong, *Principles of Marketing*, p. 97 et seq., Mercer, *Marketing*, p. 208 et seq., 214. The product determines to a very large extent the weights of each of the other elements of the marketing mix within the particular marketing strategy, O'Shaughnessy, *Competitive Marketing*, p. 99.

9 The definition of commercial communication in Directive 2000/31 quoted above, however, applies to business-to-business relationships as well. See moreover for the relationship of fair trading to competition law *infra* at 2.2.2.

10 See Chapter 5 at 3. 'Fair trading' was the term originally used by the Commission. The project for a new legislative proposal started out by the announcement of the Commission in its Consumer Policy Action Plan 1999-2001, COM (98) 696 final, p. 17 that it will 'examine the feasibility of a general legislative framework on fair trading'.

11 See Chapter 1 at 4.2.1.

it is a prerequisite for its analysis that this law applies to consumers as well.[12] Moreover, also in these cases only the consumer dimension will be considered.[13]

2.1.2 Principle

In a legal system, rules and principles can be regarded as the two basic embodiments of norms. While rules tend to set out specific conditions that make their application necessary and attach legal consequences to them, principles constitute the rules' conceptual fundament and explain the reasons for their existence. They are ideas with a considerable degree of abstraction that argue in a particular direction and have to be taken into account in the application of rules.[14]

Multiple rules relating to fair trading can be found in secondary law. What seems to be missing is a legal principle which underlies them. In national legal systems, these principles are mostly incorporated into general clauses featuring concepts as *bonos mores*, good or fair marketing practices, or unlawfulness.[15] In Community law, it seems, such a principle has not been spelled out. It is thus the aim of the study to detect the general conceptual fundament of Community fair trading law. This is what is understood by 'principle of fair trading'.

Before the discussion of the ambit of the principle in Chapter 4 the term 'general principle' of fair trading is deliberately avoided in order not to confuse it with so-called general principles of Community law. While a 'principle' of Community law comprises a general legal concept, it is suggested that a 'general principle' of Community law comprises a general legal concept which, additionally, is universally applicable within the entire realm of Community law. The extent of the field of application of the principle of fair trading is discussed in Chapter 4.

2.1.3 Community law

It is the intention of this work to establish a principle of fair trading in Community law.[16] This requires clarification insofar as this means

---

[12] Several directives contain rules on market behaviour which apply to consumer recipients and business recipients alike.

[13] For example, in the case of the imitation of a product, it would only be considered whether and to what extent consumers would be misled, while possible abuse of intellectual property rights in this context would be ignored.

[14] Cf. Dworkin, *Taking Rights Seriously*, p. 24 et seq.

[15] See the overview in the Green Paper on European Union Consumer Protection, COM (2001) 531, p. 6, and the analysis in Bultmann/Howells/Keßler/Micklitz/Radeideh/Reich/Stuyck/Voigt, *Fair Trading Vol. III*, p. 285 et seq. See also Alpa in Collins, *Directive on Unfair Commercial Practices*, p. 91 at p. 106.

[16] See for the exclusion of national law *infra* at 2.2.1.

that only legal and legally binding sources are examined. Political sources (such as declarations) and legally non-binding sources (such as recommendations) are referred to, however, where it seems appropriate.

As a matter of fact, it is Internal Market law as a sub-category of Community law, which is at the centre of this study.[17] Given that fair trading has been described as concerning market behaviour, the link to the Internal Market results from the very notion itself. Fair trading is therefore particularly related to Internal Market law as a part of Community law as a whole.[18] In particular when it comes to the field of application of the principle of fair trading, the legal analysis is complemented by some market-theoretical and economic considerations with regard to the Internal Market.[19] This is justified since the legal dimension of the Internal Market is closely connected to the objective of a properly functioning market in the economic sense.

In this context, it is necessary to clarify the use of the term 'Internal Market'. The notion has found its way into the Treaty by the Single European Act and is defined in the current Article 14(2) as 'an area without internal frontiers in which the free movement of goods, persons, services and capital is ensured in accordance with the provisions of this Treaty'. According to Article 3(1)(c) it is 'characterised by the abolition, as between Member States, of obstacles to the free movement of goods, persons, services and capital'. The original notion, which still today is to be found in the Treaty, is that of the 'Common Market'. The establishment of the Common Market is the 'first principal means' for the achievement of the objectives of the Community according to Article 2 and can be said to embrace in particular the Internal Market, a system ensuring undistorted competition, and a common commercial policy.[20] The Single Market, by contrast, is a notion which does not appear in the Treaty, but is used in more recent documents emanating from the Community institutions. It can be regarded as synonymous to the Internal Market.[21]

Strictly speaking, the Internal Market is thus a concept which is different from the wider concept of the Common Market. The legal relevance of the distinction becomes apparent in particular in connection with harmonisation. While harmonisation aiming at the establishment and functioning of the Common Market on the basis of Article 94 requires unanimity, qualified majority is sufficient for harmonisation aiming at the establishment and functioning of the Internal Market on the basis of Article 95. However, it is submitted, in the

---

17 See for the exclusion of competition law *infra* at 2.2.2.

18 See also Chapter 1 at 3., Chapter 3 at 4.2., Chapter 4 at 2.

19 See Chapter 4 at 2.2.

20 Kapteyn/VerLoren van Themaat, *Law of the European Communities*, 3rd ed., p. 122.

21 See Mortelmans (1998) 35 *CML Rev.* 101 at 107, who points out that there is a difference between the terms in English ('Internal Market', 'Single Market') and French ('marché intérieur', 'marché unique'), but only one term is used in German ('Binnenmarkt') and Dutch ('interne markt').

field at issue the difference plays virtually no role in practice, and the concept of the Internal Market is clearly dominant. Not only has Article 95 become the leading basis for harmonisation in consumer matters,[22] also in the reasoning of the Court the differences have vanished. For instance, the Court clearly applies competition reasoning in the context of the Internal Market,[23] which finds support in Article 3(1)(g).[24] For the present purposes, it will therefore be stuck to the notion of the Internal Market.[25]

2.2 Negative delimitation

2.2.1 National law

Fair trading is a concept which, indeed, has its origins in the national legal orders of the Member States.[26] It is suggested, however, that the mere reason for this is that the national orders predate the Community legal order. It is the aim of this work to establish a principle of fair trading genuinely stemming from Community law itself, which is legally independent from national law.[27] The legal source to be examined is therefore Community law and not the laws of the Member States.

Of course, the Community may develop its law by borrowing from national concepts. This is a well-known approach of the Court of Justice with regard

---

22 For fair trading legislation, Article 94 has not played any role since the introduction of Article 95 into the Treaty.

23 Case C-300/89 *Commission v Council ('Titanium Dioxide')* [1991] ECR I-2867 at 23, Case C-376/98 *Germany v Parliament and Council ('Tobacco Advertising')* [2000] ECR I-8419 at 106. For a critical reaction to the Court's inclusion of undistorted competition into the concept of the Internal Market, i.e. its 'continuing failure to draw a clear distinction between the concept of a common market and the concept of the internal market', see Gormley, (2002) 13 *EBLR* 517.

24 The Court concludes from Article 3(1)(g) that 'Article 85 [81] of the Treaty constitutes a fundamental provision which is essential for the accomplishment of the tasks entrusted to the Community and, in particular, for the functioning of the internal market', Case C-126/97 *Eco Swiss China Time Ltd v Benetton International NV* [1999] ECR I-3055 at 36, Case C-453/99 *Courage Ltd v Bernard Crehan and Bernard Crehan v Courage Ltd et al.* [2001] ECR I-6297 at 12.

25 Likewise Davies, *Internal Market Law*, p. 3.

26 For compilations concerning the legal situations in the Member States, including historical backgrounds, see e.g. Micklitz/Keßler, *Marketing Practices*, Schotthöfer, *Handbuch des Werberechts*, Schricker, *Recht der Werbung*, Schulze/Schulte-Nölke, *Analysis of National Fairness Laws*. The legislative roots of European national fair-trading law can be located in the law of torts of the French *code civil*, in particular its Article 1382, see Keßler/Micklitz, *Harmonisierung des Lauterkeitsrechts*, p. 30 et seq., Radeideh/Franck in Micklitz/Keßler, *Marketing Practices*, p. 76.

27 The legal independence of Community law from national law is settled case law since Case 6/64 *Flaminio Costa v E.N.E.L.* [1964] ECR 1141.

to several general principles of Community law, such as fundamental rights. National law then serves as a source to expose these legal concepts, which, ultimately, are considered proper principles of Community law. This, however, is clearly not the approach taken in the context of fair trading.[28] It will be demonstrated that Community law itself has been the origin for what has emerged as a concept of fair trading. This does not mean that secondary law may not have been inspired by national ideas on fair trading. However, being a source of inspiration does not render national law a genuine legal source for a principle of fair trading in Community law.

2.2.2 Competition law

The study does not deal with competition law in the strict sense. Community competition law consists of the 'rules on competition' as set out in the Treaty in Chapter 1 of Title VI (rules applying to undertakings and aides granted by States).[29] These rules aim at establishing and retaining undistorted competition within the Community, watching over the positions of undertakings in the market.[30] Although the Treaty does not further define the concept of competition,[31] its competition rules clearly apply to 'undertakings' and the Member States.[32] They do not, however, directly regulate market conduct of undertakings towards consumers,[33] which is what rules on fair trading do. Accordingly, 'fair trading' is not 'fair competition', a notion which appears in the Preamble of the Treaty and alludes to the goal of an efficiently competitive market from the competitor's perspective. Essentially, rules of competition law tend to focus on the conduct of competitors (sellers) towards each other, in order to maintain competition.[34] A concept of 'fair' competition can be said to aim at realising further political objectives, such as the support of small business.[35] In

---

28 See also Chapter 3 at 1.

29 Hildebrand, *Economic Analysis*, p. 8. See Kapteyn/VerLoren van Themaat, *Law of the European Communities*, 3rd ed., p. 773 for a wide understanding of competition policy, including the provisions on harmonisation.

30 See for the evolution of competition law in Europe beginning in the nineteenth century and based on the idea of protecting the freedom of competition Gerber, *Law and Competition*, p. 16 et seq. Cf. also Jones/Sufrin, *EC Competition Law*, p. 4 with an emphasis on effective competition.

31 See also Goyder, *EC Competition Law*, p. 9.

32 See Articles 81 et seq. and Articles 87 et seq. Cf. also Vogelaar/Stuyck/van Reeken, *Competition Law*, p. 17.

33 However, they do take into account the effects for consumers, see Article 81(3), Article 82(1)(a) and Article 82(1)(b). See also Reich in Gormley, *Current and Future Perspectives*, p. 127 at p. 133 et seq., Monti, (2002) 39 *CML Rev.* 1057 at 1075 et seq., Grundmann in Collins, *Directive on Unfair Commercial Practices*, p. 209 at p. 211.

34 Goyder, *EC Competition Law*, p. 9.

35 Nihoul, *Concurrence*, p. 15 names the objective of social cohesion.

a system of 'fair' competition it is thus not merely competition as such which is protected, but competition law serves as well to protect certain traders in order to guarantee fair market conditions for all competitors.[36] Fair trading, by contrast, takes the consumers' perspective and aims at guaranteeing fair market conditions for consumers.

The strict distinction between (fair) trading and (fair) competition is in line with the doctrine that notions of Community law must normally be given a uniform interpretation and one independent from national meanings.[37] This is important to note, since national connotations of 'competition law' may include the aspect of fair trading with consumers.[38] The national legal background obviously plays an important role in this context. This is why a purely Community law understanding of terms is proposed in this book in general.[39]

On the other hand, it is fairly uncontroversial that a system of effective competition is ultimately for the benefit of consumers.[40] This idea is taken up in some market-theoretical considerations of this study, given that the Treaty acknowledges undistorted competition in the Internal Market as being essential for the objectives of the Community (Article 3(1)(g)).[41] However, it is suggested that the question whether and to what extent Community competition law actually meets the standards of a framework for effective competition which then also guarantees fair trading (so that a separate fair-trading law would be superfluous) would have to be the subject of a separate study.

---

[36] Cf. Jones/Sufrin, *EC Competition Law*, p. 16.

[37] See Case 327/82 *Ekro BV Vee- en Vleeshandel v Produktschap voor Vee en Vlees* [1984] ECR 107 at 11. Subsequently, see Case C-287/98 *Luxemburg v Berthe Linster et al.* [2000] ECR I-6917 at 43, Case C-357/98 *R. v Secretary of State for the Home Department, ex parte Nana Yaa Konadu Yiadom* [2000] ECR I-9265 at 26, Case C-151/02 *Landeshauptstadt Kiel v Norbert Jaeger* [2003] ECR I-8389 at 58, Case C-236/01 *Monsanto Agricoltura Italia SpA et al. v Presidenza del Consiglio dei Ministri et al.* [2003] ECR I-8105 at 72.

[38] The terms get particularly mixed up in English texts by German authors. This can be explained by the fact that the German prohibition of – literally translated – 'unfair competition' (as codified in the German *Gesetz gegen den unlauteren Wettbewerb (UWG)*) comprises, *inter alia*, fair trading in the presently defined sense. By contrast, the French concept of *concurrence déloyale*, for instance, has not been developed for the interests of consumers, but is meant to protect competitors only, Calais-Auloy in Balate, *Unfair advertising*, p. 85 at p. 88. See Cseres, (2001) *REDC* 221 at 228 et seq. on how fair trading law has developed out of competition law in national legal orders.

[39] The term 'fair trading' is likewise largely used from the viewpoint of consumers' interest in Harvey/Parry, *Consumer Protection and Fair Trading*. Hermann/Jones, *Fair Trading*, by contrast, include cartels, mergers, and also intellectual property rights.

[40] Cf. Nihoul, *Concurrence*, p, 25 et seq. and p. 85 et seq., Vogelaar/Stuyck/van Reeken, *Competition Law*, p. 16.

[41] See Chapter 4 at 2.2.2.1. See also *supra* footnote 24 and footnote 33.

2.2.3 Contract law

There is no doubt that European contract law is a very popular subject these days among European legal academics. While it received much less attention in the early days of the integration process, European contract law is today even considered 'the core area not only for private law, but also of the internal market process'.[42] This judgment is based on the correct assumption that the Treaty's fundamental freedoms can practically only be fully exercised by the instrument of (cross-border) contracts.[43]

Much research has been done in order to establish a common European contract law.[44] It is suggested that all relevant approaches can in principle be traced back to two basic legal sources, that is common principles of the Member States and principles of the *acquis communautaire*. It is in particular the latter approach, which recognises that at the moment considerable elements of a European contract law already exist and do not need to be created.[45] The Commission's 2001 Communication on European contract law and its follow-ups granted the subject a prominent place on the political agenda and further stimulated the debate.[46]

---

42 Grundmann/Kerber/Weatherill in Grundmann/Kerber/Weatherill, *Party Autonomy*, p. 3 at p. 5 with further references.

43 It should be noted in this context, however, that the Court has proved reluctant so far to apply Article 28 to rules of contract law, see Case C-93/92 *CMC Motorradcenter v Pelin Baskiciogullari* [1993] ECR I-5009 with regard to the German principle of *culpa in contrahendo* (at 12: 'the restrictive effects which the said obligation to provide information might have on the free movement of goods are too uncertain and too indirect to warrant the conclusion that it is liable to hinder trade between Member States'). Rules of contract law may furthermore usually be 'certain selling arrangements' in the sense of Joined Cases C-267/91 and C-268/91 *Criminal proceedings against Bernard Keck and Daniel Mithouard* [1993] ECR I-6097 at 16, which excludes them under the specified conditions from the field of application of Article 28. See also Rott, (2003) 40 *CML Rev.* 1107 at 1113 et seq.

44 The literature on this subject is abundant. Any list of references within the limitations of the present study must necessarily be incomplete and is therefore omitted. See instead the recent overview on the various international research projects and networks by Wurmnest, (2003) 11 *ZEuP* 714 with further references. See also Alpa, (2003) 14 *EBLR* 379, who not only portrays the projects and results, but also clarifies what 'European Private Law' actually concerns. Staudenmayer, (2004) 27 *JCP* 269 discusses the place of the consumer within the process on European contract law with regard to recent initiatives taken by the Commission.

45 See also Micklitz, (1998) 6 *ZEuP* 253 and Micklitz in Grundmann/Kerber/Weatherill, *Party Autonomy*, p. 197 at p. 203.

46 Commission Communication on European Contract law, COM (2001) 398 final, OJ 2001 C 255/1. See also Commission Communication 'A more coherent European contract law – An action plan', COM (2003) 68 final, OJ 2003 C 63/1 and Commission Communication 'European Contract Law and the revision of the *acquis*: the way forward', COM (2004) 651 final.

Fair-trading law, as it is understood here, must be differentiated from contract law in the strict sense. Fair trading concerns the pre-contractual relationship between business and consumers rather than their contractual relationship. While fair trading relates to the conduct of business that eventually may or may not lead to the conclusion of a contract (the goal of making the consumer conclude the contract must be seen as the actual motivation of the business conduct),[47] contract law obviously deals with aspects related to the contract itself. Contractual fairness, for instance, which is the central subject matter of Directive 93/13 on unfair contract terms in consumer contracts,[48] is therefore outside the scope of this study. Fair trading concerns the way to the contract, not the contract itself. Sticking to the example of contract terms this implies the following: while contract law is concerned with banning unfair terms in consumer contracts, fair trading is concerned with informing consumers about the terms of the contract which they are going to conclude, so that they can make their economic decision.[49] The quality of the terms and the legal consequence of their use is a matter of contract law. The difference between contract law and fair trading law corresponds to a difference in their underlying objectives. While consumer protection in contract law aims at the compensation of unequal bargaining power,[50] fair trading aims at the proper functioning of the market.[51] Fair trading is relevant already before the bargaining situation.

---

47 Contract or any kind of transaction, see *supra* at 2.1.1. Most of the ubiquitous advertising presumably does not lead to the conclusion of a contract at all.

48 Directive 93/13/EEC on unfair terms in consumer contracts, OJ 1993 L 95/29, see especially the general clause in Article 3(1) of this Directive. For an evaluation of the practical effects of this Directive, based on an analysis of the European Database on Case Law about Unfair Contractual Terms (CLAB Europa), see Micklitz/Radeideh, (2003) 11 *ZEuP* 85.

49 Wilhelmsson in Schulze/Ebers/Grigoleit, Informationspflichten, p. 245 at p. 259 et seq. points out that Directive 93/13 indirectly contains pre-contractual information requirements in the form of the principle of transparency (Article 5) and the provision in no. 1(i) of the Annex, according to which a term is (indicated to be) unfair which aims at 'irrevocably binding the consumer to terms with which he had no real opportunity of becoming acquainted before the conclusion of the contract'. Indeed, some overlapping with fair trading can be seen here. However, also these provisions still remain focussed on the contractual sphere rather than on the pre-contractual one: Article 5 is actually a rule of interpretation (of contractual terms), and the consequence of an unfair clause (in the sense of No. 1(i) of the Annex or in any other way according to Article 3(1) of the Directive) is that it is not binding on the consumer according to Article 6 of the Directive. On this subject, see also Wolf in Grundmann/Kerber/Weatherill, *Party Autonomy*, p. 313.

50 In the case of standard contract terms, the bargaining power of the consumer is virtually reduced to zero. See also Joined Cases C-240/98 to C-244/98 *Océano Grupo Editorial SA v Rocío Murciano Quintero* [2000] ECR I-4941 at 25.

51 Reich, (2000) 164 *ZHR* 433 at 437. Schulte-Nölke in Schulze/Ebers/Grigoleit, *Informationspflichten*, p. 85 at 89 et seq. emphasises the market integration function of existing EC contract law. For the functions of contract law, see also the conceptual framework developed by Wilhelmsson in Wilhelmsson, *Critical Contract Law*, p. 9.

Of course, the pre-contractual phase plays also a role in contract law.[52] For example, pre-contractual statements may affect the question whether the good to be delivered will be in conformity with the contract.[53] Unfair pre-contractual behaviour may result in contractual liability, because a fiduciary relationship between the parties is assumed.[54] Inducing consumers into entering a contract by misleading them about certain details may not only constitute unfair trading, but may also affect the validity of the contract itself, because the declaration of intent was provoked by deception. However, this dimension of contract law, which is currently still predominantly governed by national law indeed, will be ignored in this study. It is the market behaviour aspect which is at the centre of focus here.

It is probably the contract-law concept of party autonomy which overlaps with fair trading to the greatest extent. Party autonomy in the Internal Market concerns the freedom to conclude (or not to conclude) contracts, to design the content of the contract, and to choose the law applicable to the contract.[55] This implies that restrictions of party autonomy are linked to restrictions of pre-contractual choices, which is what fair trading is about, as will be demonstrated. Both concepts are of crucial importance for the Internal Market process as such, since they are a necessary condition to take full advantage of the Treaty's fundamental freedoms.[56] Both concepts are concerned with the sovereignty of contractual parties as market actors.[57] Party autonomy looks at matters from the contractual perspective, fair trading from the market behavioural perspective. In addition, fair trading, within the meaning of the present study, is only

52 Collins in Collins, *Directive on Unfair Commercial Practices*, p. 1 at p. 36 et seq. speaks of the 'mutual interference' between the systems. Such a mutual interference will all the more be assumed, if the process of contracting under Community law is understood as a 'continuum', lasting from the first contact, over the pre-contractual stage, up to the conclusion of the contract and the post-contractual stage, see Micklitz, (2002) 13 *EBLR* 583 at 595, Micklitz/Keßler, (2003) 49 *WRP* 919 at 931. By contrast, Pfeiffer in Schulze/Ebers/Grigoleit, *Informationspflichten*, p. 103 at 110 et seq. stresses the necessity for a 'magic moment' of contract conclusion in view of legal certainty.

53 Cf. in particular Article 2(2)(d) of Directive 1999/44/EC on certain aspects of the sale of consumer goods and associated guarantees, OJ 1999 L 171/12. See Wilhelmsson in Collins, *Directive on Unfair Commercial Practices*, p. 223 at p. 229 et seq., who explains the liability for non-conformity of goods as a method of contract law enforcement of provisions on marketing.

54 Cf. the principle of *culpa in contrahendo* under German law (now § 311(2) BGB).

55 See e.g. Grundmann/Kerber/Weatherill in Grundmann/Kerber/Weatherill, *Party Autonomy*, p. 3 at p. 4 et seq.

56 See Grundmann, (2002) 39 *CML Rev.* 269 at 270, for markets in general, see Kötz (2000) 9 *EJLE* 5 at 11.

57 Market-actor sovereignty is complex and depends on other factors as well. Prerequisite, for instance, is a system respecting individual property rights, cf. Kerber/Vanberg in Grundmann/Kerber/Weatherill, *Party Autonomy*, p. 49 et seq. Market-actor sovereignty may be considered a corollary of a democratic system, Keßler/Micklitz, *Harmonisierung des Lauterkeitsrechts*, p. 21, Nihoul, *Concurrence*, p. 50.

concerned with consumer sovereignty. However, the clear overlapping of both concepts entails that to a certain extent similar considerations are taken into account in this study to those relevant from the party-autonomy viewpoint. Nevertheless, these considerations fall here under the label 'fair trading'.

2.2.4 Enforcement

The study does not specifically deal with the enforcement of fair trading. Access to justice and effective legal protection of consumers are themselves subjects of such a magnitude that they could not possibly be dealt with adequately within the boundaries of this work.

The actual reason for the exclusion of enforcement, however, is related to the difference between rules and principles as suggested previously.[58] Rules may directly be enforced, provided that they grant enforceable rights and enforcement mechanisms are provided.[59] Principles, it is submitted, may not directly be enforced, but, by their function as an authoritative source of interpretation, serve as a vehicle for the enforcement of rules which they underlie. The study is concerned with the identification of a principle of fair trading. From an enforcement point of view, the question to be asked is therefore not how a principle of fair trading can be enforced, but which rules it underlies that, in turn, could be enforced. This means that it is necessary to ascertain the field of application of a possibly detected principle of fair trading. If it is determined which rules it underlies, the question of enforcement is then linked to those rules. Consequently, in this book not the enforcement but the ambit of the principle of fair trading will be discussed.[60]

3 Methodology and structure of this work

The examination of the existence of a principle of fair trading is guided by the two basic regulatory levels in Community law, namely primary law and secondary law. The distinction between the two levels in the analysis is of fundamental significance, since primary law constitutes the framework for the harmonisation of fair trading by secondary law. Accordingly, in Chapter 1 fair trading in the EC Treaty is explored, and in Chapter 2 fair trading in secondary law is analysed. Case law is not understood as a separate regulatory level, but, in accordance with Article 220, as a legal source of interpretation of both primary and secondary law. It follows from the scarce and vague indica-

---

58 See *supra* at 2.1.2.

59 This is the context in which the discussion of the relationship of rights and remedies in EC Law takes place, see Eilmansberger, (2004) 41 *CML Rev.* 1999.

60 See Chapter 4.

tions on fair trading in the Treaty that case law plays a far more significant role in the context of the analysis of primary law than in that of secondary law. As a consequence, Chapter 1 actually focuses on the case law on the free movement of goods and services. Besides, in Chapters 1 and 2 attention is paid to particular characteristics of the respective regulatory level, which are of importance not only for the content of a principle of fair trading but even more so for conclusions concerning its ambit.

After having analysed the fragmentary appearance of Community fair-trading law in Chapters 1 and 2, Chapter 3 provides a conclusion on the existence and the content of a principle of fair trading in the *acquis communautaire*. A concrete principle of fair trading is defined and its existence is demonstrated by means of a systematic reference to present fair trading rules. In Chapter 4 the ambit of the principle of fair trading is identified. For this purpose the field of application of the principle's legal sources, the methodology of the Court's reasoning, and the function of fair trading within Internal Market law are taken into account. Chapters 3 and 4 both feature conclusions on the principle of fair trading in EC law from a different perspective respectively (content and ambit). They are therefore to be understood as complementing each other.

Finally, in Chapter 5 a look at future legislative developments is taken in the light of the study's previous findings. For this purpose, the current proposal for an Unfair Commercial Practices Directive, which is to provide a general legislative framework for fair trading, is examined in its version of the Common Position adopted by the Council. The general concept comprised in the Directive is moreover compared with the Internal Market law principle of fair trading which has been ascertained, and the question is asked whether and to what extent the adoption of the Directive would entail added value.

CHAPTER I

Fair Trading in Primary Community Law

1 The significance of primary law

Typically, Community fair-trading law is contemplated on the basis of Community legislation. The number of directives relating to fair trading has grown substantially in the last decades, and their substance has become fairly dense. This makes secondary law an obvious source for analysis, and, indeed, Community fair-trading law from the perspective of secondary law will also thoroughly be examined separately in this study.[1]

Much less attention, by contrast, is paid to primary law, even though primary law is the first logical approach to fair trading in Community law in accordance with the hierarchy of legal norms. The fact that the Treaty is quite silent as far as direct statements on fair trading are concerned must not act as a deterrent to close analysis, since the gaps are impressively filled by case law. In fact, with the help of the case law of the Court of Justice the Treaty is revealed to be the key source when it comes to determining a principle of fair trading in Community law.[2]

The particular significance of primary law lies in its determination of the outer boundaries of the content and the ambit of a potential principle of fair trading.[3] Its analysis has logically priority over that of secondary law, since primary law sets the legal framework for secondary law.[4] The fundamental principle of conferred powers, codified in Article 5(1), is crucial in this respect. The Community institutions have no inherent powers, but they possess only those powers conferred on them and they must not go beyond these powers,[5] which makes it the leading principle for the division of powers between the Community and the Member States.[6]

The most obvious implication of the doctrine of conferred powers is that Community-created law requires a legal basis in primary Community law.[7] This aspect has recently received fresh impetus by the judgment of the Court

---

1 See Chapter 2.

2 See also Drexl, (2002) 13 *EBLR* 557 at 565 et seq.

3 This is further discussed in Chapter 4 at 2.1.1.

4 Simon, *Système juridique*, p. 211.

5 See e.g. Case C-327/91 *France v Commission* [1994] ECR I-3641, Case C-426/93 *Germany v Council* [1995] ECR I-3723; Hartley, *Foundations*, p. 105 et seq.; Kapteyn/VerLoren van Themaat, *Law of the European Communities*, 3rd ed., p. 233 et seq.

6 Slot, (2002) 13 *EBLR* 1 at 7. The idea of limited government by the principle of conferred powers is undermined, however, by the doctrine of implied powers, Douglas-Scott, *Constitutional Law*, p. 160. See also Case 8/55 *Fédération Charbonnière de Belgique v High Authority* [1954] ECR 245 at 299, Joined Cases 281, 283, 284, 285 and 287/85 *Germany v Commission* [1987] ECR 3203 at 28.

7 E.g. Joined Cases 80/77 and 81/77 *Société Les Commissionnaires Réunis SARL v Receveur des douanes* and *SARL Les fils de Henri Ramel v Receveur des douanes* [1978] ECR 927. See also Douglas-Scott, *Constitutional Law*, p. 163 et seq.

in *Tobacco Advertising*, which delimited the powers to legislate on the basis of the general harmonisation competence of Article 95,[8] and which has revived the general debate about the constitutional boundaries for harmonisation, particularly with regard to European private law.[9] The issue of the legal basis for harmonisation will extensively be discussed in connection with fair trading in secondary law.[10]

As an indirect consequence the concept of conferred powers assigns further significance to the case law of the Court, which observes the interpretation and application of Community law according to Article 220. With regard to fair trading, the Court therefore assumes a chief role not only in moulding a fair trading concept on the basis of the Treaty provisions, but also in determining the boundaries of secondary fair trading law: existing piecemeal legislation as well as a future general legislative framework for fair trading must not conflict with principles inherent in primary law as interpreted by the Court of Justice. The Court has developed the idea of dependence of secondary law on primary law further by holding that Community legislation cannot be interpreted as authorising Member States to impose conditions contrary to the Treaty rules.[11] This has then been further refined to the doctrine that all secondary law must be interpreted in the light of the Treaty rules on free movement.[12] In turn, this is coherent with the rule that not only national measures must obey free movement but also measures adopted by the Community institutions.[13]

It follows from the above that the understanding of the concepts inherent in primary law, as interpreted by the Court, is indispensable for the correct

---

8 Case C-376/98 *Germany v Parliament and Council ('Tobacco Advertising')* [2000] ECR I-8419.

9 Although the Commission's Communication on European contract law (COM (2001) 398 final, OJ 2001 C 255/1) does not refer to this aspect – it instead highlights possible problems of subsidiarity and proportionality – legal doctrine has indeed brought the logically prior question into focus of whether the Treaty is even able to provide a constitutional basis for a European contract law, see esp. Weatherill, (2001) 24 *JCP* 339 at 364 et seq., cf. also more generally Möstl, (2002) *EuR* 318 at 324 et seq. For an earlier analysis, see Picod in Osman, *Code européen de la consommation*, p. 73 et seq.

10 See Chapter 2 at 1.1.

11 Case C-47/90 *Établissements Delhaize frères et Compagnie Le Lion SA v Promalvin SA and AGE Bodegas Unidas SA* [1992] ECR I-3669 at 26. Subsequently, see e.g. Case C-14/00 *Commission v Italy* [2003] ECR I-513 at 66.

12 Case C-315/92 *Verband Sozialer Wettbewerb e.V. v Clinique Laboratoires SNC and Estée Lauder Cosmetics GmbH* [1994] ECR I-317 at 12. Subsequently, see e.g. Joined Cases C-427/93, C-429/93 and C-436/93 *Bristol-Myers Squibb et al.* [1996] ECR I-3457 at 27, Case C-220/98 *Estée Lauder Cosmetics GmbH & Co. OHG v Lancaster Group GmbH ('Lifting')* [2000] ECR I-117 at 25. See also Meyer in Schricker/Henning-Bodewig, *Neuordnung des Wettbewerbsrechts*, p. 93 at p. 107.

13 Case 15/83 *Denkavit Nederland BV v Hoofdproduktschap voor Akkerbouwprodukten* [1984] ECR 2171 at 15, Case C-51/93 *Meyhui NV v Schott Zwiesel Glaswerke AG* [1994] ECR I-3879 at 11, Case C-169/99 *Hans Schwarzkopf GmbH & Co. KG v Zentrale zur Bekämpfung unlauteren Wettbewerbs e.V.* [2001] ECR I-5901 at 37.

interpretation and application of Community fair-trading legislation. More importantly, however, primary law constitutes the legal backdrop against which a principle of fair trading must be considered.

2 From the laconic Treaty to expressive case law

The first source of reference in search of either a specific rule or a broader principle of Community law is undoubtedly the Treaty itself. At first glance it turns out, however, that 'the basic constitutional Charter'[14] of the European Community, is not very illuminating with regard to fair trading. This is true, at least, as far as direct statements are concerned. As a matter of fact, the Treaty does not contain a single provision which deals explicitly with fair trading.

Consumer protection provisions

Given that fair trading concerns trading with consumers, the Treaty provisions concerning consumer protection appear to be closest to the subject.

Formally, the only genuine consumer protection provision in the Treaty is Article 153. It is the only Article under Title XIV headed 'Consumer Protection' and was inserted by the Treaty of Maastricht (as ex Article 129a) and modified by the Treaty of Amsterdam. So far, however, this provision has had a limited impact on the development of consumer law.[15] Referring in Article 153(3)(a) to the general harmonisation provision of Article 95 on the one hand and restraining in Article 153(3)(b) further measures to supporting, supplementing and monitoring national consumer policies on the other hand, Article 153 has served political initiatives rather than as a legal basis for consumer-protection legislation.[16] However, the importance of Article 153 must not be underestimated as far

---

[14] Case 294/83 *Parti écologiste 'Les Verts' v European Parliament* [1986] ECR 1339 at 23, see also Opinion 1/91 [1991] ECR I-6079 at 1.

[15] Stuyck, (2000) 37 *CML Rev.* 367 at 379 et seq. Shortly after its introduction by the Treaty on European Union Micklitz/Weatherill, (1993) 16 *JCP* 285 at 298 et seq. had expected the provision to be of greater influence.

[16] Up to now, Directive 98/6/EC on consumer protection in the indication of the prices of products offered to consumers, OJ 1998 L 80/27 is the only directive exclusively based on Article 153, see Chapter 2 at 2.4. Advocate General Lenz has pointed out in his Opinion to Case C-192/94 *El Corte Inglés SA v Cristina Blázquez Rivero* [1996] ECR I-1281 at 29 et seq. that Article 153(3)(a) served in the first place to refer to the possibilities already available in the context of the completion of the Internal Market, with the difference that this provision committed the Community as a whole, while Article 95 only put the Commission under this duty. He further submitted that the competence provided by Article 153(3)(b) authorised the Community only to support and supplement the policy pursued by the Member States and hence to act only on an ancillary basis. Bearing in mind the principle of subsidiarity, it becomes clear that the impact of Article 153(3)(b) can only be limited. See also Amtenbrink/Schneider, (1999) 14 *VuR* 293 at 294.

as the role of consumer protection as a Community policy is concerned.[17] From a substantive point of view, Article 153 does not provide clear indications on fair trading. In the first paragraph it instructs the Community to contribute to protecting the economic interests of consumers, which can at least be construed as a link to the idea of fair trading. However, apart from the fact that such an interpretation allows to relate fair trading to the Community consumer policy, Article 153 does not further enlighten fair trading as a substantive Community concept.[18]

The second provision in this context, Article 95, is practically much more significant.[19] According to paragraph 3 of this general legal basis for harmonisation which has as object the establishment and functioning of the Internal Market, Commission proposals concerning consumer protection are to take as a base a high level of protection. The vast majority of European consumer legislation is based on Article 95, which underlines the fundamental connection between an operational Internal Market and a strong position of the consumer. However, also Article 95 does not define fair trading.

It will be demonstrated that Article 153 and Article 95 are indeed central Treaty provisions with regard to a principle of fair trading. Both provisions will be examined more closely with regard to their functions as legal bases for harmonisation,[20] the information they provide on the interrelationship between consumer protection and the Internal Market,[21] and whether and to what extent they allow conclusions concerning fair trading.[22] For the moment, however, suffice to establish that the Treaty's provisions dealing with consumer protection do not themselves directly suggest a Treaty concept of fair trading. Besides, these provisions' function as legal bases for Community legislation entails that relevant case law only deals with them with regard to that function. It is therefore submitted that there is no case law in which a substantive principle of fair trading is derived from those provisions.

Free movement provisions

The situation differs fundamentally as regards the Treaty's free movement provisions. Although, on the surface, they may seem less related to fair trading than the consumer protection provisions, it is on their basis that Court has developed substantial case law allowing sound conclusions on a principle of fair trading.[23]

---

[17] See also Chapter 4 at 2.1.3.1.

[18] The function of the consumers' 'right to information' is dealt with separately in Chapter 3 at 5.1.

[19] Added to the Treaty by the 1986 Single European Act as Article 100a.

[20] Chapter 2 at 1.1.

[21] Chapter 4 at 2.1.3.

[22] Chapter 3 at 5.1.

[23] See for example the overview of fair-trading related free-movement case law given by Lenz, (1994) 2 *ZEuP* 624 at 625 et seq.

A plain explanation for this development may be that the free movement provisions preceded the existence of those on consumer protection, given that they were included in the original Treaty. The main reason, however, is that fair trading turns out to concern significantly the Internal Market, which comprises an area of free movement according to Article 14(2). Alternatively, seen from the opposite side, fair trading is a perfect example that 'in the Internal Market, as in the Common Market, the consumer is envisaged as the ultimate beneficiary of the more efficiently functioning market'.[24]

The Treaty's free movement provisions have served as a basis for the Court to decide on national fair-trading rules, where those were applied in a cross-border context.[25] As a result, the interpretation of the Treaty's free movement provisions to permit national obstacles to trade justified on the ground of the prevention of unfair practices, which had begun as an interim protection of the interest or value concerned pending the adoption of Community legislation,[26] has become a fundamental yardstick when it comes to fair trading. Still today, with the existence of piecemeal Community legislation, case law therefore assumes a pivotal role among the sources of a principle of fair trading.

Given its vital function for finding a principle of fair trading in primary law, the rest of this chapter is dedicated to the case law of the Court. It will be demonstrated how the Court has developed a principle of fair trading on the basis of the concept of free movement. The actual analysis of the cases (section 5) is preceded, firstly, by an elaboration on the relationship between fair trading and free movement (section 3) and, secondly, by an outline of the conceptual framework in which the Court acts, which is to shed light on the Court's theoretical potential for developing a principle of fair trading (section 4).

---

[24] Howells/Weatherill, *Consumer Protection Law*, p. 84 (with reference at p. 83 to the 1992 Internal Market project as outlined in the 1985 Commission White Paper 'Completing the Internal Market' (COM (85) 310 final)). The Commission has continued to emphasise the benefits of a functioning Internal Market for the consumer ever since, e.g. in the Sutherland Report 'The Internal Market after 1992 – Meeting the Challenge', LET (1992) 3697, Follow-up, SEC (92) 2277 final. It has done so more recently in its Communication adopted on 24 November 1999 which sets out 'The Strategy for Europe's Internal Market' for the next five years (based on the consultative Communication COM (1999) 464) and in the 'Consumer Policy Strategy 2002–2006', COM (2002) 208 final, OJ 2002 C 137/2, welcomed by the Council Resolution in OJ 2003 C 11/1 (the Council recalled the positive impact of a well-functioning Internal Market in no. 3).

[25] Cf. Grundmann, *Europäisches Schuldvertragsrecht*, p. 48.

[26] Cf. Gormley, *Prohibiting Restrictions*, p. 52 et seq. and Gormley (1989) *LIEI* 9 at 20. See also Weatherill, (1999) 36 *CML Rev.* 51 at 82.

3 The relationship between fair trading and free movement

The Treaty's free movement provisions are the cornerstone of the Internal Market, their objective consisting in the abolition of obstacles to trade between Member States (Article 3(1)(c)). Despite their fundamental function for the Internal Market, the relationship between them and fair trading is not *per se* obvious. It will therefore be delineated which of the freedoms are relevant in this context and how the Court established the connection between them and fair trading.

3.1 The relevant freedoms

It follows from Article 3(1)(c) and Article 14(2) that the Internal Market comprises four freedoms, respectively relating to goods, persons, services, and capital.[27] Fair trading has been defined as setting behavioural standards for commercial communication targeted by business at consumers.[28] This implies that only those freedoms can reasonably be relevant which affect people in their quality as consumers. This, in turn, depends on the understanding of 'consumers'.[29] Yet, although the notion of consumers appears a couple of times in the Treaty,[30] a legal definition is missing. In secondary law, by contrast, consumers are usually defined, albeit often differently, according to the socio-economic context and functional criteria.[31] However, in order to determine the relevant freedoms for fair trading, a definition at Treaty level is necessary. It is suggested that in this context the consumer notion has to be brought down to its very basic idea, which is that consumers 'consume'.[32] The objects of consump-

---

27 In the same way Davies, *Internal Market Law*, p. 1 et seq. For the classification of the free movement of payments as a fifth freedom, see Kapteyn/VerLoren van Themaat, *Law of the European Communities*, 3rd ed., p. 575 et seq. and p. 765 et seq.

28 See Introduction at 2.1.1.

29 What matters in this context is the formalistic definition of consumers, i.e. which group of people is concerned, see also Chapter 3 at 3.1. This has to be distinguished sharply from the standard of the consumer, the so-called 'consumer image'. This standard, which serves as a yardstick for fair trading, applies only to those which are considered as 'consumers' in the first place, according to the formalistic definition of 'consumers'. The image of the consumer is dealt with *infra* at 5.3. and synthetically in Chapter 3 at 3.2.

30 Article 3(1)(t), Article 33(1)(e), Article 34(2), Article 81(3), Article 82(b), Article 87(2)(a), Article 95(3), Article 153, Article 257.

31 See Chapter 3 at 3.1.

32 Or they 'use'. This aspect becomes clearly apparent in other translations of the consumer notion in the Treaty: Article 33(1)(e) (Dutch: 'verbruikers'), Article 34(2) (Dutch: 'verbruikers'), Article 81(3) (Dutch: 'gebruikers', French: 'utilisateurs'), Article 82(b) (Dutch: 'verbruikers'), Article 87(2)(a) (Dutch: 'verbruikers'). The literal translations of 'consumers' would be 'consumenten' (Dutch) and 'consommateurs' (French).

tion are products, that is to say either goods, being material products, or services, being non-material products.[33] Adding to this the idea that consumers are people acting for private rather than professional purposes, consumers can be defined as 'every person who acquires goods or services in the Internal Market for private consumption'.[34] Thus concentrating on the consumption aspect as the decisive characteristic of consumers, it can be concluded that the free movement of goods and services are the only relevant fundamental freedoms with regard to fair trading.[35] This explains why, indeed, these are freedoms on the basis of which the Court has developed its fair trading case law. Hence, they are the freedoms analysed in this study.[36]

Although both freedoms are theoretically relevant, the amount of cases concerning the free movement of services is almost negligible compared to those concerning the free movement of goods.[37] It can sincerely be claimed that, at the level of primary law, fair trading case law is predominantly free movement of goods case law.[38] This corresponds to the common view that the free movement of goods is the archetype of the Treaty's free movement scheme, and that it has served as the prime basis for achieving market integration by the Court.[39] On the other hand, taking into account that the starting point of Article 28 is the prohibition of quantitative restrictions on imports of goods, it is less evident that its scope of application comprises commercial communication, given that commercial communication is immaterial. One explanation for the predominance of goods case law over services case law is certainly that, according to Arti-

---

33 It can be said that the free movement of goods and the free movement of services relate to products, while the other freedoms relate to production factors, cf. Snell, *Goods and Services*, p. 16 and Snell/Adenas in Adenas/Roth, *Services and Free Movement*, p. 69 at 71.

34 Reich in Gormley, *Current and Future Perspectives*, p. 127 at p. 127. Reich points out that consumer interests, on the other hand, are not easily defined. He states at p. 127 that they 'must be regarded as *diffuse interests* which cannot be described with relation to a specific group of persons but which are inherent to every person who acquires goods or services in the Internal Market for private consumption'. See also Reich in Wilhelmsson, *Critical Contract Law*, p. 55 at p. 55.

35 Of course, consumers can be at the same time workers, self-employed, or investors. However, these are coincidences. The point of reference of the other freedoms does not affect people in their specific quality as consumers. On the situation of citizens as consumers, see Reich, *Bürgerrechte*, p. 262 et seq.

36 This approach does not deny that there is an interrelationship between the freedoms. For instance, the free movement of services includes the freedom for the recipients of the service to go to another Member State to receive a service there (e.g. as tourists), see Joined Cases 286/82 and 26/83 *Luisi and Carbone v Ministero del Tesoro* [1984] ECR 377 at 16 and Case 186/87 *Ian William Cowan v Trésor public* [1989] ECR 195 at 15. However, it is still the service as the object of consumption, which is the point of reference and which implies further rights.

37 Cf. Schmid, *Dienstleistungsverkehr*, p. 257 et seq.

38 Cf. Beater, *Schutzzweckdenken*, p. 48, Henning-Bodewig/Schricker, (2002) 25 *E.I.P.R.* 271 at 272.

39 Cf. Craig/de Búrca, *EU Law Materials*, p. 613, Weatherill/Beaumont, *EU Law*, p. 500.

cle 50(1), the free movement of services is subsidiary to the other freedoms.[40] However, it has to be examined more closely in the following section how the Court has interpreted the scope of the free movement of goods so as to cover fair trading related rules. This is essential for the understanding of the Court's case law, because the Court can possibly express itself on fair trading only if the respective free movement scheme applies in the first place.

3.2 Fair trading and the scope of free movement

On the basis of the free movement of goods, as the principal freedom in this context, it will be examined to what extent fair trading comes under free movement. The question is therefore to what extent rules concerning commercial practices are covered by Article 28.

3.2.1 The basic principle

The pivotal notion for the Court's wide interpretation of the ambit of Article 28 is 'measures having equivalent effect' (to quantitative restrictions on imports). In *Dassonville* the Court held that

> '[a]ll trading rules enacted by Member States which are capable of hindering, directly or indirectly, actually or potentially, intra-Community trade are to be considered as measures having an effect equivalent to quantitative restrictions'.[41]

This broad definition of measures having equivalent effect, which is still today the 'basic principle of the free movement of goods',[42] could hardly exclude rules concerning sales promotion. A national rule requiring the adjustment of the marketing method of imports is certainly capable of hindering intra-Community trade. *Dassonville* itself concerned rules on the designation of imported goods, which is in fact a marketing issue. However, it took a few years until this was also noted more explicitly by the Court.[43] In *Oosthoek* it held with regard to a

---

40 See also Segnana, (2001) 9 *JTDE* 11.

41 Case 8/74 *Procureur du Roi v Benoît and Gustave Dassonville* [1974] ECR 837 at 5.

42 Gormley, *Prohibiting Restrictions*, p. 20.

43 Directive 70/50/EEC on the abolition of measures which have an effect equivalent to quantitative restrictions on imports, OJ 1970 L 13/29, the purpose of which was to abolish certain measures which were operative at the date of entry into force of the EEC Treaty has taken up the marketing question much earlier. Article 3 of the Directive reads: 'This Directive also covers measures governing the marketing of products which deal, in particular, with shape, size, weight, composition, presentation, identification or putting up and which are equally applicable to domestic and imported products, where the restrictive effect of such measures on the free movement of goods exceeds the effects intrinsic to trade rules. This is the case, in particular, where: the restrictive effects on the free movement of goods are out of proportion to their purpose; the same objective can be attained by other means which are less of a hindrance to trade'.

Dutch law which prohibited the offering or giving of free gifts for sales promotion purposes that

> '[l]egislation which restricts or prohibits certain forms of advertising and certain means of sales promotion may, although it does not directly affect imports, be such as to restrict their volume because it affects marketing opportunities for the imported products'.[44]

This observation, which has been confirmed in *Buet*[45] and subsequent judgments,[46] can be seen as the basic test in order to determine which of the fundamental freedoms applies. If the sales promotion concerns goods (and the national rule therefore affects the cross-border movement of goods), Article 28 applies. If the sales promotion concerns services (and the national rule therefore affects the cross-border movement of services), Article 49 applies.[47] It is thus not the quality of the sales promotion which is decisive, but the quality of its target (good or service).[48]

3.2.2 The *Keck* doctrine

With the introduction of the *Keck* doctrine the Court has restricted the scope of application of the free movement of goods and consequently confined its own potential to express itself on fair trading. In the landmark judgment *Keck and Mithouard* the Court namely held that

---

44 Case 286/81 *Oosthoek's Uitgeversmaatschappij B.V.* [1982] ECR 4575 at 15.

45 Case 382/87 *R. Buet and Educational Business Services (EBS) v Ministère public* [1989] ECR 1235 at 7.

46 For instance, in Case C-362/88 *GB-INNO-BM v Confédération du commerce luxembourgeois* [1990] ECR I-667 at 7, Case C-369/88 *Delattre* [1991] ECR I-1487 at 50, Case C-239/90 *SCP Boscher, Studer and Fromentin v SA British Motors Wright and others* [1991] ECR I-2023 at 14, Joined Cases C-1/90 and C-176/90 *Aragonesa de Publicidad Exterior SA and Publiva SAE v Departamento de Sanidad y Seguridad Social de la Generalitat de Cataluña* [1991] ECR I-4151 at 10 and Case C-126/91 *Schutzverband gegen Unwesen in der Wirtschaft e.V. v Yves Rocher GmbH* [1993] ECR I-2361 at 10.

47 See e.g. Case C-275/92 *Her Majesty's Customs and Excise v Gerhart Schindler and Jörg Schindler* [1994] ECR I-1039 at 37. This is to be distinguished from the situation where advertising itself is a service, i.e. in the relationship between the advertiser and the person whose products are advertised. This is a (contractual) business-to-business relationship, which has nothing to with fair trading in the present sense.

48 This is compatible with the Court's statement in Case C-71/02 *Herbert Karner Industrie-Auktionen GmbH v Troostwijk GmbH* [2004] ECR I-nyr at 47 that the dissemination of advertising is not an end in itself, but a secondary element in relation to the sale of the goods in question.

> '[...] contrary to what has previously been decided, the application to products from other Member States of national provisions restricting or prohibiting certain selling arrangements is not such as to hinder directly or indirectly, actually or potentially, trade between Member States within the meaning of the *Dassonville* judgment, so long as those provisions apply to all relevant traders operating within the national territory and so long as they affect in the same manner, in law and in fact, the marketing of domestic products and of those from other Member States'.[49]

It appears that, by taking rules on 'certain selling arrangements' out of the scope of Article 28 under certain conditions, the *Oosthoek* principle, according to which rules on marketing practices come under the free movement provisions, has become obsolete. However, two aspects have to be carefully differentiated. The first is the general interrelationship between trade practices and free movement. It is submitted that the *Keck* doctrine has not changed anything in this respect. The *Oosthoek* statement that rules on sales promotion can potentially affect the free movement of goods and services is as true as ever before.[50] Depending on whether the sales promotion is targeted at goods or services, the Treaty scheme on free movement of goods or free movement of services applies.

The novelty of *Keck and Mithouard* concerns a second aspect, which is that 'certain selling arrangements' fulfilling the conditions of the *Keck* proviso[51] are considered not to affect the integrating process of the Internal Market, so that regulatory diversity may prevail.[52] It follows from this aspect that certain rules on marketing practices have been excluded from judicial assessment. The effects of this exclusion with regard to a principle of fair trading (in particular the question whether the Court's pre-*Keck* findings are still good law post-*Keck*) will be carefully discussed at a later stage.[53] It is submitted that for an adequate assessment of the influence of the *Keck* doctrine on the case law on fair trading and on a principle of fair trading further knowledge of the pre-*Keck* situation is indispensable. Not before a picture of fair trading in case law has been drawn, it can be assessed in what ways this could be affected by *Keck*. For the moment it is therefore sufficient to establish that, as a matter of principle, rules on sales promotion are not as such excluded from the scope of Article 28 by *Keck*.

---

49 Joined Cases C-267/91 and C-268/91 *Criminal proceedings against Bernard Keck and Daniel Mithouard* [1993] ECR I-6097 at 16.

50 This is the reason why *Oosthoek* is at times still cited post-*Keck*, e.g. Case C-448/98 *Criminal proceedings against Jean-Pierre Guimont* [2000] ECR I-10663 at 21. See also the analysis by Greaves (1998) 23 *E.L.Rev.* 305 at 308 et seq., which is backed by the same idea.

51 The so-called *Keck* proviso is to be found in *Keck and Mithouard* at 16: '[...] so long as those provisions apply to all relevant traders operating within the national territory and so long as they affect in the same manner, in law and in fact, the marketing of domestic products and of those from other Member States'.

52 See Weatherill, *Cases and Materials*, p. 399.

53 See *infra* at 5.4.

4 The conceptual framework of the Court's judgments

The Court's contribution to a principle of fair trading has to be contemplated against the backdrop of the conceptual framework of its judgments. The external boundaries of this framework are represented by the concept of negative integration, which sets structural limits for the Court to express itself on fair trading (section 4.1). The internal margins are set by the source of a principle of fair trading in the Court's reasoning (section 4.2). The effective analysis of the fair trading case law requires the clear prior identification of this source.

4.1 Negative integration

The Court's potential of contributing to the substance of a principle of fair trading is linked to its market integrative power. In the context of Community market integration two fundamentally different concepts have to be distinguished from each other, which are commonly captured by the terms 'positive integration' and 'negative integration'.[54] Unlike Community legislation, which positively sets up particular standards and values with the intention of creating a common regulatory structure, i.e. in order to harmonise diverging national laws, the case law of the Court performs integration in a negative way.[55] It gets involved into the process of integration by dealing with national rules which restrict free movement within the Community. While enforcing the Treaty's free movement provisions, which contain prohibitions and not obligations, the Court may basically decide between two alternatives:

- it may uphold a restrictive national rule, because it does not contravene Community law (i.e. it does not interfere with Community law at all, or it is justified),
- it may outlaw a national measure, because it contravenes Community law (i.e. it constitutes a barrier to inter-Community trade which cannot be justified).

---

[54] The terms 'positive integration' and 'negative integration' can be traced back to the definitions given by Tinbergen, *International Economic Integration*, p. 76, according to whom 'negative integration' are measures consisting of the abolition of a number of impediments to the proper operation of an integrated area, whereas 'positive integration' is the creation of new institutions and their instruments or the modification of existing instruments. Cf. Kapteyn/VerLoren van Themaat, *Law of the European Communities*, 2nd ed., p. 79.

[55] See Howells/Weatherill, *Consumer Protection Law*, p. 85 et seq., Franzen, *Privatrechtsangleichung*, p. 10 et seq., Weatherill/Beaumont, *EU Law*, p. 554 et seq. Cf. Kapteyn/VerLoren van Themaat, *Law of the European Communities*, 3rd ed., p. 288 et seq. on the role of the Court in the process of integration in general.

In the first case, the fragmentation of legal rules in the Internal Market is maintained. In the second case, the Court does in principle approximate diverging national rules, however, not by creating a new common rule, but in a negative way by eliminating national regulatory differences, and only for cross-border situations.

Starting from the concept of negative integration inherent in free movement case law, it is therefore not self-evident that the Court delivers its own – positive – contribution to a principle of fair trading. This all the more the case taking into account that the particular measure at issue in a case before the Court represents a national standard of fairness: the starting point for the Court's assessment is thus a national one. By eliminating those rules incompatible with free movement the Court certainly evens out heterogeneous national rules affecting inter-Member-State trade. But it remains open whether and to what extent the Court is moreover capable of adding its own conceptions of fair trading, i.e. conceptions of a specifically Community-law nature.

This question is linked to the underlying nature of the Court's decision-making. Is the Court not more than the mouthpiece of the Treaty, as the wording of Article 220 may suggest? Or are the Court's statements rather policy-making beyond the mere application of the Treaty provisions? In fact, it is widely accepted that policy-making by the Court of Justice is a reality and, given the vagueness of some of the Treaty provisions, is actually inevitable.[56] There is, however, some controversy as to when and to what extent it is appropriate.[57] According to Rasmussen, three situations or degrees of policy-making can be distinguished.[58]

- In the first situation, the provision of Community law gives wide discretion to the Court. Considerable vagueness or ambiguity of wording provides the judges with more rationally defendable alternatives based on a public-policy decision. For instance, the interpretation of 'measures having equivalent effect' in Article 28 belongs to this category.[59]
- The second situation concerns silences in the Treaty on important points of law. The filling of these *lacunae* is much more problematic. It might

---

56 Cf. the analysis of the Court's legal reasoning by Benegoetxea/MacCormick/Moral Soriano in de Búrca/Weiler, *Court of Justice*, p. 41. As van Gerven in Hartkamp et al., *European Civil Code*, p. 91 at p. 92 notes, the Court's interpretation of directives is typically of a more limited nature, given their usually more precise wording compared to the Treaty provisions.

57 Cf. Arnull, *Court of Justice*, p. 38 et seq. and Kapteyn/VerLoren van Themaat, *Law of the European Communities*, 3rd ed., p. 291, both with further references. Constantinesco in O'Keeffe/Bavasso, *Liber Amicorum Lord Slynn of Hadley Vol. I*, p. 73 most elegantly sums up the factual situation as well as the discussion about it in the title of his paper: 'The ECJ as a Law-Maker: *Praeter aut Contra Legem?*'.

58 Rasmussen, *Law and Policy*, p. 25 et seq.

59 Gormley, *Prohibiting Restrictions*, p. 52 et seq. regards the creation of the rule of reason as an exception to the basic principle of the free movement of goods as a reflection of the *lacunae* in the Treaty.

well be just 'usual judicial business',[60] but it could as well be a transgression of judicial power. As an example of this category Rasmussen mentions the doctrine of the supremacy of Community law over national law.[61]

- In the third situation, the most grave judicial policy involvement, the Court reaches a decision in contrast to the textual indication in the Treaty. The Court's decisions on the European Parliament's status in the legislative process and its access to justice despite of the clear wording of the pre-Maastricht Article 173 EEC (now the amended Article 230) are a good example of this.[62] Yet, however far the Court may depart from the textual indications of a specific provision, it usually seeks to found its decisions on other indications rooted in the Treaty, be they as vague as the 'spirit' and the 'scheme' of the Treaty.[63]

These findings on the Court's approach of interpreting the Treaty provisions help to answer the initial question whether the concept of negative integration allows the Court to contribute to a Community concept of fair trading in deciding on national rules. Given that the Treaty remains significantly silent in matters of fair trading, not much can be expected from the Court regarding straight textual interpretation. The free movement provisions, on the other hand, belonging to Rasmussen's first category and giving wide discretion, induce the Court to go beyond mere application of provisions and pass to a considerable degree of policy making. This is the place where the Court devel-

---

60 Rasmussen, *Law and Policy*, p. 28.

61 In Case 6/64 *Flaminio Costa v E.N.E.L.* [1964] ECR 585 the Court developed this doctrine on the basis of a purposive and contextual interpretation of the Treaty. A much more crucial variation arose in Case C-213/89 *R. v Secretary of State for Transport, ex parte: Factortame Ltd et al.* [1990] ECR I-2433 on whether putative Community law rights have supremacy over clear provisions of national law. The Court answered the question in the affirmative by using the policy argument of the effectiveness of Community law which otherwise would be impaired (at 21).

62 In Case 294/83 *Parti écologiste 'Les Verts' v European Parliament* [1986] ECR 1339 the Court has accepted the admissibility of an action to review the legality of an act of the European Parliament – *légitimation passive* (because the Community is based on the rule of law, *Les Verts* at 23). In Case C-70/88 *European Parliament v Council ('Chernobyl')* [1990] ECR I-2041 the Court decided that the absence of a provision enabling the Parliament to bring an action for annulment (*légitimation active*) was a procedural gap that could not prevail over the fundamental interest in the maintenance and observance of the institutional balance laid down in the Treaty (*Chernobyl* at 26; here the Court departed from its decision of less than two years before in Case 302/87 *European Parliament v Council ('Comitology')* [1988] ECR 5615). Gormley in O'Keeffe/Bavasso, *Liber Amicorum Lord Slynn of Hadley Vol. I*, at p. 195 et seq. points out that the Court also considers itself to have the power to determine which of the effects of an annulled directive or decision should be declared definitive, although this conflicts with the wording of Article 231.

63 See e.g. Case 294/83 *Parti écologiste 'Les Verts' v European Parliament* [1986] ECR 1339 at 25.

ops Community trade law between the lines of the Treaty provisions. It is thus particularly in the context of free movement that the Court may contribute to a Community law principle of fair trading within the framework of negative integration.

4.2 The source of a principle of fair trading in the Court's reasoning

It has been demonstrated that statements on fair trading can be expected from the Court despite the limits of negative integration. Yet, it remains to be seen where within the line of the Court's reasoning they can possibly originate from. For an adequate analysis of the case law concerning fair trading, it seems necessary first to examine more carefully the underlying logic of the Court's reasoning.[64] This logic is primarily determined by the concrete provisions the Court has to interpret, that being, in the context of fair trading, the free movement provisions and the discretion they give.

4.2.1 Justification of a national rule as the starting point

Obstacle to trade

Due to the lack of specific rules on fair trading in primary Community law, the legal basis for the Court's judgment consists essentially in the free movement provisions of the Treaty, which are to ensure a functioning Internal Market by eliminating barriers to trade. The Court thus measures a national rule – in the present context a rule claimed to guarantee fair trading at the national level – against these Treaty provisions.[65] As long as the national rule does not produce an obstacle to intra-Community trade it is hardly necessary for the Court to further tackle the rule and elaborate in any way on the fairness standard it sets up.[66] Given that the Court of Justice is entrusted with the interpretation of Community law (Article 220), an assessment of a national rule which does not interfere with Community law would even rather fall outside the Court's jurisdiction. A closer inspection of the national rule is, as a matter of

---

64 This logic is going to be presented abstractly for the most part in this section. The following case law analysis will provide the practical references.

65 This typically happens under the mechanism of references for a preliminary ruling established by Article 234, which is 'the jewel in the Crown of the Community system' according to Gormley, (2001) 4 *Cam. YBELS* 167 at 168. Much more rarely, the review of national fair trading rules takes place in the context of an infringement proceeding under Article 226 (e.g. Case C-391/92 *Commission v Greece* [1995] ECR 1621, Case C-217/99 *Commission v Belgium ('Belgian Notification Numbers')* [2000] ECR I-10251, Case C-325/00 *Commission v Germany ('German quality label')* [2002] ECR I-9977).

66 This is exactly the point where the Court's doctrine developed in *Keck and Mithouard* comes into play. This will specifically be addressed *infra* at 5.4.

fact, only of relevance, if it is considered to be an obstacle to free movement. It is in this setting that the Court is likely to pronounce itself on fairness from the European perspective.

Justification

The existence of an obstacle to trade obviously brings up the question of a possible justification of the national measure.[67] It is precisely at this stage – the examination of whether the existence of the national rule can be justified, even though it impedes intra-Community trade – at which the actual assessment of the national measure takes place. It is also the stage at which reasoning on fair trading can be expected, since in order to assess the validity of a national rule the Court must take a stand on which interests the Member State can legitimately pursue and balance this interest to the objective of free movement.[68] A closer look will therefore be taken at the general reasoning behind the justification of a national measure. This allows the Court's views on fair trading to be identified as precisely as possible.

To begin with, it should be mentioned that justification under Article 30 plays virtually no role in connection with fair trading, as the legitimate interests of Article 30 are different from fair trading.[69] It is the so-called 'rule of reason' which assumes the crucial function. It serves as an additional possibility of justification of indistinctly applicable measures, alongside Article 30.[70] The rule of reason originates in *Dassonville*, where the Court held:

> 'In the absence of a Community system guaranteeing for consumers the authenticity of a product's designation of origin, if a Member State takes measures to prevent unfair practices in this connexion, it is however subject to the condition that these measures should be reasonable and that the means of proof required should not act as a hindrance to trade between Member States and should, in consequence, be accessible to all Community nationals'.[71]

It becomes clear from this formula that, in the absence of Community legislation, the free movement of goods is not absolutely and boundlessly guaranteed, but can very well be restricted beyond the possibility of justification according to

---

67 See Amtenbrink in Nordhausen, *Entwicklungen*, p. 53 at 58 et seq. for the relationship between the fundamental freedoms and public interests as a justification for their restrictions.

68 Dougan, (2000) 37 *CML Rev.* 853 at 857.

69 Of course this has not kept the Member States from relying on Article 30 in order to justify their restrictive 'fair trading' rules, e.g. by public health arguments as in *Cassis de Dijon* (see *infra* at 5.2.2) and *German Beer* (see *infra* at 5.3.1).

70 Cf. Gormley, *Prohibiting Restrictions*, p. 56 et seq.

71 Case 8/74 *Procureur du Roi v Benoît and Gustave Dassonville* [1974] ECR 837 at 6.

Article 30 by 'reasonable' national measures.[72] However, requiring the measures at the same time 'not to act as a hindrance to trade between Member States' sets an extremely high standard, which factually seems hardly possible to be met. In view of this, the rule-of-reason doctrine of *Dassonville* can be regarded as being not yet fully developed.[73] Nevertheless, *Dassonville* undoubtedly recognised that the prevention of unfair practices relating to consumers is a legitimate interest which may justify restrictions of the free movement of goods.

In *Cassis de Dijon*[74] the Court examined a German provision fixing the minimum alcohol content of specified categories of liqueurs and refined the rule of reason as follows:

> 'In the absence of common rules relating to the production and marketing of alcohol [...] it is for the Member States to regulate all matters relating to the production and marketing of alcohol and alcoholic beverages on their own territory. Obstacles to movement within the Community resulting from disparities between the national laws relating to the marketing of the products in question must be accepted in so far as those provisions may be recognized as being necessary in order to satisfy mandatory requirements relating in particular to the effectiveness of fiscal supervision, the protection of public health, the fairness of commercial transactions and the defence of the consumer'.[75]

Cassis de Dijon has thus not only refined the rule of reason as such but also the legitimate interests of justification, among them explicitly being 'the fairness of commercial transactions' and the 'the defence of the consumer'.[76] It is exactly

---

72 The Court added that the 'reasonable' restrictions 'must not, in any case, constitute a means of arbitrary discrimination or a disguised restriction on trade between Member States', *Dassonville* at 7. Moreover, it should be noted that in Case 33/74 *van Binsbergen v Bestuur van de Bedrijfsvereniging voor de Metaalnijverheid* [1974] ECR 1299 the rule of reason has for the first time been applied to the free movement of services. At 12 the Court held: 'However, taking into account the particular nature of the services to be provided, specific requirements imposed on the person providing the service cannot be considered incompatible with the Treaty where they have as their purpose the application of professional rules justified by the general good – in particular rules relating to organization, qualifications, professional ethics, supervision and liability – which are binding upon any person established in the State in which the service is provided, where the person providing the service would escape from the ambit of those rules being established in another Member State'.

73 Cf. Davies, (2003) 3 *ERA-Forum* 55 at 56. The question is whether measures must cumulatively be 'reasonable' and 'not act as a hindrance to trade' or whether 'reasonable' measures by design do 'not act as a hindrance to trade'. Since the Court has clarified the rule of reason in *Cassis de Dijon* an exhaustive discussion of the *Dassonville* conditions is obsolete.

74 Case 120/78 *Rewe-Zentral AG v Bundesmonopolverwaltung für Branntwein ('Cassis de Dijon')* [1979] ECR 649.

75 *Cassis de Dijon* at 8.

76 The list of mandatory requirements given in *Cassis de Dijon* is open.

these grounds of justification which constitute the relevant basis for the Court to articulate on fair trading.[77] It is striking, in this regard, that consumer protection and fair trading – these are the expressions regularly used in judgements subsequent to *Cassis de Dijon*[78] – are usually referred to as one fixed phrase by the Court. Efforts have been made to draw a clear distinction between the mandatory requirements of consumer protection and fair trading, and the way they are cited by the Court.[79] However, such a distinction seems, at least in the present context, quite artificial and does not help the elaboration of a synthetical portrait of fair trading.[80] It may occasionally happen that the Court – after confirming consumer protection and fair trading together to be mandatory requirements – only refers explicitly to consumer protection in its reasoning.[81] Yet, although the Court is not dependent solely upon the arguments which the parties choose to put before it,[82] in these cases it simply takes up the one-dimensional argumentation of the Member State, sometimes merely bringing up the objective of 'consumer protection', which the Court then elaborates on.[83] Although very rarely, this may also happen the other way around.[84]

---

77 Joliet, (1994) 43 *GRUR Int.* 1 at 11. See also Perau, *Werbeverbote*, p. 137.

78 The term 'fair trading' has first been used while applying the *Cassis de Dijon* rule-of-reason formula in Case 130/80 *Fabriek voor Hoogwaardige Voedingsprodukten Kelderman BV* [1981] ECR 527 at 6 and Case 193/80 *Commission v Italy ('Italian Vinegar')* [1981] ECR 3019 at 21 (it has been used before, but not in the *Cassis* formula, e.g. Case 27/80 *Fietje* [1980] ECR 3839 at 3. It has now more or less replaced the original term 'fairness of commercial transactions'.

79 See Ahlfeld, *Zwingende Erfordernisse*, p. 99 et seq.

80 Ahlfeld, *Zwingende Erfordernisse*, p. 99 et seq. admits that a clear demarcation line between the two mandatory requirements does not appear to exist and that in some judgments, at best, a certain tendency towards one or the other can be exposed. Cf. also Lettl, (2004) 50 *WRP* 1079 at 1084.

81 See also Niemöller, *Verbraucherleitbild*, p. 173 et seq. who argues that this is due to the Court's understanding of 'misconception' as implying consumer protection, which therefore makes consumer protection the core of the proportionality test in the misleading advertising cases.

82 However, the Court requires that the party at least claims the existence of a mandatory requirement justifying the obstacle; the Court does not conceive one by itself, cf. Case C-143/03 *Commission v Italy* [2004] ECR I-nyr at 32.

83 This is the case for example in Case 382/87 *R. Buet and Educational Business Services (EBS) v Ministère public* [1989] ECR 1235 (at 10 naming both consumer protection and fair trading, from 11 on focussing on consumer protection as the nationally offered ground of justification) and in Case C-362/88 *GB-INNO-BM v Confédération du commerce luxembourgeois* [1990] ECR I-667 (at 10 naming both consumer protection and fair trading, from 11 on focussing on consumer protection as the nationally offered ground of justification). Both judgments are cited by Ahlfeld, *Zwingende Erfordernisse*, p. 100 as only being considered from the point of view of consumer protection.

84 In Case 182/84 *Criminal proceedings against Miro BV* [1985] ECR 3731, for instance, the Court examined the Dutch prohibition to sell imported 'Jenever' with an alcohol content of less than 35 % solely under the requirement of fair trading. It did so, however, because the national court itself considered that the

4.2.2 Proportionality as the central source

The focal point of the judicial reasoning at the stage of justification can be narrowed down even further. Fair trading and consumer protection, being acknowledged legitimate objectives for the justification of a measure of equivalent effect, are themselves not questioned by the Court. Accordingly, if the national rule is claimed (usually by the national government) to aim at consumer protection and fair trading, the Court does not challenge these objectives, given that they are legitimate *per se*.[85] The reasoning rather focuses on the next step of the examination, namely whether the objectives are reasonably attained by the measure in issue.[86] This makes the question of proportionality the decisive stage of the compatibility test of a national fair trading rule with Community law.[87] It is the stage where the national fair trading standard is actually

---

prohibition was not justified by mandatory requirements of consumer protection (at 15). Fair trading was therefore the only remaining argument in the case. The Court nevertheless left no doubt that fair trading was connected with consumer protection ('purchaser is provided with proper information' at 25), although this was challenged by the Commission (at 19). In Case 407/85 *3 Glocken GmbH and Gertraud Kritzinger v USL Centro-Sud and Provincia autonoma di Bolzano* [1988] ECR 4233 the Court examined consumer protection and fair trading separately as two grounds of justification. However, it thereby merely took up the line of reasoning of the Italian Government. Consumer protection was related to transparency (at 16) and fair trading to the prevention of a misrepresentation (at 21). These are aspects which were jointly considered under consumer protection and fair trading in other judgments, as the following analysis will show.

85 These objectives have also not been challenged by the Court in Case 178/84 *Commission v Germany ('German Beer')* [1987] ECR 1227 on the German purity requirement (*Reinheitsgebot*) for beer. The rejection of the 'German Government's argument that Article 10 of the Biersteuergesetz is essential in order to protect German consumers [...]' (at 31) is just the introduction to the proportionality test ('essential' equivalent to 'necessary'). See also Case C-166/03 *Commission v France ('Gold Alloy')* [2004] ECR I-nyr (at 18: 'the provision [...] in question is admittedly intended to ensure fair trading and consumer protection'. At 19 the Court starts the proportionality reasoning: 'However [...].).

86 Advocate General VerLoren van Themaat pointed out in his Opinion in Case 286/81 *Oosthoek's Uitgeversmaatschappij B.V.* [1982] ECR 4590 at 4598 that the grounds justifying a restriction were primarily classified not under national law, but under Community law. In the context of the compatibility of the Dutch prohibition of free gifts he had raised doubts as to whether the criterion of related consumption or use – one of the exceptions to the Dutch prohibition – could justify the restriction of the free gifts scheme, since it appeared not to be based on the objective of fair trading, but rather on the protection of undertakings, which usually offered the gifts as part of their normal range of products. Both objectives had been forwarded by the Dutch side. The Court, however, did not question the validity of any of the objectives, but proceeded to examine the proportionality of the rule with regard to those objectives (at 17 and 20 of the judgment).

87 Accordingly, it is not the end (consumer protection and fair trading) which is the problem, but the means to achieve this end (i.e. it must be proportionate), Weatherill, *Consumer Law and Policy*, p. 48. See also Davies, *Nationality Discrimination*, p. 39.

evaluated and commented on from a Community law perspective, and which is consequently the origin of a Community concept of fair trading in case law. Therefore, the examination of the case law has to focus especially on this part of the reasoning.[88]

The principle of proportionality is one of the leading general principles of Community law. It was one of the earliest general principles articulated by the Court,[89] although its origin was not always clearly exposed.[90] The principle of proportionality is today reflected in Article 5(3) of the Treaty.[91]

Notwithstanding its central role, proportionality is far from being a uniform concept in Community law. In fact, the concept of proportionality appears in a number of different contexts in EC law, and its content varies depending on the context. According to Usher, three fundamental categories can be established where the principle of proportionality plays a leading role:[92]

- the determination of the competence or legislative capacity of the Community and its institutions,
- the legality of the burdens imposed on those subject to Community law,
- the legality of Member States' measures interfering with Community law.

The first category is the one to which the principle of proportionality as captured by Article 5(3) belongs. According to this provision, any action by the Community shall not go beyond what is necessary to achieve the objectives of the Treaty.[93] The definition given by the Court is somewhat more comprehensive:

---

88 See also Fezer, (2001) 47 *WRP* 989 at 992 et seq.

89 De Búrca in Bernitz/Nergelius, *General Principles*, p. 95; Emiliou, *Principle of Proportionality*, p. 134. As far as one can tell, the first case in which the Court referred to the principle of proportionality was Case 8/55 *Fédération Charbonnière de Belgique v High Authority* [1954] ECR 245 at 299.

90 National constitutional principles (in particular the German and French principles of proportionality), general principles of Community law, and specific Treaty provisions have been suggested as a source of the principle of proportionality in Community law. In early judgments, neither the Advocates General nor the Court discussed the origin of proportionality. The probably broadest discussion about the source of the principle of proportionality can be found in the Opinion of Advocate General Dutheillet de Lamothe Case 11/70 *Internationale Handelsgesellschaft mbh v Einfuhr- und Vorratsstelle für Getreide und Futtermittel* [1970] ECR 1140 at 1146 et seq.). See the overview given by Emiliou, *Principle of Proportionality*, p. 134 et seq.

91 The principle of proportionality has been introduced into the EC Treaty by the Treaty of Maastricht as ex Article 3b(3), together with the principle of subsidiarity (Article 5(2), ex Article 3b(2)). Both principles have been complemented by the Protocol on the application of the principles of subsidiarity and proportionality annexed by the Treaty of Amsterdam.

92 See Usher, *General Principles*, p. 37 et seq.

93 The Protocol on the application of the principles of subsidiarity and proportionality provides exactly the same definition in No. 1.

> '[...] the principle of proportionality requires that measures taken by the Community institutions should be appropriate to achieve the objective pursued without going beyond what is necessary to that end'.[94]

The second category (the consequences of a Community action) is much more governed by the case-law doctrine of proportionality. In *Fedesa*, which involved the question of the validity of Directive 88/146,[95] the Court held that by virtue of the principle of proportionality,

> '[...] the lawfulness of the prohibition of an economic activity is subject to the condition that the prohibitory measures are appropriate and necessary in order to achieve the objectives legitimately pursued by the legislation in question; when there is a choice between several appropriate measures recourse must be had to the least onerous, and the disadvantages caused must not be disproportionate to the aims pursued'.[96]

This concept alludes to the German constitutional principle of proportionality (*Verhältnismäßigkeitsprinzip*), which is derived from the principle of the rule of law (*Rechtsstaatsprinzip*),[97] and which requires the executive measure to be appropriate (suitable for the legitimate aim pursued), necessary (no less restrictive means available for the same effect) and proportionate in the narrow sense (adequate or fair means to the end, not excessive).[98]

The last category (the assessment of the conduct of Member States when they are acting within the scope of Community law) is the crucial one in the context of this study. Here, the question of proportionality largely arises in connection with national measures which, in principle, may be permissible under Community law but which restrict the exercise of the Treaty freedoms. A comprehensive summary of the application of the principle of proportionality in this area was given in *Gebhard*.[99] With regard to Italian legislation laying down the conditions for the use of the professional title of *avvocato*, the Court stated that national

94 Case C-359/92 *Germany v Council* [1994] ECR I-3681 at 44 referring to settled case law, in particular Case C-174/89 *Hoche* [1990] ECR I-2681 at 19.

95 Directive 88/146/EEC prohibiting the use in livestock farming of certain substances having a hormonal action, OJ 1988 L 70/16.

96 Case C-331/88 *R. v Minister of Agriculture, Fisheries and Food and Secretary of State for Health, ex parte: Fedesa and others* [1990] ECR I-4023 at 13.

97 Article 20(3) in connection with Articles 1(3), 19(4) and 28(1) first sentence of the German Constitution (*Grundgesetz*).

98 See Stern, *Staatsrecht, Bd. I*, § 20 IV 7 (p. 861 et seq.) with numerous references to the case law of the German Constitutional Court (*Bundesverfassungsgericht*).

99 Case C-55/94 *Reinhard Gebhard v Consiglio dell'Ordine degli Avvocati e Procuratori di Milano* [1995] ECR I-4165.

measures liable to hinder or make less attractive the exercise of fundamental freedoms guaranteed by the Treaty

> '[...] must be suitable for securing the attainment of the objective which they pursue and they must not go beyond what is necessary in order to attain it [...]'.[100]

More recently, the Court slightly modified this and held that administrative measures or penalties, which restricted the free movement of persons,

> '[...] must not go beyond what is strictly necessary for the objectives pursued and a penalty must not be so disproportionate to the gravity of the infringement that it becomes an obstacle to the freedoms enshrined in the Treaty [...]'.[101]

The definitions provided here for each category reflect the general tendency of the content of the principle of proportionality in the respective context, but it must be borne in mind that there are multiple variations on this principle – and that the Court itself is not very systematic in its approach of applying it.[102] However, a deeper doctrinal exploration of the principle of proportionality is neither fully feasible within the framework of this study,[103] nor is it required for its purpose. The significance for the present purpose lies in the understanding of the function of proportionality test as a 'weighing mechanism'.[104] It is used to weigh the national interest against the Community interest with the help of balancing standards, such as 'suitability', 'necessity' and 'appropriateness'. Those standards may be applied in various combinations and with different emphasis, but the underlying idea of weighing seemingly conflicting interests

---

[100] *Gebhard* at 37. The same formula is used e.g. in Case C-212/97 *Centros Ltd v Erhvervs- og Selskabsstyrelsen* [1999] ECR I-1459 at 34 and Case C-255/97 *Pfeiffer Großhandel GmbH v Löwa Warenhandel GmbH* [1999] ECR I-2835 at 23. The idea of the rule being 'suitable for securing the attainment of the objective pursued' can also be expressed differently, like e.g. being 'of such a nature as to protect [...]' in Joined Cases C-1/90 and C-176/90 *Aragonesa de Publicidad Exterior SA and Publiva SAE v Departamento de Sanidad y Seguridad Social de la Generalitat de Cataluña* [1991] ECR I-4151 at 14.

[101] Case C-262/99 *Paraskevas Louloudakis v Elliniko Dimosio* [2001] ECR I-5547 at 67.

[102] Kapteyn/VerLoren van Themaat, *Law of the European Communities*, 3rd ed., p. 656. See, on the other hand, the attempt of Jarvis to construe a two-stage test to which all the variations come down, but who admits difficulties regarding the relationship between those stages, Jarvis, *Application of EC Law*, p. 203 et seq.

[103] For a more comprehensive analysis, see in particular Emiliou, *Principle of Proportionality*.

[104] See Case C-169/91 *Council of the City of Stoke-on-Trent and Norwich City Council v B & Q plc.* [1992] ECR I-6635 at 15: 'Appraising the proportionality of national rules which pursue a legitimate aim under Community law involves weighing the national interest in attaining that aim against the Community interest in ensuring the free movement of goods'. See also de Búrca in Bernitz/Nergelius, *General Principles*, p. 95 at p. 97 'balancing principle'.

against each other (and thereby reconciling them) remains the same. This weighing process, which implies a judicial assessment of policy interests, is the point where fair trading is considered from a Community law perspective.[105]

In accordance with the aforesaid, the following examination of free movement case law is going to expose the idea of fair trading implied in the assessment of national rules by the Court using the mechanism of proportionality.

5 Free movement case law

5.1 The selection and presentation of the cases

As has been pointed out, the Treaty's provisions on the free movement of goods and services are the Court's gateway to pronounce itself on fair trading under primary law.[106] Therefore, it is the case law on these two fundamental freedoms which has to be further examined in order to come to grips with the content of a principle of fair trading.[107]

5.1.1 Selection

It is submitted that the main judgments that substantively contribute to a principle of fair trading are those in which the Court assesses the national measure explicitly in relation to the overriding requirements of consumer protection and fair trading.[108] These are the 'leading cases', which will be discussed in detail. Other cases, which are marketing related, but where the Court reasons on the basis of other grounds of justification, fulfil a supplementary function in the analysis or even have been left aside, since their substantive contribution to the shape of the Community law concept of fair trading is very much restricted.[109] This point can be illustrated by *German quality label*.[110]

---

[105] This idea is further developed in Chapter 4 at 2.1.2.2. in connection with the discussion of the ambit of the principle of fair trading. It is suggested that proportionality is used as a tool to redefine the national fair trading interest as a Community interest.

[106] See *supra* at 3.

[107] The case law relating to secondary law is examined in the context of the analysis of secondary law, see Chapter 2.

[108] In practice, this means that only those cases are concerned where consumer protection and fair trading have been advanced by the national governments (or sometimes the referring national court) as the underlying objective of the measure at issue.

[109] This strategy is derogated where exceptionally an added value has been attributed to other judgments, such as *Belgian Notification Numbers*, see *infra* at 5.2.6.

[110] Case C-325/00 *Commission v Germany ('German quality label')* [2002] ECR I-9977. The case is a modern variation of Case 249/81 *Commission v Ireland ('Buy Irish')* [1982] ECR 4005, Case 222/82 *Apple and*

German quality label involved the awarding of a quality label for produce made in Germany which fulfilled certain quality standards.[111] This scheme was easily recognised by the Court as a restriction on the free movement of goods, since it might encourage consumers to buy German products with the quality label to the exclusion of imported products. When it came to the possible justification of the contested scheme the Court did not lose a single word on whether it could be justified on the grounds of consumer protection and fair trading, although the information about the origin and quality of the product could have been claimed to be necessary for consumer protection and fair trading in that it enables the consumer to make an informed choice. As the German Government merely argued that the measure was justified by Article 30 as coming within the derogation for the protection of industrial and commercial property, the Court solely contemplated this aspect, which it finally dismissed.[112] Compared with the cases which reason on the basis of consumer protection and fair trading, the reasoning of a case such as *German quality label* obviously does not provide enormously constructive input to the definition of a Community principle of fair trading.[113]

Pear Development Council v K. J. Lewis Ltd. [1983] ECR 4083 and Case 207/83 *Commission v United Kingdom* [1985] ECR 1201. The cases are linked by the idea that campaigns to promote the purchase of domestic products or the mere origin-marking of products influences consumers' purchase choices to the detriment of imported products, which is contrary to Article 28.

111 The quality label was awarded by a limited liability company. However, the Court classified this scheme as a public measure attributable to the State. As to this aspect, see Jarvis, (2003) 40 *CML Rev.* 715 at 721 et seq.

112 Advocate General Jacobs briefly considered the application of Regulation 2081/92 on the protection of geographical indications and designations of origin for agricultural products and foodstuffs, OJ 1992 L 208/1, Opinion of Advocate General Jacobs Case C-325/00 *Commission v Germany ('German quality label')* [2002] ECR I-9977) at 37.

113 To this category of cases belong furthermore e.g. Case 16/83 *Criminal proceedings against Karl Prantl* [1984] ECR 1299 (no substantive elaboration on consumer protection and fair trading, but rather on public policy and protection of industrial and commercial property as grounds of justification under Article 30), Joined Cases C-1/90 and C-176/90 *Aragonesa de Publicidad Exterior SA and Publiva SAE v Departamento de Sanidad y Seguridad Social de la Generalitat de Cataluña* [1991] ECR I-4151 (public health as ground of justification under Article 30), Joined Cases C-321–324/94 *Criminal proceedings against Jacques Pistre et al.* [1997] ECR I-2343 (protection of industrial and commercial property as ground of justification under Article 30), Case C-368/95 *Vereinigte Familiapress Zeitungsverlags- und vertriebs GmbH v Heinrich Bauer Verlag* [1997] ECR I-3689 (press diversity as overriding requirement of public interest), Case C-405/98 *Konsumentombudsmannen (KO) v Gourmet International Products AB (GIP)* [2001] ECR I-1795 (public health as ground of justification under Article 30).

5.1.2 Presentation

It appears inappropriate to divide the presentation of the case law according to goods and services for a conceptual and a methodological reason.

It is the aim of the study to establish a principle of fair trading. Obviously, this is to be a universally applicable concept, irrespective of whether goods or services are commercially communicated. Goods and services are both products, the difference being that goods are material products and services are immaterial products.[114] It would make no sense for a principle of fair trading to attach different requirements to the commercial communication of goods and services just because they formally belong to either one or the other group of products. The idea of a principle of fair trading is that it attaches the same fairness requirements to the trading of all products. If the materiality of goods and the immateriality of services imply that the requirements of the fair trading principle are not met in the same way or that they are more difficult to meet for either of the categories,[115] this is just a consequence. It does not, however, affect the principle of fair trading as a uniform concept.

Moreover, the separation of goods and services case law is not methodologically indicated in the present context. It has been argued that the crucial moment for fair trading reasoning in the case law of the Court is the point of justification of a national measure. However, the justification of obstacles to the two freedoms follows the same pattern. This is suggested by *Gebhard* where the Court has put forward a common system of justification for all the fundamental freedoms.[116] It has recently been confirmed by Snell's comprehensive comparison of the relationship between the free movement of goods and the free movement of services. Snell demonstrated that, in spite of the differences that can be found in the schemes of the free movement of goods and services with regard to the notion of restriction and the addressee of Article 28 and Article 49, the Court's approach to the justification of measures falling within the scope of the freedoms is similar in both fields.[117] Not only has the Court interpreted the

[114] This reasoning also underlay the 1985 Commission White Paper 'Completing the Internal Market' with regard to 'financial products' (COM (85) 310 final at paragraph 102). The Court followed this reasoning e.g. in Case 205/84 *Commission v Germany* [1986] ECR 3755 at 46 by accepting, in principle, that the requirement of an authorisation for the provision of insurance services may be justified on grounds relating to the protection of the consumer in the sense of *Cassis de Dijon* (given the absence of Community legislation on the matter at the time).

[115] E.g. because goods convey certain information to consumers due to their mere physical presence, while in the context of services this information must actively be provided in order to achieve the same effect.

[116] See Case C-55/94 *Reinhard Gebhard v Consiglio dell'Ordine degli Avvocati e Procuratori di Milano* [1995] ECR I-4165 at 37.

[117] Snell, *Goods and Services*, in particular p. 169 et seq., p. 223 et seq.

differently worded Treaty exceptions in Article 30 and Article 46 similarly,[118] but, more importantly in the present context, it can be said that the system of judicially created exceptions is the same for both freedoms.[119]

The following presentation of the cases trails the two basic lines of reasoning to either of which, it is submitted, all the fair trading reasoning can be attributed. These are market transparency and the information of the consumer on the one hand, and a particular image of the consumer on the other hand. The case law suggests that transparency and consumer image are strongly interlinked, and, indeed, both aspects often appear jointly in the reasoning. However, they are emphasised to different degrees within the individual judgments, and the presentation tries to follow this emphasis.

5.2 Market transparency and consumer information

5.2.1 The start of fair trading reasoning

In *Dassonville*[120] the possibility of the justification beyond Article 30 of a national marketing practice rule was raised for the first time.[121] It is therefore also in *Dassonville* where the Court's fair trading reasoning commences.

The Court dealt with a Belgian provision prohibiting the import of goods bearing a designation of origin where such goods were not accompanied by an official document issued by the government of the exporting country certifying their right to such designation. The question of the compatibility of this rule with Community law was raised in criminal proceedings instituted in Belgium against traders who duly acquired a consignment of Scotch whisky in free circulation in France and imported it into Belgium without being in possession of a certificate of origin from the British customs authorities. The Court did believe the Belgian rule to pursue the objective of preventing unfair practices by guaranteeing for consumers the authenticity of a product's designation of origin. However, in the absence of Community measures in the field, such a measure had to fulfil certain objectives in order not to be prohibited: it had to be reasonable and the means of proof required had not to act as a hindrance to trade between Member States and, in consequence, to be accessible to all Community nationals.[122]

It can be deduced from the reasoning that a national rule preventing unfair marketing practices, and thus defending fair marketing practices, had to be

---

118 Snell, *Goods and Services*, p. 172 et seq., p. 223 et seq.

119 Snell, *Goods and Services*, p. 181 et seq., p. 223 et seq.

120 Case 8/74 *Procureur du Roi v Benoît and Gustave Dassonville* [1974] ECR 837.

121 See *supra* at 3.2.1.

122 *Dassonville* at 6. It has become clear subsequently that this applies to all, not just Community nationals.

reasonable (i.e. proportionate) and non-discriminatory in order to be compatible with Community law. This has allowed national intervention for the purpose of fair trading under those – not further expanded – conditions. Yet, the requirement that the measure should not act as a hindrance to trade between Member States, did not leave much room at that stage for any fair-trading legislation having inter-Member-State effects. If the importing Member State imposed obligations which are not imposed by the Member State of exportation, this would always mean some kind of hindrance to free movement. But despite the limited elucidation of the characteristics of a justified fair-trading measure, this judgment clearly marks the starting point of the European fair trading case law, which argues in favour of information rather than prohibition.

5.2.2 Information rather than prohibition

It has been pointed out before that since *Cassis de Dijon*[123] the 'fairness of commercial transactions and the defence of the consumer' have explicitly been recognised as overriding requirements of public interest within the rule of reason and that the original formula has evolved to a general justification test of consumer protection and fair trading.[124] Having started the information oriented reasoning of the Court, *Cassis de Dijon* has contributed more to fair trading than just coining the basic formula.

The Court had to decide on the compatibility with Community law of a German rule relating to the marketing of alcoholic beverages fixing a minimum alcoholic strength for various categories of alcoholic products. Whereas the fruit liqueur 'Cassis de Dijon' was freely marketed as such in France with an alcohol content of between 15% and 20%, the product was not allowed to be marketed under the same name in Germany, unless it had a minimum alcohol content of 25%. Regarding the protection of consumers against unfair commercial practices,[125] the German Government had claimed that the fixing of a lower limit for the alcohol content of certain liqueurs was designed to protect the consumer against unfair practices on the part of producers and distributors of alcoholic beverages. It submitted that the lowering of the alcohol content would secure a competitive advantage in relation to beverages with a higher alcohol content, as alcohol constituted the most expensive constituent of beverages due

[123] Case 120/78 *Rewe-Zentral AG v Bundesmonopolverwaltung für Branntwein ('Cassis de Dijon')*, [1979] ECR 649.

[124] See *supra* at 4.2.1.

[125] Arguments defending the German provision for its protection of public health have quickly been dismissed by the Court. The purpose of the fixing of minimum alcohol contents by national legislation in order to avoid the proliferation of alcoholic beverages on the national market were not decisive, since the consumer could obtain on the market an extremely wide range of weakly or moderately alcoholic products, *Cassis de Dijon* at 11.

to high taxes. In addition, the German Government feared that the fulfilment only with the legal requirements of the Member State of origin would have the effect of imposing as a common standard within the Community the lowest alcohol content permitted in any of the Member States,[126] and even of rendering any requirements in this field inoperative since a lower limit of this nature was foreign to the rules of several Member States.[127]

The Court did not really react to those arguments. It rather took up the reasoning of the Commission, according to which the fixing of limits in relation to the alcohol content of beverages might lead to the standardisation of products placed on the market and of their designations, which was in the interests of a greater transparency of commercial transactions and offers for sale to the public. The Court concluded, however, that the mandatory fixing of minimum alcohol contents was not an essential guarantee of the fairness of commercial transactions, since it was a simple matter to ensure that suitable information was conveyed to the purchaser by requiring the display of an indication of origin and of the alcohol content on the packaging of products.[128] The German requirement of a minimum alcoholic strength for 'Cassis de Dijon' did therefore not serve a purpose being in the general interest.

---

[126] *Cassis de Dijon* at 12. The argument that the principle of mutual recognition would lead to the acceptance of the lowest common denominator has rightly been countered by Gormley (1981) 6 *E.L.Rev.* 458. Gormley pointed out that stricter national standards could still be justified, if they were proportionate – or, described from another perspective, if the standards of the exporting country, with which the product in question complied, did not 'suitably and satisfactorily' fulfil the legitimate objectives of the importing Member State (the expression 'suitably and satisfactorily' has been borrowed from the Commission's Communication concerning the consequences of the judgment in *Cassis de Dijon*, OJ 1980 L 256/2, which was the central subject of Gormley's article). For the limits of the mutual-recognition approach, see also Case 188/84 *Commission v France ('French woodworking machines')* [1986] ECR 419 at 16 (decisive is an equivalent level of protection, not the adherence to exactly the same rules) and Case C-293/93 *Houtwipper* [1994] ECR I-4249 at 18–22 (self-testing and self-hallmarking of precious metal by the producers is not equivalent to a public guarantee by an independent body). The latter case is commented by Gormley (1996) 21 *E.L.Rev.* 44. See also Gormley in Bernitz/Nergelius, *General Principles*, p. 113 at p. 117.

[127] It should be noted that the 'race-to-the-bottom' argument has prevailed ever since. However, it has not the same weight in the mutual-recognition situation as in the context of the country of origin principle. Whereas in the first situation justification is in principle still possible, as has just been demonstrated (footnote 126), the country of origin principle does not allow this anymore. The country of origin principle has been perfected in some pieces of Community legislation, see notably Art. 2a(1) of Directive 89/552/EEC concerning the pursuit of television broadcasting activities ('Television without frontiers'), OJ 1989 L 298/23 as amended by Directive 97/36/EC, OJ 1997 L 202/60 and Art. 3 of Directive 2000/31/EC on certain legal aspects of information society services, in particular electronic commerce, in the Internal Market (Directive on electronic commerce), OJ 2000 L 178/1. See Chapter 2 at 1.5.

[128] *Cassis de Dijon* at 13.

In terms of proportionality, the Court established that information requirements constituted a less stringent means of ensuring fair commercial transactions than the mandatory requirement of minimum alcohol contents, which was equivalent to a prohibition of goods not meeting this condition. Regarding the content of a principle of fair trading, it becomes quite clear that a national fair trading provision interfering with the supply of the market in an indirectly discriminatory way by determining the quality of a product cannot defy Community law. A rule, however, requiring the provision of information about the quality of the product, and thereby possibly also hindering the free movement of goods, is considered compatible with Community law, since it is proportionate in pursuing the legitimate objective of fair trading.[129] Information thus seems to be a component of fair trading. The reasoning of *Cassis* advocates the transparency of the market, a concept the Court especially focused on in *Oosthoek*.[130]

Similar to *Cassis de Dijon*, *Fietje* concerned the designation of alcoholic products.[131] The Dutch law on the designation of liqueurs (*likeurbesluit*) required the use of the word 'likeur', or certain variations of this word, in the case of the beverages therein defined. A number of exceptions to the obligation had been named, one of them relating to products 'described with the help of a description generally used under normal commercial practice to describe a liqueur', provided that those liqueurs had an alcoholic strength of not less than 24% by volume and the director of the appropriate government department has given his approval. The designation requirement had been based on the Netherlands legislation on goods (*warenwet*), which provided *inter alia* for regulations pursuing the protection of public health or fair trading.[132] Yet, the Court considered whether the Dutch rule might be justified on grounds of public interest in consumer protection, which underlay the rule, according to the observations of the Netherlands Government and according to the *warenwet*.[133] The discussion of the law, presented as fair trading legislation, under the objective of consumer protection hints once more at the fact that, for the Court, fair trading and consumer protection go hand in hand. They can be seen as two features of the same idea.

The Court acknowledged the potential necessity to extend national obligations to imported products in order to give consumers effective protection, where those obligations required to use a description that is sufficiently precise to inform the purchaser of the nature of a given product and to enable it to be distinguished from products with which it might be confused. The Court

---

[129] See also Usher in Grundmann/Kerber/Weatherill, *Party Autonomy*, p. 151 at p. 157.

[130] See *infra* at 5.2.3.

[131] Case 27/80 *Fietje* [1980] ECR 3839.

[132] *Fietje* at 3.

[133] *Fietje* at 10.

pointed out that Community legislation recognised this possibility in several directives relating to foodstuffs.[134] There was, however, no longer any need for such protection, if the details given on the original label of the imported product included at least the same information and if it was just as capable of being understood by consumers in the importing State as the description prescribed by the rules of that State.[135] It was for the national court to establish whether there was such equivalence. The fact that the Dutch rule provided for exemptions to be granted by the competent authority did not alter the Court's reasoning. It merely underlined that exceptions must not lead to the favouring of domestic products, because this would constitute arbitrary discrimination against or a disguised restriction on products imported from other Member States.

The quality of information and its reception by consumers are the key aspects of the assessment of the national fair-trading rule. The starting point is the application of the principle of mutual recognition. Information considered sufficient in the Member State of origin must, in principle, be considered to inform consumers in the Member State of importation sufficiently. Although it is not the wording of the designation which is decisive, but the information it conveys to the consumer, information is generally preferable to prohibition. This preference remains also in situations where the provision of information seems too difficult, because the goods cannot be labelled.[136]

5.2.3 Market transparency as the underlying concept

Market transparency has been highlighted in *Oosthoek*.[137] The Court had to decide on compatibility with EC law of the Dutch Act on the restriction of free gift schemes (*Wet beperking cadeaustelsel 1977*), which prohibited the offering or giving of products as free gift within the framework of a commercial activity. The Act allowed certain exceptions to that prohibition, in particular it permitted a free gift to be offered or given, provided that (1) it was

---

[134] In particular Directive 2000/13/EC [ex Directive 79/112/EEC] on the approximation of the laws of the Member States relating to the labelling, presentation and advertising of foodstuffs, OJ 2000 L 109/29. See Chapter 2 at 2.5.3.1, where it is also dealt with the *Piageme* case law concerning language.

[135] See e.g. also Case 788/79 *Criminal proceedings against Herbert Gilli and Paul Andres* [1980] ECR 2071 at 7.

[136] Impossibility of information disclosure has for example been claimed for foodstuffs which are sold in restaurants. For the Court, however, also in these situations 'it is possible to establish a system for informing the consumer', see Case 407/85 *3 Glocken GmbH and Gertraud Kritzinger v USL Centro-Sud and Provincia autonoma di Bolzano* [1988] ECR 4233 at 18. The same holds true for foodstuffs sold by vending machines or in catering establishments, Case 216/84 *Commission v France ('Milk substitutes')* [1988] ECR 793 at 10. See also *infra* note 187 on *German Beer.*

[137] Case 286/81 *Oosthoek's Uitgeversmaatschappij B.V.* [1982] ECR 4575.

usually used or consumed at the same time as all the products in respect of the purchase of which it was offered or given (so-called 'related consumption or use'), or (2) that it bore a mark which was indelible and clearly visible when it was used in the normal way and which clearly showed that it was intended for advertising purposes, or (3) that its value did not exceed 4% of the sale price of all the products in respect of the purchase of which it was offered or given. Proceedings were instituted against the company Oosthoek in the Netherlands for infringement of that Act, because that company offered in its printed advertisements a dictionary, a universal atlas or a small encyclopaedia as a free gift to all subscribers to an encyclopaedia, which was partly manufactured by a company in Belgium and then imported into the Netherlands by Oosthoek.

The Court emphasised that legislation which restricted or prohibited certain forms of advertising and certain means of sales promotion might, although it did not directly affect imports, be such as to restrict their volume because it affected marketing opportunities for the imported product, which had been contested by the Governments of Denmark and Germany. Within the rule of reason the Court examined whether the prohibition of a free gift scheme might be justified by requirements relating to consumer protection and fair trading. With reference to the objectives of the free gifts scheme as established by the national court, the Court of Justice considered it undeniable that the offering of free gifts as a means of sales promotion might mislead consumers as to the real prices of certain products and thus impaired market transparency. Therefore, legislation which restricted or even prohibited such commercial practices was seen as capable of contributing to consumer protection and fair trading. With regard to the criterion of related consumption or use (which defined the scope of one of the exceptions of the offering of free gifts), it did not appear to the Court to be unrelated to the objectives of the Dutch legislation or, in particular, to the desire to achieve market transparency to the extent considered necessary for the protection of consumers and to ensure fair trading.[138]

By examining the Dutch free-gifts prohibition with Community law, the Court further revealed the character of a European concept of fair trading in a key aspect. An essential link is established between consumer protection and fair trading on the one hand, and market transparency on the other. According to *Oosthoek*, a rule which protects consumers from being misled about the real value of a product, i.e. which prevents them from resting uninformed about what they are really offered, meets Community law requirements of fair trading. Fair trading in the Community sense thus aims at keeping the transaction transparent for consumers by protecting them from being misled about what they are offered.[139] Whether and to what extent this requires the positive disclosure of information to the consumer is not further discussed in *Oosthoek*,

[138] *Oosthoek* at 18–20.

[139] See also Case C-166/03 *Commission v France ('Gold Alloy')* [2004] ECR I-nyr at 19.

but the judgment suggests that market transparency is the decisive underlying concept of fair trading, no matter how it is achieved.

5.2.4 Access to consumer information

The *Oosthoek* doctrine, according to which restrictions of advertising may affect marketing opportunities for imported goods, has been extended in *GB-INNO*.[140] Not only had the unrestricted access to imported goods to be guaranteed, but also the access to advertising itself.

The Belgian company GB-INNO, which operated supermarkets in Belgian territory (some near the Belgian-Luxembourg border) had distributed advertising leaflets on Luxembourg territory as well as on Belgian territory. These leaflets were contrary to Luxembourg law, according to which sales offers involving a temporary price reduction may not state the duration of the offer or refer to previous prices.

From the Luxembourg side it was put forward that the prohibitions in question were justified on the grounds of consumer protection. The purpose of the prohibition concerning the duration of the special offer was to avoid the risk of confusion between special sales and half-yearly clearance sales, the timing and duration of which were restricted under Luxembourg legislation. The prohibition against allowing the previous price to appear in the offer was necessary according to the Luxembourg Government, because the consumer was not normally in a position to check whether a previous reference price was true.[141] In addition, the marking of a previous price was claimed to exert excessive psychological pressure on the consumer.

This set of arguments was firmly rejected by the Court. It stressed that under Community law concerning consumer protection the provision of information to the consumer was considered one of the principal requirements,[142] which it demonstrated by extensive reference to non-binding Community policy programmes on the subject. Moreover, the Court referred to its case law, according to which a prohibition against importing certain products into a Member State was contrary to Article 28 where the aim of such a prohibition might be attained by appropriate labelling of the products concerned which would 'provide the consumer with the information he needs and enable him to make his choice'.[143] Article 28 could therefore in no way be interpreted as meaning that national legislation denying the consumer 'access to certain kinds of infor-

---

140 Case C-362/88 *GB-INNO-BM v Confédération du commerce luxembourgeois* [1990] ECR I-667.

141 As a matter of fact, the Luxembourg prohibition did not, however, distinguish between true and false price indications.

142 *GB-INNO* at 18.

143 *GB-INNO* at 17. The Court referred to Case 193/80 *Commission v Italy ('Italian Vinegar')* [1981] ECR 3019 at 27 and Case 178/84 *Commission v Germany ('German Beer')* [1987] ECR 1227 at 35.

mation' might be justified by mandatory requirements concerning consumer protection.[144] It should be noted that the Community legislator has meanwhile tackled the issue of price comparisons in connection with special offers in Directive 97/55 relating to comparative advertising.[145]

In *GB-INNO* the Court unambiguously held that the protection of trading with consumers cannot be justified by non-information of consumers. Fair trading and the suppression of information obviously do not go together from a Community law point of view. The Court was less clear in explaining what 'certain kinds of information' these were to be, the access to which must not be denied. Working on the assumption of an active cross-border consumer,[146] the Court pointed out generally that the free movement of goods concerned not only traders, but also individuals, which required, particularly in frontier areas, that consumers resident in one Member State might travel freely to the territory of another Member State to shop under the same conditions as the local population.[147] This freedom for consumers was compromised, if they were deprived of access to advertising available in the country where purchases were made.[148] Besides acknowledging a right of consumers to (access) information,[149] *GB-INNO* seems to suggest a duty to inform, albeit still unrefined. The European Consumers' organisation BEUC[150] has criticised *GB-INNO* for not clearly seeing the difference between sales promotion and the giving of information.[151] This criticism implies that not all information is necessarily to the benefit of the consumer so that a duty to inform must specify to which details this duty applies. However, the Court clearly referred to information consumers need in order to be able to make their choice in full knowledge of the facts.[152] Even

---

144 *GB-INNO* at 18.

145 Directive 97/55/EC amending Directive 84/450/EEC concerning misleading advertising so as to include comparative advertising, OJ 1997 L 290/18. Article 3a(1)(c) of the amended Directive 84/450 allows objective price comparisons as a matter of principle. Besides, Article 3a(2) reads: 'Any comparison referring to a special offer shall indicate in a clear and unequivocal way the date on which the offer ends or, where appropriate, that the special offer is subject to the availability of the goods and services, and, where the special offer has not yet begun, the date of the start of the period during which the special price or other specific conditions shall apply'.

146 See also *infra* at 5.3.1.

147 The Court thus highlights the close connection between the access to the marketplace and the freedom of the demand side in a market, Paefgen, (2003) 11 *ZEuP* 266 at 275.

148 *GB-INNO* at 8.

149 See Stuyck, (2000) 37 *CML Rev.* 367 at 384, according to whom the 'right to information is undoubtedly the most fundamental specific consumer right, i.e. a right vested in all citizens in their capacity as consumers'.

150 Bureau Européen des Unions des Consommateurs.

151 Reported by Schmitz, (1993) 16 *JCP* 394.

152 Micklitz in Reich/Heine-Mernik, *Umweltverfassung*, p. 65 at p. 87 doubted the idea that *GB-INNO* could be generalised as suggesting a European principle of truthfulness of advertising.

though this statement does not specify concretely which information particulars this comprises, it does imply that not just any information provision is considered to be adequate.

In *Alpine Investments* the Court took a similar view as earlier in *GB-INNO.*[153] A Dutch provider of financial services was prevented by Dutch rules from contacting potential customers by telephone without their prior written consent (the practice of 'cold calling'). This ban on cold calling for financial services was applicable to offers made to people both inside and outside the Netherlands.

According to the Dutch Government, the prohibition of cold calling in off-market commodities futures trading sought both to safeguard the reputation of the Netherlands financial markets and to protect the investing public. Although the protection of consumers in the other Member States was not, as such, a matter for the Dutch authorities, the Court found that maintaining the good reputation of the national financial sector constituted an imperative reason of public interest, because the nature and extent of the protection of consumers did nonetheless have a direct effect on the good reputation of Dutch financial services.[154] It thus seems that the protection of consumers was not itself considered the decisive imperative reason of public interest by the Dutch Government, but that it served as a vehicle to defend another public interest, namely the preservation of the good reputation of the national financial sector. However, in its reasoning, the Court somewhat capriciously referred to different objectives of the national prohibition, thus leaving it fairly vague in the end what it actually was or to which objective the justification referred to exactly.

In the present context the Court's statements on the appropriateness of the imposed requirements to ensure the achievement of the intended aim are of particular interest.[155] The Court agreed with the submissions of the Dutch Government according to which, in the case of cold calling, the individual, generally caught unawares, was neither in a position to ascertain the risks inherent in the type of transactions offered to him nor to compare the quality and price of the caller's services with competitors' offers. The Court therefore considered a rule appropriate which intends to counter the restriction in comparing other offers, which is nothing else but a variation of the lack of sufficient access to information for consumers. The Court thus expressed its policy to support the provision of consumers with the information they need in order to enable them to make their choice in full knowledge of the facts. Even though the reasoning is less obvious, the message is clear enough. The access of the consumer to information is clearly a benchmark for the justification of a national fair-trading measure.

---

[153] Case C-384/93 *Alpine Investments BV v Minister van Financiën* [1995] ECR I-1141.

[154] *Alpine Investments* at 43 and 44.

[155] *Alpine Investments* at 46 to 49. As to the statements on the necessity of the measure, see *infra* at 5.3.4. with regard to the image of the consumer.

5.2.5 No suppression of correct information

The *GB-INNO* reasoning has been confirmed in *Yves Rocher*,[156] which places the emphasis on the correctness of the information provided, and which marks the end of the line of pre-*Keck* leading cases relating to fair trading. A provision of the German law against unfair competition (*Gesetz gegen den unlauteren Wettbewerb, UWG*) prohibited advertisements making use of individual comparisons between old and new prices, if those were 'eye-catching'[157]. This prevented the use of an integrated marketing strategy for the company Yves Rocher which distributed mail order catalogues throughout the Community, which contained eye-catching price comparisons within the meaning of the German law.

The Court rejected the arguments of the German Government, which considered the measure necessary to protect consumers from being misled regarding the correctness of the comparison between the old and the new prices and regarding the attractiveness of the prices of other products not advertised for. In *Oosthoek* the Court, indeed, accepted the Dutch prohibition on free gifts, because it protected consumers from being misled about the real value of a product. In *Yves Rocher*, however, the Court drew attention to the fact that the prohibition applied wherever price comparisons caught the eye, whether or not they were correct. Therefore, advertising was prohibited not because it was alleged to be incorrect, but only because it was eye-catching. The prohibition was thus not even suitable for attaining the aim pursued.[158] Moreover, the prohibition of comparisons of prices actually charged could not be misleading. Such a comparison could even 'be of considerable use in that it enables the consumer to make his choice in full knowledge of the facts'.[159]

The Court made it very clear that, as the provision of correct information cannot be misleading, the prohibition of information irrespective of its correctness cannot be necessary in the name of fair trading.[160] This renders the connection between the information of the consumer and fair trading incontestable. Although the incompatibility with Community law of the suppression of (correct) information can easily be inferred from the judgment, the positive duty to provide information is less evident. Nevertheless, it seems a logical

[156] Case C-126/91 *Schutzverband gegen Unwesen in der Wirtschaft e.V. v Yves Rocher GmbH* [1993] ECR I-2361.

[157] In German: *blickfangmäßig*.

[158] Advocate General Darmon provocatively (and rightly) argued in his Opinion on *Yves Rocher* that the prohibition of 'eye-catching' (a term he considered far too vague) advertising would mean the prohibition of any (good) advertising in the end (at 44 et seq.).

[159] *Yves Rocher* at 17.

[160] Today, Directive 97/55 amending Directive 84/450 concerning misleading advertising so as to include comparative advertising (see footnote 145) reflects this idea by allowing objective price comparisons.

consequence where necessary information is lacking. It follows from the reasoning that the yardstick for the existence and the quality of information is that it enables consumers to make their choice in 'full knowledge of the facts'. This allows the conclusion that it has to concern true information and information which is vital for the active consumers' decision-making. However, the Court is hesitant to become more concrete about the exact facts consumers need to know. In *Guimont*, for instance, which concerned the French prohibition to give a cheese without rind the name 'Emmenthal', the Court likewise vaguely referred to the 'necessary information' the consumer or purchaser should be provided with.[161]

5.2.6 The quality of the information

The Court has been more precise on the quality of the information in *Belgian Notification Numbers*.[162] Belgian legislation required foodstuffs placed on the national market to which nutrients had been added to indicate on the labelling of the product the notification number issued by the national inspection service. The Belgian Government contended that the obligation to indicate the notification number on the labelling of the products did not constitute a barrier to the free movement of goods, since the extra costs which might arise as a result of the requirement to alter the packaging were borne by Belgian consumers.[163] The Court dismissed this argument, because the mere prospect of having to lay out those costs constituted a barrier for traders, since it was capable of acting as a disincentive to those of them who were contemplating marketing the products concerned in Belgium. The question therefore arose whether the obstacle could be justified.

Unlike the judgments dealt with so far, the basis for justification in this case was the protection of public health under Article 30. Although not the mandatory requirements of consumer protection and fair trading were the yardsticks, the Court expressed itself rather precisely on what kind of information the consumer needs to be protected, which makes this judgment also relevant for the understanding of the Court's perception of fair trading. The Court stated that

---

[161] Case C-448/98 *Criminal proceedings against Jean-Pierre Guimont* [2000] ECR I-10663 at 31. See also Case C-12/00 *Commission v Spain* [2003] ECR I-459 at 86, Case C-14/00 *Commission v Italy* [2003] ECR I-513 at 81.

[162] Case C-217/99 *Commission v Belgium ('Belgian Notification Numbers')* [2000] ECR I-10251.

[163] To the effect that different labelling produces additional packaging cost, which then causes a barrier to intra-Community trade, see Case C-51/93 *Meyhui NV v Schott Zwiesel Glaswerke AG* [1994] ECR I-3879 at 13 and Case C-33/97 *Colim NV v Bigg's Continent Noord NV* [1999] ECR I-3175 at 36.

> '[...] the value of including the notification number on the labelling of the products concerned as a means of giving consumers information must be ascertained, by considering, in particular, whether that number provides consumers with any information enabling them to adapt their consumption of those products in such a way as to take precautionary measures for the protection of their health'.[164]

The Court continued:

> 'Such information, even if it provides consumers with an assurance that a file has been notified to the competent authorities, is not capable of enabling them to decide whether or not they should consume the product and, if they do consume it, in what quantities. It is not sufficiently useful to them for its inclusion to be fully justified on grounds of the protection of public health'.[165]

Consequently, the Court has considered the requirement of including the notification numbers on the packaging of foodstuffs not even useful for the protection of public health.[166] The Court argued from the perspective of the decision-making process of a consumer who wants to buy a product, which makes its statements affect fair trading. What had been indicated in *Yves Rocher,* namely that consumers should be able to make their decisions in full knowledge of the facts, has been put in somewhat more concrete terms in *Belgian Notification Numbers*: the basic facts consumers must know are those which enable them to make a qualified decision for or against a product and to decide in which quantity they should consume this product. The latter aspect is certainly particularly relevant from the public health perspective, but the idea can be generalised, since the purchase of any good implies a decision which good is to be purchased and in which quantity.

The reasoning reveals a parallel to the *essentialia negotii* known from contract law. Just as a contract must cover basic elements to render it valid, so too a transactional decision (which is usually the decision on the conclusion of a contract) requires basic facts in order to become effective. Just as each type of a contract requires very specific elements,[167] so too different types of decisions require different facts as a decision-making basis. The Court may still be far away from elaborating such a differentiated system, but its foundation is clearly laid. In *Belgian Notification Numbers*, the Court found it necessary to consider 'in particular', whether the notification number provided consumers with any

[164] *Belgian Notification Numbers* at 25.

[165] *Belgian Notification Numbers* at 26.

[166] The necessity of the labelling of the notification numbers has likewise been rejected, *Belgian Notification Numbers* at 26–29.

[167] For instance, in the case of a classic sales contract this would be the determination of the parties (buyer and seller), the good to be sold, and the price of this good.

information enabling them to adapt their consumption in such a way as to take precautionary measures for the protection of their health. As public health is probably the most vital public interest conceivable and concerns all consumers,[168] it may be concluded that information disclosure must always take into account the consumers' health. Fair trading, it is submitted, involves the respect for the consumers' health.

5.2.7 Limits to consumer information

The concepts of, first, the availability of information that is necessary for consumers in order to make their choice and, second, the preference, as a matter of principle, of information over prohibition can be regarded as fundamental. However, as the case law concerning lotteries shows, there are also limits to them.

Schindler concerned the UK prohibition of the dispatch of advertisements and application forms for a lottery organised in Germany to United Kingdom nationals.[169] After the Court established that lottery activities were services within the meaning of the Treaty and that the UK prohibition constituted an obstacle to their free movement it examined the possible justification of the rule. The objectives of the UK legislation, as the Court understood it, were 'the protection of the recipients of the service and, more generally, of consumers as well as the maintenance of order in society'.[170] Without any application of the principle of mutual recognition[171] and without seriously engaging the principle of proportionality[172] the Court acknowledged that, *inter alia*, the high risks of crime and fraud involved in large-scale lotteries and the damaging individual and social consequences of spending incitement justify national authorities having a sufficient degree of latitude to determine what is required to protect the players and, in the light of specific social and cultural features of each Member

---

[168] This link between public health and consumer protection becomes also apparent in Case C-358/01 *Commission v Spain* [2003] ECR I-nyr where both interests seem to be considered in a combined way (at 39, 45 et seq., 49 et seq.).

[169] Case C-275/92 *Her Majesty's Customs and Excise v Gerhart Schindler and Jörg Schindler* [1994] ECR I-1039.

[170] *Schindler* at 58. This is the Court's own summary of the objectives of the legislation as submitted by the national court. The judgment is not unequivocal, but it seems that the Court examined the objectives commonly under the rule of reason. Accordingly, Stuyck in Micklitz, *Rechtseinheit oder Rechtsvielfalt*, p. 331 at p. 337 considers 'order in society' to be the creation of a new ground of justification. For Gormley, (1994) 19 *E.L.Rev.* 644 at 652 'the maintenance of order in society' is a expression of public policy as specified in Article 46(1).

[171] Gormley, (1994) 19 *E.L.Rev.* 644 at 651.

[172] Straetmans, (2000) 37 *CML Rev.* 991 at 991 and 1000.

State, to maintain order in society.[173] Consequently, the Court also accepted prohibiting restrictions, provided that the restrictions not be discriminatory.

It does not become very clear whether the Court has placed the 'maintenance of order in society' above consumer protection, or whether a particularly high level of danger for consumers automatically means a danger for the social order. In any case, the Court accepted that fair trading might not be guaranteed by the information of consumers, but that a prohibition might be adequate. However, the fact that the Court assigned such a high degree of latitude to the Member States according to their specific social and cultural features suggests that it has to a substantial extent simply been reluctant to interfere with this sensitive policy area.[174]

Schindler has been confirmed, extended to various types of gambling activities,[175] and refined in *Läärä*,[176] *Zenatti*,[177] *Anomar*,[178] *Gambelli*,[179] *Lindmann*,[180] and *Omega*.[181] Although the condition of proportionality has been emphasised more strongly in the latter cases,[182] the Court has still kept far behind the concrete criteria that it has provided in its other case law. Moreover, *Schindler* remains the only judgment in the lotteries case law which deals (also) with advertising, the subsequent judgments concerning the free movement of the service itself. In conclusion, it is submitted that this restrictive reasoning with regard to the information of consumers has remained an exception for the particular sector of lotteries.

5.3 The image of the consumer

The concept of market transparency, the idea that consumers must be enabled to make informed choices, can be considered not only from the point of view of the quality or quantity of available information, but likewise from the perspective of the consumer, i.e. the recipient of the information. The

173 *Schindler* at 60 et seq.

174 Straetmans, (2000) 37 *CML Rev.* 991 at 991 and 1001.

175 However, in Case C-368/95 *Vereinigte Familiapress Zeitungsverlags- und vertriebs GmbH v Heinrich Bauer Verlag* [1997] ECR I-3689 at 21 et seq. the Court rejected the application of the *Schindler* case law to small scale prize draws in newspapers.

176 Case C-124/97 *Markku Juhani Läärä et al. v Kihlakunnansyyttäjä (Jyväskylä) et al.* [1999] ECR I-6067.

177 Case C-67/98 *Questore di Verona v Diego Zenatti* [1999] ECR I-7289.

178 Case C-6/01 *Associação Nacional de Operadores de Máquinas Recreativas (Anomar) et al. v Estado português* [2003] ECR I-8621.

179 Case C-243/01 *Criminal proceedings against Piergiorgio Gambelli et al.* [2003] ECR I-nyr.

180 Case C-42/02 *Diana Elisabeth Lindman* [2003] ECR I-nyr.

181 Case C-32/02 *Omega Spielhallen- und Automatenaufstellungs-GmbH v Oberbürgermeisterin der Bundesstadt Bonn* [2004] ECR I-nyr.

182 Cf. Straetmans, (2004) 41 *CML Rev.* 1409 at 1420 et seq.

Court has followed this second approach in another set of judgments. Although both lines of reasoning go hand in hand in the judgments and mutually complement each other, there seems, in fact, to be a slight tendency of the Court to argue increasingly on the perception of information by the consumer rather than on the information itself. The result is reflected in a fairly elaborate image of the consumer.

5.3.1 Cross-border variety and evolution

German Beer, concerning the German purity requirements for beer (*Reinheitsgebot*), nicely illustrates the interrelationship between the image of the consumer and market transparency.[183] In an infringement action, Germany was alleged to be in breach of Article 28, because it prohibited the marketing on its territory of beer lawfully produced and marketed in other Member States, if the beer failed to comply with the provisions of the *Biersteuergesetz* of 1952. The law, which applied equally to imports and to nationally produced beer, provided that the name *Bier* (beer) could be used only for products brewed using malted barley, hops, yeast and water alone (i.e. brewed according to the German purity requirements for beer, the so-called *Reinheitsgebot*). This implied that that the use of other ingredients such as maize did not preclude the marketing of the finished product, but it could not be sold as *Bier*.

The German Government had first sought to justify its rules on public health grounds, maintaining that the use of raw materials other than those permitted by the law would inevitably entail the use of additives. However, at the hearing the German Government conceded that the rule in question, which was merely a rule on designation, was exclusively intended to protect consumers. In its view, consumers associated the designation *Bier* with a beverage manufactured from only the raw materials listed in the provision. Consequently, it was necessary to prevent them from being misled as to the nature of the product.

The Court started the examination of a possible justification of the German prohibition under the mandatory requirement of consumer protection by firstly pointing out that consumers' conceptions, which varied from one Member State to the other, were also likely to evolve in the course of time within a Member State, not least due to the contributions to the establishment of a Common Market.[184] Legislation of the kind contained in the *Biersteuergesetz* prevented such a development from taking place, which distinguished it from rules protecting consumers against misleading practices. The Court referred to its decision in *Beer and Wine*[185] where it held in the context of tax arrangements

---

[183] Case 178/84 *Commission v Germany ('German Beer')* [1987] ECR 1227.

[184] *German Beer* at 32.

[185] Case 170/78 *Commission v United Kingdom ('Beer and Wine')* [1983] ECR 2265 (interlocutory judgment [1980] ECR 417).

applying to wine that the legislation of a Member State must not 'crystallize given consumer habits so as to consolidate an advantage acquired by national industries concerned to comply with them'.[186]

The Court made clear that it was legitimate to seek to enable consumers who attribute specific qualities to beers manufactured from particular raw materials to make their choice in the light of that consideration. However, that possibility might perfectly be ensured by means which did not prevent the importation of products which have been lawfully manufactured and marketed in other Member States and, in particular, by the compulsory affixing of suitable labels giving the nature of the product sold. The indication of the raw materials utilised in the manufacture of beer would enable the consumer to make his choice in full knowledge of the facts and would guarantee transparency in trading and in offers to the public.[187] The German Government thus had failed to fulfil its obligations under Article 28 of the Treaty.[188]

The Court has taken a negative view of consumer protection rules which factually prohibited the import of specific product categories, where the same effect could be reached by effectively informing the consumer. Thus, rules protecting consumers against misleading practices must not strengthen existing consumer habits, but allow consumers to evolve and to become acquainted with foreign Community products, which may differ from what they are used to from their national markets.[189] That means that national fair trading rules have to reflect the diversity of the Internal Market. They have to do so, because consumers are considered to be flexible and capable of evolution, so long as they are adequately informed. The diversity of the Internal Market thus fosters the diversity of consumers, who are considered to be open and ready for development in consumption habits. This image of the consumer is perfectly complemented by the Court's assumption of active cross-border consumers as presented in *GB-INNO*,[190] i.e. consumers who do not restrict themselves to the national market, but actively access foreign markets and therefore are receptive to cross-border advertising.

---

[186] *Beer and Wine* at 8 (interlocutory judgment at 14).

[187] *German Beer* at 35. Moreover, the Court dismissed the German Government's desperate attempt to uphold the archaic *Reinheitsgebot* by drawing attention to the fact such a system of consumer information is feasible, even where beers are sold on draught, where the requisite information could appear on the casks or the beer taps (which was provided for, in respect of certain beers, in the law in question itself).

[188] There was a second limb of the rules, which involved an absolute ban on the marketing of beers containing additives, wherever the beers have been produced. Arguments relating to the protection of public health had been dismissed by the Court, because the rules were disproportionate.

[189] Cf. *Beer and Wine*, footnote 186.

[190] See *supra* at 5.2.4.

These traits of the consumers' character, which come along with the Internal Market, must not be counteracted by restrictive national trading rules. *German beer* shows that such rules therefore cannot resist Community law in the name of fair trading. The idea rather is that fair-trading rules contribute to the information of consumers about national as well as foreign Community products, allowing them to make autonomous choices on the supply of the Internal Market as a whole. The case thus suggests that transparency in trading, fair trading and a self-responsible and flexible consumer basically are different features of the same idea. The fact that the Court does accept that consumer habits differ within the Community but that it does not accept that those habits are cemented by national rules may suggest the existence of multiple consumer images. However, it is submitted that this is actually just one image of the consumer, which includes the idea of differing consumer habits, i.e. differing facets of consumers.

5.3.2 The complexity of determining factors

In *Buet*[191] the Court examined the compatibility with Article 28 of a French prohibition of canvassing at private dwellings for the purpose of selling educational material. In the line of the *Oosthoek* reasoning the Court considered the sales method of canvassing to be a measure of equivalent effect, but which could possibly be justified by the need to satisfy mandatory requirements, such as the protection of consumers and fair trading. Taking up the French legislature's concern to protect consumers against the risk of ill-considered purchases,[192] the Court examined in the framework of the proportionality test whether France had at its disposal less restrictive means of obtaining the same goal. Here, the Court drew a remarkably differentiated picture of the interrelation between different types of consumers and different situations they face.

According to the Court, canvassing at private dwellings exposed the potential customer to the risk of making an ill-considered purchase. To guard against that risk it was normally sufficient to ensure that purchasers have the right to cancel a contract concluded in their home.[193] The Court deemed it necessary, however, to point out that there was greater risk of an ill-considered purchase when the canvassing was for enrolment for a course of instruction or the sale of educational material, since the potential purchaser often belonged to a category of people who, for one reason or another, were behind with their education and were seeking to catch up. The Court thus clearly made a distinction between

---

[191] Case 382/87 *R. Buet and Educational Business Services (EBS) v Ministère public* [1989] ECR 1235.

[192] This explains why the Court continues arguing from the point of view of consumer protection only.

[193] *Buet* at 12. The right to cancel the contract within a certain period of time is also the central content of Directive 85/577/EEC to protect the consumer in respect of contracts negotiated away from business premises (Articles 4 and 5), OJ 1985 L 372/31.

different *types of consumers*, who are, due to their personal (intellectual) capacities, in need of more or less protection. These less capable consumers, the Court continued, were particularly vulnerable when faced with salesmen of educational material who attempted to persuade them that if they use that material they would have better employment prospects. A distinction is thus made according to the *type of situation*, which might require different degrees of protection. Finally, the Court stressed that since teaching was not a consumer product in daily use, an ill-considered purchase could cause the purchaser harm other than mere financial loss that could be longer lasting. It had to be acknowledged that the purchase of unsuitable or low-quality material could compromise the consumer's chances of obtaining further training and thus consolidating his position on the labour market. The Court thus observed that the *type or gravity of effect* could have different consequences concerning what can be considered necessary in order to protect consumers and guarantee fair trading.[194] The Court concluded that in 'those circumstances' it was permissible for the national legislature of the Member State to consider that giving consumers a right of cancellation was not sufficient protection and that it was necessary to ban canvassing at private dwellings.[195]

It can be inferred from the reasoning that a rule on fair trading must take into account those consumer-related conditions in order to be compatible with Community law. The Court acknowledged that the relationship between market circumstances and consumers is complex: there are different kinds of acting consumers, faced with diverse situations, and these situations can have different effects. The Court suggested that these factors are interwoven, and that only the case-by-case assessment of this interplay allows a judgment on what can legally defend consumer protection and fair trading under EC law. The more vulnerable consumers are in relation to the marketing situation with which they are confronted, and the more serious the effects of the potential transaction could possibly be for the consumer in question (which indicates a subjective approach), the more restrictive a measure may be in order to assure fair transactions. In *Buet*, even a prohibition was acceptable. Where a prohibition was not proportionate, the adequate information of consumers would obviously be a

194 *Buet* at 13–14.

195 *Buet* at 15. Strikingly, not before the end of the rule-of-reason test the Court (at 16) referred to Directive 85/577, which partially harmonised doorstep selling. The Directive, which requires Member States to ensure that consumers have the right to cancel a contract of sale concluded at their home, allows (being a classical minimum harmonisation directive) in Article 8 the State to adopt or maintain more favourable provisions to protect consumers. This provision as well as the last recital of the preamble to the Directive, where the Council expressly recognised that Member States might introduce or maintain a total or partial prohibition on the conclusion of contracts away from business premises, have been cited by the Court as confirmation of the legality of a total prohibition of canvassing in connection with door-to-door sales.

less restrictive means for attaining the objective. Thus transferring the Court's reasoning to the idea of market transparency, a parallel can be developed of, on the one hand, the relationship between the characteristic of the consumer, the marketing situation and the possible effects, and, on the other hand, the extent and quality of the information necessary for fairness in consumer transactions.

5.3.3 The relevance of misconceptions and the image of the consumer

The case law suggests that the mere possibility of the promotion of a product to mislead the consumer is not sufficient to justify a restrictive national fair-trading rule. Thus, misconceptions which are not liable to influence the decision-making process of the consumer in any reasonable respect are considered to be irrelevant.[196] This has to do with the image of a consumer, who is able to cope with the complexity of the Internal Market.

Pall reveals more of the Court's conceptual starting point when it comes to the assessment of the consumer.[197] P. J. Dahlhausen & Co marketed in Germany blood filters which it had imported from Italy. The Italian producer placed on the filters themselves and on their packaging the trade mark, followed by the symbol ®. The competitor Pall Corp. applied *inter alia* for an injunction restraining Dahlhausen from using, in Germany, the symbol ® after the trade mark, on the grounds that this trade mark was not registered in Germany, but only in Italy. The German court took the view that under German law the injunction had to be granted, because the use of the symbol ® in those circumstances constituted misleading advertising, which was prohibited under the German law against unfair competition (*Gesetz gegen den unlauteren Wettbewerb, UWG*).

The Court considered the prohibition to be capable of impeding intra-Community trade, because it could force the proprietor of a trade mark that has been registered in only one Member State to change the presentation of his products according to the place where it is proposed to market them and to set up separate distribution channels. Consideration therefore had to be given to the question whether such a prohibition could be justified by the mandatory requirements of consumer protection and fair trading.

The prohibition could not, however, be justified on the grounds that the use of the symbol would mislead consumers, since it had not been established that in practice the symbol was generally used and understood as indicating that the trade mark was registered in the country in which the product was marketed.[198] The mere hypothetical possibility seemed thus not to be deemed sufficient. However, the Court went into the assumption that consumers, or some of them,

---

[196] Niemöller, *Verbraucherleitbild*, p. 178.

[197] Case C-238/89 *Pall Corp. v P. J. Dahlhausen & Co.* [1990] ECR I-4827.

[198] *Pall* at 18.

might be misled on that point, but held that such a risk could not justify so considerable an obstacle to the free movement of goods, since consumers were more interested in the qualities of a product than in the place of registration of the trade mark.[199]

Although it may leave that impression at first glance, the judgment is not inconsistent with *Buet*, which seemingly had been more differentiated in drawing an image of the consumer and finally assumed a weak consumer in need of protection. *Pall* rather complements this image. It shows that the Court basically starts from a reasonable consumer who is not easily misled. This does not rule out that there are consumers who are more susceptible to misleading or unfair marketing behaviour. This is, however, not self-evident. The Court indicated that there must be adequate signs that consumers are actually misled; mere speculation is not sufficient. In addition, the Court asks for a logical link between the consumers' (economic) interest and the goal of protection of the restriction in question. A measure cannot be upheld in the name of consumer protection and fair trading, when it essentially does not defend what consumers are really concerned about. According to the Court, symbols of trademark registration are a message not so much to consumers (who, if they are interested at all in the fact of registration, are certainly even less interested in the place of registration, as Advocate General Tesauro rightly emphasised)[200] but basically to other traders. Fair trading is therefore strongly determined by the (economic) interests of consumers.

In *Mars*[201], in the framework of a publicity campaign covering the whole of Europe, ice-cream bars were presented in wrappers marked '+10%' and the quantity of each product was as well increased by 10%, which had been considered unfair under German law.

In order to examine whether the prohibition might be justified as being necessary in order to satisfy overriding requirements relating to consumer protection and fair trading, the Court considered two arguments that had been raised in the main proceedings. Firstly, the argument was rejected that the consumer was bound to assume that the advantage indicated by the marking

---

199 *Pall* at 19. The Court also rejected the argument that the use of the symbol ® in the present circumstances could be regarded as unfair competition vis-à-vis competitors, since prudent economic operators with an interest in knowing whether or not a trade mark was registered could determine the legal situation concerning the trade mark in question at the public register. Finally, since the prohibition had been found not to be justified by imperative requirements relating to consumer protection and fair trading, it could also find no basis in Directive 84/450/EEC relating to misleading advertising, OJ 1984 L 250/17, which was confined to a partial harmonisation of the national laws on misleading advertising (*Pall* at 22).

200 Opinion of Advocate General Tesauro Case C-238/89 *Pall Corp. v P. J. Dahlhausen & Co.* [1990] ECR I-4827 at 6.

201 Case C-470/93 *Verein gegen Unwesen in Handel und Gewerbe Köln e.V. v Mars GmbH* [1995] ECR I-1923.

was granted without any price increase. Apart from the fact that Mars had not actually profited from the promotional campaign in order to increase its sale prices and that there was no evidence that retailers had themselves increased their prices, the Court stressed that, in any case, the mere possibility that importers and retailers might increase the price was not sufficient to justify a general prohibition which might hinder intra-Community trade.[202] Moreover, the principle of freedom of retail trade in the matter of the fixing of prices might not justify an obstacle to intra-Community trade such as that in question. The constraint imposed on the retailer not to increase his prices was in fact favourable to the consumer. The second argument, according to which the prohibition should be justified, because a significant number of consumers would be induced to believe that the increase was larger than that represented (the band bearing the '+10%' marking actually occupied more that 10% of the total surface area of the wrapping), was likewise firmly rejected by the Court. Reasonably circumspect consumers might be deemed to know that there was not necessarily a link between the size of publicity markings relating to an increase in a product's quantity and the actual size of that increase.

Here, like in *Pall*, the Court establishes a connection between the probability of consumers being mistaken and the intensity of protection (i.e. barriers to trade) justified. Assuming a reasonably circumspect consumer, who is not easily misled, there is little necessity for interference with intra-Community trade for the sake of fair trading.

In *Sauce hollandaise*[203] the same pattern was followed. The German legislation on foodstuffs and products for human consumption[204] required that, in order to be marketed in Germany, foodstuffs containing an ingredient which did not conform to the traditional German recipe had to carry a trade description with an additional statement indicating that the substance in question had been used, even if that substance was already included in the list of ingredients. The Court had therefore to decide on the compatibility with EC law of the German prohibition of the marketing of *sauce hollandaise* or *sauce béarnaise* prepared from vegetable fats. The prohibition had been defended with the argument that consumers were led to believe that those products had been made with butter and eggs following the traditional recipe in Germany.

Once more, the Court did not share the German Government's view that the obstacle was justified by the need to protect consumers and to ensure fair trading.[205] Although it could not be ruled out that in certain cases the requirement

---

[202] *Mars* at 19.

[203] Case C-51/94 *Commission v Germany ('Sauce hollandaise')* [1995] ECR I-3599.

[204] *Gesetz über den Verkehr mit Lebensmitteln, Tabakerzeugnissen, kosmetischen Mitteln und sonstigen Bedarfsgegenständen (LMBG).*

[205] Not without reason has the German Government aptly been described as 'the advocate of nanny consumer protection', Gormley (1997) *EFLR* 1 at 5.

that an additional statement accompany the trade description was necessary in order to avoid any confusion on the part of consumers, that risk remained minimal and could not therefore justify the obstacle created to the free movement of goods.[206] Secondly, the Court determined whether the measures were justified by the need to ensure fair trading.[207] It rejected, however, the argument that certain producers might derive a competitive advantage from the use of less expensive products. Consumers were heedful of the composition of the product and could process the sufficient information by way of the list of ingredients, which made them able to distinguish between the various methods of manufacture.[208]

Again, the connection between the probability of being mistaken and the legitimate gravity of obstruction to intra-Community trade becomes obvious. Given the existence of a reasonable and responsible consumer, the risk of being misled is, however, deemed rather low.[209] The Court obviously assumes quite a high capability of consumers to process information.

5.3.4 European diversity of consumers

In *Clinique*,[210] a judgment shortly handed down after *Keck*, the Court has confirmed the consumer image as it had previously been developed. This happened in contrast to the Opinion of Advocate General Gulmann, who appeared to have paved the way with his reasoning for a further evolution of the concept of the European consumer. The case concerned, yet again, a German measure against misleading advertising,[211] which had the effect of preventing the sale of cosmetics under the name 'Clinique', as this could make consumers believe that the products in question had medicinal properties.

---

[206] *Sauce hollandaise* at 34.

[207] This makes *Sauce hollandaise* an exception for the use of the notion 'fair trading' in order to refer to the particular relation between competitors.

[208] *Sauce hollandaise* at 36.

[209] The Court has argued similarly in Case C-465/98 *Verein gegen Unwesen in Handel und Gewerbe Köln e.V. v Adolf Darbo AG* [2000] ECR I-2297 concerning the German prohibition to use the term *naturrein* (naturally pure) on the labels of strawberry jam, if certain additives exceeded a particular quantity. Legal basis for the decision was Directive 2000/13/EC [ex Directive 79/112/EEC] on the approximation of the laws of the Member States relating to the labelling, presentation and advertising of foodstuffs, OJ 2000 L 109/29.

[210] Case C-315/92 *Verband Sozialer Wettbewerb e.V. v Clinique Laboratoires SNC and Estée Lauder Cosmetics GmbH* [1994] ECR I-317.

[211] § 3 of the German law against unfair competition (*Gesetz gegen den unlauteren Wettbewerb, UWG*) and its correlative § 27 of the law on foodstuffs and products for human consumption *Gesetz über den Verkehr mit Lebensmitteln, Tabakerzeugnissen, kosmetischen Mitteln und sonstigen Bedarfsgegenständen, LMBG*).

Despite the existence of secondary Community law on the issue in form of Directive 84/450[212] and Directive 76/768,[213] the Court basically performed an Article 28 analysis, since the Directives had to be interpreted in the light of the Treaty rules on the free movement of goods. As the measure, in its application, concerned requirements as to designation, labelling and packaging, Article 28 was still considered applicable in accordance with *Keck*.[214] The Court held, however, that the prohibition of the use of the name 'Clinique' could not be justified in the interests of consumer protection and fairness of commercial transactions or the objective of protecting human health. As the cosmetic products were sold exclusively in perfumeries and cosmetic departments and not in pharmacies, as those products were presented as cosmetic products and not as medicinal products and as they were ordinarily marketed in other countries under the name 'Clinique' apparently without misleading consumers, the prohibition of the use of that name in Germany did not appear necessary.

In *Clinique* the picture of the reasonable self-responsible consumer is only indirectly sketched, but it there is no doubt that the Court worked on the assumption that the consumer is able to judge independently the setting of the market and to come to a sensible conclusion. The striking point about *Clinique* is that the Court makes no difference between the consumers' national backgrounds at all, but clearly generalises the consumer image.[215] Advocate General Gulmann had taken a different view.[216] He considered that it was primarily a matter for national legislatures to determine the level of protection desired in each country. There might be specific differences in linguistic, social and cultural conditions, which had the result that something which did not mislead consumers in one country might do so in another.[217] With his line of reasoning, the Advocate General anticipated the Court's approach in *Graffione* and in the more famous *Lifting*, which refined the image of the consumer.

In *Graffione*[218] the Court had to decide on the compatibility with Community law of the Italian prohibition to sell toilet paper under the name 'Cotonelle', since this would mislead consumers into believing that the product actually contained cotton.[219] The product was legally marketed in other Member States.

[212] Directive 84/450/EEC relating to misleading advertising, OJ 1984 L 250/17.

[213] Directive 76/768/EEC relating to cosmetic products, OJ 1976 L 262/169.

[214] *Clinique* at 13.

[215] Critically, Weatherill, (1999) 36 *CML Rev.* 51 at 56 et seq.

[216] Opinion of Advocate General Gulmann Case C-315/92 *Verband Sozialer Wettbewerb e.V. v Clinique Laboratoires SNC and Estée Lauder Cosmetics GmbH* [1994] ECR I-317.

[217] Opinion of Advocate General Gulmann at 18.

[218] Case C-313/94 *Fratelli Graffione SNC v Ditta Fransa* [1996] ECR I-6039.

[219] The case implied as well a trade-mark law dimension, and considerations have been made with regard to Directive 89/104/EEC relating to trade marks, OJ 1989 L 40/1. Here, only the reasoning relating to Article 28 is examined.

The Court considered whether the barrier to the free movement of goods might be justified in order to protect consumers against the misleading nature of the trade mark, although the same trade mark was not believed to be misleading in other Member States. It came to the conclusion that it was possible that because of 'linguistic, cultural and social differences between the Member States' a trade mark which was not liable to mislead a consumer in one Member State might be liable to do so in another.[220] Proportionality required, however, that the national court must, in particular, examine whether the risk of misleading consumers (i.e. the risk in relation to the group of consumers concerned) was 'sufficiently serious' to be able to override the requirements of the free movement of goods.[221]

Lifting concerned the German prohibition to use the term 'lifting' in the name of a firming cream for the skin.[222] It had been argued that the term 'lifting' was misleading, because it gave purchasers the impression that the use of the product would obtain results which, overall in terms of their lasting effects, were identical or comparable to surgical lifting, whereas this was not the case as far as the cream in question was concerned. Directive 76/768 on cosmetic products was again interpreted in the light of the free movement of goods, which meant that measures restricting the freedom of trade in cosmetic products had to be taken in the interests of consumer protection and fair trading.[223] With reference to *Gut Springenheide and Tusky*[224] the Court emphasised that in order to determine whether a particular description, trade mark or promotional description or statement was misleading, it was necessary to take into account the presumed expectations of an average consumer who was reasonably well informed and reasonably observant and circumspect. It expressed that this test was actually based on the principle of proportionality.[225] In order to apply that test it had to be determined in particular whether 'social, cultural or linguistic factors' might justify the term 'lifting', used in connection with a firming cream, meaning something different to the German consumer as opposed to consumers in other Member States, or whether the instructions for the use of the product were in themselves sufficient to make it quite clear that its effects were short-lived. Therefore, it concluded that Community law did not preclude the prohibition in cases where the average consumer, reasonably well informed and reasonably observant and circumspect, was misled.[226]

---

[220] *Graffione* at 22. This corresponds to the observations of Advocate General Jacobs at 10 of his Opinion on this case.

[221] *Graffione* at 24, 26, 27.

[222] Case C-220/98 *Estée Lauder Cosmetics GmbH & Co. OHG v Lancaster Group GmbH ('Lifting')* [2000] ECR I-117.

[223] *Lifting* at 25.

[224] Case C-210/96 *Gut Springenheide GmbH and Rudolf Tusky v Oberkreisdirektor des Kreises Steinfurt – Amt für Lebensmittelüberwachung* [1998] ECR I-4657.

[225] *Lifting* at 27 and 28, see also Case C-358/01 *Commission v Spain* [2003] ECR I-nyr at 53.

[226] See also Case C-99/01 *Criminal proceedings against Gottfried Linhart and Hans Biffl* [2002] ECR I-9375 at 31.

Still, the average consumer is regarded as reasonable and circumspect as a matter of principle. It becomes clear, however, that what is 'average' is nationally influenced, and that the social, cultural and linguistic diversity in Europe is mirrored by a diversity of consumer perception regarding trading situations. The application of the test of the average consumer has thus to take into account this socio-cultural dimension.[227] In *Lifting*, it was consequently up to the national Court to further clarify the justification of the prohibition, if necessary with the help of experts or a survey of the public opinion.[228]

The Court had ruled similarly in the above-mentioned *Gut Springenheide and Tusky*,[229] which concerned the German prohibition to market eggs ready-packed under the description 'six-grain – 10 fresh eggs', where the six varieties of cereals accounted for only 60% of the feed mix used to feed the hens. The Court held that in order to determine whether a statement or description designed to promote sales of eggs was liable to mislead the purchaser, the national court had to take into account the presumed expectations which it evoked in an average consumer who was reasonably well-informed and reasonably observant and circumspect.[230] However, Community law did not preclude the possibility that, where the national court had particular difficulty in assessing the misleading nature of the statement or description in question, it might have recourse, under the conditions laid down by its own national law, to a consumer research poll or an expert's report as guidance for its judgment.[231] The Court did not, however, suggest a particular method for establishing the misleading nature of the statement.[232] Yet, with reference to *Nissan*[233] the Court pointed out that the national court had to bear in mind the type of consumers to which the advertising was addressed.[234] Unlike in *Lifting*, no explicit indication was made to linguistic, social and cultural conditions.

Also from *Alpine Investments*, in the context of the free movement of services, a differentiated approach of the Court towards European consumers can be inferred.[235] When it examined the necessity of the Dutch ban on cold calling in the financial services sector,[236] the Court focussed on the objective of restoring

---

227 See Chapter 3 at 3.2.

228 Such an assessment certainly poses considerable difficulties for national courts (of first instance). It should be noted that the Court has rejected opinion polls in earlier case law (where they did not produce objectively assessable results), see Case 12/74 *Commission v Germany* [1975] ECR 181 at 12.

229 See footnote 224.

230 *Gut Springenheide and Tusky* at 37. Similarly in Case C-303/97 *Verbraucherschutzverein e.V. v Sektkellerei G.C. Kessler GmbH und Co.* [1999] ECR I-513 at 36.

231 *Gut Springenheide and Tusky* at 37, see also *Sektkellerei Kessler* at 37.

232 Niemöller, *Verbraucherleitbild*, p. 188 et seq.

233 Case C-373/90 *Criminal proceedings against X ('Nissan')* [1992] ECR I-131.

234 *Gut Springenheide and Tusky* at 34.

235 Case C-384/93 *Alpine Investments BV v Minister van Financiën* [1995] ECR I-1141.

236 *Alpine Investments* at 50 to 54. As to the statements on the appropriateness of the measure, see *supra* at 5.2.4 with regard to the access to information.

and maintaining investor confidence. The necessity of a general prohibition of cold calling had been denied by the company 'Alpine Investments' with reference to less stringent measures adopted in another Member State (recording of unsolicited telephone calls). The Court made clear, however, that the fact that one Member State imposes less strict rules than another Member State did not mean that the latter's rules were disproportionate and hence incompatible with Community law. Relating this to the cultural diversity of consumers within the European Union, it can be established that the Court recognises different levels of 'necessary' protection of consumers in matters of fair trading, depending on the cultural background. Besides, the Court underlined that the rules at issue were, indeed, limited in scope: only cold calling (i.e. only without prior written consent) was prohibited, whereas other techniques for making contact were still permitted; furthermore, the prohibition of unsolicited telephone calls was limited to the sector of the commodities futures market. Consequently, the Dutch prohibition, was regarded as proportionate and compatible with Article 49. In sum, also *Alpine Investments* illustrates that access to information, as a constituent element of a principle of fair trading, is complemented by the yardstick of a consumer image, which recognises the diversity of consumers.

5.4 The impact of the *Keck* doctrine

With the Court's decision in *Keck and Mithouard* the wide scope of application of Article 28 has been restricted to some extent.[237] As Weatherill has put it: '*Keck* reflects the Court's concern to establish where regulatory diversity does not affect the integrative process for the purposes of application of Article 28 and where, accordingly, States remain free to make their own regulatory choices unhindered by the demands of EC trade law'.[238]

In the foregoing analysis, pre-*Keck* and post-*Keck* cases have been analysed together, and it has been tried to draw a coherent picture of the Court's fair trading reasoning. However, the majority of the 'leading cases' were pre-*Keck* cases, which maybe would not have been decided under Article 28 post-*Keck*. It must therefore be asked whether and to what extent *Keck* affects pre-*Keck* reasoning with regard to a principle of fair trading. It will be seen, however, that while until today the exact consequences of the *Keck* decision have not yet been fully resolved, its impact should not be overstated.[239]

[237] Joined Cases C-267/91 and C-268/91 *Criminal proceedings against Bernard Keck and Daniel Mithouard* [1993] ECR I-6097.

[238] Weatherill, *Cases and Materials*, p. 399.

[239] See also Jarvis, *Application of EC Law*, p. 118, Tesauro, (1995) 15 *YEL* 1 at 6.

5.4.1 The judgment

The judgment concerned the French prohibition of reselling products in an unaltered state at prices lower than their actual purchase price (resale at a loss). The Court admitted that such legislation might restrict the volume of sales, and hence the volume of sales of products from other Member States,[240] but it doubted whether such a possibility was sufficient to characterise the legislation in question as a measure having equivalent effect to a quantitative restriction on imports. It then made the following distinction.

In paragraph 15 of the judgment the Court partly confirmed the basic principle in *Dassonville* as refined in *Cassis de Dijon*. It stated that

> '[...] in the absence of harmonization, obstacles to free movement of goods which are the consequence of applying, to goods coming from other Member States where they are lawfully manufactured and marketed, rules that lay down requirements to be met by such goods (such as those relating to designation, form, size, weight, composition, presentation, labelling, packaging) constitute measures of equivalent effect'.

The confirmation of the definition of measures having equivalent effect is hence restricted to 'requirements to be met by goods'. What the Court intended to exclude by contrast was attempted to be indicated in paragraph 16, according to which

> '[...] contrary to what has previously been decided, the application to products from other Member States of national provisions restricting or prohibiting certain selling arrangements is not such as to hinder directly or indirectly, actually or potentially, trade between Member States within the meaning of the *Dassonville* judgment, so long as those provisions apply to all relevant traders operating within the national territory and so long as they affect in the same manner, in law and in fact, the marketing of domestic products and of those from other Member States'.

Without seriously applying the test suggested in paragraph 16, the Court then simply established that Article 28 was to be interpreted as not applying to legislation imposing a general prohibition on resale at a loss.

It is quite apparent that the Court's new course in *Keck* means a certain clash with the *Oosthoek* and *Buet* line of reasoning, which had left it no doubt that measures of equivalent effect in the sense of the *Dassonville* formula could perfectly well comprise those relating to sales promotions. Although it can easily be ascertained that this is no longer entirely true according to the statement

---

[240] *Keck* has actually concerned a wholly internal situation. This aspect is not going to be discussed.

contained in paragraph 16 of *Keck*, it has not yet been fully resolved to what extent exactly the *Keck* approach has modified the previous jurisprudence, especially because the Court has not stated which of its case law can be considered overruled.[241]

In this context, it seems useful and necessary to recall that also pre-*Keck* case law did not at all automatically consider restrictive marketing related rules to be measures having equivalent effect.[242] In *Blesgen* the ban on keeping and consuming certain spirits in places open to the public was not deemed a measure of equivalent effect, because the restrictive effect of this measure on the free movement of goods did not exceed the effects intrinsic to trade rules. As such a legislative measure did not, in fact, have a connection with the importation of the products, it was not of such a nature as to impede trade between Member States.[243] In *Oebel* the German prohibition of nightwork in bakeries and the prohibition of the delivery of bakery products to consumers and retailers at night were not considered to restrict imports or exports between Member States.[244] In *Forest* the Court held that the French milling quota system did not constitute a restriction on flour production and did not affect the possibilities of importing flour from other Member States.[245] In *Quietlynn* the Court construed Article 28 as meaning that national provisions prohibiting the sale of lawful sex articles from unlicensed sex establishments do not constitute a measure having an effect equivalent to a quantitative restriction on imports, since legislation governing the marketing of certain products which applied without distinction to imported and domestic products and was not intended to regulate trade in goods within the Community had in fact no connection with intra-Community trade, provided that the products might be marketed through other channels.[246]

With *Keck and Mithouard* the Court claimed to 'clarify' its incoherent case-law.[247] Yet, this statement can hardly be understood as anything different to the

[241] Cf. that *Oosthoek* has also been cited post-*Keck* e.g. Case C-448/98 *Criminal proceedings against Jean-Pierre Guimont* [2000] ECR I-10663 at 21.

[242] For an overview and discussion of pre-*Keck* case law and the scope of Article 28, see Gormley, (1989) 9 *YEL* 197, Gormley, (1990) 27 *CML Rev.* 825. White, (1989) 26 *CML Rev.* 235 at 246 et seq. has developed a very similar definition of measures of equivalent effect from the pre-*Keck* case law as the Court as later introduced in *Keck and Mithouard*. White argued that the 'distinction between the *characteristics* required of imported products and the *circumstances* in which they may be sold is implicit in the case-law of the Court of Justice'. National measures relating to 'circumstances' would not be covered by the notion of measures having equivalent effect.

[243] Case 75/81 *Joseph Henri Thomas Blesgen v Belgian State* [1982] ECR 1211 at 8 et seq.

[244] Case 155/80 *Summary proceedings against Sergius Oebel* [1981] ECR 1993 at 20.

[245] Case 148/85 *Direction générale des impôts et procureur de la République v Marie-Louise Forest, née Sangoy, and Minoterie Forest SA* [1986] ECR 3449 at 11 and 17.

[246] Case C-23/89 *Quietlynn Limited and Brian James Richards v Southend Borough Council* [1990] ECR I-3059 at 9 et seq.

[247] *Keck and Mithouard* at 14.

proclamation of a goal which has not been achieved. Although the judgment lacks the clarity it pretends to possess, it can safely be claimed that the *Keck* doctrine's impact on a principle of fair trading is less intense than it seems on the surface. A distinction has to be drawn between, on the one hand, the consequences concerning the potential scope of fair trading reasoning by the Court, which is related to the scope of free movement itself, and, on the other hand, the effects on the substance of the fair trading reasoning. Both aspects are to be examined separately (section 5.4.2 and section 5.4.3). It is not necessary in this context to repeat all the controversial discussions about *Keck* in literature.[248] Rather it is aimed at developing an own interpretation in the specific context of this study.

5.4.2 The impact on the scope of fair trading reasoning

5.4.2.1 Rules that lay down requirements to be met by goods

According to paragraph 15 of the *Keck* judgment, which is to confirm prior case law, rules that lay down requirements to be met by imported goods are still considered measures of equivalent effect and therefore are in principle prohibited by Article 28. While it is true that this is merely a partial confirmation of the *Dassonville/Cassis de Dijon* doctrine, the examples given as an illustration are quite revealing. Rules relating to designation, presentation, labelling and packaging, for instance, are deemed to belong to the category of goods-related requirements and thus may still constitute measures of equivalent effect. These trading rules – which are frequently claimed by the national governments to pursue an objective of consumer protection and fair trading – played an important role before *Keck*, and they have continued to assume a most significant part after *Keck*. As far as the pre-*Keck* era is concerned, it should be recalled that, for example, the probably most influential pre-*Keck* free movement cases, *Dassonville* and *Cassis de Dijon*, concerned exactly this kind of trading rules. In *Dassonville* it was the Belgian prohibition of scotch whisky bearing a designation of origin without an official certificate. In *Cassis de Dijon* it was the German prohibition to market a fruit liqueur under the designation 'Cassis de Dijon', if a specific minimum content of alcohol had not been attained.

After *Keck*, national measures affecting the designation, packaging and labelling of goods still come under Article 28. Post-*Keck* case-law has shown that those labelling cases constitute a significantly high proportion of the relevant case law. The most prominent cases may be *Clinique* and *Mars*. In *Clinique* the

---

[248] See in general e.g. Gormley, (1994) 5 *EBLR* 63, Joliet, (1994) 43 *GRUR Int.* 979, Reich, (1994) 31 *CML Rev.* 459, Roth, (1994) 31 *CML Rev.* 845, Stuyck (1994) 30 *CDE* 431, Gormley (1996) 19 *Fordh. Int. L.J.* 866, Weatherill, (1996) 33 *CML Rev.* 885. For more references to the abundant literature, see Kapteyn/VerLoren van Themaat, *Law of the European Communities*, 3rd ed., p. 631.

German prohibition to market a cosmetic product under the name 'Clinique' fell within the ambit of Article 28 as it concerned the designation of a product.[249] In *Mars* the German prohibition to market ice-cream bars marked '+ 10%' during a publicity campaign equally was within the scope of Article 28 as it related to the packaging of products.[250] These judgments are not at all a somewhat lax interpretation of the *Keck* doctrine, but they are on the contrary a perfectly straightforward application of it (i.e. of paragraph 15 of *Keck*). Other significant cases in this respect are for example:[251] *Expiry Dates*[252] (packaging of medicinal products), *Sauce hollandaise*[253] (designation and labelling of sauces and pastry products), *Gut Springenheide and Tusky*[254] (labelling of packs of eggs), *Lifting*[255] (designation of a firming cream for the skin), *Guimont*[256] (labelling of Emmenthal cheese) *Ruwet*[257] (labelling of pre-packaged liquids), *Belgian Notification Numbers*[258] (obligation to include notification number on labelling of foodstuffs), *Schwarzkopf*[259] (labelling of cosmetic products), *Familiapress*[260] (prize competitions advertised in periodicals).

Recently, *Morellato* has specified, however, that the good-related rule must apply to the state of the good at the moment of its importation in order to fall under Article 28 according to paragraph 15 of *Keck*.[261] Under Italian law bread obtained by completing the baking of partly baked bread had to be distributed and put on sale in compartments separate from those for fresh bread, and in pre-prepared packaging displaying certain information, while bread obtained by baking fresh dough could be displayed and sold without this packaging. Obviously, this requirement would more likely affect imported partly baked bread.

---

[249] Case C-315/92 *Verband Sozialer Wettbewerb e.V. v Clinique Laboratoires SNC and Estée Lauder Cosmetics GmbH* [1994] ECR I-317.

[250] Case C-470/93 *Verein gegen Unwesen in Handel und Gewerbe Köln e.V. v Mars GmbH* [1995] ECR I-1923.

[251] It must be emphasised that this is a strictly exemplary list and by no means complete. For labelling cases in the foodstuffs sector, see furthermore Gormley (1997) *EFLR* 1.

[252] Case C-317/92 *Commission v Germany* [1994] ECR I-2039.

[253] Case C-51/94 *Commission v Germany ('Sauce hollandaise')* [1995] ECR I-3599.

[254] Case C-210/96 *Gut Springenheide GmbH and Rudolf Tusky v Oberkreisdirektor des Kreises Steinfurt – Amt für Lebensmittelüberwachung* [1998] ECR I-4657.

[255] Case C-220/98 *Estée Lauder Cosmetics GmbH & Co. OHG v Lancaster Group GmbH ('Lifting')* [2000] ECR I-117.

[256] Case C-448/98 *Criminal proceedings against Jean-Pierre Guimont* [2000] ECR I-10663.

[257] Case C-3/99 *Cidrerie Ruwet SA v Cidre Stassen SA and HP Bulmer Ltd.* [2000] ECR I-8749.

[258] Case C-217/99 *Commission v Belgium ('Belgian Notification Numbers')* [2000] ECR I-10251.

[259] Case C-169/99 *Hans Schwarzkopf GmbH & Co. KG v Zentrale zur Bekämpfung unlauteren Wettbewerbs e.V.* [2001] ECR I-5901.

[260] Case C-368/95 *Vereinigte Familiapress Zeitungsverlags- und vertriebs GmbH v Heinrich Bauer Verlag* [1997] ECR I-3689.

[261] Case C-416/00 *Tommaso Morellato v Comune di Padova* [2003] ECR I-9343.

Although packaging was concerned, the Court established that since the pre-baked bread, as imported, had not to be altered in order to comply with the Italian requirement, it concerned a certain selling arrangement, which fell outside the scope of Article 28, provided it did not constitute discrimination.[262]

In sum, the *Keck* doctrine still allows for the examination under Article 28 of an important part of national rules, which relate to fair trading. Consequently, the Court can continue making statements on fair trading on the basis of those labelling and designation provisions as ever before. Besides, the role of this category of cases must not be underestimated. As the case law analysis has shown, providing the consumer with correct and necessary information is the core feature of fair trading as shaped by the Court's case law. When the packaging and labelling situations still come under Article 28 after *Keck and Mithouard* this does signify nothing less than that the rules concerning the most central information transmitters are still subject to EC law assessment. This leaves the door open for the Court to pronounce itself on fair trading as it did pre-*Keck*.

5.4.2.2 'Certain' selling arrangements

In paragraph 16 of the *Keck* decision, the Court excludes rules restricting 'certain' selling arrangements from the *Dassonville* formula. This wording strongly suggests that not all kinds of selling arrangements are to be banned from the application of Article 28.[263] But which are the ones that are precluded?[264] The textual interpretation allows two different conclusions: either the use of the word 'certain' merely reinforces the statement in paragraph 15 of the judgment and therefore does not allude to other conceivable types of selling arrangements, or it has an own quality and indicates that there are 'certain' other selling arrangements which do not escape Article 28.

Are all selling arrangements taken out of the scope of free movement?

The Court might have referred to 'certain' selling arrangements just as a contrast to the rules that lay down 'certain' requirements to be met by goods (paragraph 15). A closer look at the examples given by the Court in paragraph 15 for product-related provisions reveals that some of them – namely presentation, labelling, and packaging – are actually hardly anything else than 'certain' other selling arrangements, i.e. promotion techniques which are associated with the substance of the good.[265] In this case, indeed, paragraph 16 would mean that all

---

[262] *Morellato* at 35 et seq.

[263] See also Schmid, *Dienstleistungsverkehr*, p. 293.

[264] Cf. the attempt of Stuyck (1994) 30 *CDE* 431 at 443 et seq. to get more clarity into the term *'modalités de vente'*. See furthermore the analysis by Heermann (1999) 48 *GRUR Int.* 579 at 582 et seq.

[265] This seems to correspond with the view expressed by Advocate General Léger in his Opinion in Case C-470/93 *Verein gegen Unwesen in Handel und Gewerbe Köln e.V. v Mars GmbH* [1995] ECR I-1923 at 28 and 29.

selling arrangements which do not coincide with the very few product-related (selling) arrangements in the sense of paragraph 15 are out of the scope of Article 28 (provided that they do not meet the criteria of the *Keck* proviso).

The reference to 'certain' selling arrangements could also be an additional emphasis of the *Keck* proviso in paragraph 16. Selling arrangements are excluded from the assessment under the free movement scheme, provided that they are not discriminatory with regard to their application and with regard to their effect. According to this reading, all non-product related trade-practice rules escape Article 28 as long as they are not discriminatory in the expressed sense.[266] Only this confinement would then be expressed by 'certain' selling arrangements.

Are 'certain' selling arrangements not taken out of the scope of free movement?

On the other hand, the stark confrontation of the *Keck* judgment's paragraphs 15 and 16 (together with the Court's express intention to amend prior case law) suggests that 'selling arrangements' is intended to signify something completely different to 'requirements to be met by goods'. This reading suggests that if only 'certain' selling arrangements are excluded from the application of Article 28, 'certain' others are not, and the latter ones do not coincide with some of the mentioned product-related practices of paragraph 15. According to this understanding, there seem thus to be 'certain' selling arrangements in the sense of paragraph 16 which are not to be excluded from Article 28.[267] The *Keck* judgment itself, however, remains silent about what kind of selling arrangements that would be.

In post-*Keck* case law, it appears, a selling arrangement has never been considered to be a measure of equivalent effect purely on the basis that it was a non-product related type of sales promotion of a specific type which did not fall out of the scope of Article 28 *per se*. Advocate General Lenz alluded to a distinction between different 'certain' selling arrangements in *Infant Milk*.[268] The Court, however, did not follow this approach. Yet, it seems significant to point out that *Keck* is indeed predisposed for such a reasoning. Even if the Court has not yet argued in this way, the wording of the judgment allows it do so in the future.

5.4.2.3 The *Keck* proviso

As has been mentioned before, not all rules on certain selling arrangements have been removed from the assessment under the free movement scheme. According to paragraph 16 of *Keck*, they are not considered to be a measure having equivalent effect only

[266] Cf. Leible, (2003) 14 *EuZW* 37 at 41.

[267] In the same way Koutrakos, (2001) 26 *E.L.Rev.* at 393. Earlier, see Roth, (1994) 31 *CML Rev.* 845 at 852.

[268] Opinion of Advocate General Lenz Case C-391/92 *Commission v Greece* [1995] ECR I-1621 at 16.

> 'so long as those provisions apply to all relevant traders operating within the national territory and so long as they affect in the same manner, in law and in fact, the marketing of domestic products and of those from other Member States'.[269]

The *Keck* proviso is actually a double discrimination test. Rules concerning certain selling arrangements are excluded so long as they are not discriminatory with regard to their application (i.e. if they are indistinctly applicable) and with regard to their legal or factual effect. Otherwise, rules concerning certain selling arrangements can perfectly well be measures of equivalent effect and thus be subject to assessment under Article 28. The distinction between requirements related to the good itself and requirements not related to the good does therefore not mechanically entail different consequences, but the test provides a flexible instrument for assessing the national measure.[270] The Court has indicated, in paragraph 17 of *Keck*, the discrimination test's underlying idea:

> 'Provided that those conditions are fulfilled, the application of such rules to the sale of products from another Member State meeting the requirements laid down by that State is not by nature such as to prevent their access to the market or to impede access any more than it impedes the access of domestic products. Such rules therefore fall outside the scope of Article 30 [28] of the Treaty'.[271]

Hence, the quality of the access of imported products to the national market is the key idea behind the *Keck* requirements. In the straightest tradition of free movement and non-discrimination it is the intention, as a matter of principle, not to have foreign products face more hindrance to access the domestic market than national products.[272] *Keck* is thus not about market access, it is about *equal* market access.[273] However, it may be seen as an '(unproven) assertion'[274] that by fulfilling the two non-discrimination conditions the national restriction is by nature not such as to prevent foreign goods' access to the market or to impede access any more than the access of domestic products.[275]

---

269 *Keck and Mithouard* at 16.

270 Cf. Koutrakos, (2001) 26 *E.L.Rev.* at 396. See also Perau, *Werbeverbote*, p. 113.

271 *Keck and Mithouard* at 17.

272 The prevention of access to the market must be understood as the most rigorous form of impeding access any more than impeding the access of domestic products.

273 Cf. also Weyer, *Freier Warenverkehr*, p. 377.

274 Barnard, (2001) 26 *E.L.Rev.* at 41.

275 Davies draws attention to the Court's jurisdiction to decide on matters of law, not on matters of fact. According to Davies, *Nationality Discrimination*, p. 96 note 10 '*Keck* is an authority for the proposition that Article 28 only extends to measures which do not prevent market access or hinder it unequally. The remark that selling arrangements have this characteristic is necessarily *obiter* given the division of functions between national and Community courts. It is for each national court, faced with particular selling arrangements, to decide their characteristics'.

Application of the Keck *proviso in the early post-*Keck *cases*

Given that the non-discrimination conditions have to be fulfilled cumulatively, one might assume that the test is not easily complied with. However, contrary to what might be expected, the Court has proven extraordinarily reluctant to actually apply the *Keck* proviso, in particular in the early post-*Keck* cases. In fact, already in *Keck* itself the Court did not apply it expressly. After the introduction of the formula the Court apparently considered it self-evident that its conditions were fulfilled.

In the judgments in which the national measures are held not to be covered by Article 28 the 'application' of the test is typically limited to the declaration of the finding that its conditions are satisfied. This is the case in *Hünermund*, which followed shortly after *Keck* and which concerned the German prohibition on advertising quasi-pharmaceutical products outside the pharmacy.[276] In *Leclerc-Siplec* the ban of televised advertising in respect of certain sectors of economic activity was likewise easily considered to fulfil the non-discrimination conditions.[277] The Court argued similarly tersely in *Infant Milk* concerning the Greek prohibition to market processed milk for infants other than by pharmacies.[278] In *Franzén*, which was about the monopoly on the retail of alcohol in Sweden, *Keck* was even not referred to at all.[279] It is true that in *Banchero*, which concerned the Italian legislation according to which the retail sale of tobacco products was reserved to authorised distributors, the Court's statements on the fulfilment of the *Keck* conditions are somewhat more detailed.[280] Still, they are presented as assertions rather than as the results of a serious application of the test.

A more serious application of the Keck *proviso*

In his Opinion in *Leclerc-Siplec*,[281] Advocate General Jacobs argued from an Internal Market point of view, claiming that the exclusion from the scope of Article 28 of measures which 'affect in the same manner, in law and in fact, the marketing of domestic products and those from other Member States' amounted to introducing, in relation to restrictions on selling arrangements, a test of discrimination. That test, however, seemed inappropriate to him. Jacobs opined that the central concern of the Treaty provisions on the free movement of goods

---

[276] Case C-292/92 *Ruth Hünermund and others v Landesapothekerkammer Baden-Württemberg* [1993] ECR I-6787 at 22.

[277] Case C-412/93 *Société d'Importation Edouard Leclerc-Siplec v TF1 Publicité SA and M6 Publicité SA* [1995] ECR I-179 at 23.

[278] Case C-391/92 *Commission v Greece* [1995] ECR I-1621 at 16.

[279] Case C-189/95 *Franzén* [1997] ECR I-5909.

[280] Case C-387/93 *Banchero* [1995] ECR I-4663 at 37, 40.

[281] Opinion of Advocate General Jacobs Case C-412/93 *Société d'Importation Edouard Leclerc-Siplec v TF1 Publicité SA and M6 Publicité SA* [1995] ECR I-179.

was to prevent unjustified obstacles to trade between Member States. Such an obstacle to inter-State trade would not cease to exist simply because an identical obstacle affected domestic trade. According to Jacobs,

> '[t]here is one guiding principle which seems to provide an appropriate test: that principle is that all undertakings which engage in a legitimate economic activity in a Member State should have unfettered access to the whole of the Community market, unless there is a valid reason for denying them full access to a part of that market'.[282]

The Court has not followed the Advocate General in his 'unfettered' market access reasoning, but rather applied more seriously the initial *Keck* proviso, which is underpinned by the idea of equal market access.[283]

The severe impediment of the access to the market for foreign goods played a role in *TK-Heimdienst Sass*.[284] The Court examined the Austrian trade rules, according to which bakers, butchers and grocers were only permitted to offer goods for sale on rounds from door to door in a particular municipality, if they carried on their trade from a permanent establishment in that same municipality or in a municipality adjacent thereto. Only goods which were offered for sale at such permanent establishments were allowed to be offered for sale on rounds. Accordingly, the Court concluded that the rules did not affect in the same manner the marketing of domestic products and that of products from other Member States in the sense of the *Keck* proviso, since such legislation imposed an obligation on traders who already had a permanent establishment in another Member State and who wished to sell their goods on rounds in a particular Austrian administrative district to set up or purchase another permanent establishment in that administrative district or in an adjacent municipality, whilst local economic operators already met the requirement as to a permanent establishment. The Austrian prohibition was therefore treated as a measure having equivalent effect.

Total marketing prohibitions were at the centre of *De Agostini and TV-Shop* and *Gourmet International*. In *De Agostini and TV-Shop*[285] the question has been raised, amongst others, whether the Swedish general ban on advertising in television aimed at children less than 12 years of age and on misleading advertising in television was compatible with the free movement scheme of the

---

[282] See the 'alternative analysis', as it is marked, of Advocate General Jacobs in his Opinion on *Leclerc-Siplec* at 38–55, the quotation is from 41.

[283] See also Oliver/Roth, (2004) 41 *CML Rev.* 407 at 416.

[284] Case C-254/98 *Schutzverband gegen unlauteren Wettbewerb v TK-Heimdienst Sass GmbH* [2000] ECR I-151.

[285] Joined Cases C-34/95, C-35/95 and C-36/95 *Konsumentombudsmannen (KO) v De Agostini (Svenska) Förlag AB and TV-Shop i Sverige AB* [1997] ECR I-3843.

Treaty.[286] The first condition of the *Keck* proviso (application of the measures to all traders operating within the national territory) was clearly fulfilled according to the Court. As regards the second condition, the Court found that it could not be excluded that an outright ban, applying in one Member State, of a type of promotion for a product which was lawfully sold there might have a greater impact on products from other Member States. It concluded, however, that such an outright ban on advertising was not covered by Article 28 of the Treaty, unless it was shown that the ban does not affect in the same way, in fact and in law, the marketing of national products and of products from other Member States. This means that in *De Agostini and TV-Shop* the advertising ban was considered *prima facie* falling out of the scope of Article 28, unless proven otherwise.[287]

The Court took a slightly different approach in *Gourmet International.*[288] The Swedish legislation practically totally prohibited the advertising of alcohol, so that the question arose whether this was compatible with Article 28. The Court considered it apparent that a prohibition on advertising such as that at issue not only prohibited a form of marketing a product, but in reality prohibited producers and importers from directing any advertising messages at consumers, with a few insignificant exceptions. It therefore felt able to conclude, without its being necessary to carry out a precise analysis of the facts, that the wide-ranging prohibition of advertising for alcohol, the consumption of which was linked to traditional social practices and to local habits and customs, was liable to impede access to the market by products from other Member States more than it impeded access by domestic products, with which consumers were instantly more familiar.[289] This reasoning suggests a further development of the practical application of the *Keck* proviso. In contrast to *De Agostini and TV-Shop,* in *Gourmet International* the national advertising ban was *prima facie* considered a measure of equivalent effect falling under Article 28, unless proven otherwise.

Two recent cases have further refined the Court's application of the *Keck* proviso. In *Morellato* the Court considered it a mere option that the Italian packaging rule for bread made from pre-baked bread discouraged their import or made them less attractive for consumers, which would cause the rule on the selling arrangement to be caught by Article 28.[290] The Court reasoned in a more

---

[286] The initial focus of the Court was of course Directive 89/552/EEC concerning the pursuit of television broadcasting activities ('Television without frontiers'), OJ 1989 L 298/23 .

[287] See also Heermann (1999) 48 *GRUR Int.* 579 at 587.

[288] Case C-405/98 *Konsumentombudsmannen (KO) v Gourmet International Products AB (GIP)* [2001] ECR I-1795, see for a critical discussion of the judgment A. Biondi (2001) 26 E.L.Rev. 616.

[289] *Gourmet International* at 21. According to Spaventa, (2004) 41 *CML Rev.* 743 at 755, the national rules challenged in *Gourmet International* 'did not prevent *access* to a foreign market, rather they prevented the very *existence* of a domestic market'. See also Case C-239/02 *Douwe Egberts* [2004] ECR I-nyr at 53.

[290] Case C-416/00 *Tommaso Morellato v Comune di Padova* [2003] ECR I-9343 at 37, see *supra* at 5.4.2.1.

authoritarian way in *DocMorris*.[291] The case concerned the German legislation according to which the sale of medicinal products for human use was restricted to German pharmacies, while the import by way of mail order through pharmacies approved in other Member States in response to individual orders placed by consumers over the Internet was prohibited. The Court recognised the distribution method via the Internet as a selling arrangement and therefore examined the prohibition under the *Keck* proviso. It then concluded that for pharmacies not established in Germany, the Internet provides a more significant way to gain direct access to the German market than for German pharmacies. Therefore, the prohibition could impede access to the market for products from other Member States more than it impeded access for domestic products and, accordingly, the prohibition did not affect the sale of domestic medicines in the same way as it affected the sale of those coming from other Member States.[292]

In conclusion, it seems that the Court bases the application of the *Keck* proviso on some kind of evidence assessment. The more evident it seems to the Court that the national restriction impedes or prevents access of foreign goods to the national market, the less latitude it leaves to the national court to make its own evaluation, and the more likely it considers the measure to fall under Article 28. In any case, both *Gourmet International* and *DocMorris* suggest that a total prohibition of advertising is, as a matter of principle, an obstacle to the free movement of goods.[293] Such a prohibition affects the marketing of products originating from other Member States more than it affects the marketing of domestic products, because they are deprived of a necessary instrument for gaining access to a market on which domestic products are already present.

5.4.2.4 *Keck* and the free movement of services

Whether the *Keck* doctrine is, should be, or can be applied to the free movement of services almost seems to be more controversial than *Keck* itself.[294] It is submitted that, at least, serious doubts must be raised as to whether the doctrine is applied to services by the Court.

Alpine Investments can be considered the central judgment, which, as a matter of fact, is used by all sides as support for their conflicting opinions.

---

[291] Case C-322/01 *Deutscher Apothekerverband e.V. v 0800 DocMorris NV and Jacques Waterval* [2003] ECR I-nyr.

[292] *DocMorris* at 74 et seq.

[293] Cf. Stuyck (2001) 37 *CDE* 683 at 700 et seq. regarding *Gourmet International*. This rule has been confirmed in Case C-71/02 *Herbert Karner Industrie-Auktionen GmbH v Troostwijk GmbH* [2004] ECR I-nyr at 42.

[294] The discussion is excellently reproduced and further stimulated by Roth in Adenas/Roth, *Services and Free Movement*, p. 1 and da Cruz Vilaça in Adenas/Roth, *Services and Free Movement*, p. 24, who, unsurprisingly, reach different conclusions.

According to the present reading, the judgment indicates quite clearly the non-application of the *Keck* doctrine, given that the Court has considered the Dutch prohibition of cold calling to be 'not analogous to the legislation concerning selling arrangements held in *Keck and Mithouard*'.[295] According to the Court, the Dutch prohibition directly affected access to the market in services in the other Member States, which distinguished it from *Keck* situations.[296] It is moreover fairly revealing that the Court does not raise the question of the application of the *Keck* doctrine in cases where it might be expected to do so. In *Schindler*, for instance, it was not questioned whether the prohibition of the advertising and distribution of tickets for large-scale lotteries was a national restriction of a certain selling arrangement in the sense of *Keck*.[297] Nor did such a consideration appear in *Corsten*,[298] which concerned the obligation for foreign service providers to be entered on the trades register in Germany, in order to perform skilled trade activities (floor laying in this case).

Despite the controversy about the application of the *Keck* doctrine to services,[299] this issue is deliberately merely touched upon in this study. For the present purposes it is unnecessary to enter deeply into the discussion. In view of the dominance of the free movement of goods for the Court's fair trading reasoning, the examination of the application of *Keck* in the goods sector is sufficient to make the point about the restrictions on the impact of the *Keck* doctrine. With regard to services, it seems therefore sufficient to establish that the Court did have the opportunity to express itself clearly on the applicability of *Keck* on services,[300] but failed to do so, which rather points towards non-application.[301] This is just another indicator that the ambit of *Keck* is more restricted for the issue of fair trading than it might seem at first glance.

---

[295] Case C-384/93 *Alpine Investments BV v Minister van Financiën* [1995] ECR I-1141 at 36.

[296] *Alpine Investments* at 38. For Tesauro, (1995) 15 *YEL* 1 at 7 *Alpine Investments* clearly demonstrates that the extension of the *Keck* doctrine on services has been ruled out by the Court.

[297] Case C-275/92 *Her Majesty's Customs and Excise v Gerhart Schindler and Jörg Schindler* [1994] ECR I-1039. See also *supra* at 5.2.7.

[298] Case C-58/98 *Josef Corsten* [2000] ECR I-7919.

[299] It should be noted that the question of the application of *Keck* is also unclear regarding other freedoms, which are not fair trading relevant in the sense of this study, see e.g. Case C-415/93 *Union royale belge des sociétés de football association ASBL v Jean-Marc Bosman* [1995] ECR I-4921 at 103 for the free movement of workers.

[300] At least this should be uncontroversial (in view of the controversial discussion).

[301] One approach in doctrine consists in attempting to 'reconcile' services case law with *Keck*, e.g. Snell, *Goods and Services*, p. 82 et seq. This is hardly satisfactory, since the question remains why the Court has not itself taken a clear position.

5.4.3 The impact on the substance of fair trading reasoning

It has been demonstrated that *Keck* indeed has consequences for the scope of fair trading reasoning by the Court, given that the field of application of Article 28 has been restricted, albeit less than it might seem. In view of the fair trading reasoning developed in the previous case law analysis, it must moreover be asked about the consequences of *Keck* for the substance of the Court's fair trading reasoning. Despite the particular significance of the question, the answer, it is submitted, is much clearer in this respect: there are no consequences. The reason for the non-influence of *Keck* on the substance of the Court's fair trading reasoning lies in the methodological framework of the reasoning, and it is empirically confirmed.

5.4.3.1 Methodological framework

It has been explained that the fair trading reasoning of the Court originates in the potential justification of a national measure, and in particular in the application of the principle of proportionality.[302] During the process of balancing the different interests at stake the Court imparts elements of a fair trading concept. Post-*Keck*, this has not changed at all. Proportionality is still the decisive balancing standard and the crucial basis for the Court's expression on fair trading. *Keck* has affected the ambit of Article 28 in that it curtailed the wide scope of the basic *Dassonville* formula. It has clearly not affected, however, the fundamental scheme of justification of a national measure. The rule of reason and the proportionality of the national restriction are still valid principles which are applied post-*Keck*, and which have not changed as such. Due to *Keck*, there may be fewer measures which are assessed under these principles. However, those measures which still fall under Article 28 – be it because they are not rules concerning certain selling arrangements, be it that they are rules concerning certain selling arrangements which do not meet the requirements of the *Keck* proviso – receive the exact same justification assessment as pre-*Keck*. This allows and, in fact, requires the Court to continue with its interest balancing. Methodologically, there is thus no indication for a change of the Court's substantive fair trading reasoning.

5.4.3.2 Empirical considerations

Next to the methodological consistency in the Court's reasoning, there are also no empirical indications why pre-*Keck* statements regarding fair trading should not be valid post-*Keck*.[303] In principle, the question could be

---

302 See *supra* at 4.2. This has become moreover apparent in the entire case law analysis.

303 See also the analysis of Alexandridou in Krämer/Micklitz/Tonner, *Law and diffuse interests*, p. 409 at p. 414 et seq.

raised whether a case that would be decided differently post-*Keck* is still good law. However, the difference would merely be that the measure would not fall under Article 28 anymore. This means it would not be assessed under Community law anymore and therefore would prevail, whereas it may have been an unjustified measure having equivalent effect pre-*Keck*. This does not, however, affect the substance of pre-*Keck* reasoning.

For instance, if a measure such as in *GB-INNO* (the prohibition of certain price comparisons) would post-*Keck* not fall under Article 28 anymore, the consequence would simply be that the Court would not express itself on such a measure anymore. This does not mean that the *GB-INNO* reasoning on the need of consumers to make informed choices would be invalid. *Clinique, Mars, Gut Springenheide and Tusky, Lifting,* or all the other labelling cases,[304] including case law on secondary law,[305] forcefully prove that consumer information and the related image of the consumer are still the crucial parameters of fair trading reasoning. The Court's views on the need of information for consumers to make their choice in full knowledge of the facts have not changed.[306] Post-*Keck* the Court merely has less opportunity to express itself on fair trading. *Keck* may have 'overruled' some previous case law in scope but not in substance.

Finally, a look at the background to the *Keck* judgment illustrates that the idea never was to change substantive reasoning, but merely to curtail the outer limits of Article 28. It can be said that the ruling in *Keck* has particularly been provoked by the growing number of Sunday trading cases for which *Torfaen* is representative.[307] The British rule prohibiting retailers from opening their premises on Sunday, which applied to imported and domestic products alike, was deemed to be incompatible with Article 28, unless justified from a Community law perspective. The implementation of certain political, social and economic choices had already been held to be legitimate aims in *Oebel*[308] and *Cinéthèque*,[309] and in *Torfaen* the prohibition of Sunday trading was considered to be an implementation of exactly that kind. Proportionality was left for the national courts to determine. Given the difficulty of the national courts to apply the proportionality test,[310] the subsequent Sunday trading cases, culminating in

---

[304] See *supra* at 5.4.2.1.

[305] E.g. Case C-373/90 *Criminal proceedings against X ('Nissan')* [1992] ECR I-131, Case C-44/01 *Pippig Augenoptik GmbH & Co. KG v Hartlauer Handelsgesellschaft mbH* [2003] ECR I-3095, see Chapter 2 at 2.3.

[306] See also Keßler/Micklitz, *Harmonisierung des Lauterkeitsrechts*, p. 48.

[307] Case C-145/88 *Torfaen Borough Council v B & Q plc* [1989] ECR 3851. Cf. the case note by Gormley, (1990) 27 *CML Rev.* 141.

[308] Case 155/80 *Summary proceedings against Sergius Oebel* [1981] ECR 1993.

[309] Joined Cases 60 and 61/84 *Cinéthèque SA and others v Fédération nationale des cinémas français* [1985] ECR 2605.

[310] Jarvis, *Application of EC Law*, p. 195 et seq.

Stoke-on-Trent, sought to resolve these conflicts.[311] Although the Sunday trading cases paved the way for the idea that certain rules could as such escape the prohibition under Article 28,[312] it appears that with the introduction of the *Keck* doctrine the Court primarily aimed at disposing of the cases concerning the non-discriminatory regulation of socio-economic life,[313] rather than it intended to change its assessment of marketing practices that would still be within the realm of Community law. This aim is reflected in the post-*Keck* Sunday trading cases, like *Punto Casa* and particularly *Semeraro Casa*.[314] It is needless to say that it has been strongly doubted whether the introduction of the *Keck* doctrine was the dogmatically proper answer in order to cope with the diversity of socio-economic rules in the Community.[315]

5.5 Concluding remarks

It will be the aim of Chapter 3 to establish a comprehensive general concept of fair trading based on the statements of the Court in interpreting primary law, and added by the indications in secondary law, which will be examined separately in the following Chapter 2. Nevertheless, at this point, it seems useful to recall very briefly the main findings concerning fair trading in the Treaty case law.

Market transparency and consumer information

It is clearly discernible from the relevant case law that consumer information plays a predominant role in the assessment of a national rule pursuing the objective of consumer protection and fair trading. The Court has left no doubt

---

311 See Case C-312/89 *Union départementale des syndicats CGT de l'Aisne v SIDEF Conforama, Socit Arts et Meubles and Socit Jima* [1991] ECR I-997, Case C-332/89 *Marchandise, Chapuis and SA Trafitex* [1991] ECR I-1027, Case C-306/88 *Rochdale Borough Council v Stewart John Anders* [1992] ECR I-6457, Case C-304/90 *Reading Borough Council v Payless DIY Ltd, Wickes Building Supplies Ltd, Great Mills (South) Ltd, Homebase Ltd, B & Q Plc* [1992] ECR I-6493, Case C-169/91 *Council of the City of Stoke-on-Trent and Norwich City Council v B & Q plc* [1992] ECR I-6635.

312 See Nihoul, (1993) 1 *JTDE* 12 at 13.

313 Gormley, (1994) 5 *EBLR* 63 at 66 et seq., Gormley, (1996) 19 *Fordh. Int. L.J.* 866 at 871 et seq. See also *Keck and Mithouard* at 14.

314 Joined Cases C-69/93 and C-258/93 *Punto Casa SpA v Sindaco del Comune di Capena et Comune di Capena and Promozioni Polivalenti Venete Soc. coop. arl (PPV) v Sindaco del Comune di Torri di Quartesolo and Comune di Torri di Quartesolo* [1994] ECR I-2355 and Joined Cases C-418/93, C-419/93, C-420/93, C-421/93, C-460/93, C-461/93, C-462/93, C-464/93, C-9/94, C-10/94, C-11/94, C-14/94, C-15/94, C-23/94, C-24/94 and C-332/94 *Semeraro Casa Uno Srl v Sindaco del Comune di Erbusco et al.* [1996] ECR I-2975 at 25.

315 See esp. Gormley, (1994) 5 *EBLR* 63; Reich, (1994) 31 *CML Rev.* 459; Gormley, (1996) 19 *Fordh. Int. L.J.* 866; Weatherill, (1996) 33 *CML Rev.* 885.

that the prohibition to provide information to the consumer is not proportionate to the aim pursued and can therefore not be justified under the mandatory requirements of consumer protection and fair trading. To put it more straightforwardly: the suppression of information to the consumer is obviously not fair in terms of a Community law standard. However, the Court expands less upon what kind of information is concerned. It is decisive, in any case, that the consumers are enabled to make their choice in full knowledge of the facts. More specifically, price transparency and product quality have been mentioned, as well as the necessity to enable consumers to take precautionary measures for the protection of their health. There are also indications in the case law suggesting a positive obligation to supply information, that is to say a duty to inform, where information is not available otherwise. However, this is less clear, due to the conceptual characteristic of negative integration: in principle, the Court does not set up obligations, but it removes obstacles.

The image of the consumer

The idea that consumers must be able to make informed choices is complemented by a certain image of the consumer, which has been developed, in particular, in cases concerning misleading advertising. The consumer image is another expression of the principle of proportionality and serves as a yardstick for assessing whether the available information actually enables consumers to make their choices. It is submitted that it is a normative concept. Although, on the surface, the consumer image may not seem entirely consistent in view of its various objective and subjective elements, it is actually a coherent concept. As a basic rule, there is the consumer who is capable of making autonomous and sensible decisions. Yet, the socio-cultural heterogeneity of European consumers involves different levels of susceptibility regarding (unfair) marketing practices, which, in turn, may justify different qualities of restrictive fair-trading measures. This could be translated into a two-stage test. The 'presumed expectations of an average consumer who is reasonably well informed and reasonably observant and circumspect' forms the basic principle. At the moment this standard is actually applied to the commercial practice national socio-cultural parameters have to be taken into account.[316]

The impact of the Keck*-doctrine*

It is submitted that the consequences of the *Keck* doctrine should not be overstated in the present context. The scope of the Court's fair trading reasoning is indeed reduced to those measures which still come under Article 28 post-*Keck*. However, in particular rules on the designation, presentation, labelling and packaging of goods, which have constituted the bulk of the case law already

---

[316] For more elaboration on the image of the consumer, see Chapter 3 at 3.2.

pre-*Keck*, are still within the scope of Article 28. In addition, a more serious application of the *Keck* proviso in recent case law suggests a tendency of rules on certain selling arrangements to fall under Article 28 after all, if they concern total advertising bans, or particularly impeding restrictions on marketing. The Court thus recognises the fundamental market access function of sales promotion.[317] Without advertising, foreign suppliers, who are naturally less present on the national markets, are deprived of their most important means of drawing attention to their products. As a matter of fact, this concept strikingly relates to the initial *Oosthoek* approach. Moreover, as results from the methodology of the Court's reasoning and from empirical considerations, *Keck* has not affected the substance of the Court's fair trading reasoning.

317 Cf. Leible, (2001) 12 *EuZW* 253 at 254.

CHAPTER 2

Fair Trading in Secondary Community Law

1 The regulatory approach

The goal of establishing a smoothly functioning Internal Market is not only an economic objective, but it clearly entails a legal implication as well. Differences in the national legal orders of the Member States always imply obstacles of some degree to free movement. These can be direct and obvious obstacles, such as marketing rules, or they may be of a more indirect and disguised nature, such as, for instance, rules regarding judicial protection. Either type undermines the consumer's confidence in performing a cross-border transaction.[1] In fact, for the existence of a true single market, as well as for its smooth functioning, the approximation of national laws is indispensable. Ideally, this means total harmonisation, or even legal uniformity.[2] Yet, as the principles of conferred powers and of subsidiarity illustrate, this is not wanted in the current stage of integration of the Community.[3] At the same time, negative integration and mutual recognition with their deregulatory and liberalising effects are merely stopgap remedies for the achievement of an Internal Market.[4] The legislation concerning fair trading perfectly reflects these conceptual conflicts.

Given that fair trading is at present not regulated by one single comprehensive legislative measure, it is necessary to have a closer look at the current regulatory approach of the Community with regard to fair trading. In fact, in order to be able to analyse adequately the existing legislative measures and potentially to infer a principle of fair trading from them, a clear awareness of the Community's regulatory approach in general is indispensable. This examination therefore precedes the actual substantive analysis of the specific legislative instruments.

---

1 Wilhelmsson, (2004) 27 *JCP* 317 at 329 et seq. highlights the practical problems and problems of access to justice, which prevent consumers from cross-border shopping. According to him, what the confident consumer really needs is easy access to a counterparty.

2 Cf. Dougan, (2000) 37 *CML Rev.* 853 at 860. See also Kurcz, (2001) 12 *EBLR* 287 at 288 and Stuyck in Krämer/Micklitz/Tonner, *Law and diffuse interests*, p. 279 at p. 281. However, the connotations of 'harmonisation' and the 'approximation of laws' indicate that the underlying concept is not designed to create uniform law, see Drexl in Grundmann/Stuyck, *Academic Green Paper*, p. 103 at p. 106 et seq. and p. 112. In support of pluralism of consumer and private law in Europe: Wilhelmsson, *Is There a European Consumer Law*, p. 21 et seq.

3 For an economic justification of the subsidiarity principle, see Wagner, (2002) 39 *CML Rev.* 995 at 999 et seq. Tilleman/Du Laing in Grundmann/Stuyck, *Academic Green Paper*, p. 81 at p. 91 et seq. report on other possible views on subsidiarity as an instrument to encourage Community action.

4 See Chapter 1 at 2. See also Grundmann/Kerber/Weatherill in Grundmann/Kerber/Weatherill, *Party Autonomy*, p. 3 at p. 7.

1.1 The legal basis for harmonisation

Article 95 – Fair trading legislation is Internal Market legislation

Since the introduction of social welfare concerns into the Treaty the focus of Community goals has widened. Consumers are not only seen as the indirect beneficiaries of a functioning Internal Market, but they have become the object of specifically targeted measures.[5] The establishment of common consumer protection standards is indeed used as a tool for guaranteeing the functioning of the Internal Market.[6] The legitimacy for positive integration – i.e. harmonisation – of fair trading is thus to be found in the creation of a functioning Internal Market featuring a high level of consumer protection.[7] Accordingly, the Community legislator generally uses Article 95 as the legal basis for harmonisation.[8] In more recent directives this is combined with Article 153(3)(a), which refers to Article 95 for consumer protection measures in the context of the completion of the Internal Market.[9] As far as the legal basis is concerned, there can be no doubt that the Community legislator regards fair trading legislation as Internal Market legislation.

The limits of Article 95 as a legal basis

Yet, Article 95 is not to be understood as *'carte blanche'* for harmonisation of the Internal Market.[10] In the past, the Community legislator has often justified the approximation of laws under Article 95 by the mere fact of the disparity of national legislation in a particular field.[11] The Court has made clear in *Tobacco Advertising* that this is not sufficient as it conflicts with the principle of conferred

---

5 According to Alpa, (2001) 12 *EBLR* 244 at 244 'consumer protection has become one of the fundamental objectives of the European Union and one of the essential tasks of E.C. policy inherent to the realisation of the internal market'.

6 Amtenbrink/Schneider, (1999) 14 *VuR* 293 at 293.

7 It has been suggested that the system of the Internal Market and of undistorted competition (Art. 3(c) and (g)) presupposes a specific fair-trading-law. In combination with the Preamble, it has further been suggested, this would allow the conclusion that the Treaty has assigned to the Community the harmonisation of sanctioning unfair commercial practices, Weinand, *Europarecht und Recht gegen den unlauteren Wettbewerb*, p. 23 with further references.

8 See also Weatherill, (2002) 31 *GAJICL* 139 at 148 et seq.

9 Measures which support, supplement and monitor the policy pursued by the Member States, for which Article 153(3)(b) constitutes an own legal basis, has proven to be of little significance. For the prominent exception, Directive 98/6, see *infra* at 2.4.

10 See Joined Opinion of Advocate General Fennelly Case C-376/98 *Germany v Parliament and Council ('Tobacco Advertising')* [2000] ECR I-8419, Case C-74/99 *R v Secretary of State for Health and others, ex parte Imperial Tobacco Ltd and others* [2000] ECR I-8419 at 89.

11 See also Micklitz in Grundmann/Kerber/Weatherill, *Party Autonomy*, p. 197 at p. 200, Weatherill, (2004) 8 *ERPL* 633 at 636 et seq.

powers in Article 5(1).[12] The shifting from unanimity to qualified majority vote, resulting in the possibility of adopting legislation against the wishes of some Member States, has made the legal issue of Community competence a practical concern of Member States being in the minority.[13] The Court has dealt with challenges of Community acts by outvoted Member States before,[14] *Tobacco Advertising*, however, is certainly a landmark judgment as regards the interpretation of Article 95. In this case the Court annulled Directive 98/43 on tobacco advertising[15] which, except for a few limited exemptions, featured a general ban on all forms of advertising and sponsorship of tobacco products, and which was based on the harmonisation provisions of Articles 47(2), 55 and 95. The Directive was obviously motivated by human health objectives, which are excluded from harmonisation by Article 152(4)(c). The circumvention of this exclusion brought the matter of Community competence into the spotlight and focussed on the question how far Article 95 reaches as a legal basis for the harmonisation of the Internal Market.[16] The Court held that a measure adopted on the basis of Article 95 'must genuinely have as its object the improvement of the conditions for the establishment and functioning of the internal market'[17]. To the rule of its *Titanium Dioxide* case law, according to which the aim of eliminating distortions of competition is conducive to the attainment of the Internal Market and thus falls within the scope of Article 95,[18] the Court added that the distortion of competition which the measure purports to eliminate must be appreciable.[19] It therefore introduced a *de minimis* requirement in order to invoke Article 95 as a legal basis.[20]

As a consequence of *Tobacco Advertising*, a mere finding of disparities between national rules and of the abstract risk of consequential obstacles to the exercise of fundamental freedoms or of distortions of competition is not

12 Case C-376/98 *Germany v Parliament and Council ('Tobacco Advertising')* [2000] ECR I-8419.

13 Cf. Slot, (2002) 13 EBLR 1 at 18.

14 See in particular Case C-84/94 *United Kingdom v Council* [1996] ECR I-5755 and Case C-233/94 *Germany v Parliament and Council* [1997] ECR I-2405. Besides the claim of adoption on the wrong legal basis the violation of general principles of Community law, such as proportionality and subsidiarity, is a favourite plea.

15 Directive 98/43/EC relating to the advertising and sponsorship of tobacco products, OJ 1998 L 213/9.

16 See the analysis by Usher (2001) 38 *CML Rev.* 1519, who, in addition to his observations concerning *Tobacco advertising*, relates Article 95 to the general Internal Market case law of the Court. See furthermore Segnana, (2001) 9 *JTDE* 9.

17 *Tobacco Advertising* at 84.

18 Case C-300/89 *Commission v Council ('Titanium Dioxide')* [1991] ECR I-2867 at 23.

19 *Tobacco Advertising* at 106.

20 Cf. Amtenbrink, (2001) 16 *VuR* 163 at 170, who notes that the *de minimis* requirement was not yet obvious from *Titanium Dioxide*, likewise Amtenbrink/Appeldoorn (2001) 49 *SEW* 413 at 417, cf. also Barents, (2000) 6 *NTER* 327 at 330.

sufficient to justify the choice of Article 95 as a legal basis. The Court's reasoning can be translated into a three-stage test. Firstly, obstacles to free movement or appreciable distortions of competition do have to exist, or it must be probable that obstacles to free movement will arise in the future. Secondly, the legislative measure has to contribute actually to eliminating obstacles to free movement or to removing appreciable distortions of competition. Finally, Article 95 cannot be used to circumvent the limits on other Treaty provisions.[21]

The Court has remained fairly laconic on the role of public interest matters within the competence to harmonise the Internal Market on the basis of Article 95.[22] According to Article 95(3) health, safety, environmental protection and consumer protection are public interests that can indeed be harmonised under the general competence of Article 95(1). In these matters the Commission shall take as a base a high level of protection in its proposals. Almost incidentally the Court remarked that, provided that the conditions for Article 95 as a legal basis were fulfilled, the Community legislature could not be prevented from relying on that legal basis on the ground that public health protection was a decisive factor in the choices to be made.[23] This reasoning suggests a vertical relationship between the Internal Market objective and the social welfare policies: only if Article 95(1) is applicable as a legal basis for the harmonisation of the Internal Market in accordance with the abovementioned criteria developed in *Tobacco Advertising*, can the social welfare objectives of Article 95(3) be pursued under that Article. In other words: public interest objectives can certainly be harmonised according to Article 95, but only if they serve the establishment and functioning of the Internal Market.[24]

One may wonder whether legislation in the field of consumer protection, due to Article 153, is freed from this hierarchy and must not obey the Internal Market objective in the same manner. This may be true for measures based on Article 153(3)(b), which is a sufficient legal basis for measures which support, supplement and monitor the policy pursued by the Member States. However, as far as measures in the context of the Internal Market are concerned, Article 153(3)(a) refers to the adoption 'pursuant to Article 95'. This can hardly be understood in another way than that the same conditions of Article 95 apply for these harmonisation measures, which are the relevant ones in the context of fair trading.

---

[21] This is a synthesis of the tests suggested by Schroeder, (2001) 12 *EuZW* 489 at 491, Usher, (2001) 38 *CML Rev.* 1519 at 1536, and Weatherill, (2004) 8 *ERPL* 633 at 644.

[22] See the discussion of this issue by Amtenbrink in Nordhausen, *Entwicklungen*, p. 53 at p. 62 et seq. This aspect is taken up again in Chapter 4 at 2.1.3.1 in connection with the discussion whether and to what extent the Treaty relates consumer protection to the Internal Market.

[23] *Tobacco Advertising* at 88; see also *British American Tobacco* (footnote 25) at 62.

[24] Amtenbrink in Nordhausen, *Entwicklungen*, p. 53 at p. 65, Weatherill, (2004) 15 *EBLR* 23 at 25. For a different view, see Reich, (2001) 16 *VuR* 203 at 204.

In *British American Tobacco* the Court confirmed its reasoning in *Tobacco Advertising.*[25] In addition, it emphasised the close relationship between the principle of subsidiarity (Article 5(2)) and the principle of conferred powers. It pointed out that

> 'the principle of subsidiarity applies where the Community legislature makes use of Article 95 EC, inasmuch as that provision does not give it exclusive competence to regulate economic activity on the internal market, but only a certain competence for the purpose of improving the conditions for its establishment and functioning, by eliminating barriers to the free movement of goods and the freedom to provide services or by removing distortions of competition'.[26]

The validity of existing law

It is settled case-law that the interpretation the Court gives to a rule of Community law clarifies and defines where necessary the meaning and scope of that rule as it must be, or ought to have been, understood and applied from the time of its coming into force.[27] It follows that the lawful adoption of previous directives based on Article 95 (or formerly Article 94) has to be seriously questioned.[28] The mere finding of disparities between national rules and of the abstract risk of obstacles to the exercise of fundamental freedoms or of distortions of competition has often been the only explanation for harmonisation in the recitals of the directives. This scanty justification does not *per se* mean that the directives are illegal. They might – totally or partially – very well meet the requirements of Article 95 as interpreted by the Court. In fact, the answer to the question of legality requires a provision-by-provision analysis. However, for the purpose of this study it is decisive that the directives constitute legislation in force. So long as they are not challenged and annulled by the Court,[29] they

---

25 Case C-491/01 *R. v Secretary of State for Health, ex parte British American Tobacco (Investments) Ltd and Imperial Tobacco Ltd.* [2002] ECR I-11453, confirming the validity of Directive 2001/37/EC concerning the manufacture, presentation and sale of tobacco products, OJ 2001 L 194/26.

26 *British American Tobacco* at 179.

27 Case 61/79 *Amministrazione delle finanze dello Stato v Denkavit italiana Srl.* [1980] ECR 1205 at 16; Joined Cases C-367/93 to C-377/93 *F. G. Roders BV and others v Inspecteur der Invoerrechten en Accijnzen* [1995] ECR I-2229 at 42; Case C-35/97 *Commission v France* [1998] ECR I-5325 at 46; Case C-481/99 *Georg and Helga Heininger v Bayerische Hypo- und Vereinsbank AG* [2001] ECR I-9945 at 51.

28 Howells/Wilhelmsson, (2003) 28 *E.L.Rev.* 370 at 377, Roth, (2002) 6 *ERPL* 761 at 764, Weatherill, (2001) 24 *JCP* 339 at 368 et seq., Weatherill, (2004) 8 *ERPL* 633 at 636 et seq. and at 645 et seq. Directive 1999/44/EC on certain aspects of the sale of consumer goods and associated guarantees, OJ 1999 L 171/12 is often named as an example of a most doubtful legality as far as the Internal-Market objective is concerned.

29 Due to passed deadlines, in most cases only an indirect challenge in the context of a preliminary ruling is conceivable.

continue to remain valid law. For the deduction of a principle of fair trading from secondary Community law it is the reality of existing legislation that matters.

1.2 Piecemeal approach and content of Community legislation

It is obvious that the co-existence of numerous Community acts[30] comes along with various inconsistencies which affect consumer law in general and fair trading law in particular.[31] This begins with the most fundamental concept of the 'consumer', which is not uniformly defined in the directives.[32] The right of cancellation, a contractual remedy which is provided for in several directives, is another well-known example of incoherence, not only regarding the cancellation periods but also concerning the legal consequences of the cancellation.[33] The latter are moreover often left to the national legal order, which results in a variety of different solutions.[34] More specifically affecting fair trading, the tremendously differing information requirements are a perfect example of an incoherent secondary law. In the case of Directive 97/7 and Directive 2000/31 the information requirements are partly even contradictory,[35] although the Directives have overlapping scopes of application.[36] The different purposes of protection (e.g. both consumers and suppliers, or consumers only) and the correspondingly different scopes of application of the directives may finally be mentioned as an example of the most obvious flaws of present fair trading legislation.[37]

The incoherent content of Community legislation may seem to render it more difficult to deduce an underlying general concept of fair trading. However,

---

30 For more elaboration on the so-called piecemeal approach, see *infra* at 1.4.1.

31 See e.g. Micklitz, (2002) 13 *EBLR* 583 at 587. For a most harsh criticism of the unsystematic consumer and private law legislation and moreover its political genesis, see Calliess, (2003) 203 *AcP* 575 at 586 et seq.

32 Howells/Wilhelmsson, *EC Consumer Law*, p. 2 et seq., Bernardeau, (2001) *REDC* 341 at 341 et seq., Blaurock, (1999) 54 *JZ* 801 at 802, Landy in Osman, *Code européen de la consommation*, p. 57 at 67 et seq. See Chapter 3 at 3.1.

33 Roth, (2002) 6 *ERPL* 761 at 767, Rott, (2001) 16 *VuR* 78 at 80.

34 Drexl in Grundmann/Stuyck, *Academic Green Paper*, p. 103 at p. 110; Tilleman/Du Laing in Grundmann/Stuyck, *Academic Green Paper*, p. 81 at p. 82.

35 Cf. Reich, (2002) 66 *RabelsZ* 531 at 537.

36 According to recital 11 of Directive 2000/31 this Directive is to complement information requirements established by Directive 97/7.

37 Fair trading legislation therefore seems to be a perfect example of insufficiently systematic EC law, which produces surprising effects in the sense of Wilhelmsson's 'jack-in-the-box theory of European Community law', see Wilhelmsson in Krämer/Micklitz/Tonner, *Law and diffuse interests*, p. 177 (in particular at p. 186).

this is by no means an inevitable consequence. Just because two specific rules may clash with each other (e.g. because of different cancellation periods), this does not necessarily mean that they are not underpinned by the same general idea. This general idea may just have been expressed with different nuances in the specific cases. It should be noted in this context that the Commission has recognised the incoherence, and in various political and preparatory documents has proclaimed as a primary goal the review and adjustment of current law in order to create more cohesion.[38]

1.3 Directive as the leading type of legislative measures

Regulations and directives are the two (relevant) types of legal measures the Community possesses in order to achieve positive integration. However, in practice, harmonisation related to consumer protection has happened virtually exclusively by means of directives. Although the insufficiencies in this area are usually discussed in the context of minimum harmonisation,[39] several weaknesses stem from the very use of directives as legislative measures.

According to Article 249(3) a directive is binding as to the result to be achieved, while it leaves to the Member States the choice of form and methods to achieve this result.[40] Therefore, despite the fact that the objective is determined, a directive, by definition, leaves some flexibility in implementation for the national legislator, which results in dissimilar rules in the Member States.[41] The dissimilarities may be minor, but as long as a directive is not transposed literally into all the national legal orders, these dissimilarities will remain and, indeed, are tolerated. Besides the variations in substantive law, there is always the national application of the implemented directives, which can differ substantially as well.[42]

It is true that modern directives have left the path of merely proclaiming the basic goals and tend to formulate meticulously the means to achieve the result,

---

[38] See e.g. the Commission White Paper on governance, COM (2001) 428 final and the Commission Action Plan on 'better regulation', COM (2002) 278 final for a general approach to the issue and the Commission 'Consumer Policy Strategy 2002–2006', COM (2002) 208 final at 15, OJ 2002 C 137/2 at 7 and the Commission Communication 'A more coherent European contract law – An action plan', COM (2003) 68 final at 15 seq. for a more specific approach.

[39] See *infra* at 1.4.2.

[40] According to Weatherill, (2002) 31 *GAJICL* 139 at 142, 'the Directive serves as the most vivid illustration of the insight that the EC governs by a model of "indirect rule"'.

[41] Cf. Drexl in Grundmann/Stuyck, *Academic Green Paper*, p. 103 at p. 107.

[42] The situation is different where the Court uses its power to define general concepts in directives not abstractly but in detail, thereby taking all the leeway of interpretation from the national courts. See e.g. Case C-168/00 *Simone Leitner v TUI Deutschland GmbH & Co. KG* [2002] ECR I-2631 on the concept of 'damage' in Directive 90/314 on package travel, critically Roth, (2003) 40 *CML Rev.* 937 at 947. For the obligation to interpret national law in conformity with directives, see Wissink, *Richtlijnconforme interpretatie*, in particular at p. 88 et seq.

so that there is not much latitude left for the national legislator.[43] However, the structural problem that comes with the approximation of laws by means of a directive persists.[44] This has been acknowledged by the Commission in its contract-law action plan,[45] where it reported the criticism concerning the uniform application of Community law with which it was confronted in the responses to its earlier communication on contract law.[46] It has been submitted by the respondents[47] that abstract legal terms[48] in directives are often either not defined or too broadly defined, which has often resulted in a very large margin of discretion for the national legislators. Although national implementation laws would be in perfect conformity with the relevant directive, they would nevertheless lead to inconsistencies in their application to similar cases in different Member States.[49] The situation is comparable where abstract terms are defined in some directives, while they are not defined in others.[50]

In conclusion, it can be argued that the excessive use of directives is at odds with the intended aim of these measures, namely the effective harmonisation of national rules.[51] Although differing national laws are to be approximated, directives tend to uphold, or in some respects even intensify, the fragmentation of the Internal Market. However, their preference in practice over regulations can be explained precisely by the fact 'that a directive is less far-reaching than a regulation'.[52] Consequently, their proportionality is more obvious,[53] and the political consensus necessary for adoption is usually easier to achieve.

---

43 Cf. Micklitz, (2003) 18 *VuR* 2 at 6 and 8.

44 The 1992 Sutherland Report has therefore recommended the successive use of regulations as legal instruments of harmonisation, see Sutherland Report 'The Internal Market after 1992 – Meeting the Challenge', LET (1992) 3697, recommendation no. 11. This recommendation has successfully been implemented with regard to the Community Customs Code, see Gormley in Emiliou/O'Keeffe, *World Trade Law*, p. 124 (in particular at p. 128).

45 Commission Communication 'A more coherent European contract law – An action plan', COM (2003) 68 final. This has been confirmed in the Commission Communication 'European Contract Law and the revision of the *acquis*: the way forward', COM (2004) 651 final, which outlines the plan for developing a 'common frame of reference', which is to provide clear definitions of legal terms, fundamental principles and coherent model rules of contract law.

46 Commission Communication on European contract law, COM (2001) 398 final, OJ 2001 C 255/1.

47 The Commission does not mention the concrete sources for all the arguments. Given the high number of reactions and the obvious weaknesses of the current Community law it can be assumed that the various respondents submitted quite similar arguments.

48 E.g. fundamental terms like 'contract', 'damage' or more specific terms like 'equitable remuneration', 'fraudulent use' or 'durable medium'.

49 COM (2003) 68 final at 19.

50 COM (2003) 68 final at 20.

51 Amtenbrink, (1996) 11 *VuR* 286 at 290.

52 Kapteyn/VerLoren van Themaat, *Law of the European Communities*, 3rd ed., p. 327.

53 See No. 6 of the Protocol on proportionality and subsidiarity.

1.4 Scope and degree of harmonisation

Harmonisation can happen to different extents, which adds to the heterogeneous nature of fair trading law. Classified according to its scope, harmonisation can be complete or partial, horizontal or vertical. Classified according to its degree, one can distinguish between minimum and maximum harmonisation.

1.4.1 Complete or partial, horizontal or vertical harmonisation – the piecemeal approach

In order to move on with the integration process, the Community legislator has adopted a piecemeal approach in areas where comprehensive regulation could not be achieved politically. Fair trading has been one of them. Consequently, those issues were picked out which could be consented on first. Others followed, and a patchwork of rules has been created as time went on.[54] Accordingly, Community fair-trading legislation is characterised by this sector-specific or vertical harmonisation approach. The piecemeal process is reinforced by the fact that the sectors are not necessarily completely harmonised, but rather only partially. Usually only specific elements are dealt with in a directive, leaving all the other aspects of regulation within the sector to the preference of the national legislature.[55] Hence, the distinction between complete or partial, horizontal or vertical harmonisation answers what has been harmonised by the Community and where, in the context of shared competence, the Member States have chosen to cease exercising their regulatory competence. From an Internal Market perspective, the combination of sector-specific with partial harmonisation is particularly delicate, since it leaves much regulatory power to the Member States, which results in legislative disparities throughout the Community.

The piecemeal situation is also reflected by the implementation of Community legislation in the national legal orders. The European patchwork of rules has correspondingly been transposed into national law in the course of time and was not always well integrated into the existing legal system, and the national rules were often not coordinated with the implemented directives.[56] As a consequence, also the national laws have become – in creation as well as in application – to a certain extent more fragmented due to European harmonisation.[57] Given its potential for obstacles to trade, the resulting co-existence of many fragmented

54 Cf. Pützhoven, (1999) 10 *EWS* 447 at 450.

55 It may therefore be wondered whether complete harmonisation must not be regarded as a fairly theoretical concept at the current stage of integration.

56 See Micklitz, (2001) 16 *VuR* 71 for a description of this situation in the context of the modernised German law of obligations and Fischer, (2003) 18 *VuR* 20 for the effects of harmonisation of consumer law on German private law in general.

57 See Roth, (2002) 6 *ERPL* 761 at 772 et seq.

and varying national laws is undoubtedly not quite promoting a smoothly functioning Internal Market.[58]

Horizontal harmonisation, by contrast approximates national laws on a broad scale, beyond specific sectors. So far, in the area of fair trading, Directive 84/450 on misleading advertising as amended by Directive 97/55 on comparative advertising is the only such horizontally harmonising directive.[59] However, the categorisation into horizontal and vertical harmonisation is not an absolute one, but subject to interpretation. It has been suggested, for instance, that Directive 2000/31 on e-commerce was a horizontal directive, because it covered any kind of activity taking place on the Internet.[60] However, taking the Internet as a medium for trading, the Directive is a vertically harmonising directive limited to this specific medium. Following the latter approach, all relevant directives can be classified into vertical groups,[61] except for the horizontal Misleading Advertising Directive. It should be noted that horizontal harmonisation does not automatically entail complete harmonisation. The horizontal Community measure, extending beyond single sectors, does not have to deal with all aspects of the regulated matter, and usually only does so partially.

1.4.2 Maximum and minimum harmonisation

Unlike the differentiation between complete or partial, horizontal or vertical harmonisation, the distinction between maximum and minimum harmonisation is not one of scope but one of degree. The vast majority of fair-trading directives are minimum-harmonisation directives, i.e. Member States are free to exceed the minimum standard of protection prescribed in the directive.[62] Hence, although the matter is in principle harmonised by the Community the Member States are given an opportunity to exceed a particular standard. Obviously, the higher standard of protection must still be compatible with primary law, i.e. in particular the fundamental freedoms.[63]

Minimum harmonisation is usually the result of a political compromise in sensitive policy matters, such as consumer protection.[64] It is the balance of

---

58 Drexl in Grundmann/Stuyck, *Academic Green Paper*, p. 103 at p. 111; Tilleman/Du Laing in Grundmann/Stuyck, *Academic Green Paper*, p. 85 et seq.

59 Directive 98/6 on price indication assumes a special, quasi-horizontal, position, see *infra* at 2.4.

60 Lopez-Tarruella (2001) 38 *CML Rev.* 1337 at 1342.

61 For the classification, see *infra* at 2.5.

62 What constitutes a higher or lower level of consumer protection is certainly disputable, see the case law discussed in Chapter 1.

63 Kemper/Rosenow, (2001) 47 *WRP* 370 at 372, Oughton/Willett, (2002) 25 *JCP* 299 at 301. In the words of Weatherill, *Law and Integration*, p. 153: 'Secondary Community law sets the floor for national action; primary Community law sets the ceiling'.

64 Antoniolli in Collins, *Directive on Unfair Commercial Practices*, p. 241 at p. 279 et seq., Rott (2003) 40 *CML Rev.* 1107 at 1108.

achieving the highest common denominator and gaining the most support for it by the Member States.[65] Minimum harmonisation, which has earlier been accepted by the Court,[66] and which is now recognised by the Treaty itself,[67] has therefore remained the predominant practice in the consumer-relevant positive-integration process, as it allows the most progress where national laws differ widely.[68] In *Tobacco Advertising*[69] the Court observed that allowing stricter requirements to the Member States in connection with prohibiting provisions of Community legislation might lead to a complete prevention of movement within the coordinated field, which it considered unacceptable.[70] Such a preclusion of movement is usually not, at least not structurally, involved in connection with positive obligations. Therefore, it may be concluded that, while minimum harmonisation in connection with prohibiting norms is objectionable, it is still acceptable regarding positive obligations as known from consumer-protection legislation.[71]

Although minimum harmonisation can fix a high minimum standard of protection, it will not assure a high level of approximation of laws within the Community. Thus, as a result of the technique of minimum harmonisation the

---

65 See Dougan (2000) 37 *CML Rev.* 853 at 863 for the impact of minimum harmonisation on the development of the Community 'towards a more multifaceted Union which combines economic integration with high standards of social protection for those relatively vulnerable groups and interests which interface with the ambitions of the Internal Market, and whose objectives can, if necessary, be achieved through 'shared competence' and 'regulatory differentiation' between the Member States rather than 'exclusive competence' and 'uniformity' across the entire territory of the Community'.

66 See Case C-361/89 *Patrice Di Pinto* [1991] ECR I-1189 at 21 et seq.

67 According to Article 153(5), measures adopted pursuant to Article 153(4) shall not prevent any Member State from maintaining or introducing more stringent protective measures. This concerns measures which support, supplement and monitor the policy pursued by the Member States in the sense of Article 153(3)(b). Strictly speaking, these are therefore not 'harmonisation' measures, but, in practice, there does not seem to be a difference, as the example of Directive 98/6/EC on consumer protection in the indication of the prices of products offered to consumers, OJ 1998 L 80/27 shows, see *infra* at 2.4. See also Weatherill, *Consumer Law and Policy*, p. 27, who uses the term 'minimum harmonization' in this context. Likewise Askham in Vaughan, *Law of the European Communities*, at paragraph 91. It should be noted, moreover, that the Court pointed out in Case C-183/00 *María Victoria González Sánchez v Medicina Asturiana SA* [2002] ECR I-3901 at 24 that the minimum harmonisation requirement of Article 153(5) did not extend to measures adopted pursuant to Article 95 in the sense of Article 153(3)(a).

68 Drexl, (2002) 13 *EBLR* 557 at 567 points out that due to Community legislation some Member States, for the first time, had to introduce specific consumer protection into their private law legislations, while others already had a high standard of protection, which they wanted to maintain.

69 See footnote 12.

70 *Tobacco Advertising* at 104.

71 Reich, (2001) 16 *VuR* 203 at 204 et seq.

convergence of the national (fair trading) laws is quite limited.[72] Not only do they often differ widely regarding their level of protection, but also regarding the density of regulation. Consequently, it is difficult for businesses to develop marketing strategies that can be applied throughout the market,[73] which in fact derogates from the idea of the market integration process.[74]

Some of the more recent legislation features maximum (or full)[75] harmonisation. The E-Commerce Directive[76] and the Directive on distance marketing of consumer financial services[77] are representative examples. Likewise, the initiative for a Directive concerning unfair commercial practices aims at maximum harmonisation,[78] and the legislation concerning sales promotions is proposed as a regulation.[79] Finally, the Consumer Policy Strategy 2002–2006 proposes the review of existing Community legislation relating to consumer protection aiming at maximum harmonisation.[80] There seems thus to be a genuine tendency towards maximum harmonisation.[81] On the other hand, it has to be taken into account that in practice the maximum harmonisation approach is less comprehensive than it might be expected. Usually, the higher harmonisa-

---

72 See Drexl in Grundmann/Stuyck, *Academic Green Paper*, p. 103 at p. 107, who points out that from the point of view of the Internal-Market objective minimum harmonisation has to be – and indeed is – complemented by the principle of mutual recognition. Yet, according to the principle of mutual recognition as articulated in the *Cassis de Dijon* case law, higher standards, which constitute obstacles to free movement, can only be upheld if they satisfy overriding requirements of public interest. See also Weatherill in Grundmann/Kerber/Weatherill, *Party Autonomy*, p. 173 at p. 186. See furthermore *infra* at 1.5.

73 COM (2003) 68 final at 50.

74 Stuyck in Krämer/Micklitz/Tonner, *Law and diffuse interests*, p. 279 at p. 281.

75 Confusingly, 'maximum harmonisation' is often also referred to as 'full harmonisation'. The term 'full harmonisation' therefore usually denotes that no national standard different from the one prescribed in the directive is accepted. The term is then not meant in the sense of 'complete harmonisation' as explained above, *supra* at 1.4.1.

76 Directive 2000/31/EC on certain legal aspects of information society services, in particular electronic commerce, in the Internal Market (Directive on electronic commerce), OJ 2000 L 178/1.

77 Directive 2002/65/EC of 23 September 2002 concerning the distance marketing of consumer financial services, OJ 2002 L 271/16.

78 See the proposal for a Directive concerning unfair business-to-consumer commercial practices in the Internal Market and amending Directives 84/450/EEC, 97/7/EC and 98/27/EC (the Unfair Commercial Practices Directive), COM (2003) 356 final. However, the Common Position adopted by the Council has watered down the strict maximum harmonisation approach to some extent, see Chapter 5 at 3.3.3.

79 Amended proposal for a Regulation concerning sales promotions in the Internal Market, COM (2002) 585 final. Original proposal COM (2001) 546 final, OJ 2002 C 75 E/11, see Chapter 5 at 2.

80 'Consumer Policy Strategy 2002–2006', COM (2002) 208 final, OJ 2002 C 137/2, point 3.1.2.2.

81 Howells in Grundmann/Stuyck, *Academic Green Paper*, p. 73 at p. 77 et seq. seems to be more inclined to assume this. See also Howells/Wilhelmsson, (2003) 28 *E.L.Rev.* 370 at 375 et seq.

tion degree comes along with a higher number of exceptions, which is well illustrated by the E-Commerce Directive.[82] The labelling Directives, for instance, typically feature a maximum harmonisation approach as well, however curtailed by numerous specific exceptions.

Besides, an important differentiation has to be made: maximum harmonisation and a harmonised high level of consumer protection are fundamentally different issues.[83] While a high level of consumer protection may be the goal, this is not necessarily to be achieved by maximum harmonisation, i.e. by not allowing national deviations from the prescribed Community standard of protection. On the contrary, maximum harmonisation means that the Member States have to stick with the political compromise reached at Community level.[84] Moreover, it has to be borne in mind that Community harmonisation measures are always determined by the omnipresent market-integration goal. Unlike national consumer-protection legislation, Community consumer protection can therefore only be adopted to the extent it serves the Internal Market,[85] which obviously restricts its potential scope.[86] In that sense, maximum harmonisation can indeed imply a lower level of protection.

1.5 The country of origin principle

It has been noted earlier that negative integration, i.e. the Court's striking down of a national rule as incompatible with Community law, plays an important role in the approximation of national laws where harmonisation (positive integration) has not yet taken place.[87] Although not approximating national laws as such, the principle of mutual recognition (or mutual acceptance) is another important concept developed by the Court in order to facilitate free circulation and thereby contributing to a smooth functioning of the Internal Market. Generalising the Court's reasoning in *Cassis de Dijon*,[88] the principle of mutual recognition denotes that one Member State must admit the free circulation of goods or services on its territory which have been lawfully produced or

---

82 See also Micklitz/Keßler (2002) 51 *GRUR Int.* 885 at 888.

83 Howells in Grundmann/Stuyck, *Academic Green Paper*, p. 74.

84 Howells/Wilhelmsson, (2003) 28 *E.L.Rev.* 370 at 376.

85 Measures adopted according to Article 153(3)(b) in connection with Article 153(4) do not have to serve the Internal-Market objective, but, according to Article 153(5), they may not be maximum harmonisation either. It has been noted earlier that it is doubtful indeed whether existing legislation has always been adopted for the sake of the Internal Market, see *supra* at 1.1.

86 Howells/Wilhelmsson, (2003) 28 *E.L.Rev.* 370 at 376 et seq. As a conclusion, Howells and Wilhelmsson reject a shift from a policy of minimum harmonisation to one of maximum harmonisation (at 379).

87 See Chapter 1 at 2. and *supra* at 1.

88 Case 120/78 *Rewe-Zentral AG v Bundesmonopolverwaltung für Branntwein ('Cassis de Dijon')* [1979] ECR 649 at 14.

marketed in another Member State, as long as overriding requirements of public interest do not justify a hindrance.[89]

The principle of mutual recognition, which is derived from primary law and generally applicable, has a counterpart in Community legislation, namely the country of origin principle.[90] Two directives which are of relevance for fair trading feature the country of origin principle, namely the Television Directive[91] (there, the principle is also known as transmission-State principle) and the E-Commerce Directive.[92] Their central provisions illustrate the country of origin principle very well.[93]

The definition of the country of origin principle

According to Article 2(1) and Article 2a(1) of the Television Directive

> 'Each Member State shall ensure that all television broadcasts transmitted by broadcasters under its jurisdiction comply with the rules of the system of law applicable to broadcasts intended for the public in that Member State'.
>
> 'Member States shall ensure freedom of reception and shall not restrict re-transmissions on their territory of television broadcasts from other Member States for reasons which fall within the fields co-ordinated by this Directive'.

---

89 Although *Cassis de Dijon* is commonly seen as the origin of the mutual recognition principle (and indeed features the first clear formulation of it) the Court has articulated it before in Joined Cases 110/78 and 111/78 *Ministère public et al. v Willy van Wesemael et al.* [1979] ECR 35 at 39 in the context of the free movement of services, see Kapteyn/VerLoren van Themaat, *Law of the European Communities*, 3rd ed., p. 579. For further application in the context of the free movement of services, see e.g. Case 279/80 *Webb* [1981] ECR I-3305 at 17 et seq. and Case C-384/93 *Alpine Investments BV v Minister van Financiën* [1995] ECR I-1141 at 30 and 44 et seq.

90 The country of origin principle is sometimes also known as the home State control principle (as distinct from host State control).

91 Directive 89/552/EEC concerning the pursuit of television broadcasting activities ('Television without frontiers'), OJ 1989 L 298/23 as amended by Directive 97/36/EC, OJ 1997 L 202/60.

92 Directive 2000/31/EC on certain legal aspects of information society services, in particular electronic commerce, in the Internal Market (Directive on electronic commerce), OJ 2000 L 178/1.

93 Directive 93/22/EEC on investment services in the securities field, OJ 1993 L 141/27 with its authorisation ('passport') system does not feature a strict country of origin principle. It is true that the home State authorises and supervises the investment services firm (in this sense it is home-State control), the Directive, however, explicitly provides for exemptions 'in the interest of the general good'. The Directive thus merely codifies the rule-of-reason justification of the free-movement case law, see Moloney, *EC Securities*, p. 395.

According to Article 3(1) and (2) of the E-Commerce Directive

> 'Each Member State shall ensure that the information society services provided by a service provider established on its territory comply with the national provisions applicable in the Member State in question which fall within the coordinated field'.
>
> 'Member States may not, for reasons falling within the coordinated field, restrict the freedom to provide information society services from another Member State'.

Unfortunately, the principle of mutual recognition and the country of origin principle (or at least their designations) are often mixed up.[94] In order to be able to grasp fully the magnitude of the country of origin principle it must be strongly emphasised, however, that the concepts differ fundamentally in a key aspect: while the principle of mutual recognition structurally allows for exceptions (i.e. the non-recognition of the rules of the Member State of origin) in the form of a justification due to an open catalogue of overriding requirements of public interest,[95] the country of origin principle does not, in principle, allow such derogations.[96] It is up to the home State to ensure that its national rules are complied with, and the receiving State has to accept that assessment.[97] The application of national rules by the host State may not add a secondary control to that exercised by the home State.[98] As a result, the country of origin principle surpasses the market integrative capacity of the principle of mutual recognition in that it ensures a less obstructive movement of goods and services and facilitates the market access for the market actors.[99] It is in principle based on the idea of mutual recognition, but it abolishes the open grounds of justification for its derogation.

---

94 Not only does legal doctrine lack a clear distinction between the two concepts, also the Explanatory Memorandum to the Commission's original Proposal concerning a Directive on unfair commercial practices spoke of the introduction of the 'principle of mutual recognition' (or the 'Internal Market clause') in the proposal's Article 4 although this provision contained the country of origin principle, see COM (2003) 356 final at 30 and 47.

95 Of course, also justifications under Article 30 are derogations from the general principle of mutual recognition, see Case 272/80 *Frans-Nederlandse Maatschappij voor Biologische Producten BV* [1981] ECR I-3277 at 11 et seq. and Case 124/81 *Commission v United Kingdom* [1983] ECR I-203 at 12 et seq.

96 In the context of the regulatory technique of the 'New Approach to technical harmonisation and standardisation' the principle of mutual recognition has been further developed in that products manufactured in compliance with harmonised standards benefit from a presumption of conformity with the corresponding essential requirements.

97 See in the context of the Television Directive Case C-11/95 *Commission v Belgium* [1994] ECR I-4155 at 34 et seq. and Case C-14/96 *Paul Denuit* [1997] ECR I-2785 at 32 et seq.

98 Joined Cases C-34/95, C-35/95 and C-36/95 *Konsumentombudsmannen (KO) v De Agostini (Svenska) Förlag AB and TV-Shop i Sverige AB* [1997] ECR I-3843 at 34 and 61.

99 Cf. Grundmann, (2003) 67 *RabelsZ* 246 at 255 et seq.

In order to complete the picture it should be pointed out that that this structural key difference is slightly watered down in practice by basically three techniques. Firstly, specific aspects may explicitly be exempted from the application of the country of origin principle.[100] Secondly, provisional derogations may be allowed in specified cases of grave infringement of certain provisions of the respective Directive.[101] Thirdly, a complete system of derogation can be established, which is done in Article 3(4) of the E-Commerce Directive.[102] According to this provision, measures which are necessary for the reasons of public policy, public health, public security, and consumer protection, and which are proportionate to those objectives, may justify a derogation from the country of origin principle. However, except for consumer protection, the accepted grounds of justification are the same as those in Article 30 of the Treaty. They are thus not implied grounds of justification, such as the rule-of-reason grounds that come along with the principle of mutual recognition, but they rather constitute a closed catalogue of 'external' derogations from the country-of-origin-principle.[103] This confirms that, unlike the principle of mutual recognition, the country-of-origin-principle does not structurally comprise the derogations. It should be noted that invoking the derogations under the E-Commerce Directive is moreover connected to a notification procedure and requires beforehand that the Member State of origin has been asked first to take the necessary measures.[104]

The function of the country of origin principle

Besides the qualities mentioned above, the cited provisions of the Television Directive and of the E-Commerce Directive characterise the country of origin principle in two further respects. First, it is not an alternative to harmonisation, but rather a supplement. It only applies in fields coordinated by the directive. In the context of the Television Directive the Court has interpreted this condition narrowly in *De Agostini and TV-Shop*, arguing that the (partial) harmonisation of these areas is a prerequisite.[105] The country of origin principle is much more far-

[100] Such exemptions from the scope of the country of origin principle can be found in the Annex of the E-Commerce Directive.

[101] See Article 2a(2) of the Television Directive.

[102] See also Arndt/Köhler, (2001) 12 *EWS* 102 at 106 et seq. regarding Article 3(4) of the E-Commerce Directive.

[103] In fact, this implements Article 95(10) of the Treaty, which allows the inclusion of safeguard clauses.

[104] Contrary to what had been expected, so far the Article 3(4) derogation has hardly been invoked by the Member States, see First Report on the application of Directive 2000/31/EC, COM (2003) 702 final, p. 8.

[105] Joined Cases C-34/95, C-35/95 and C-36/95 *Konsumentombudsmannen (KO) v De Agostini (Svenska) Förlag AB and TV-Shop i Sverige AB* [1997] ECR I-3843 at 32–34. The Court thus considered 'coordinated' to be tantamount to 'regulated'. Advocate General Jacobs had opined, however, that 'coordinated' and 'regulated' were two distinct issues which must not be confused (at 80 of his Opinion). See also Drijber, (1999) 36 *CML Rev.* 87.

reaching in the E-Commerce Directive. According to its Article 2(h), the coordinated field[106] not only incorporates the Member State legislation as harmonised by the Directive, but *every* legal requirement applicable to *any* of the services provided on the Internet, i.e. also rules that are not specifically designed for information society services, rules that are not harmonised but purely national (e.g. general rules on sales promotion).[107] However, this wide approach is put into perspective by the numerous exclusions to the principle in the Directive's Annex, the exclusion of 'contractual obligations concerning consumer contacts' being one of them.

As a second characteristic, the country of origin principle assumes the function of determining the law applicable to a certain situation. It therefore serves to prevent a potential conflict of laws rather than to approximate laws. This makes the country of origin principle a possible counterpart to rules of (conventional) private international law,[108] which feature the application of the law of the country of residence for certain consumer contracts in the absence of choice (i.e. the law of the host State applies and not that of the home State).[109] This

[106] Article 2(h) of the E-Commerce Directive defines 'coordinated field' as 'requirements laid down in Member States' legal systems applicable to information society service providers or information society services, regardless of whether they are of a general nature or specifically designed for them'.

[107] Henning-Bodewig, (2001) 47 *WRP* 771 at 772 and 774, Lopez-Tarruella, (2001) 38 *CML Rev.* 1337 at 1343, Ohly, (2001) 50 *GRUR Int.* 899 at 900.

[108] The opinions differ widely with regard to the relationship between the country of origin principle in Directive 2000/31 and private international law. The problem arises particularly from Article 1(4) of the Directive which states that 'This Directive does not establish additional rules on private international law nor does it deal with the jurisdiction of Courts'. Recital 23 adds that 'provisions of the applicable law designated by rules of private international law must not restrict the freedom to provide information society services as established in this Directive'. For the purposes of unveiling a general principle of fair trading the exhaustive discussion of this paradox is, however, not very fruitful. From the literature relating to the E-Commerce Directive and the conflicts which arise regarding private international law, see e.g. Grundmann, (2003) 67 *RabelsZ* 246 at 293 et seq., Hellner, (2004) 8 *ERPL* 193, Mankowski, (2001) 100 *ZVglRWiss* 137 at 140 et seq., Lopez-Tarruella, (2001) 38 *CML Rev.* 1337 at 1348 et seq., Puurunen, (2003) 11 *ZEuP* 789 at 806 et seq., Thünken, (2001) *IPRax* 15. More generally on the country of origin principle as a conflict of law rule Ohly, (2001) 50 *GRUR Int.* 899. It should be noted, moreover, that also the general principle of mutual recognition as implied in the free movement provisions may be in conflict with traditional rules of private international law. Therefore the discussion may fall short of the mark, if it is reduced to the country of origin principle, see Fezer/Koos (2000) 20 *IPRax* 349 at 350 et seq. For a discussion of this aspect, see Katzenberger in Schricker/Henning-Bodewig, *Neuordnung des Wettbewerbsrechts*, p. 218 at 227 et seq., who rejects the idea that the free movement provisions have a conflict-of-law content.

[109] See Article 5 of the Convention on the law applicable to contractual obligations (Rome Convention), OJ 1998 C 27/34 (publication of a consolidated version). The solution in the Convention still stems from a time when distance selling techniques were not yet well developed. In its Green Paper on the conver-

possible conflict can arise although the underlying objectives of the concepts differ: while the purpose of the country of origin principle is to guarantee the smooth functioning of the Internal Market and to prevent a conflict of laws, the rules of private international law are to solve (i.e. not to prevent) a conflict of laws. However, a country of destination principle does not meet the needs for legal certainty and economic efficiency that come along with modern, globally applied means of distance communication. Accordingly, the specific significance of the country of origin principle stems from 'multistate advertising' with modern cross-border media, i.e. a situation where the advertising act emanating from one country affects the markets of other countries at the same time. It is economically and legally unreasonable, and it seems technically impractical, to adapt 'multistate advertising' to the laws of all potential recipient countries, which in the case of the global Internet would mean all legal orders of the world. The advantage for traders of applying the law of the home State is accompanied by some risk for consumers. As the directives provide for minimum harmonisation only, and the level of protection may therefore vary, traders might be incited to launch their marketing from those Member States with the lowest standards ('race to the bottom').[110] Therefore, it is desirable to have either a high level of protection in combination with the country of origin principle or to have maximum harmonisation. With regard to the degree of harmonisation the country of origin principle is fairly ambivalent indeed. On the one hand, from a market-integration and consumer-protection perspective, the application of this principle asks for a high degree of harmonisation in order to eliminate the risk of different treatment according to the place of establishment (business) and the place of living (consumers) respectively.[111] On the other hand, the principle itself does actually not encourage maximum harmonisation. In fact, it is the very divergence of the Member States' laws which even assigns the country of origin principle its specific significance, i.e. if the national laws were identical there would be no need for the country of origin principle.

---

sion of the Rome Convention into a Community instrument and its modernisation the Commission opens the discussion for a revision of Article 5 in order to give the mobile consumer proper protection and to adapt it to modern techniques of distance selling, COM (2002) 654 final at section 3.2.7. It should be noted that national rules of private international law are of course not exempt from compliance with the free-movement provisions of the Treaty, and the considerations underlying those rules can only be taken into account in terms of justified exceptions to Community freedoms, cf. Joined Cases C-369/96 and C-376/96 *Jean-Claude Arblade & Fils SARL and Bernhard Leloup et al. SARL* [1999] ECR I-8453 at 31, see Fallon, (2000) 10 *RCDIP* 728 at 733.

110 Alexandridou in Wilhelmsson/Tuominen/Tuomola, *Information Society*, p. 103 at p. 104, Arndt/Köhler, (2001) 12 *EWS* 102 at 105, Boehme-Neßler, (2001) 12 *EWS* 149 at 156, Henning-Bodewig, (2001) 47 *WRP* 771 at 772.

111 Le Berre/Arnould/Derenne, (2002) 10 *JTDE* 113 at 117.

The appropriate approach for regulation

In conclusion, in a situation where national laws still differ, a high degree of harmonisation in combination with the country-of-origin principle is most appropriate to guarantee a high level of consumer protection on the one hand and to ensure maximum freedom of movement on the other hand.[112] Even though in a maximum-harmonisation situation the (theoretical) level of protection may be the same, national laws are likely to differ to some extent. This potential of obstructing free movement can substantially be reduced or even eliminated by the application of the country of origin principle.

1.6 The conclusiveness of secondary law for a principle of fair trading

The portrayed deficiencies that come with the current practice of harmonisation give rise to the question to what extent secondary law actually allows safe conclusions about a principle of fair trading. However, the difficulty in grasping hold of a general fair-trading concept and the authority of the legislative statements have to be strictly differentiated. It is true that the piecemeal approach renders it ostensibly more difficult to find a common denominator or an underlying general rule. On the other hand, the type of legislative measures used and their scope and degree of harmonisation does not mean that their content is less conclusive or of less impact. The fact that directives, particularly those involving partial and minimum harmonisation, are indeed questionable with regard to an effective approximation of the laws of the Member States and a successful implementation of the Internal Market objective does not prevent the rules contained in those measures from reflecting legally binding elements of a general Community concept of fair trading. In case of minimum harmonisation, the Member States may go further, but the directives prescribe the binding minimum Community concept. The potential flaws that come with the national implementation of the imperfect European definition of this concept are a different issue. This aspect is rather related to the ambit of the fair trading principle, which is addressed separately.[113]

It should be recalled in this context that the Court of Justice also plays an important role in giving force to the directives' principles.[114] Some light has already been cast on the Court's role in delimiting the Community's competence of adopting secondary law,[115] as well as on the principle of interpreting Community legislation in the light of the Treaty.[116] The Court's methods of interpreta-

[112] See also Micklitz in Collins, *Directive on Unfair Commercial Practices*, p. 43 at p. 57 et seq.

[113] Chapter 4.

[114] See Rösler, (2003) 18 *VuR* 12 at 15.

[115] See *supra* at 1.1.

[116] Chapter 1 at 1. See also Alexandridou in Krämer/Micklitz/Tonner, *Law and diffuse interests*, p. 409 at p. 411, who calls the interpretation of national laws in the light of the Treaty the 'Europeanisation of the national laws'.

tion of secondary law are in principle the same as for primary law, contextual and teleological interpretation becoming more and more dominant.[117] Due to their minimum harmonisation approach and often vague wording the directives may sometimes have a weak starting point for consumer protection. However, by the development of the *effet utile* doctrine,[118] the Court has strongly amplified the impact of the directives.[119] The Court vigorously enforces them by interpreting their provisions closely according to the objective of the directive and its most effective achievement.[120] This very powerful and flexible technique has not without reason been called 'a sacred method of interpretation'.[121]

2 Fair trading as shaped by Community legislation

2.1 The historical background

The study of Ulmer

The idea of implementing the concept of fair trading into the legal order of the European Community has existed since the early days of the Community itself.[122] The most remarkable testimony of this period is the study by Ulmer,[123] which was conducted in the early 1960s and published in 1965.[124]

---

[117] Brown/Jacobs/Kennedy, *Court of Justice*, p. 322 et seq. Cf. also Jacobs, (2004) 41 *CML Rev.* 303 at 304 et seq. See in general Kutscher, *Methods of Interpretation*. For recent case law, see e.g. Case C-12/00 *Commission v Spain* [2003] ECR I-459 at 55, Case C-14/00 *Commission v Italy* [2003] ECR I-513 at 48.

[118] The *effet utile* doctrine has been developed in the context of the direct effect of directives. It has its roots in Case 9/70 *Franz Grad v Finanzamt Traunstein* [1970] ECR 825 at 5 and has been confirmed and refined in Case 41/74 *Yvonne van Duyn v Home Office* [1974] ECR 1337 at 12. In Case 48/75 *Jean Noël Royer* [1976] ECR 497 at 72 the Court held that the 'freedom left to the Member States by Article 189 [249] as to the choice of forms and methods of implementation of Directives does not affect their obligation to choose the most appropriate forms and methods to ensure the effectiveness of the Directives'. See moreover Snyder, (1993) 56 *MLR* 19 (in particular at 41 et seq.)

[119] On information duties and *effet utile*, see Schwintowski in Schulze/Ebers/Grigoleit, *Informationspflichten*, p. 267. Recent applications of the *effet utile* doctrine in the sphere of contract law (Directive 93/13 on unfair terms in consumer contracts) are to be found in Joined Cases C-240/98 to C-244/98 *Océano Grupo Editorial SA v Rocío Murciano Quintero* [2000] ECR I-4941 at 26 and Case C-473/00 *Cofidis SA v Jean-Louis Fredout* [2002] ECR I-10875 at 35.

[120] Cf. Micklitz, (2003) 18 *VuR* 2 at 6. For a critical point of view, see Nourissat, (2003) 179 *Rec. Dalloz* 486.

[121] Rasmussen, *Court of Justice*, p. 31.

[122] See also the historical overview by Cseres, (2001) *REDC* 221 at 232 et seq., Henning-Bodewig (2004) 53 *GRUR Int.* 183 at 186, and Ohly in Schricker/Henning-Bodewig, *Neuordnung des Wettbewerbsrechts*, p. 69 et seq.

[123] Eugen Ulmer was the director of the *Max-Planck-Institut für ausländisches und internationales Patent-, Urheber- und Markenrecht* (nowadays the *Max-Planck-Institut für geistiges Eigentum, Wettbewerbs- und Steuerrecht*) in Munich, Germany.

Ulmer examined on behalf of the European Commission the Member States' laws relating to fair trading and unfair competition, the latter field being in the actual focus of the study. The central piece of his work is the comparative analysis of the national rules, including suggestions for harmonisation. Ulmer envisaged a general clause, in principle based on Article 10bis(2) of the Paris Convention for the Protection of Industrial Property of 1883[125] (however with a larger scope of application), and complemented by specific marketing rules.[126] His vision of a relatively comprehensive legislative framework for unfair competition and fair trading at Community level, however, has still not come true.

Ulmer's work has had a great impact though and stimulated the discussion of the issue in the late 1960s and in the 1970s. The long and intensive debate, which was accompanied by surveys, and which produced numerous working documents, memoranda and reports climaxed in the Commission proposal of 1978 for a Directive concerning misleading and unfair advertising.[127] This shift from the competition-oriented approach, for which Ulmer's study is representative, to the consumer-oriented approach, for which the notion 'fair trading' stands, is documented by the first consumer protection programme of 1975.[128] Under the leitmotif of the protection of consumer interests the programme established that

> 'practices which were once regarded in many countries as unfair solely in terms of competition between producers (misleading advertising, for example), are now also considered from the point of view of relations between producers and consumers'.[129]

---

[124] Ulmer, *Recht des unlauteren Wettbewerbs*. The first volume contains the comparative presentation of the laws of the then six Member States together with suggestions for harmonisation of fair-trading and unfair-competition law. The subsequent volumes contain country reports and have been published until the 1990s.

[125] Article 10bis(2) of the Paris Convention for the Protection of Industrial Property of 1883 reads: 'Any act of competition contrary to honest practices in industrial or commercial matters constitutes an act of unfair competition'.

[126] Ulmer, *Recht des unlauteren Wettbewerbs*, Vol. I, p. 249 et seq.

[127] Proposal for a Council Directive relating to the approximation of the laws, regulations and administrative provisions of the Member States concerning misleading and unfair advertising (Submitted by the Commission to the Council on 1 March 1978), OJ 1978 C 70/4, amendment in OJ 1979 C 194/3.

[128] Council Resolution on a preliminary programme for a consumer protection and information policy, OJ 1975 C 92/1 (the consumer protection programme is attached as Annex).

[129] Programme for a consumer protection and information policy at 7.

In this context, it set as the Community's priorities the protection of consumers against false or misleading advertising and from unfair commercial practices.[130] Moreover, it featured consumer information as one of the core principles.[131]

The 1978 proposal

The 1978 proposal was based on Article 94 of the Treaty and, according to its recitals, was to promote the establishment and the functioning of the Common Market, to prevent the distortion of competition and to provide for consumer protection. The objective of the proposed directive was defined in Article 1, which assumed the function of a general clause:

> 'The objective of this Directive is to protect consumers, persons carrying on a trade, business or profession, and the interests of the public in general against unfair and misleading advertising'.

Article 2 defined in detail the terms 'advertising', 'misleading advertising' and 'unfair advertising'. 'Advertising' was considered to be

> 'the making of any pronouncement in the course of a trade, business or profession for the purpose of promoting the supply of goods or services'.

This definition is particularly significant, as it determines the basic scope of application of the proposed directive. By concerning 'advertising' the directive may seem confined to just a part – although a very large and important one – of fair trading issues, since not all types of sales promotions are necessarily linked to a 'pronouncement' in the sense of a spoken of written manifestation. However, the ambit would have been a matter of interpretation of the term 'pronouncement'. Sales promotions, indeed, are necessarily linked to some sort of communication from business to consumers. This is the reason why the more modern term of 'commercial communication', as used e.g. in the E-Commerce Directive, is much more appropriate.[132] It is wider as it comprises 'any form

---

[130] Programme for a consumer protection and information policy at 22 and at 24.

[131] Programme for a consumer protection and information policy at 34.

[132] Directive 2000/31/EC on certain legal aspects of information society services, in particular electronic commerce, in the Internal Market (Directive on electronic commerce), OJ 2000 L 178/1. The Directive defines in Article 2(f): 'commercial communication': any form of communication designed to promote, directly or indirectly, the goods, services or image of a company, organisation or person pursuing a commercial, industrial or craft activity or exercising a regulated profession. The following do not in themselves constitute commercial communications: - information allowing direct access to the activity of the company, organisation or person, in particular a domain name or an electronic-mail address, - communications relating to the goods, services or image of the company, organisation or person compiled in an independent manner, particularly when this is without financial consideration.

of communication' aimed at sales promotion, i.e. also non-verbal types. The seventh recital of the 1978 proposal, however, takes into account modern communication techniques and thus suggests that the old term 'advertising' was to have a similarly broad meaning as today's notion of 'commercial communication'.[133]

'Misleading advertising' was defined as

> 'any advertising which is entirely or partially false or which, having regard to its total effect, including its presentation, misleads or is likely to mislead persons addressed or reached thereby, unless it could not reasonably be foreseen that these persons would be reached thereby'.

'Unfair advertising' was defined as

> 'any advertising which (a) casts discredit on another person by improper reference to his nationality, origin, private life or good name, or (b) injures or is likely to injure the commercial reputation of another person by false statements or defamatory comments concerning his firm, goods or services, or (c) appeals to sentiments of fear, or promotes social or religious discrimination, or (d) clearly infringes the principle of the social, economic and cultural equality of the sexes, or (e) exploits the trust, credulity or lack of experience of a consumer, or influences or is likely to influence a consumer or the public in general in any other improper manner'.

The respective definitions[134] reflect the underlying assumption of an elemental difference between the concepts of misleading and unfair advertising. Whereas the first is based on a misconception of facts, the latter implies the violation of fundamental and common values and ethical considerations.[135] Although the linguistic connotations do imply a different emphasis of the effects on the recipient, it must be questioned, whether such a sharp distinction between unfair and misleading advertising is sensible.[136] In the reality of sales promotion both aspects will blend, and a misled consumer is certainly also influenced in an 'improper manner'. It can be said that in the later adopted Directive 84/450 on misleading advertising this fact has to some extent been acknowledged, since its

---

133 The seventh recital reads: 'Whereas, in view of modern techniques of communication, the definition of 'advertising' must be worded broadly [...]'.

134 In fact, 'unfair advertising' is less defined than just illustrated by an enumeration of examples, which, however, was meant to be exhaustive.

135 The list fits into the classification by Stuyck in Balate, *Unfair advertising*, p. 111 at p. 131 et seq.: ethical rules, social-ethical rules, social values, public-interest rules, and rules concerning aspects unfair to the potential consumer.

136 See the critical considerations of Bernitz in Balate, *Unfair advertising*, p. 53 at p. 55.

defined purpose is to 'protect [...] against misleading advertising and the unfair consequences thereof'.[137] Moreover, cases like *Clinique* and *Yves Rocher*, where alleged misrepresentations have been assessed under fairness considerations,[138] show that also the Court does not make a rigid distinction in the sense of an exclusivity of the concepts, but rather considers misleading advertising as being covered by the more global concept of unfairness.[139]

Article 3 served as a guideline, indicating which elements were particularly to be taken into consideration in order to determine whether advertising was misleading or unfair. Emphasis was laid on the characteristics of the goods or services, the condition of supply of the goods and services, and the nature, attributes and rights of the advertiser. As a kind of subordinate general clause Article 4 provided:

> 'Comparative advertising shall be allowed, as long as it compares material and verifiable details and is neither misleading nor unfair'.

Furthermore, the proposal contained rules in Article 5 on the judicial protection of persons affected by misleading or unfair advertising, which included the right of public interest associations to take legal action and which provided for injunction and summary proceedings. Article 6 imposed the burden of proof on the advertisers of all factual claims they would make. Article 7 regulated judicial protection in the case of self-regulation of misleading and unfair advertising.

The substantive approach to the regulation of unfair advertising was a rather comprehensive and ambitious one, setting a high standard. However, the proposed directive merely pursued minimum harmonisation, as was stipulated in Article 8. The directive, had it come into effect, would therefore not have completely eliminated the differences in the national unfair-advertising laws. Yet, compared to the piecemeal approach that has followed, the directive would certainly have constituted a veritable milestone in Community harmonisation.

The non-adoption of the 1978 proposal and the beginning of the piecemeal approach

The 1978 proposal faced fierce resistance on the part of some Member States. The strongest opposition concerning the element of unfair advertising came from the United Kingdom, which feared that the proposed fairness system headed by a general clause was not compatible with the tradition of Common Law and self-regulation.[140] Bearing in mind that Article 94 requires unanimity,

[137] Article 1 of Directive 84/450. See also *infra* at 2.3.

[138] See the case law analysis in Chapter 1 at 5.

[139] In the same way Bernitz in Balate, *Unfair advertising*, p. 53 at p. 55.

[140] Cf. Lawson in Balate, *Unfair advertising*, p. 69. For an overview of the traditionally critical attitude towards a general principle of fair trading in the UK legal system, see, Ohly, *Richterrecht und Generalklausel*, p. 73 et seq.

six years later in 1984, only the Directive on misleading advertising could be adopted,[141] which was obviously the highest common denominator at the time. Given the rather broad definition of unfair advertising in the original proposal, the non-adoption must be considered a major drawback. The Misleading Advertising Directive has been amended by the Directive on comparative advertising in 1997.[142] It had already been announced in the sixth recital of the original Directive 84/450 that the issue of 'unfair advertising, and (as far as necessary) comparative advertising' should be dealt with at a second stage. The wording implies that comparative advertising was seen as a kind of subcategory of unfair advertising, the latter being the much wider concept. The adoption of Directive 97/55 on comparative advertising can therefore be considered as merely another small compromise on the long path towards a general legal framework for fair trading.

In accordance with the above, harmonisation of fair-trading law has happened on a strictly sectoral basis. Before the adoption of Directive 84/450 this was in order to get at least parts of the harmonisation process on the way, as long as more was not feasible politically. After the harmonisation of the national laws concerning misleading advertising by Directive 84/450 it was in order to tackle at least those fair-trading issues where compromises could be found, as long as a general harmonisation could still not be consented on. This remedy by sector-specific harmonisation led to a patchwork of fair-trading rules in various Directives and finally to the current piecemeal situation. The Court has left no doubt, however, about the horizontal nature of Directive 84/450, which makes it remain applicable next to the vertical directives.[143]

2.2 The selection and presentation of Community legislation

There are political commitments and non-binding legal measures, such as recommendations, that relate to fair trading. However, in accordance with the aim to elaborate a legally binding principle of fair trading in the *acquis communautaire*, only legally binding Community instruments have been taken into consideration for closer analysis.[144]

---

[141] Directive 84/450/EEC relating to the approximation of the laws, regulations and administrative provisions of the Member States concerning misleading advertising, OJ 1984 L 250/17.

[142] Directive 97/55/EC amending Directive 84/450/EEC concerning misleading advertising so as to include comparative advertising, OJ 1997 L 290/18.

[143] E.g. Joined Cases C-34/95, C-35/95 and C-36/95 *Konsumentombudsmannen (KO) v De Agostini (Svenska) Förlag AB and TV-Shop i Sverige AB* [1997] ECR I-3843 at 37. Of course, Directive 84/450 is subsidiary with regard to specific provisions in other directives, see. e.g. Case C-99/01 *Criminal proceedings against Gottfried Linhart and Hans Biffl* [2002] ECR I-9375 at 20.

[144] In line with what has been said earlier (see *supra* at 1.3) these are almost exclusively directives.

Different ways of categorising secondary legislation are conceivable.[145] The guiding criterion should be to optimise the groundwork for drawing conclusions on a principle of fair trading. However, unlike the examined Court cases on primary law, legislative Community instruments do not focus on one or a few particular legal statement(s), but they establish a much more complex regulatory framework for the subject matter they concern. It is true that they start from regulating a particular issue, but regarding this issue they deal with a whole variety of questions that come along with it. This makes the categorisation not only more difficult, but it actually renders it less crucial for later conclusions, since the sectors overlap to a far greater extent in their regulated substance. Making a distinction between distant and direct communication techniques, for instance, does not *per se* clarify the picture, since similar information requirements or cooling-off periods play a role in both contexts. Possibly different functions of the same or similar requirements must therefore be clarified at a second stage anyway. This second stage then also involves conclusions concerning the substance of a principle of fair trading. In preference to establishing somewhat artificial categories, it seems therefore most appropriate to reflect the actual regulatory approach of the Community as closely as possible in the following examination. In order to do so the analysis will take up the fundamental classification of horizontal and vertical harmonisation. The analysis will then constitute a solid basis for the separate step of drawing general conclusions regarding a principle of fair trading.[146]

It is assumed that Directive 84/450 as amended is the only true horizontally harmonising directive concerning fair trading at present, while the other directives belong to the group of vertically harmonising directives. Directive 98/6 is of a special kind and very close to horizontal harmonisation. It has therefore been classified in-between horizontal and vertical harmonisation, i.e. as quasi-horizontal harmonisation.

As far as vertical harmonisation is concerned, the presentation and analysis will mirror the Community's sectoral approach.[147] Those legal instruments have been selected which either regulate trade practices as such or which deal with pre-contractual commercial communications between business and consumers in another context. Single provisions in very different legislative measures, other than those analysed here, may slightly touch upon the area of fair trading. Their

[145] In Bultmann/Howells/Keßler/Micklitz/Radeideh/Reich/Stuyck/Voigt, *Fair Trading Vol. III*, for instance, categories have been made according to communication policies, distribution policies, price policies, product policies and public-interest policies. Micklitz in Reich/Micklitz, *Europäisches Verbraucherrecht*, at § 6 takes up these categories, preceded by the misleading advertising Directive as a separate category. Howells/Wilhelmsson, *EC Consumer Law*, p. 17 distinguish between 'a relatively general scope' and 'more specific rules'.

[146] See Chapter 3.

[147] For the criteria of categorisation of the vertical directives, see *infra* at 2.5.

meticulous exposure and discussion, however, would hardly enlighten the characterisation of the Community's approach and the determination of a principle of fair trading any further. It can therefore be claimed that the selection made comprehensively covers the substantive realm of fair trading as laid down by Community legislation.

It follows from the underlying objective of the study that the instruments are only analysed with regard to their fair-trading characteristics and not in their every facet.

2.3 Horizontal harmonisation – Misleading and comparative advertising

General remarks

Directive 84/450 on misleading advertising[148] and Directive 97/55 on comparative advertising[149] are often referred to separately, although they constitute in fact one Directive, since the latter has amended the former so as to include comparative advertising.[150]

The purpose of the Directive is set out in Article 1:

> 'The purpose of this Directive is to protect consumers, persons carrying on a trade or business or practising a craft or profession and the interests of the public in general against misleading advertising and the unfair consequences thereof and to lay down the conditions under which comparative advertising is permitted'.

The Directive thus features a modern concept of integrated protection of consumers, traders and the general public interest, aiming at balancing possibly conflicting interests.[151] Although the Directive goes far beyond pure consumer protection it may be argued that, by starting the enumeration with consumers, the legislator intended to lay specific emphasis on this group of market participants. This interpretation is backed by an analysis of the recitals, which particularly highlight the group of consumers. Recitals 3 to 7 of Directive 84/450 and the second recital of Directive 97/55 leave no doubt that advertising is considered to affect the economic welfare of consumers, and that they have to be protected at a minimum level from taking decisions prejudicial to them.

---

[148] See footnote 141.

[149] See footnote 142.

[150] The following references to Articles are to Directive 84/450 as amended by Directive 97/55. Of course, each of the Directives has its own recitals.

[151] Henning-Bodewig, (2001) 47 *WRP* 771 at 773. This can be said to coincide with the three protective objectives of competition law, cf. Reich in Gormley, *Current and Future Perspectives*, p. 127 at p. 127.

The substantive rules of the Directive and the role of information

The substantive core of the Directive is linked to the purpose as set out in Article 1: misleading advertising is prohibited, whereas comparative advertising is permitted, provided that the conditions for it are met.

The impact of this rule is obviously closely related to the fundamental definitions, which are provided in Article 2 of the Directive:

> '1. 'advertising' means the making of a representation in any form in connection with a trade, business, craft or profession in order to promote the supply of goods or services, including immovable property, rights and obligations;
>
> 2. 'misleading advertising' means any advertising which in any way, including its presentation, deceives or is likely to deceive the persons to whom it is addressed or whom it reaches and which, by reason of its deceptive nature, is likely to affect their economic behaviour or which, for those reasons, injures or is likely to injure a competitor;
>
> 2a. 'comparative advertising' means any advertising which explicitly or by implication identifies a competitor or goods or services offered by a competitor;
>
> 3. 'person' means any natural or legal person'.

The definition of 'advertising' is slightly broader than in the 1978 proposal. What was then called 'any pronouncement' has transformed into 'representation in any form', which assures that also non-verbal sales promotions are covered.[152] Only private advertising[153] or non-economic advertising[154] are excluded, which gives the Directive a fairly comprehensive scope of application, including online commercial communication. However, it has to be borne in mind that the Directive merely provides for minimum harmonisation, as far as misleading advertising is concerned (Article 7(1)),[155] yet it does provide for full harmonisation regarding 'comparative advertising as far as the comparison is concerned' (Article 7(2)). The objective of removing prohibitions of comparative advertising – which follows the general aim not to suppress, but rather to disclose

---

152 The French version reads 'toute forme de communication', which leaves no doubt that the scope of the Directive covers all forms of communication. The French text indeed anticipates the notion 'commercial communication' as defined in Article 2(f) of Directive 2000/31 (there: 'toute forme de communication', 'any form of communication'). The German 'jede Äußerung' and the Dutch 'iedere mededeling', by contrast, recall the expression 'any pronouncement' in the 1978 proposal.

153 I.e. advertising not connected with a trade, business, craft or profession. This is not to be confounded with individual advertising, which is included, cf. De Cock Buning/Hondius/Prins/de Vries, (2001) 24 *JCP* 287 at 295.

154 E.g. with general social or political aims.

155 The Commission has highlighted the significant differences in the laws of the Member States concerning misleading advertising in its Green Paper 'Commercial Communications in the Internal Market', COM (96) 192 final, p. 21 et seq.

information – cannot be reasonably achieved by minimum harmonisation. The subtle distinction between 'comparative advertising' and 'comparison' has been resolved by the Court in *Toshiba*.[156] Advertising does not itself have to compare in order to constitute comparative advertising, but it is sufficient that the recipient of the information can use this information in order to compare.

Indeed, information is the key concern of the Directive. Unlike unfair advertising, misleading advertising necessarily implies a clash between the representation and reality.[157] It thus happens by a deception based on facts, and information is the communication of facts. Although the Directive does not provide for concrete information requirements as do many of the later fair trading directives, the disclosure or non-disclosure of information is the pivotal point with regard to misleading advertising. It is self-evident that also comparative advertising is based on the (more or less apparent) confrontation of facts.

Misleading advertising

Article 3 of the Directive clearly shows the information-related approach. In determining whether advertising is misleading, information concerning the characteristics of goods or services, the price or the manner in which it is calculated, the conditions on which the goods are supplied or the services provided, and the nature, attributes and rights of the advertiser, shall particularly be taken into account. Article 3 provides furthermore that actually all the features of the advertising in question have to be taken into account. Therefore, also non-verbal information, e.g. the form of the good as such, can be misleading.[158]

With regard to the definition of misleading advertising in Article 2(2) two aspects are particularly significant. First, the advertising must not actually deceive, but it is sufficient if it is likely to deceive the persons to whom it is addressed or whom it reaches. This *ex ante* approach affects the burden of proof, as it has not to be proved that a person has in fact been deceived.[159] Second, the deception must be likely to affect the addressed people's economic behaviour.[160] This narrows down the wide definition to some extent, but the influence of the addressed person's economic behaviour should easily be assumed as it is to a certain extent inherent in the notion of 'misleading'. However, as the object of reference is the consumer who can potentially be misled, the exact definition of what misleading advertising constitutes is fundamentally correlated with the image of the consumer. The well-informed and educated consumer might be less easily misled than the uneducated and vulnerable one. The Directive remains silent about the applicable standard. Given that the consumer image

---

[156] See footnote 169.

[157] Cf. Case C-358/01 *Commission v Spain* [2003] ECR I-nyr at 60.

[158] Cf. Howells/Wilhelmsson, *EC Consumer Law*, p. 137.

[159] See also Springer, *Irreführungsverbot*, p. 59.

[160] See also Evrard, (1993) 1 *JTDE* 11 at 12.

differs widely in the national legal orders of the Member States, the application of the national laws implementing the Directive should differ correspondingly. The Court provided interpretation on this and other aspects of the Directive.

In *Nissan*,[161] concerning the parallel import of cars, the Court focussed on the interpretation of misleading advertising. According to French law, it was prohibited to advertise cars with the words 'buy your new vehicle cheaper' and 'one year manufacturer's guarantee', where these cars were imported to France from Belgium, and had been registered for import purposes but never had been driven. The Court argued that such advertising was not misleading in the sense of the Directive on three grounds.

Firstly, the claim that the cars were new could not be considered misleading just because the cars were registered before importation. According to the Court, a car loses its character as a new car when it is first driven on a public highway and not when it is registered. The Court considered it possible, however, that the advertising could be misleading insofar as it sought to conceal the fact of the previous registration. Yet, it was for the national court to ascertain the circumstances of the particular case and to bear in mind the consumers to which the advertising was addressed, i.e. with regard to whether the advertising sought to conceal the fact that the cars were registered before importation and with regard to whether that fact would have deterred a significant number of consumers from making a purchase, had they known it.[162] The affection of the consumers' economic behaviour in the sense of Article 2(2) of the Directive is thus clearly related to their purchase choice. The Court did actually not clearly commit itself to a specific type of consumer, but rather presumed that consumers might react differently to the advertising.

Secondly, the Court dealt with the claim that the cars were cheaper. It held that this could only be considered misleading, if it was established that a significant number of consumers would decide to buy the cars in ignorance of the fact that the lower price of the vehicles corresponded to the smaller number of accessories on the cars sold by the parallel importer.[163] This is compatible with Article 2(2) of the Directive, which demands that the deceptive advertising 'is likely to affect their economic behaviour'.[164] There is thus a parallel to the Treaty case law which requires the relevance of the consumer's misconception.[165]

---

[161] Case C-373/90 *Criminal proceedings against X ('Nissan')* [1992] ECR I-131.

[162] *Nissan* at 13 to 15.

[163] *Nissan* at 16.

[164] In fact, the Court's statement in *Nissan* at 16 caused some bewilderment among the commentators of the judgment, since, depending on the language version, the Court seemed to have argued *contra legem* to Article 2(2) of the Directive. For instance, the English version ('if it is established that the decision to buy [...] was made in ignorance of the fact') and the German version ('wenn nachweislich [...] die Kaufentscheidung in Unkenntnis dessen getroffen wurde') strongly suggest that it has to be proven that a significant number of consumers actually already have made such a decision, instead of this just being

Finally, with regard to the claim about the manufacturer's guarantee, the Court clearly pointed out that such information cannot be considered as misleading advertising, if it was true.[166] This, as well, is an analogy to the Court's reasoning in the free movement cases, represented by *GB-INNO* and *Yves Rocher*,[167] where the Court held that the disclosure of true information could not be considered unfair and could therefore not be prohibited in the name of consumer protection and fair trading. Information is advantageous for the active consumer rather than dangerous, provided that it is correct.[168]

Comparative advertising

The Directive's concept of comparative advertising is somewhat ambiguous. The basic definition of comparative advertising in Article 2(2a) is complemented by Article 3a, which provides a detailed list of conditions under which comparative advertising 'as far as the comparison is concerned' shall be permitted. As Article 2(2a) does not refer to a 'comparison', but defines comparative advertising as 'any advertising which explicitly or by implication identifies a competitor or goods or services offered by a competitor' uncertainty has arisen to what extent 'comparative advertising' has actually to 'compare'. In *Toshiba* and in *Pippig Augenoptik* the Court has clarified the notion.

In *Toshiba* a company advertised spare parts and consumable items that could be used with the photocopiers distributed by Toshiba Europe.[169] In the advertising for its spare parts it referred next to its own product number to the original product number of Toshiba's corresponding product. It depended on the interpretation of 'comparative advertising' in the sense of the Directive whether this practice was legal under Community law. The Court confirmed the dilemma resulting from the Directive's definition of comparative advertising.[170] While the relevant Article 3a(1)(c) permitted advertising so long as it objectively 'compared' one or more material, relevant, verifiable and representative features of the goods and services, which may include price, Article 2(2a) did not require such a 'comparing' element. The assessment of the provisions led the Court

---

'likely'. The cause for this confusion, however, is to be found in a bad translation of the French original ('dans l'hypothèse où il serait établi que la décision d'achat [...] est prise dans l'ignorance'), which was the authentic language of the case. The wording leaves no doubt that the Court meant the hypothetical assumption of consumers making their choice in ignorance of the facts ('est prise' is passive voice and not past tense). See also Deutsch, (1997) 99 GRUR 44.

165 See Chapter 1 at 5.3.3 and Niemöller, *Verbraucherleitbild*, p. 182 et seq.

166 *Nissan* at 17.

167 Case C-362/88 *GB-INNO-BM v Confédération du commerce luxembourgeois* [1990] ECR I-667 and Case C-126/91 *Schutzverband gegen Unwesen in der Wirtschaft e.V. v Yves Rocher GmbH* [1993] ECR I-2361.

168 Schulte-Nölke/Schulze/Jones, *Casebook*, p. 63 and p. 77.

169 Case C-112/99 *Toshiba Europe GmbH v Katun Germany GmbH* [2001] ECR I-7945.

170 See to this dilemma Sack, (2002) 48 *WRP* 363 at 364 et seq.

to the conclusion that 'on a literal interpretation, they would render unlawful any reference enabling a competitor, or the goods or services which he offers, to be identified in a representation which did not contain a comparison within the meaning of Article 3a'[171]. With reference to Directive 89/104[172] relating to trade marks and the judgment in *BMW*[173] the Court recalled that that the use of another person's trade mark was legitimate where it was necessary to inform the public of the nature of the products or the intended purpose of the services offered. In order to resolve the conflict between the Directives the Court based its reasoning on the objectives of the Advertising Directive, which according to the second recital of Directive 97/55 is to help demonstrate objectively the merits of the various comparable products. The Court thus concluded that the indication of the product numbers did constitute a positive statement that the two products had equivalent technical features and thus were a comparison of features within in the meaning of Article 3a(1)(c) of the Directive and constituted 'comparative advertising'.[174] Putting the Courts findings more abstractly, the advertising does not itself have to compare in order to be comparative advertising in the sense of the Directive, but it is sufficient that it provides information which allows the consumer to compare the products.[175]

Pippig Augenoptik concerned advertising leaflets of an Austrian commercial company whose branches had optical shelves where spectacles were sold.[176] In these leaflets the lower prices were compared with those of the same spectacles (but lenses of a different brand) sold by another company operating specialist opticians' shops. The Court rejected doubts as to the extent of maximum harmonisation of comparative advertising which arose from a textual contradiction in the Directive. The Court emphasised that the Directive carried out an exhaustive harmonisation of the conditions under which comparative advertising in Member States might be lawful. This implied by its nature that the lawfulness of comparative advertising throughout the Community was to be assessed solely in the light of the criteria laid down by the Directive. Therefore, stricter national provisions on protection against misleading advertising could not be applied to comparative advertising as regards the form and content of the comparison.[177] The Court underlined furthermore that the comparison may rely on all kinds of conceivable objective features, relating to the advertiser's offer, the competitor's

---

[171] *Toshiba* at 33.

[172] Directive 89/104/EEC relating to trade marks, OJ 1989 L 40/1, cf. Article 6(1)(c) of the Directive.

[173] Case C-63/97 *Bayerische Motorenwerke AG (BMW) and BMW Nederland BV v Ronald Karel Deenik* [1999] ECR I-905 at 58 to 60.

[174] *Toshiba* at 39 and 40.

[175] See also *Pippig Augenoptik* at 35.

[176] Case C-44/01 *Pippig Augenoptik GmbH & Co. KG v Hartlauer Handelsgesellschaft mbH* [2003] ECR I-3095.

[177] *Pippig Augenoptik* at 44.

offer or the relationship between those offers. The (repetitive) use of objective features could therefore not have denigrating effects, which were prohibited by the Directive.[178] The underlying reason for the Court to leave comparative advertising as unrestricted as possible is that it is considered to be designed to enable consumers to make the best possible use of the Internal Market.[179] On the other hand, the Court acknowledged that it was possible that the omission of a statement in an advertising message involving a comparison might mislead or was capable of misleading, thereby making it 'misleading' within the meaning of the Directive.[180]

The consumer image in the context of the directive

With regard to the underlying consumer image it can be established that whereas in *Nissan* the Court clearly worked on the assumption of a diversity of consumers who might react differently to the advertising in question, in *Toshiba* the Court asked the national judge to take into account the perception of an 'average individual who is reasonably well informed and reasonably observant and circumspect'[181] in order to determine whether the equipment manufacturer's product numbers are 'distinguishing marks' within the meaning of the Directive. In *Pippig Augenoptik* the Court similarly asked the national court to take into account the 'presumed expectations of an average consumer who is reasonably well informed and reasonably observant and circumspect'[182]. Although the standard is formulated in a very general way, in *Toshiba* the Court recognised differences in appreciation as well. It namely added that account should be taken of the type of persons at whom the advertising is directed. In the present case, those persons appeared to be 'specialist traders who are much less likely than final consumers to associate the reputation of the equipment manufacturer's products with those of the competing supplier'.[183] The case law concerning the Directive on misleading and comparative advertising shows that the Court's standard bears in mind the different recipients of the advertising. Hence, the consumer image corresponds to the one in the free movement case law.[184] The basic standard is that of an average consumer who is 'reasonably well informed and reasonably observant and circumspect'. However, it is the average member of the target group, which is decisive. Moreover, at the stage of the application of the test particularities of the actual recipients must be taken into account.[185]

---

178 *Pippig Augenoptik* at 80 et seq.

179 *Pippig Augenoptik* at 64.

180 *Pippig Augenoptik* at 52.

181 *Toshiba* at 52.

182 *Pippig Augenoptik* at 55.

183 *Toshiba* at 52.

184 See Chapter 1 at 5.3 and at 5.5.

185 See also Chapter 3 at 3.2.

2.4 Quasi-horizontal harmonisation – Price indications

General remarks

Next to its quality, the price of a good or service is certainly of the utmost concern to the consumer. Moreover, in synallagmatic contracts an agreement on the price will be an indispensable element of the contract itself, as the amount of money paid is the consumer's exchange for the good or service to be received. There is no doubt that the average consumers want to know the price they have to pay for the product in order to make their purchase decision. This makes the price an indispensable component of the information consumers need 'in order to enable them to make their choice in full knowledge of the facts'.[186] However, it is not only the price of the product itself, which is of particular interest to consumers, but the actual final amount of money they have to pay, including additional charges, such as taxes, fees or delivery costs. Cost transparency (i.e. not only price transparency) must therefore be a central element of any fair-trading policy. Cost transparency is dealt with in virtually all sectoral legislation relating to pre-contractual information requirements. The costs addressed depend on the specific sector.[187]

Directive 98/6[188] on the indication of the prices of products offered to consumers reflects this extraordinary importance of cost transparency. It harmonises cost transparency in a quasi-horizontal way. There are two reasons why it is 'quasi-horizontal harmonisation' rather than horizontal harmonisation.

First, it does not cover services, since it employs the term 'product' as meaning goods only.[189] Relating it to other legislation, however, it turns out that this is the only directive to cover price indications of all goods offered to consumers, whereas other directives contain rules on price and cost indication with regard to just a specific good or service or a particular sales method. Taking into account this relation, it can therefore be said that the Directive almost pursues a horizontal purpose. Its quasi-horizontal aim becomes furthermore apparent taking into account that it substitutes the repealed vertical Directives 79/581 and 88/314,[190] thereby merging the requirements for price indications of food and non-food products.

---

[186] Case C-362/88 *GB-INNO-BM v Confédération du commerce luxembourgeois* [1990] ECR I-667 at 17; Case C-126/91 *Schutzverband gegen Unwesen in der Wirtschaft e.V. v Yves Rocher GmbH* [1993] ECR I-2361 at 17.

[187] Delivery costs, for instance, typically play a role in distance selling situations.

[188] Directive 98/6/EC on consumer protection in the indication of the prices of products offered to consumers, OJ 1998 L 80/27.

[189] The term 'product' is not defined in the Directive. However, the measurements referred to for product units (kilogramme, litre, metre, square metre or cubic metre) clearly hint at goods only. This interpretation is confirmed by the exception in Article 3(2) of the Directive relating to 'products supplied in the course of the provision of a service', see also Micklitz in Reich/Micklitz, *Verbraucherrecht*, at 9.11.

[190] Directive 79/581/EEC concerning the indication of prices of certain foodstuffs, OJ 1979 L 158/19 and Directive 88/314/EEC concerning the indication of prices of non-food products, OJ 1988 L 142/19.

Second, doubts may be expressed whether the Directive constitutes 'harmonisation' at all. Atypically, it is exclusively based on Article 153 and not on Article 95.[191] It is thus not considered to be harmonisation for the purpose of the Internal Market, but rather a contribution to a high level of protection by 'specific action which supports and supplements the policy pursued by the Member States regarding precise, transparent and unambiguous information for consumers on the prices of products offered to them'.[192] While it was not clear whether 'specific actions' in the sense of ex Article 129a(1)(b) would include legislative 'measures', Article 153(3)(b) now confirms the direction taken by Directive 98/6.[193] Although, strictly speaking, measures which 'support, supplement and monitor the policy pursued by the Member States' do not 'harmonise', there does not seem to be a difference in practice as the substance of Directive 98/6 shows.[194]

Substance

The purpose of the 'Unit Prices Directive', as this instrument is commonly referred to, is to stipulate indication of the selling price and the price per unit of measurement of products offered by traders to consumers in order to improve consumer information and to facilitate comparison of prices (Article 1).

As a general rule, the selling price – i.e. the final price for a unit of the product, or a given quantity of the product, including VAT and all other taxes – and the unit price – i.e. the final price, including VAT and all other taxes, for one single unit of quantity (e.g. kilogramme, litre, metre, etc.) which is widely and customarily used in the Member State concerned[195] – shall be indicated for all products. For products sold in bulk, only the unit price must be indicated. The obligation of price indication not only applies to products offered on the spot, but Article 3(4) provides that also any advertisement which mentions the selling price of products must indicate the unit price.

The Directive takes care of the quality of the information as well. As a general obligation, Article 4(1) provides that the selling price and the unit price must be unambiguous, easily identifiable and clearly legible. However, the Community legislator is aware of the fact that price transparency is not only

[191] As Micklitz in Reich/Micklitz, *Verbraucherrecht*, at 9.7 and Stuyck, (2000) 37 *CML Rev.* 367 at 380 note this has remained an exceptional practice. The proposal for the Directive did not further discuss the choice of the legal basis, see COM (95) 276 final, OJ 1995 C 260/5 at point 24.

[192] See recital 2 of Directive 98/6 and the wording of ex Article 129a(1)(b).

[193] Reich, (1999) 14 *VuR* 3 at 9.

[194] See furthermore *supra* footnote 67.

[195] As the UK case *Thoburn et al. v Sunderland City Council et al.*, [2002] 1 C.M.L.R. 1461, known as the 'metric martyrs case' vividly demonstrates, somewhere in Europe one small group of indomitable believers in the imperial system still tries to hold out against the Community invaders imposing on them the metric system. See the case note by Boyron, (2002) 27 *E.L.Rev.* 771.

a matter of visual characteristics, but that the quality is closely related to the comprehensibility of the information. Consequently, according to Article 5(1), Member States may waive the obligation to indicate the unit price of products for which such indication would not be useful because of the products' nature or purpose or would be liable to create confusion, for instance when indication of the quantity is not relevant for price comparison purposes, or when different products are marketed in the same packaging.

On a second level of information, the Member States have to inform all persons concerned of the national law transposing this Directive (Article 7).

2.5 Vertical harmonisation

Contrary to horizontal harmonisation, vertical harmonisation approximates the laws according to a specific sector. Regarding fair trading, the Community legislator has chosen as objects of regulation either a selling technique (direct and distant), a communication medium, a good or service, or a particular public interest. The directives often combine some of these objectives, but usually one of them is prevailing. In order to reflect the Community approach as closely as possible, in the following examination, the directives shall be categorised according to their leading objective.

2.5.1 Selling technique as the leading object

Specific selling techniques business avails itself of in order to sell its goods and services to consumers can be distinguished from general commercial communication. Given the fairly direct link of these selling methods to what can be understood by 'trading', this group might be expected to be governed by a lot of Community measures. However, the Directives concerning doorstep selling and distance selling are the only two in this category so far. They are complemented by the Directive on the distance marketing of consumer financial services, which, although featuring a particular product, is actually a special supplement to the general Distance-Selling Directive. The Directives aim specifically at the protection of the consumers' position in the context of those marketing practices. They are characterised by a subtle combination of private law rules with fair trading rules,[196] which cannot always be separated from one another.

[196] Micklitz in Grabitz/Hilf, *Recht der EU*, Vor A2 at 1.

2.5.1.1 Doorstep selling

General remarks

Directive 85/577,[197] a classic minimum harmonisation directive (Article 8),[198] belongs to the set of pioneer directives relating to consumer protection and fair trading. It has its roots in the first consumer protection programme of 1975,[199] a first proposal having been published in 1977.[200] The Directive covers consumer contracts negotiated away from business premises. Article 1 names explicitly those contracts concluded during an excursion or those concluded during a visit by a trader to the consumer's home or place of work, where the visit does not take place at the express request of the consumer. In case of requested visits, the Directive still applies to contracts for the supply of goods or services other than those for which the consumer requested the visit of the trader, provided the consumer did not know, or could not reasonably have known, at the time of the request, that the supply of those other goods or services formed part of the trader's commercial or professional activities.

The scope is extended to further modalities of contract conclusion referred to in Article 1(3) and (4), which involve the offer made by the consumer. As the Court has emphasised in *Travel Vac*, according to the fourth recital of the Directive, the special feature of contracts concluded away from the business premises of the trader is that it is the trader who initiates the contract negotiations.[201] This suggests that the initiation by the trader is the most general underlying idea for the scope of application regarding modalities of contract conclusion.[202]

Several types of contracts are excluded from the scope in Article 3(2). The Court's settled case law, according to which derogations from Community rules for the protection of consumers must be interpreted strictly,[203] is also reflected in the rulings relating to the Doorstep-Selling Directive.[204] In *Dietzinger* the Court had to decide whether the conclusion of a contract of guarantee secur-

---

[197] Directive 85/577/EEC to protect the consumer in respect of contracts negotiated away from business premises, OJ 1985 L 372/31.

[198] In Case C-361/89 *Patrice Di Pinto* [1991] ECR I-1189 at 21 et seq. the Court has explicitly accepted minimum harmonisation for this Directive.

[199] Council Resolution on a preliminary programme for a consumer protection and information policy, OJ 1975 C 92/1, item 24 of the annex.

[200] Proposal for a Council Directive to protect the consumer in respect of contracts which have been negotiated away from business premises, COM (1976) 544 final, OJ 1977 C 22/6.

[201] Case C-423/97 *Travel Vac SL v Manuel José Antelm Sanchis* [1999] ECR I-2195 at 34.

[202] See also *Travel Vac* at 36: an excursion is 'organised' by the trader where the initiative for such an excursion comes from the trader.

[203] See Case C-203/99 *Henning Veedfald v Århus Amtskommune* [2001] ECR I-3569 at 15.

[204] The Doorstep-Selling Directive can be considered as 'the ECJ's vehicle for developing the case law on consumer issues', Karsten/Sinai, (2003) 26 *JCP* 159 at 160.

ing performance of a credit agreement by the principal debtor was covered by Directive.[205] Whereas most language versions of Article 1 of the Directive suggest that it is sufficient for the trader to be a supplier of goods or services in general so that the actual contract does not have to concern the sale of goods or services,[206] the English version clearly refers to 'contracts under which a trader supplies goods or services to a consumer'. Consequently, the terms of most language versions suggest a contract of guarantee to be covered by the Directive, whereas the English one excludes it, since the contract does not itself concern a service.[207] The Court did not, however, get involved into a discussion about the different language versions at all.[208] It rather argued that the Directive was designed to protect consumers by enabling them to withdraw from a contract concluded on the initiative of the trader rather than of the customer, where the customer might have been unable to see all the implications of his act. It did not matter that the goods or services purchased were intended for the use of the third party standing outside the contractual relationship.[209] However, the guarantee at issue was nevertheless not covered by the Directive, because the wording of Article 1 and the ancillary nature of guarantees implied that the Directive covered only a guarantee ancillary to a contract whereby, in the context of 'doorstep selling', a consumer assumed obligations towards the trader with a view to obtaining goods or services from him. Furthermore, since the Directive was designed to protect only consumers, the guarantor must have entered into the commitment in his quality as a consumer as well, i.e. for a purpose unconnected with his trade or profession (which was not the case in *Dietzinger*).[210] The wide interpretation of the scope of the Directive with regard to the contract type is therefore somewhat narrowed down by its particular focus on consumer protection.[211]

Directive 85/577 can be applicable next to other consumer protection directives. The Court held in *Travel Vac* that time-share contracts negotiated away

---

[205] Case C-45/96 *Bayerische Hypotheken- und Wechselbank AG v Edgard Dietzinger* [1998] ECR I-1199. The case concerned a German 'Bürgschaft'.

[206] E.g. German: 'Verträge, die zwischen einem Gewerbetreibenden, der Waren liefert oder Dienstleistungen erbringt, und einem Verbraucher geschlossen werden', French: 'contrats conclus entre un commerçant fournissant des biens ou des services et un consommateur', Dutch: 'overeenkomsten die tussen een handelaar die goederen levert of diensten verricht, en een consument worden gesloten'.

[207] It is notable that the French and the German Governments relied on the English version in their argument, *Dietzinger* at 14 et seq.

[208] Advocate General Jacobs did discuss the incoherence, because he thought that distinction might be crucial in this case, at 17 of his Opinion. See also Edelmann, (1998) 13 *VuR* 179 at 180.

[209] *Dietzinger* at 19.

[210] *Dietzinger* at 22.

[211] See also Micklitz, (1998) 9 *EuZW* 253 at 254, Schulte-Nölke/Schulze/Jones, *Casebook*, p. 187 et seq.

from business premises were not only covered by Directive 94/47,[212] but that the Doorstep-Selling Directive did in principle apply as well.[213] In *Heininger* the Court held that security credit agreements on immovable property were not to be considered as concerning a right relating to immovable property for the purposes of Article 3(2)(a) of the Directive, which has the purpose to protect consumers as broadly as possible in connection with contracts concluded away from business premises.[214] The Consumer Credit Directive[215] is therefore not a *lex specialis* which prevents the application of the Doorstep-Selling Directive.[216]

Substance

The substantive core of Directive 85/577 is the right of cancellation provided for in Article 4. In fact, this is a central fairness element in doorstep selling, compensating the surprise effect and restriction of consumer choice due to lack of information. Providing for a modality of contract termination, this right directly interferes with the private legal orders of the Member States. This makes it a good example of the hybrid nature of fair trading and private law rules in Community legislation. As with any other right conferred on consumers by this Directive, they may not waive their right of cancellation (Article 6).

Traders are required to give consumers written notice of their right of cancellation, together with the name and address of a person against whom that right may be exercised. Such notice has to be dated and to state particulars enabling the contract to be identified. The decisive time at which the notice has to be given to the consumer is the moment at which the binding effect of the future contract has its origin. This can be the conclusion of the contract itself, or a situation in which the consumer is bound by his offer. According to Article 5, the consumer has at least seven days from receipt of the notice to cancel the contract.[217] As the Court has made clear in *Travel Vac*, the Member States are

---

212 Directive 94/47/EC on the protection of purchasers in respect of certain aspects of contracts relating to the purchase of the right to use immovable properties on a timeshare basis, OJ 1994 L 280/83.

213 *Travel Vac* at 26. With regard to the exception in Article 3(2)(a) the Court held in *Travel Vac* at 25 that where the time-share contract 'does not only concern the right to use a time-share apartment, but also concerns the provision of separate services of a value higher than that of the right to use the property, that contract is not covered by the exception provided for in Article 3(2)(a) of Directive 85/577'.

214 Case C-481/99 *Georg and Helga Heininger v Bayerische Hypo- und Vereinsbank AG* [2001] ECR I-9945 at 32 to 34. The case concerned a German *Sicherungsgrundschuld.*

215 Directive 87/102/EEC for the approximation of the laws, regulations and administrative provisions of the Member States concerning consumer credit, OJ 1987 L 42/48.

216 *Heininger* at 37 to 39.

217 The Directive mentions the 'right of cancellation' in Article 4 and the 'right to renounce the effects of his undertaking' in Article 5. In Article 7 the English version reads: 'If the consumer exercises his right of renunciation, the legal effects of such renunciation shall be governed by national laws [...], whereas the German version reads: 'Übt der Verbraucher sein Rücktrittsrecht aus, so regeln sich die Rechts-

free to determine that the notice of renunciation is not subject to any condition as to form, such as having to be given in writing. The Directive thus allows the notice to consist of unequivocal acts.[218] Article 5(2) provides that, in the event of renunciation, the consumer is released from any obligations under the cancelled contract. According to *Travel Vac*, this provision rules out that after cancellation of the contract there can be an obligation to pay damages if the contract is not performed. The payment of such damages would be equal to imposing a penalty on the consumer for exercising his right of renunciation, which would be contrary to the purpose of the Directive, according to which the consumer is to be prevented from undertaking financial obligations without being prepared for them.[219]

The Directive leaves it open to the Member States to determine the consequences in case the trader does not give the required written notice of the consumers' right to cancellation. Article 4(3) merely requires 'appropriate consumer protection measures' in these cases. The Court has admitted in *Faccini Dori* that 'Articles 4 and 5 allow the Member States some latitude regarding consumer protection when information is not provided by the trader'.[220] Yet, it specified that this did not affect the precise and unconditional nature of the provisions of the Directive, since the required minimum level of protection could be determined. Accordingly, the Member States have chosen for a variety of different legal consequences to the exercised right of cancellation.[221] The crucial point is: what is an 'appropriate' consumer protection measure in the sense of Article 4(3)? The Court has given an initial shape to the notion in *Heininger.*[222] The German law prescribed a period of one year from the conclusion of the contract for the exercise of the right of cancellation of security credit agreements on immovable property, even in situations covered by the Doorstep-Selling Directive. This was rejected by the Court. It argued that if the consumer was not aware of the existence of the right of cancellation, he would not be able to exercise that right.[223] For the Court, the wording and the purpose of Article 5 did not allow an interpretation of Article 4(3) which would permit restriction of the time in which the consumer can exercise his cancellation right to one year. Although the Court does not make more concrete statements, it seems, in fact,

folgen des Widerrufs nach einzelstaatlichem Recht [...]', *Rücktritt* and *Widerruf* being totally different concepts of contract termination under German law. These inconsistencies in terms of national legal concepts suggest a functional interpretation of the Directive's provisions, according to which it is decisive that the consumer is released from any obligations under the contract, see Article 5(2).

218 *Travel Vac* at 50 et seq.

219 *Travel Vac* at 59.

220 Case C-91/92 *Paola Faccini Dori v Recreb Srl.* [1994] ECR I-3325 at 17.

221 For the national implementations of Directive 85/577, see Rott, *Haustürwiderrufsrichtlinie.*

222 See *supra* footnote 214.

223 This is reflected by Article 5(1) 'not less than seven days from receipt by the consumer of the notice'.

that it does not consider any time limitation whatsoever to be 'appropriate'. It rejected the argument that the restriction of the period within which the right of cancellation might be exercised was essential for reasons of legal certainty, because, first, this would imply a limitation of the rights expressly conferred on consumers by the Doorstep-Selling Directive,[224] and, second, the traders could easily safeguard both the interests of consumers and their own requirements as to legal certainty by complying with their duty to supply consumers with information.[225]

As far as the role of information in the context of the Doorstep-Selling Directive is concerned, two relevant levels can be distinguished. These are alluded to in the Directive's recitals, which themselves are often referred to by the Court in the above-cited judgments to support its interpretation. On a first level, the Directive assumes that the special feature of contracts concluded away from the business premises of the trader is that the consumer is unprepared and that he is often unable to compare the quality and price of the offer with other offers (recital 4). The Directive, by its substantive provisions, does not actually directly improve this information deficit, which is the initial trading weakness. It rather tackles the symptoms by granting the right of cancellation, in order to enable the consumer to assess the obligations arising under the contract (recital 5). On a second level, the Directive requires the information of the consumer about this cancellation right. It sets high standards by requiring qualified information in writing together with details about the addressee of that right.

2.5.1.2 Distance selling in general

General remarks

Directive 97/7 on distance selling was the first far-reaching consumer-protection answer of the Community to a market more and more relying on modern means of distance communication.[226] However, it is also applicable to more traditional activities, like mail order selling. The recitals emphasise the general importance of quantity and quality of information provided to the consumer in various types and stages of distance sales, information being a key underlying principle of the Directive.[227] The Directive goes far beyond the information requirements of the Doorstep-Selling Directive. One reason may be that it is a modern piece of legislation. The main explanation is, however, that distant communication bears more risks for consumers than direct communication, because they lack knowledge about the dealer and cannot assess the quality of

---

[224] The Court thus acknowledges a subjective right to the consumer, Reich, (2002) 13 *EuZW* 87. See generally Reich, *Bürgerrechte*, p. 272 et seq.

[225] *Heininger* at 45 to 47.

[226] Directive 97/7/EC on the protection of consumers in respect of distance contracts, OJ 1997 L 144/19.

[227] Recitals 11 to 13.

the product before the conclusion of the contract.[228] The Directive also pursues public-interest policy issues by protecting the consumer from particularly intrusive distance selling techniques.

The Directive applies to almost all contracts between consumers and suppliers concluded by, in principle, any means of distance communication as further defined in Article 2. Some contracts, however, are entirely exempted by Article 3(1),[229] and Article 3(2) excludes the core information provisions from application to specific contracts relating to everyday consumption and seasonal services. In practice, contracts of a mixed type play an important role. Such contracts have direct marketing elements, relating to the Doorstep-Selling Directive, as well as distance communication characteristics, e.g. in situations where the consumer is approached for the first time at an organised selling party, and where the conclusion of the contract takes place at a later stage via modern means of distance communication. It is not very clear whether and to what extent these contracts are covered by Directive 97/7. Its definition of distance contracts is based on the 'exclusive use of one or more means of distance communication up to and including the moment at which the contract is concluded'. Sticking close to the wording, this seems to exclude the use of any direct communication from the very initial contact until the conclusion of the contract.[230] But also an interpretation is conceivable which puts the emphasis on the actual process of contract conclusion instead of on the whole contact between the supplier and the consumer.[231] Such an interpretation would substantially widen the scope of the Directive. In fact, if the consumer has had no possibility of seeing the goods during the initial direct contact with the supplier, he is in a similar situation of information deficit to where there is distance communication only, thus deserving similar protection.

The controversially exempted contracts relating to financial services are now covered by Directive 2002/65.[232] Distance communication via the Internet is

---

[228] The consumer buys 'in the dark', Dickie, (1998) 21 *JCP* 217 at 217, 220; see also Salaün in Nihoul, *Telecommunications and broadcasting networks*, p. 103 at p. 114 et seq.

[229] Contracts relating to financial services, contracts concluded by means of automatic vending machines or automated commercial premises, contracts concluded with telecommunications operators through the use of public payphones, contracts concluded for the construction and sale of immovable property or relating to other immovable property rights, except for rental, and contracts concluded at an auction.

[230] Cf. Micklitz, (2001) 12 *EuZW* 133 at 134 et seq.

[231] See Dickie, (1998) 21 *JCP* 217 at 219.

[232] Directive 2002/65/EC concerning the distance marketing of consumer financial services, OJ 2002 L 271/16. See *infra* at 2.5.1.3.

specifically regulated in the E-Commerce Directive,[233] teleshopping is covered by the Television Directive.[234]

Substance

Article 4(1) requires detailed information the consumer has to be provided with in 'good time prior to the conclusion of the contract'. This concept is not further specified, but the underlying idea is obviously that the consumer has sufficient time to consider adequately the disclosed information before entering into the agreement.[235] The Directive remains silent, however, about the language to be used for this information, which according to the eighth recital, is a matter for the Member States. The information to be disclosed concerns the identity of the supplier, the characteristics and the price of the goods or services (including supplementary costs, like taxes or delivery), and further details which surpass the items commonly regarded necessary to be agreed upon for a valid sales contract. Amongst others, the consumer has to be informed about the existence of a right of withdrawal and about the cost of using the means of distance communication. Article 4(3) provides that in the case of telephone communications, the identity of the supplier and the commercial purpose of the call have to be made explicitly clear at the beginning of any conversation with the consumer. This is an indication of the disclosure of the information at a very early stage of the contact also for other means of distance communication.

Article 4(2) sets the standards for the quality of the information. It must be provided in a clear and comprehensible manner in any way appropriate to the means of distance communication used, and the commercial purpose of the information must be made clear to the consumer. The Directive requires the information to obey the principles governing the protection of those who, under national law, are unable to give their consent, and, generally, to respect 'the principles of good faith in commercial transactions'. The idea of 'good faith', which is rather unfamiliar to common law, has been introduced into Community legislation by the Directive on self-employed commercial agents.[236] However, it has received its actual recognition from Article 3 of the Unfair Terms Directive,[237] where it directly affects contract law. The German and the French versions of the Directives illustrate the difference of the notion as used in the different

---

[233] Directive 2000/31/EC on certain legal aspects of information society services, in particular electronic commerce, in the Internal Market (Directive on electronic commerce), OJ 2000 L 178/1. See *infra* at 2.5.2.2.

[234] Directive 89/552/EEC concerning the pursuit of television broadcasting activities ('Television without frontiers'), OJ 1989 L 298/23 as amended by Directive 97/36/EC, OJ 1997 L 202/60. See *infra* at 2.5.2.1.

[235] Micklitz in Reich/Micklitz, *Verbraucherrecht*, at 15.24.

[236] Article 3(1) and Article 4(1) of Directive 86/653/EEC relating to self-employed commercial agents, OJ 1986 L 382/17.

[237] Article 3(1) of Directive 93/13/EEC on unfair terms in consumer contracts, OJ 1993 L 95/29.

contexts. In Directive 93/13 the used terms are *Treu und Glauben* and *bonne foi*, typical concepts of contract law. The translations in Directive 97/7 are *Grundsätze der Lauterkeit bei Handelsgeschäften* and *principes de loyauté en matière de transactions commerciales*. These concepts are related to the pre-contractual phase and, in fact, are much closer to what can be called a 'principle of fair trading'.

One of the characteristics of distance sales is that means of distance communication are of a transitory nature, and so is usually the information provided via these means. Article 5 responds to this situation by providing for written confirmation or confirmation on another durable medium of the most required information under Article 4. The consumer must receive this confirmation 'in good time' during the performance of the contract or at the latest at the time of delivery. Services which are performed through the use of a means of distance communication are exempted, where they are supplied on only one occasion and are invoiced by the operator of the means of distance communication. The consumer must still be able, however, to obtain the address of the place of business of the supplier to which he may address any complaints.

In addition, the Distance-Selling Directive bestows on the consumer a right of withdrawal from the contract, which is regulated in great detail in Article 6. Whereas in the context of doorstep selling the aim is to give consumers a chance for reflection on the obligations arising under the contract, which they may not have had in a surprise situation, the reason in the context of distance selling is rather to be found in a chance to assess the quality of the product, which was unknown before. The main ideas are a minimum period of seven working days and a withdrawal without penalty (only the direct cost of returning the goods can be charged) and without giving any reason. The period for exercise of this right begins, in the case of goods, from the day on which the consumer receives the goods where the information confirmation obligations have been fulfilled, otherwise the period for exercise of the right of withdrawal extends to three months. Some contracts are exempted from the compulsory right of withdrawal.

Unlike the Doorstep-Selling Directive, Directive 97/7 also provides for the effects of the exercised right of withdrawal: the consumers have to be reimbursed the costs within 30 days. The only charge that may be made to consumers because of the exercise of their right of withdrawal is the direct cost of returning the goods.[238] Article 8 protects the consumers from fraudulent use of their payment cards, in case of which they can request the cancellation of a payment. In practice, however, this right will be of limited value, since the consumers are not relieved from the burden of proof.

---

[238] It is disputed whether and to what extent the consumer must still pay for having used the goods before sending them back, Rott, (2001) 16 *VuR* 78 at 80 et seq.

The practice of unsolicited supply of goods or services (inertia selling) is specifically dealt with in Article 9. At the pre-contractual level, the Member States have to prohibit this practice, where the supply involves a demand for payment, at the private-law level they have to exempt the consumer from the provision of any consideration in cases of unsolicited supply, the absence of a response not constituting consent.

Finally, Article 10 contains restrictions for certain means of distance communication, which are characterised by their automatism and their intrusion into the private sphere of the consumer. The use of automatic calling machines and faxes require the prior consent of the consumer (opt-in). Other means of distance communication, which allow individual communications, may be used only where there is no clear objection from the consumer (opt-out). As a result, there is the somewhat unsatisfying situation from the consumer's perspective that automatic 'cold calling' is in principle prohibited whereas the actually no less intrusive manual 'cold calling' is lawful under the Directive as long as the consumer has not opted out.

It should be noted that consumer information does not only play a role in the pre-contractual relationship between suppliers and consumers, but that the consumer information approach is also reflected in the implementation process. The consumer has to be informed of the national law transposing this Directive, and the Member States must encourage professional organisations to inform consumers of their codes of practice (Article 16).

2.5.1.3 Distance selling in particular: financial services

Emerging from a lengthy legislation process,[239] Directive 2002/65 on the distance marketing of consumer financial services finally covers the important product group of financial services, which was excluded from Directive 97/7 for lack of political consent.[240] Therefore, although Directive 2002/65 applies to a specific product group it must basically be understood as a follow-up to the general Distance-Selling Directive, so that it seems justified to deal with it in the same category, i.e. that of selling techniques.

General remarks

It follows from the fact that Directive 2002/65 was meant to supplement the original Directive on distance sales that, next to the common objectives and purposes, there are many substantive similarities between the two pieces of legislation. Obviously, Directive 2002/65 contains specific adjustments for the important and often complex area of marketing financial products to which

239 See Van Huffel, (2001) *REDC* 295.

240 Directive 2002/65/EC concerning the distance marketing of consumer financial services and amending Council Directive 90/619/EEC and Directives 97/7/EC and 98/27/EC, OJ 2002 L 271/16.

consumers are particularly vulnerable. In principle, the Directive aims at maximum harmonisation of the distance marketing of consumer financial services, unless otherwise specifically indicated (recital 13).[241] The permission of Article 4(2) to allow more stringent requirements for information of the consumer prior to the conclusion of the distance contract than provided for in the Directive may be considered the most important exception to the maximum harmonisation approach.

Substance

The pre-contractual disclosure of information clearly constitutes a fundamental pillar of the Directive. Article 3 is much denser than the similar provision in Directive 97/7 and can be said to set new standards as regards the extent and the detail of pre-contractual information disclosure.[242] It explicitly distinguishes between information concerning the supplier, the financial service, the distance contract, and the redress, which has to be provided '[in] good time before the consumer is bound by any distance contract or offer'.[243] These four categories – parties, product, contract, remedies – can be claimed with good reason to be the essential elements of interest for consumers during the whole contractual relationship, beginning with the initial contact and continuing until after-sales matters. Hence, knowledge of these issues is certainly most significant for the consumer's economic choice.

The information concerning the supplier is to ensure that the consumer can identify him, his business and his representatives, and that the consumer can contact him. The characteristics of the financial service have to be described in a most accurate way, including all costs attached to the transaction and potential risks connected to the service. The distance contract must be described in its temporal and substantive dimension. Specific importance is attached to the possibilities and circumstances of terminating the contract, particularly the right of withdrawal. The information about the redress concerns out-of-court complaints and alternative compensation arrangements.

The requirements as to the clearness of the information and the respect of the principles of good faith in commercial transactions are the same as in Directive 97/7. In the case of telephone communications the consumer may explicitly consent to the disclosure of just the information considered most

---

[241] See also the considerations of Kieninger in Nordhausen, *Entwicklungen*, p. 13 et seq. relating to the scope and degree of harmonisation of the Directive.

[242] Micklitz/Schirmbacher, (2003) 3 *EUREDIA* 457 at 466.

[243] Unlike Directive 97/7, which mentions the conclusion of the contract as the decisive time of reference, Directive 2002/65 refers to the moment the consumer is bound by an offer. Depending on the national legal construction this may signify a shift to a slightly earlier point of time. In any case, it emphasises that the information has to be provided at a stage at which it can still be considered before entailing a legal consequence, cf. Härting/Schirmbacher, (2002) *CR* 809 at 813.

essential by the Directive, provided that he is informed about other information available on request. Article 3(4) explicitly requires that the information communicated during the pre-contractual phase is in conformity with the contractual obligations of the potentially later concluded contract.

According to Article 4, additional information requirements in existing Community legislation continue to apply, and the pre-contractual information requirements of this Directive are minimum harmonisation. In order to create a high level of transparency the Commission shall ensure, on a second information level, that the national provisions are communicated to consumers and suppliers.

Like Directive 97/7, Directive 2002/65 aims at compensating the lack of physical information that comes along with the use of means of distance communication. Directive 2002/65 is, however, much stricter as it requires *all* the contractual terms and conditions and the pre-contractual information to be communicated on paper or another durable medium. This is reasonable, because the financial service will typically only be materialised by a contract. The communication has to happen 'in good time before the consumer is bound by any distance contract or offer' (Article 5(1)), which is certainly a rather vague concept. Assuming, however, that the information has to be communicated early enough for consumers to consider their commitment before they are bound, this duty perfectly compensates the previous use of non-physical means of communication. In fact, it even produces more favourable circumstances than most typical direct-communication situations.

The consumer has a period of 14 calendar days in which to withdraw from the contract without penalty and without giving any reason (Article 6(1)). The period is 30 calendar days in distance contracts relating to life insurance and personal pension operations. As the financial services sector often involves short-term deals and is very sensitive to economic fluctuations, the Member States may provide for exemptions from the right of withdrawal for a number of specified contracts. Again, at a second level of information stream, the exemptions have to be communicated to the Commission, which shall ensure that is available to consumers and suppliers who request it. The Community thus assigns itself its own share of the information duty.

As in Directive 97/7, the effects of the exercised right of withdrawal are regulated in Article 7, with special emphasis laid on the payment of the service provided before withdrawal. The fraudulent use of the consumer's payment card is addressed in Article 8, which gives the right to request cancellation of a payment and the re-crediting of the sum paid.

The supply of unsolicited financial services including a request for payment is prohibited and must not result in any obligation for the consumer (Article 9). Unsolicited communications are governed by Article 10, which submits the use of automatic calling machines and faxes to an opt-in regime. Other means of distance communication which allow individual communications, may either be subject to an opt-in system, or they may only be used if the consumer has not expressed his manifest objection. This approach to the protection of consumers' privacy and decision-making is confronted, however, with the factual difficulties to express their manifest objection efficiently.[244]

2.5.2 Medium as the leading object

Television and the Internet are the media the Community has brought into particular focus with regard to fair trading. It has been mentioned earlier that the respective legal instruments feature a country of origin principle in order to cope with the multistate nature of these media. It comes along with taking the medium of communication as an objective of harmonisation that diverse issues, which are linked to this medium, can be dealt with. The Television Directive and the E-Commerce Directive thus both cover a broad range of fair-trading concerns.

Both legal instruments form part of a system of regulation of electronic communications networks and services.[245] This system distinguishes between the regulation of transmission and the regulation of content. The transmission is governed by the framework Directive 2002/21 and further specific Directives.[246] The Television Directive and the E-Commerce Directive form part of the regulation of the content.

2.5.2.1 Television

General remarks

Even in the Internet Age television remains an enormously important audiovisual medium, which, next to its cultural functions, plays a significant role as a platform for trading and continues to receive much attention by the Community.[247] The leading instrument in the present context is Directive 89/552,[248] which is well-known as the 'Television without frontiers' Directive.

---

[244] Scherer, (2001) 47 *WRP* 1255 at 1258.

[245] For a comprehensive analysis of the rules applicable to electronic communications networks and services within the European Union, see Nihoul/Rodford, *EU Electronic Communications Law.*

[246] Directive 2002/21/EC on a common regulatory framework for electronic communications networks and services (Framework Directive), OJ 2002 L 108/33. Directive 2002/22/EC on universal service and user's rights relating to electronic communications networks and services (Universal Services Directive), OJ 2002 L 108/51, one of the specific Directives, provides in Article 20 which minimum details must be specified in a contract with consumers (however, this being contract law rather than fair-trading law).

[247] See Communication on the future of European regulatory audiovisual policy, COM (2003) 784 final.

[248] Directive 89/552/EEC concerning the pursuit of television broadcasting activities ('Television without frontiers'), OJ 1989 L 298/23.

It has been amended by Directive 97/36 in order to adapt it to developments in the field of television broadcasting and to clarify certain definitions and obligations under the Directive.[249] Television without frontiers was motivated by the Court's ruling in *Debauve*,[250] in which it held that in the absence of harmonisation a Member State might lawfully prevent the retransmission of television adverts from other Member States on grounds of public interest.[251] The Court has recently confirmed this case law for (advertorial) television transmissions which do not fall within the fields coordinated by the Directive, and which have therefore to be measured against the free movement of services.[252]

Featuring a principle of country of origin – the transmission-State principle – the Directive is based on the concept of free circulation of television transmissions that comply with a minimum of common standards in the coordinated fields (Article 2a). These standards concern, in the context of advertising, consumer protection, protection of morals and human dignity, protection of minors, and human health.

Article 3(1) provides that the Member States remain free to require television broadcasters under their jurisdiction to comply with more detailed or stricter rules in the areas covered by the Directive. Although it appears to follow from recital 27 of the original Directive 89/552 that this minimum clause was meant to justify stricter rules in the interests of consumers alone, the Court held in *Leclerc-Siplec* that Article 3(1) did not preclude the justification of restrictions on the grounds of the protection of interests other than those of consumers (e.g. certain economic interests).[253] The Commission has established that, indeed, there are a remarkable number of differences regarding the rules on advertising at the level of the Member States.[254] This situation and new advertising tech-

---

[249] Directive 97/36/EC amending Directive 89/552/EEC concerning the pursuit of television broadcasting activities, OJ 1997 L 202/60. Consequently, the references made here concern Directive 89/552 in its amended version.

[250] Case 52/79 *Procureur du Roi v Marc J.V.C. Debauve and others* [1980] ECR 833.

[251] The Court held earlier in Case 155/73 *Giuseppe Sacchi* [1974] ECR 409 at 6 that the transmission of television signals, including those in the nature of advertisements, came within the free movement of services, see also Westphal, (2002) 13 *EBLR* 459 at 461 and 481.

[252] Case C-262/02 *Commission v France* [2004] ECR I-nyr and Case C-429/02 *Bacardi France SAS v Télévision française 1 SA (TF1) et al.* [2004] ECR I-nyr. Both judgments concerned the so-called "Loi Evin", the French prohibition of television advertising for alcoholic beverages marketed in France, in the case of indirect television advertising resulting from the appearance on screen of hoardings visible during the retransmission of bi-national sporting events taking place in other Member States. The Court considered the prohibition to be 'indirect television advertising' (see *infra* footnote 257), which was out of the scope of the Directive, and which was justified on the grounds of protecting public health. See on the French "Loi Evin" Radeideh/Franck in Micklitz/Keßler, *Marketing Practices*, p. 76 at p. 90 et seq.

[253] Case C-412/93 *Société d'Importation Edouard Leclerc-Siplec v TF1 Publicité SA and M6 Publicité SA* [1995] ECR I-179 at 43–47.

[254] See Fourth report on the application of Directive 89/552, COM (2002) 778 final at p. 12 et seq.

niques (such as interactive advertising or split-screen advertising) have proved it necessary to review the Directive and in particular its advertising provisions.[255]

Substance

One of the most important concerns of the Directive is certainly to assure the distinction of promotional broadcasts from other television broadcasts.[256] The Directive therefore sets out at the very beginning of its advertising section (Chapter IV) that television advertising (i.e. any form of announcement broadcast in return for payment or for similar consideration)[257] and teleshopping (i.e. direct offers broadcast with a view to the supply of goods or services)[258] must be readily recognisable as such and kept quite separate from other parts of the programme service by optical and/or acoustic means. Moreover, isolated advertising and teleshopping spots must remain the exception. Subliminal techniques and surreptitious advertising and teleshopping are entirely prohibited (Article 10). Furthermore, advertising and teleshopping spots must not become rampant. As a basic principle, television advertising must be inserted between programmes. It may be inserted during programmes only on condition that certain principles are observed, namely that the advertising breaks do not adversely affect either the integrity or the value of the programmes (Article 11(1)).[259] Accordingly, the Directive establishes a sophisticated system determining the types of programmes which may be interrupted for advertising spots, the intervals of the spots and the proportion of transmission time devoted

[255] Cf. the work programme for the review of the 'Television without frontiers' Directive annexed to the report mentioned in footnote 254. The Commission is aware of the fact that coherence and compatibility with the future Directive on unfair commercial practices has to be ensured, see p. 35 of the report. Although the European Parliament approves the review of the Directive it favours as far as advertising is concerned, a less prescriptive and more flexible approach than that adopted in the current Directive, leaving responsible broadcasting to 'intelligent broadcasters', Report of 25 June 2003 on Television without frontiers, A5-0251/2003 at paragraph 11 of the explanatory statement.

[256] See also in general the Commission's interpretative communication on certain aspects of the provisions on televised advertising in the 'Television without frontiers' Directive, OJ 2004 C 102/2.

[257] In Case C-429/02 *Bacardi France SAS v Télévision française 1 SA (TF1) et al.* [2004] ECR I-nyr at 28 the Court held with regard to the prohibition in the French "Loi Evin" (see *supra* footnote 252) that such indirect television advertising could not be regarded as 'television advertising' within the meaning of the Directive.

[258] These are broadcasts presenting products which may be ordered directly by telephone, mail or videotext and which are delivered to viewers at home, Joined Cases C-320/94, C-328/94, C-329/94, C-337/94, C-338/94 and C-339/94 *Reti Televisive Italiane SpA (RTI) et al. v Ministero delle Poste e Telecomunicazioni* [1996] ECR I-6471 at 31.

[259] Case C-245/01 *RTL Television GmbH v Niedersächsische Landesmedienanstalt für privaten Rundfunk* [2003] ECR I-nyr at 52.

to advertising and teleshopping (from 15% to 20% of the daily transmission time).[260]

Under a general public interest objective, advertising and teleshopping, shall not prejudice respect for human dignity, include any discrimination on grounds of race, sex or nationality, be offensive to religious or political beliefs, encourage behaviour prejudicial to health or to safety, or encourage behaviour prejudicial to the protection of the environment (Article 12).

The product-related rules are governed by health-protection goals. All forms of television advertising and teleshopping for cigarettes and other tobacco products are prohibited, and sponsorship is not allowed by undertakings whose principal activity is the manufacture or sale of tobacco products (Article 13).[261] The same applies for advertising and sponsorship for medicinal products and medical treatment available only on prescription (Article 14).[262] Advertising and teleshopping for alcoholic beverages must not be aimed specifically at minors and must not suggest to enhance physical performance, to contribute towards social or sexual success, or to have therapeutic qualities. It must also not encourage immoderate consumption of alcohol or place emphasis on high alcoholic content as being a positive quality of the beverages (Article 15).

The protection of minors plays a significant role in the Directive. This is without equivalence in any other piece of Community legislation pertaining to fair trading. In Article 16 a set of criteria is established with specific emphasis on the relationship minors have to their parents or teachers in order to prevent advertising from causing moral or physical detriment to minors. In addition, advertising must not exploit the minors' inexperience or credulity or unreasonably show them in dangerous situations. The Directive contains furthermore a separate Chapter on the protection of minors and public order (Chapter V). Most of those provisions, which, however, concern television broadcasts of programmes (e.g. programmes that involve pornography or gratuitous violence) as opposed to advertising, can justify provisional derogations from the transmission-State principle. This does not apply to television advertising aimed at

---

[260] For the number of advertising slots to be allowed during the broadcasting of audiovisual works, the method of calculation and the duration of advertisements to be taken into account, see Case C-6/98 *Arbeitsgemeinschaft Deutscher Rundfunkanstalten (ARD) v PRO Sieben Media AG* [1999] ECR I-7599, for the quality of television programmes to be interrupted, see Case C-245/01 *RTL Television GmbH v Niedersächsische Landesmedienanstalt für privaten Rundfunk* [2003] ECR I-nyr. See the review of the scope of the Television Directive's Article 11 concerning the permitted frequency of advertising by Woods/Scheuer, (2004) 29 *E.L.Rev.* 366.

[261] In *Tobacco Advertising* the Court has implicitly acknowledged the legality of this prohibition, Case C-376/98 *Germany v Parliament and Council ('Tobacco Advertising')* [2000] ECR I-8419 at 98. See Amtenbrink/Appeldoorn (2001) 49 *SEW* 413 at 416.

[262] This has become a generally applicable principle by extending it to other media by Article 88(1) of Directive 2001/83, see *infra* at 2.5.3.3.

minors. The Court held in *De Agostini and TV-Shop* that the receiving Member State may no longer, under any circumstances, apply provisions specifically designed to control the content of television advertising with regard to minors, since this would add a secondary control to the control which the broadcasting Member State must exercise under the Directive.[263]

Finally, sponsored television programmes must be clearly identified as such and may not encourage the purchase or rental of the products or services of the sponsor or a third party, in particular by making special promotional references to those products or services (Article 17).

2.5.2.2 The Internet

General remarks

Directive 2000/31[264] is the sectoral reaction of the Community to the ever growing importance of the Internet as a medium for trade in the information society. Unlike the United States of America, the European Union relies less on a customary or self-regulatory system, but prefers to control e-commerce legally.[265]

All the potential advantages of this medium on the one hand, such as the great variety of choices or lower prices of the products offered, are faced with a lack in consumer confidence on the other hand.[266] Consumers are not able to judge their contractual party or the product offered, they have no influence on the correct delivery, and they cannot be sure what happens to their data. E-commerce as such thus comprises a variety of different questions, covering, *inter alia*, the whole range of the contractual relationship (from the initial contact to after-sales issues, including, for instance, questions of digital signature,[267] online payment, etc.), liability, data protection, and (judicial) remedies.[268] The E-Commerce Directive is complementing other legislation (Article 1(3)) and tackles only some of the relevant issues, (pre-contractual) disclosure of information being the most interesting in the present context.[269]

---

[263] Joined Cases C-34/95, C-35/95 and C-36/95 *Konsumentombudsmannen (KO) v De Agostini (Svenska) Förlag AB and TV-Shop i Sverige AB* [1997] ECR I-3843 at 60–61.

[264] Directive 2000/31/EC on certain legal aspects of information society services, in particular electronic commerce, in the Internal Market (Directive on electronic commerce), OJ 2000 L 178/1.

[265] Boehme-Neßler, (2001) 12 *EWS* 149 at 150 et seq. For custom as a source of Internet regulation, see Polanski, (2002) 9 *ECLR* 165.

[266] See Noll, (2002) 9 *ECLR* 207.

[267] See Directive 1999/93/EC on a Community framework for electronic signatures, OJ 2000 L 13/12.

[268] Cf. Alpa, (2001) 12 *EBLR* 244 at 244 and Grundmann, (2003) 67 *RabelsZ* 246 at 249.

[269] It has been suggested that binding Internet law is less suitable to regulate e-commerce than custom, see Polanski, (2002) 9 *ECLR* 165.

However, the Directive is not primarily consumer-protection legislation. Its main purpose is to contribute to the proper functioning of the Internal Market by ensuring the free movement of 'information society services' between the Member States, Article 1(1).[270] Thus, trading is subject to certain rules regardless of whether the service provider deals with commercial clients or with consumers. Nevertheless, the recitals reveal that the framework to cover certain legal aspects of electronic commerce in the Internal Market shall ensure legal certainty and consumer confidence.[271] The Directive is also without prejudice to the level of protection for consumer interests, as established by other Community acts.[272] It is especially meant to complement information requirements established by earlier legislation, in particular Directive 97/7, and later legislation, such as Directive 2002/65. It can reasonably be suggested that the Internet has probably become the leading means of distance communication to which those Directives apply. Also the Directive on misleading and comparative advertising, for instance, which originally has been developed for traditional means of communication, applies to online trading. This makes the e-commerce sector a perfect example of the fragmentary situation of European fair-trading legislation.

It has been noted earlier that the Directive features a country of origin principle in order to cope with the multistate nature of the medium Internet.[273] It provides rules for 'commercial communication', which is the pivotal term of Directive 2000/31 in connection with fair trading.[274] This wide notion basically comprises 'any form of communication' aimed at sales promotion, and it is therefore a technology-neutral definition.[275] Some activities of information society services are exempted from the application of the Directive, among them gambling activities which involve wagering a stake with monetary value in games of chance, including lotteries and betting transactions (Article 1(5)(d)).

[270] Directive 2000/31/EC refers to the definition of 'information society service' in Directive 98/34/EC laying down a procedure for the provision of information in the field of technical standards and regulations, OJ 1998 L 204/37 as amended by Directive 98/48/EC, OJ 1998 L 217/18. An information society service is therefore 'any service normally provided for remuneration, at a distance, by electronic means and at the individual request of a recipient of services'.

[271] For a critical evaluation of the 'consumer confidence' argument as a justification for harmonisation, see Wilhelmsson, (2004) 27 *JCP* 317 at 324 et seq.

[272] See recital 11 for a detailed list of other acts.

[273] See *supra* at 1.5. However, the Annex of the Directive excludes from the scope of application of the country of origin principle, *inter alia*, contractual obligations concerning consumer contacts and the permissibility of unsolicited commercial communications by electronic mail.

[274] Via 'commercial communication' the issue of fair trading belongs to the core of the coordinated field of the Directive and thus is covered by the country of origin principle, see also Grundmann, (2003) 67 *RabelsZ* 246 at 270 et seq.

[275] Cf. *supra* at 2.1, esp. footnote 132.

However, according to recital 16, this exemption is not to cover promotional competitions or games where the purpose is to encourage the sale of goods or services and where payments, if they arise, serve only to acquire the promoted goods or services.

Substance

The Directive tackles disclosure of information and unfair commercial practices at the pre-contractual level, at the level of contract conclusion and throughout the whole contact between the information service provider and the recipient.

According to Article 5, general information has to be provided regarding the service provider. More than any other means of distance communication the Internet conceals the person in the background of the communication. Therefore, as a minimum basis, the name of the service provider, his geographic address and other details permitting rapid, direct and effective contact have to be provided (including his electronic mail address). In specified cases (e.g. where the service provider is registered in a trade or similar public register) additional information is required. The disclosure of this information is in no way related to the later conclusion of a contract, but must happen in any case.[276] Moreover, it must be easily, directly and permanently accessible, which could be realised, for instance, by a hyperlink on every page of the website leading to the display of the information. Relating this to a (possible) contract conclusion, this means that the information concerning the service provider must be available throughout the whole transactional process, i.e. during the whole contact between the service provider and the recipient, not only at just one particular stage of the contractual negotiations. Directive 2000/31 thus goes beyond Directive 97/7, which requires suppliers to reveal their identity prior to the conclusion of the contract.

At the pre-contractual level, commercial communication must obey a scheme of utmost recognisability and clarity, which is set out in an almost redundant way in Article 6. This is of particular significance, since the Internet, more than any other medium, is capable of blurring the borderline between editorial and commercial communication.[277] Accordingly, in addition to other information requirements, commercial communication must be clearly identifiable as such, and the natural or legal person on whose behalf the commercial communication is made must likewise be clearly identifiable. Promotional offers, such as discounts, premiums and gifts must be clearly identifiable as such, and the conditions which are to be met to qualify for them shall be easily

---

[276] Le Berre/Arnould/Derenne, (2002) 10 *JTDE* 113 at 114.

[277] De Cock Buning/Hondius/Prins/de Vries, (2001) 24 *JCP* 287 at 298, De Nayer in Wilhelmsson/Tuominen/Tuomola, *Information Society*, p. 117 at p. 122.

accessible and be presented clearly and unambiguously.[278] Promotional competitions or games have to be clearly identifiable as such, and the conditions for participation must be easily accessible and be presented clearly and unambiguously. According to Article 5(2), where information society services refer to prices, these are to be indicated clearly and unambiguously and, in particular, must indicate whether they are inclusive of tax and delivery costs.

Unsolicited commercial communication by e-mail ('spamming') is not only an intrusion into the recipients' privacy, but also involves costs not to be underestimated.[279] This practice has been regulated differently in the past. Spamming is, in principle covered by Article 10 of Directive 97/7, according to which there must be an opt-out possibility. The E-Commerce Directive left it to the Member States to decide whether or not spamming is admissible. It required in Article 7 that such unsolicited commercial communication must be identifiable clearly and unambiguously as such as soon as it is received by the recipient. In addition, service providers had to consult regularly and respect the opt-out registers in which natural persons not wishing to receive such commercial communications could register themselves. With the adoption of Directive 2002/58,[280] however, the previous rules can largely be regarded as obsolete. Article 13 of the latter Directive has clearly introduced an opt-in scheme for e-mail for the purposes of direct marketing, allowing exceptions only where the trader has obtained from his customers their electronic contact details in the context of a previous sale (and in compliance with data protection legislation), in case the customer has not initially refused such use and always with the possibility of opting out. In any event, spamming which conceals the identity of the sender on whose behalf the communication is made or which does not supply a valid address to which the recipient may send a request that such communications cease has to be banned.[281]

According to the E-Commerce Directive, the national legal systems must in general allow contracts to be concluded by electronic means. This can involve a technical procedure that leaves it ambiguous when and with which content the contract is concluded. At the level of contract conclusion, Article 10 of the Direc-

---

278 This is a good example of the effect of the country of origin principle: promotional offers meeting the minimum requirements of Directive 2000/31 may be provided through the Internet to all Member States, irrespective of whether they are prohibited in the receiving Member States. Cf. De Cock Buning/Hondius/Prins/de Vries, (2001) 24 *JCP* 287 at 297.

279 According to Gauthronet/Drouard, p. 67 Internet subscribers world-wide are unwittingly paying an estimated €10 billion a year in connection costs just to receive 'junk' e-mails.

280 Directive 2002/58/EC concerning the processing of personal data and the protection of privacy in the electronic communications sector (Directive on privacy and electronic communications), OJ 2002 L 201/37.

281 Other unsolicited communications for purposes of direct marketing, such as SMS-messages are subject to the same rules, see *infra* at 2.5.4.1.

tive therefore establishes minimum information requirements to be met by the service provider in a clear, comprehensible and unambiguous way, which allows no derogations if the recipient is a consumer. Although, these requirements are essentially of a pre-contractual nature, they reach far into the process of contract conclusion itself, which can involve several technical steps.[282] The information concerns:[283]

- the different technical steps to follow to conclude the contract,
- whether or not the concluded contract will be filed by the service provider and whether it will be accessible,
- the technical means for identifying and correcting input errors prior to the placing of the order,[284]
- the languages offered for the conclusion of the contract.

If the service provider subscribes to relevant codes of conduct,[285] which is encouraged by the Directive, he has to indicate them to consumers and inform them on how those codes can be consulted electronically. However, these information duties do not apply to contracts concluded exclusively by exchange of electronic mail or by equivalent individual communications, i.e. only if the contract is concluded via the website. Contract terms and general conditions provided to the recipient must be made available in a way that allows him to store and reproduce them. The recipient's order has to be confirmed without undue delay and by electronic means according to Article 11.[286]

---

[282] This is a functional description of the conclusion of a contract. Legally speaking, a contract is concluded at a very particular moment, when all the necessary requirements are fulfilled. Cf. also Pfeiffer in Schulze/Ebers/Grigoleit, *Informationspflichten*, p. 103 at 110 et seq.

[283] The information requirements in Article 10 have been criticised of not providing any new protection from a contract law point of view, since a contract is formed in a certain way according to national contract law, Hultmark Ramberg, (2001) 26 *E.L.Rev.* 429 at 438 et seq. It is submitted that the these information requirements are actually of a pre-contractual nature, serving fair trading practices 'prior to the placing of the order' (Article 10(1)(c)), i.e. before the legally binding conclusion of the contract.

[284] Article 11(2) requires that consumers must also have appropriate, effective and accessible technical means allowing them to identify and correct input errors, prior to the placing of the order.

[285] Cf. e.g. the 'Webtrader' trust scheme, which has a twofold objective: facilitate access of (small and medium sized) enterprises in e-commerce by improving consumer confidence in buying online. The scheme is based on the online certification of business and the grant of a 'Webtrader' label upon compliance with a code of conduct, which aims to guarantee that transactions will be completed in a fair way (according to national and Community standards). The 'Webtrader' scheme operates in a decentralised manner, aiming at European harmonisation and is supported (like other so-called 'e-confidence' programmes) by the Commission.

[286] See Hultmark Ramberg, (2001) 26 *E.L.Rev.* 429 at 439 et seq. for a discussion on how this confirmation affects the moment of the conclusion of the contract.

2.5.3 Good or service as the leading object

The Community's vertical approach to harmonisation has mostly happened according to product sectors, 'product' to be broadly understood as comprising both goods and services. The majority of legal measures can be found in this category.

As far as goods are concerned, the relevant provisions concern labelling aspects, which basically is information attached to the good. For instance, there is labelling legislation on household appliances,[287] footwear,[288] dangerous substances,[289] or textile names.[290] For this analysis a selection has been made, such as to include legislation concerning foodstuffs, cosmetic products, medicinal products, and tobacco products. These areas illustrate best the close interrelationship between the consumers' health and safety, and the protection of their economic interests. Moreover, the Court of Justice has frequently dealt with these areas in its case law.

As far as services are concerned, disclosure of information plays an important role as well. Naturally, due to the non-materialisation of the product this has to happen separately from the service. The examined legislation concerns consumer credit, investment services, insurance mediation, package travel, and timesharing.

2.5.3.1 Foodstuffs

General remarks

Foodstuffs, which have also played a role in a lot of cases before the Court,[291] are regulated in countless legislative measures, often concerning just one particular product.[292] The foodstuffs sector is, in fact, a highly volatile area of legislation. New health risks, new scientific innovations and growing

[287] Directive 92/75/EEC on the indication by labelling and standard product information of the consumption of energy and other resources by household appliances, OJ 1992 L 297/16.

[288] Directive 94/11/EC relating to labelling of the materials used in the main components of footwear for sale to the consumer, OJ 1994 L 100/37.

[289] Directive 67/548/EEC relating to the classification, packaging and labelling of dangerous substances, OJ 1967 L 196/1.

[290] Directive 96/74/EC on textile names, OJ 1997 L 32/38.

[291] See the case law review by Gormley (1997) *EFLR* 1, who identifies a shift from case law to legislation in the foodstuffs sector (at 9).

[292] Cf. e.g. for beef: Regulation 1760/2000/EC establishing a system for the identification and registration of bovine animals and regarding the labelling of beef and beef products, OJ 2000 L 204/1 and Regulation 1825/2000/EC laying down detailed rules for the application of Regulation 1760/2000/EC as regards the labelling of beef and beef products, OJ 2000 L 216/8. For chocolate: Directive 2000/36/EC relating to cocoa and chocolate products intended for human consumption, OJ 2000 L 197/19.

public awareness entail frequent amendments of existing and continuing creation of new Community rules. Taking into account the complexity and density it has developed, it is justified to speak of European food law as an own area of law.[293] Besides, food safety is probably the sector which has the closest points of contact between health and consumer protection.

The foodstuffs sector is particularly interesting from the perspective of fair trading. It is considered a fundamental objective to enable consumers to make their choice of what food to buy and to eat on the basis of clear and accurate information, usually by mandatory labelling.[294] The priorities in pursuing this objective are food labelling in general, nutritional labelling in particular and lately also rules concerning food claims. Besides, in recent years the marketing of genetically modified food has come more and more into the centre of focus.[295] This issue is particularly controversial, not only because of the ethical, environmental and health aspects, but also because of its trade implications with the United States of America, the latter having chosen for a far less restrictive framework for genetically modified food. The aspect of protected geographical indications (PGIs) and protected designations of origin (PODs) will be ignored in the analysis. Although consumer information is certainly one of the objectives, the underlying concept is more familiar to trademark protection, which is beyond the scope of this work.[296]

Nutrition labelling

Directive 90/496[297] lays down common rules on nutrition labelling, taking into account the growing public interest in the relationship between diet and health and in the choice of an appropriate diet to suit individual needs, and the fact that the knowledge of the basic principles of nutrition and appropriate nutrition labelling of foodstuffs contributes significantly towards enabling consum-

---

[293] See e.g. the work of O'Rourke, *European Food Law.*

[294] See the comprehensive article concerning the economics of food labelling by Golan/Kuchler/Mitchell/Greene/Jessup, (2001) 24 *JCP* 117, who find that mandatory food-labelling requirements are best suited to alleviating information asymmetries.

[295] For an overview of Community policy relating to labelling of genetically modified food, see MacMaoláin, (2003) 28 *E.L.Rev.* 865.

[296] The framework is laid down in the frequently amended Regulation 2081/92/EC on the protection of geographical indications and designations of origin for agricultural products and foodstuffs, OJ 1992 L 208/1. See for recent case law Joined Cases C-321–324/94 *Criminal proceedings against Jacques Pistre et al.* [1997] ECR I-2343, Case C-66/00 *Dante Bigi* [2002] ECR I-5917, Case C-469/00 *Ravil SARL v Bellon import SARL and Biraghi SpA* [2003] ECR I-5053 and Case C-108/01 *Consorzio del Prosciutto di Parma et al. v Asda Stores Ltd et al.* [2003] ECR I-5121. See the case note on *Ravil* and *Prosciutto di Parma* by Enchelmaier, (2004) 41 *CML Rev.* 825.

[297] Directive 90/496/EEC on nutrition labelling for foodstuffs, OJ 1990 L 276/40, as amended.

ers to make their choice.[298] At present, nutrition labelling is merely voluntary, unless a 'nutrition claim' is being made, i.e. a representation or advertising message which states, suggests or implies that a foodstuff has particular nutrition properties due to the energy it provides or the nutrients it contains. The Directive is currently in the process of revision in order to make its provisions obligatory.[299]

Food claims

Specific legislation on food claims, namely nutrition and health claims, has been proposed.[300] The increased interest of consumers in nutrition and health has been responded by industry by providing nutrition and health labelling on foods and by highlighting the nutritional and health-related value of products through claims in their advertising (e.g. 'low fat', 'light', 'preserves youth' etc.). Using claims as a marketing tool entails risks for consumers, who might be unduly influenced in their purchase decision. The purpose of the proposed regulation is therefore to prohibit false or misleading claims and to provide for requirements for a fair use of claims.[301]

Genetically modified organisms and food

The Community distinguishes between genetically modified food ingredients and different types of unnaturally modified food (so-called 'novel food'). A genetically modified organism – GMO – is defined in Article 2 of Directive 2001/18[302] as 'an organism, with the exception of human beings, in which the genetic material has been altered in a way that does not occur naturally by mating and/or natural recombination'. Genetically modified food means food containing, consisting of or produced from GMOs (Article 2(6) of Regulation 1829/2003).[303] Finally, other types of novel food, not containing, consisting of or produced from GMOs are covered by Regulation 258/97.[304]

---

[298] Cf. the second and the fourth recital of the Directive and Case C-40/02 *Margareta Scherndl v Bezirkshauptmannschaft Korneuburg* [2003] ECR I-nyr at 26.

[299] A consultation was started in January 2003.

[300] Proposal for a Regulation on nutrition and health claims made on foods, COM (2003) 424 final.

[301] See Gorny, (2003) 30 ZLR 253 for a fierce criticism of the proposed regulation and concerns about its legality.

[302] Directive 2001/18/EC on the deliberate release into the environment of genetically modified organisms and repealing Council Directive 90/220/EEC, OJ 2001 L 106/1.

[303] Regulation 1829/2003/EC on genetically modified food and feed, OJ 2003 L 268/1. See also Regulation 641/2004/EC on detailed rules for the implementation of Regulation 1829/2003/EC, OJ 2004 L 102/14.

[304] Regulation 258/97/EC concerning novel foods and novel food ingredients, OJ 1997 L 43/1. Regulation 1829/2003 has amended Regulation 258/97, reducing its applicability to non-GMO novel food, e.g. foods and food ingredients with a new or intentionally modified primary molecular structure, or foods

In principle, novel food has to be labelled according to the general food labelling rules of Directive 2000/13. Article 8 of Regulation 258/97 provides for additional specific labelling requirements in order to ensure that the final consumer is informed of:

- any characteristic which renders a novel food or food ingredient no longer equivalent to an existing food or food ingredient,
- the presence of material which is not present in an existing equivalent foodstuff and which may have implications for the health,
- the presence of material which is not present in an existing equivalent foodstuff and which gives rise to ethical concerns.[305]

Regulation 1829/2003 contains comprehensive labelling requirements in Article 13 for genetically modified foods delivered to final consumers and mass caterers, being applicable without prejudice to other requirements under Community law. The idea is that the consumer is informed as precisely as possible about the nature of the products. Furthermore, the food must not mislead the consumer (Article 4(1)(b)), and the labelling must mention further characteristics or properties where a food is different from its conventional counterpart or where it may give rise to ethical or religious concerns (Article 13(2)). The legislative framework is complemented by Regulation 1830/2003,[306] which establishes a system to trace and label GMOs through the production and distribution chains. Article 4(B) of this Regulation provides for specific labelling texts in order to inform about the genetically modified nature of the products.

General food labelling – Directive 2000/13

The general legal framework for food labelling was created by Directive 79/112,[307] which, after numerous amendments was repealed and consolidated

and food ingredients to which has been applied a production process not currently used, where that process gives rise to significant changes in the composition or structure of the foods or food ingredients which affect their nutritional value, metabolism or level of undesirable substances (cf. the various definitions in Article 1 of Regulation 258/97).

305 The provision has been criticised for not containing any guidance on how these labelling rules will apply in practice, cf. O'Rourke, *European Food Law*, p. 162 et seq. Some guidance came later by Regulation 1139/98/EC concerning the compulsory indication of the labelling of certain foodstuffs produced from genetically modified organisms of particulars other than those provided for in Directive 79/112/EEC, OJ 1998 L 159/4, which applies to food containing genetically modified soya or genetically modified maize.

306 Regulation 1830/2003 concerning the traceability and labelling of genetically modified organisms and the traceability of food and feed products produced from genetically modified organisms and amending Directive 2001/18/EC, OJ 2003 L 268/24.

307 Directive 79/112/EEC relating to the labelling, presentation and advertising of foodstuffs for sale to the ultimate consumer, OJ 1979 L 33/1.

in Directive 2000/13.[308] Due to its framework character with rules applicable to basically all foodstuffs put on the market the legislator considered the Directive to be of a horizontal nature (recitals 4 and 10). As it focuses on the marketing of one product category (foodstuffs), it remains justified, however, to classify it as sectoral harmonisation in the present context.

Directive 2000/13 concerns the labelling and certain aspects relating to the presentation and advertising of foodstuffs to be delivered as such to the ultimate consumer, and it applies in addition to foodstuffs intended for supply to restaurants, hospitals, canteens and other similar mass caterers. It affects the three major purposes of food labelling: product identification, consumer information, and product marketing.[309]

The labelling provisions of Directive 2000/13 differ in one essential way from those relating to advertising. The Directive allows the Member States to lay down rules in addition to those laid down by Directive. With regard to labelling, the limits of the power retained by the Member States are set by the Directive itself in so far as it lists exhaustively, in Article 18(2), the grounds on which the application of non-harmonised national provisions prohibiting trade in foodstuffs may be justified. Those grounds include, *inter alia*, the protection of public health, the prevention of fraud, and the prevention of unfair competition.[310] However, that provision is not applicable to advertising. The question whether in this field Community law precludes the application of national rules in addition to those laid down by the Directive must be considered in the light, in particular, of the provisions of the Treaty's free movement provisions.[311]

The information rules of Directive 2000/13 operate in different directions. Next to a general clause prohibiting misleading advertising, it provides for compulsory labelling particulars, and finally takes care of the presentation of the labelling.

---

308 Directive 2000/13/EC relating to the labelling, presentation and advertising of foodstuffs, OJ 2000 L 109/29. Again, the Directive has been subject to frequent amendment, last by Directive 2003/89/EC amending Directive 2000/13/EC as regards indication of the ingredients present in foodstuffs, OJ 2000 L 308/15.

309 O'Rourke, *European Food Law*, p. 30.

310 It is not always obvious whether or not national provisions are harmonised under the Directive, i.e. whether national restrictions may be justified under Article 18(2). In Case C-229/01 *Susanne Müller* [2003] ECR I-2587 the Court has accepted the national rule providing that, where the period of minimum durability of a foodstuff expired, that fact must be indicated separately, clearly and in a generally intelligible manner. The rule was a non-harmonised national provision justified on the ground of prevention of fraud.

311 See to that effect Case C-241/89 *SARPP v Chambre syndicale des raffineurs et conditionneurs de sucre de France et al.* [1990] ECR I-4695 at 15, Case C-221/00 *Commission v Austria* [2003] ECR I-1007 at 38, and Case C-239/02 *Douwe Egberts* [2004] ECR I-nyr at 34.

Assuming the function of a general clause, Article 2 requires the labelling, presentation and advertising of foodstuffs not to be misleading to a material degree as to the characteristics and effects of the foodstuff. This does not justify the total prohibition of a statement, which alludes to properties of which only some are misleading.[312] The Court has made clear that also in the context of the Foodstuffs Labelling Directive the presumed expectations of an average consumer who is reasonably well informed and reasonably observant and circumspect are to be taken into account when assessing whether an advertising statement may be misleading. Therefore, notwithstanding the presence of traces or residues of lead, cadmium and pesticides in jam, the term 'naturally pure' used on the label of the packaging of that foodstuff was not liable to mislead consumers as to its characteristics, because in view of land and air pollution consumers expected there to be remnants of toxic substances in food.[313]

Moreover, Article 2(1)(b) provides that the labelling, presentation and advertising must not attribute to foodstuff properties for the prevention, treatment or cure of a human disease, or refer to such properties.[314] Consequently, whereas foodstuffs whose labelling contains non-misleading health-related information must be regarded as complying with the Directive, all statements relating to human diseases are prohibited, regardless of whether or not they are liable to mislead consumers. This does also mean that a general national prohibition of health-related information on the labelling of foodstuffs for general consumption and by subjecting the display of such information to a prior authorisation procedure restricts the importation of goods lawfully manufactured and marketed in another Member State. It is not proportionate to that purpose and therefore incompatible with the Directive.[315]

As far as active disclosure of information is concerned, detailed labelling is required in order to enable consumers to make their choice in full knowledge of the facts. Therefore the labelling of foodstuffs must indicate the following particulars (Article 3):

---

312 Case C-241/89 *SARPP v Chambre syndicale des raffineurs et conditionneurs de sucre de France et al.* [1990] ECR I-4695 at 18, where the Court considered the prohibition of any statement alluding to the word 'sugar' or to the physical, chemical or nutritional properties of sugar in the labelling of artificial sweeteners to exceed the requirements laid down in the Directive. It held that in order to prevent the consumer from being misled it was sufficient to prohibit any particulars which indicate, suggest or lead one to believe that artificial sweeteners possess properties similar to those of sugar when in fact they do not. It had to be considered, however, that also artificial sweeteners had a sweetening effect.

313 Case C-465/98 *Verein gegen Unwesen in Handel und Gewerbe Köln e.V. v Adolf Darbo AG* [2000] ECR I-2297 at 20 et seq.

314 Except for natural mineral waters and foodstuffs intended for special diets, which are covered by specific Community provisions.

315 Case C-221/00 *Commission v Austria* [2003] ECR I-1007 at 35–37, 48–55 and Joined Cases C-421/00, C-426/00 and C-16/01 *Renate Sterbenz and Paul Dieter Haug* [2003] ECR I-1065 at 27–30, 37–42.

- the name under which the product is sold,
- the list of ingredients,
- the quantity of certain ingredients or categories of ingredients,
- in the case of prepackaged foodstuffs, the net quantity,
- the date of minimum durability or, in the case of highly perishable foodstuffs the 'use by' date,
- any special storage conditions or conditions of use,
- the name or business name and address of the manufacturer or packager, or of a seller established within the Community,[316]
- place of origin or provenance where failure to give such particulars might mislead the consumer,
- instructions for use where appropriate,
- with respect to beverages containing more than 1,2 % by volume of alcohol, the actual alcoholic strength by volume.

The exact form of indication of those particulars is further specified in detail in the Directive, and the Court has accepted some information to be conveyed by the use of pictograms or signs other than words, if this happens effectively and can be understood by the persons for whom it is intended.[317] Community legislation applicable to specified foodstuffs may provide for derogations in exceptional cases. The Court has emphasised that the information required on the labelling under the Directive is intended to inform consumers as to the characteristics of the product concerned, the need to inform and to protect consumers thus being the prime consideration for any rules on the labelling of foodstuffs.[318] Information imposed by national public authorities which made it possible to verify that the product was produced in accordance with the relevant rules, however, did not have that aim.[319] The objective of providing consumers with effective information which they can understand does not mean that the label has to contain an exhaustive list of the ingredients used in the manufacturing process, but not being present in the finished product. This would be more likely to mislead consumers than to help them.[320]

---

[316] Doubts arose as to whether in the absence of a seller established in the Community, the manufacturer and/or the packager must be established in the Community. The Court of Justice rejected this. As regards manufacturers and packagers, the label on the packaging may indicate details of either one or the other, whether established within the Community or outside; as regards sellers, the label may only indicate details of a trader established within the Community, Case C-83/96 *Provincia autonoma di Trento and Ufficio del medico provinciale di Trento v Dega di Depretto Gino SNC* [1997] ECR I-5001 at 19.

[317] Cf. Case C-33/97 *Colim NV v Bigg's Continent Noord NV* [1999] ECR I-3175 at 29. See also *infra* concerning the *Piageme* case law.

[318] Case C-17/93 *Van der Veldt* [1994] ECR I-3537 at 28.

[319] Case C-285/92 *Coöperatieve Zuivelindustrie 'Twee Provinciën' WA* [1993] ECR I-6045 at 16–17.

[320] Case C-144/93 *Pfanni Werke Otto Eckart KG v Landeshauptstadt München* [1994] ECR I-4605 at 16–18.

Finally, the content of the labelling has to be presented in a certain way. With regard to the presentation of the particulars Article 13(2) provides that they shall be easy to understand and marked in a conspicuous place in such a way as to be easily visible, clearly legible and indelible. They shall also not in any way be hidden, obscured or interrupted by other written or pictorial matter. According to Article 16(1), the Member States have to ensure that the sale of foodstuffs is prohibited where the particulars do not appear in a language easily understood by the consumer, unless the consumer is in fact informed by means of other measures as regards one or more labelling particulars.[321] Article 16(2) provides that within its own territory, a Member State may require that those labelling particulars must be given in one or more official Community languages. However, the labelling may be in several languages in any case.

The Court gave guidelines on the use of language in its *Piageme* case law, which is underpinned by a strong free movement reasoning and therefore quite restrictive regarding a right of consumers to their own language.[322] According to *Piageme I*, the Directive precludes a national rule requiring the exclusive use of a specific language for the labelling of foodstuffs, even if it seems to be the most easily understood in a particular region, without allowing for the possibility of using another language easily understood by purchasers or of ensuring that the purchaser is informed by other measures. This is to follow not only from the wording of the provision in question but also from the objective of the Directive, namely to eliminate the differences which exist between national provisions and which hinder the free movement of goods.[323] In *Piageme II* the Court confirmed that the conveying of the compulsory particulars of the Directive must not actually be in a traditional language easily understood by purchasers, but that possible other measures could be designs, symbols or pictograms. It added, however, that it was necessary that the compulsory information was accessible not only at the time of purchase, but also at that of consumption. Therefore, consumer protection was not ensured by measures other than labelling, such as information supplied at the sales point or as part of wide-ranging advertising campaigns.[324]

---

[321] The determination of other means happens according to Article 20(2) of the Directive, which provides for the application of Council Decision 1999/468/EC laying down the procedures for the exercise of implementing powers conferred on the Commission, OJ 1999 L 184/23. This procedure involves the Commission assisted by the Standing Committee on Foodstuffs (see Decision 69/414/EEC setting up a Standing Committee for Foodstuffs, OJ 1969 L 291/9; since Directive 2003/89 [see *supra* footnote 308] it is called 'Standing Committee on the Food Chain and Animal Health'). The original Directive 79/112 did not require such a procedure. There it was sufficient that 'other measures have been taken to ensure that the purchaser is informed' (Article 14(2) of Directive 79/112).

[322] See Micklitz, (2003) 11 *ZEuP* 635 at 644 et seq.

[323] Case C-369/89 *Piageme and others v BVBA Peeters* [1991] ECR I-2971 at 14–17.

[324] Case C-85/94 *Piageme and others v Peeters NV* [1995] ECR I-2955 at 24–27, confirmed in Case C-385/96 *Hermann Josef Goerres* [1998] ECR I-4431 and Case C-366/98 *Yannick Geffroy and Casino France SNC*

The *Piageme* case law supports the idea of responsible consumers, who can deal with information that is not necessarily in their native language, provided that it is conveyed in another comprehensible manner. The case law moreover compellingly demonstrates that it is the comprehensibility of information that matters, not the language. Language is just one means among many others to convey information in a comprehensible manner.

Although the *Piageme* doctrine has indeed been applied to other sectors,[325] it should be recalled that the *Piageme* cases concern specifically the Foodstuffs Labelling Directive, and that their wide concept of information transfer cannot automatically be generalised.[326] In *Meyhui*,[327] for instance, the Court confirmed the compatibility of Directive 69/493[328] with Article 28 of the Treaty. According to this Directive, for certain categories of low quality crystal glass and crystalline only the description in the language or languages of the country in which the goods are marketed may be used. The Court held that in these cases the difference in the quality of the glass used was not easily discernible to the average consumer for whom the purchase of crystal glass products was not a frequent occurrence. It was therefore necessary for consumers to be given the clearest information possible as to what they were buying. The prescription of the language to use in order to protect consumers was not considered disproportionate to the goal pursued.[329] It can thus be concluded that it depends on the particular circumstances whether comprehensibility can be achieved non-verbally, verbally, or only in the consumer's own language. The main point remains, however, that comprehensibility is to be achieved.

General principles and requirements of food law – Regulation 178/2002

Next to the patchwork of foodstuffs-related legislation, the Community legislator made an effort to create a framework for European food law by Regulation 178/2002.[330] The Regulation gives horizontally applicable definitions and, *inter alia*, lays down general principles and requirements of food law. The codification of these principles, however, is rather an attempt to structure the intricacy of the existing rules than to establish new principles.

[2000] ECR I-6579. See for the obligation not to exclude the possible use of other means of informing consumers, such as designs, symbols or pictograms in the field of technical standards and regulations Case C-33/97 *Colim NV v Bigg's Continent Noord NV* [1999] ECR I-3175 at 41.

325 For the use of language regarding cosmetic products, see *infra* at 2.5.3.2.

326 Cf. also Micklitz, (2003) 11 *ZEuP* 635 at 648 et seq.

327 Case C-51/93 *Meyhui NV v Schott Zwiesel Glaswerke AG* [1994] ECR I-3879.

328 Council Directive 69/493/EEC relating to crystal glass, OJ 1969 L 326/36.

329 *Meyhui* at 18–20.

330 Regulation 178/2002 laying down the general principles and requirements of food law, establishing the European Food Safety Authority and laying down procedures in matters of food safety, OJ 2002 L 31/1.

The most interesting provision in the present context is Article 8, which virtually contains a general clause for fair trading in the foodstuffs sector. It states that food law

> 'shall aim at the protection of the interests of consumers and shall provide a basis for consumers to make informed choices in relation to the foods they consume'.

Given the existence of the various specific provisions of food law which contain positive information duties, Article 8 defines the means to realise this aim in a negative way by banning fraudulent or deceptive practices, the adulteration of food, and any other practices which may mislead the consumer.

According to Article 16 the labelling, advertising and presentation of food or feed, including their shape, appearance or packaging, the packaging materials used, the manner in which they are arranged and the setting in which they are displayed, and the information which is made available about them through whatever medium, must not mislead consumers.

The principle of transparency in Article 10 of the Regulation obliges public authorities to take appropriate steps to inform the general public of the nature of a possible risk to health, identifying to the fullest extent possible the food or feed, or type of food or feed, the risk that it may present, and the measures which are taken or about to be taken to prevent, reduce or eliminate that risk.

2.5.3.2 Cosmetic products

General remarks

The labelling of cosmetic products has attracted much attention in the Community legal order, which is reflected by the Court's case law interpreting the Cosmetic-Products Directive in the light of the Treaty provisions on the free movement of goods.[331] The extremely frequently amended Directive 76/768 concerns the composition, labelling and packaging of cosmetic products.[332] The largest part of the Directive is dedicated to the composition of cosmetics,[333] which is motivated by safeguarding public health and, at the same

---

331 Cf. in particular Case C-315/92 *Verband Sozialer Wettbewerb e.V. v Clinique Laboratoires SNC and Estée Lauder Cosmetics GmbH* [1994] ECR I-317 and Case C-220/98 *Estée Lauder Cosmetics GmbH & Co. OHG v Lancaster Group GmbH ('Lifting')* [2000] ECR I-117, see Chapter 1 at 5.3.4. See also Case C-99/01 *Criminal proceedings against Gottfried Linhart and Hans Biffl* [2002] ECR I-9375.

332 Directive 76/768/EEC of 27 July 1976 relating to cosmetic products, OJ 1976 L 262/169.

333 This is represented by the extensive Annex listing categories of cosmetic products, substances which must not form part of the composition of cosmetic products, substances which cosmetic products must not contain except subject to the restrictions and conditions laid down, and colouring agents and preservatives UV filters which cosmetic products may contain.

time, by the delimitation from pharmaceutical specialities and medicinal products, to which the Directive does not apply.[334]

Substance

The fair-trading rules contained in Directive 76/768 fit into three categories: first, a general health-protection clause, which refers, *inter alia*, to the risks of the presentation and the labelling of the cosmetic product, second, the obligation of compulsory labelling of certain particulars, and third, the prohibition of misleading advertising.

Article 2 provides as a general rule that a cosmetic product put on the Community market must not cause damage to human health when applied under normal or reasonably foreseeable conditions of use, taking into account, in particular, the product's presentation, its labelling, any instructions for its use and disposal as well as any other indication or information provided by the manufacturer or his authorised agent or by any other person responsible for placing the product on the Community market.

According to the exhaustive[335] list in Article 6(1), cosmetic products may be marketed only if the container and (in certain cases also) the packaging bear the following information in indelible, easily legible and visible lettering:[336]

- the name or style and the address or registered office of the manufacturer or the person responsible for marketing the cosmetic product who is established within the Community,
- the nominal content at the time of packaging, given by weight or by volume, except in specified cases,
- the date of minimum durability,
- particular precautions to be observed in use,
- the batch number of manufacture or the reference for identifying the goods,
- the function of the product, unless it is clear from the presentation of the product,
- a list of ingredients in descending order of weight at the time they are added (may be indicated on the packaging alone).

The Member States may require, according to Article 7(2), that specific particulars be expressed at least in their own national or official language or languages,

---

334 In doubtful cases, where the definitions of a medicinal product and a cosmetic product overlap, a product which has the characteristics of a medicinal product does still not fall within the scope of Directive 76/768, because the stricter rules for medicinal products are preferred to apply exclusively, Case C-112/89 *Upjohn Company and Upjohn NV v Farzoo Inc. and J. Kortmann* [1991] ECR I-1703 at 30.

335 See Case C-150/88 *Kommanditgesellschaft in Firma Eau de Cologne & Parfümerie-Fabrik, Glockengasse n. 4711 v Provide Srl* [1988] ECR I-3891 at 17.

336 This is a very much simplified reproduction of the enumeration in Article 6(1) of the Directive.

and that the list of ingredients be expressed in a language easily understood by the consumer. As a general rule, however, the Court held in *Schwarzkopf* in analogy to the *Piageme* doctrine that the use of pictograms or signs other than words was acceptable where the required information could be effectively conveyed this way.[337]

Article 6(3) prohibits misleading advertising by requiring that, in the labelling, putting up for sale and advertising of cosmetic products, text, names, trade marks, pictures and figurative or other signs may not be used to imply that these products have characteristics which they do not have. The Court has understood this provision to define the measures to be taken in the interests of consumer protection and fair trading in the sense of the imperative requirements which may justify restrictions on the free movement of goods.[338] As a result of the exhaustive nature of the Directive, the Member States are no longer permitted to adopt more stringent national measures intended to prevent misleading advertising relating to the characteristics of cosmetic products.[339] Therefore, Article 6(3) does not authorise Member States to require information not provided for in the Directive on the labelling or packaging of those products.[340] In *Clinique* the Court interpreted this provision in the light of Article 28 of the Treaty and came to the conclusion that the clinical or medical connotations of the word 'Clinique' were not sufficient to make that word so misleading as to justify the prohibition of its use on cosmetic products.[341] The Court held in *Unilever* that national rules which require authorisation for the advertising of cosmetic products, even though they are not likely to mislead consumers, constituted a disproportionate obstacle to the free movement. It was possible to ensure the protection of consumers, public health and fair trading by adopting less restrictive measures, like an obligation requiring the manufacturer or distributor of the product, in the event of any uncertainty, to furnish evidence of the accuracy of the advertisements concerned.[342]

Finally, the Directive provides explicitly that advertising with reference to testing on animals must not be misleading either. In view of an increased awareness for the protection of animals, consumers are to be prevented from making their choice for a particular product on the incorrect assumption that it stems from an 'animal friendly' manufacture process.

---

337 Case C-169/99 *Hans Schwarzkopf GmbH & Co. KG v Zentrale zur Bekämpfung unlauteren Wettbewerbs e.V.* [2001] ECR I-5901 at 40.

338 Case C-220/98 *Estée Lauder Cosmetics GmbH & Co. OHG v Lancaster Group GmbH ('Lifting')* [2000] ECR I-117 at 25.

339 Case C-99/01 *Criminal proceedings against Gottfried Linhart and Hans Biffl* [2002] ECR I-9375 at 24.

340 *4711* (*supra* footnote 335) at 19.

341 Case C-315/92 *Verband Sozialer Wettbewerb e.V. v Clinique Laboratoires SNC and Estée Lauder Cosmetics GmbH* [1994] ECR I-317, see Chapter 1 at 5.3.4.

342 Case C-77/97 *Österreichische Unilever GmbH v Smithkline Beecham Markenartikel GmbH* [1999] ECR I-431 at 33–37.

2.5.3.3 Medicinal products

General remarks

The market of medicinal products is undoubtedly of a particularly sensitive nature and therefore has always been highly regulated by the Member States as well as at Community level.[343] There have been lots of directives relating to the different aspects of a free and safe marketing of pharmaceuticals in the Community.[344] The most important ones in the present context were the Labelling Directive 92/27 and the Advertising Directive 92/28.[345] Meanwhile, the former legislation has been repealed and integrated into the 'Community code relating to medicinal products for human use', which is Directive 2001/83.[346] The Directive contains more than 130 partly fairly detailed Articles including three annexes, which shows that this area is given a high priority, and that speaking of a 'code' is not an exaggeration.

The essential aim of the Directive is to safeguard public health by harmonising the rules governing the production, distribution and use of medicinal products in the Internal Market. One aspect is to guarantee that the provisions governing the information supplied to users provide a high degree of consumer protection, ensuring that medicinal products may be used correctly on the basis of full and comprehensible information (recital 40). This goal is pursued by Title V ('labelling and package leaflet'), Title VIII ('advertising') and Title VIIIa ('information and advertising') of the Directive.

Substance

The Directive contains many provisions concerning the labelling of medicinal products, with differentiations made according to the outer packaging, the

---

[343] Cf. Bouckaert/Waelbroeck, (1993) 1 *JTDE* 8.

[344] The first important legal instrument was Directive 65/65/EEC relating to proprietary medicinal products, OJ 1965 L 22/369, which still today is the point of reference for the definition of medicinal products in contrast to food, see Article 2(e) of Regulation 178/2002 laying down the general principles and requirements of food law, establishing the European Food Safety Authority and laying down procedures in matters of food safety, OJ 2002 L 31/1, and see Köhler, (2002) 104 GRUR 844 for possible demarcation problems between medicinal products and foodstuffs after Regulation 178/2002. See Gormley in Smit Sibinga et al., *Good Manufacturing Practice*, p. 59 et seq. on human blood and human blood products as medicinal products and the legal Community framework relating to consumer protection and product liability.

[345] Directive 92/27/EEC on the labelling of medicinal products for human use and on package leaflets, OJ 1992 L 113/8 and Directive 92/28/EEC on the advertising of medicinal products for human use, OJ 1992 L 113/13.

[346] Directive 2001/83/EC on the Community code relating to medicinal products for human use, OJ 2001 L 311/67. The Directive has been amended by Directive 2004/24/EC, OJ 2004 L 136/85, and above all by Directive 2004/27/EC, OJ 2004 L 136/34.

immediate packaging and the package leaflet. The outer packaging is the most interesting from a fair-trading point of view, because this is the part of the product the consumer gets in touch with while making a purchase decision. On the outer packaging (where there is no outer packaging, on the immediate packaging) the following particulars shall appear (Article 54):

- the name of the medicinal product[347] followed by its strength and pharmaceutical form, and, if appropriate, whether it is intended for babies, children or adults,
- a statement of the active substances expressed qualitatively and quantitatively per dosage unit,
- the pharmaceutical form and the contents by weight, by volume or by number of doses,
- a list of those excipients known to have a recognised action or effect,
- the method and, if necessary, the route of administration (space must be provided for the prescribed dose to be indicated),
- a special warning that the medicinal product must be stored out of reach of children,
- a special warning, if necessary,
- the expiry date in clear terms (month/year),
- special storage precautions, if any,
- specific precautions relating to the disposal of unused medicinal products or waste, where appropriate, as well as reference to any appropriate collection system in place,
- the name and address of the marketing authorisation holder and, where applicable, the name of the representative appointed by the holder to represent him,
- the number of the authorisation for placing the medicinal product on the market,
- the manufacturer's batch number,
- in the case of non-prescription medicinal products, instructions for use.

By way of derogation, Member States may also require the labelling to indicate the price, the reimbursement conditions, the legal status for supply to the patient and other details for identification and authentication (Article 57).

All the labelling particulars have to be easily legible, clearly comprehensible and indelible (Article 56). Unlike other directives, special emphasis is put on language (Articles 62 and 63). The particulars for labelling must namely appear in the official language or languages of the Member State where the product is placed on the market, without precluding the indication in several languages, provided that the same particulars appear in all the languages used. When the product is not intended to be delivered to the patient for self-administration

[347] The name must also appear in Braille format, according to Article 56a of the Directive.

exemptions can be granted. Symbols or pictograms designed to clarify certain information and other information compatible with the summary of the product characteristics which is useful for health education may be included as far as there is no element of a promotional nature. Whereas in the foodstuffs sector symbols or pictograms can in certain cases absolutely replace language information, in the case of medicinal products they may only assume a supplementary function.

The advertising rules are particularly detailed, so that only an outline can be given here. Different rules apply to advertising, depending on whether it is directed at consumers or at professionals. It is the first group that matters here. Advertising within the meaning of the Directive comprises, any form of door-to-door information, canvassing activity or inducement designed to promote the prescription, supply, sale or consumption of medicinal products (Article 86). According to the general principle underlying all the further provisions, advertising has to meet a positive and a negative requirement (Article 87). Firstly, it shall encourage the rational use of the medicinal product, by presenting it objectively and without exaggerating its properties. Secondly, it shall not be misleading.

The Directive prohibits advertising to the general public, *inter alia*, of medicinal products which are available on prescription only (Article 88).[348] It thus turns the rule of the Television Directive into a general advertising principle by applying it to other media.[349] Where advertising to the general public is allowed it must be set out in such a way that it is clear that the message is an advertisement and that the product is clearly identified as a medicinal product (Article 89). Moreover, it has to include the following minimum information:

- the name of the medicinal product, as well as the common name, if it contains only one active substance,
- the information necessary for correct use,
- an express, legible invitation to read carefully the instructions on the package leaflet or on the outer packaging.

Article 90 lists a number of situations of unlawful advertising. They concern mainly misleading statements as to various characteristics and effects of the medicinal product, which imply health risks. The prohibition of advertising directed exclusively or principally at children constitutes an exception in the list, as it expressly protects a particularly vulnerable target group.

---

[348] This provision cannot be interpreted as precluding advertising for the sale by mail order of medicines on the basis of the alleged need for a pharmacist to be physically present, Case C-322/01 *Deutscher Apothekerverband e.V. v 0800 DocMorris NV and Jacques Waterval* [2003] ECR I-nyr at 144.

[349] Article 88(1). See Article 14(1) of the Television Directive and *supra* at 2.5.2.1.

2.5.3.4 Tobacco

General remarks

The Community's anti-tobacco policy is expressed in various legislative measures and especially in many political texts which accompany smoking prevention campaigns.[350] Due to the Community's very restricted legislative competence in human health matters, the idea of regulating health protection is mainly approached from an Internal Market perspective, amongst others by way of labelling and advertising rules. The legal difficulties resulting from this approach – which have been exposed exactly in the field of tobacco advertising – have been discussed earlier.[351]

Fair trading is tackled from two sides, which both are represented by one key Directive respectively. Directive 2001/37[352] – which recasts earlier and frequently amended Directives in the interest of clarity[353] – concerns the labelling and presentation aspect of tobacco products, whereas Directive 2003/33[354] relates to the advertising and sponsorship of tobacco products.

Directive 2001/37, the legality of which has been confirmed by the Court in *British American Tobacco*,[355] aims at, *inter alia*, protecting human health by harmonising the warnings regarding health and other information to appear on unit packets of tobacco products. Directive 2003/33 has replaced the annulled Directive 98/43.[356] The Court recognised in an *obiter dictum* in *Tobacco Advertising* that a directive prohibiting the advertising of tobacco products in printing media as well as prohibiting certain forms of sponsorship could, in principle, be adopted on the basis of Article 95.[357] Given the general nature of the prohibition of advertising and sponsorship of tobacco products laid down by Directive 98/43,[358] however, the Court annulled it in its entirety. Directive 2003/33 now

---

350 See in general Hervey, (2001) 26 *E.L.Rev.* 101.

351 See *supra* at 1.1.

352 Directive 2001/37/EC concerning the manufacture, presentation and sale of tobacco products, OJ 2001 L 194/26.

353 Directive 89/622/EEC concerning the labelling of tobacco products and the prohibition of the marketing of certain types of tobacco for oral use, OJ 1989 L 359/1 (as substantially amended by Directive 92/41/EEC, OJ 1992 L 158/30) and Directive 90/239/EEC concerning the maximum tar yield of cigarettes, OJ 1990 L 137/36.

354 Directive 2003/33/EC relating to the advertising and sponsorship of tobacco products, OJ 2003 L 152/16.

355 Case C-491/01 *R. v Secretary of State for Health, ex parte British American Tobacco (Investments) Ltd and Imperial Tobacco Ltd.* [2002] ECR I-11453, see *supra* at 1.1.

356 Directive 98/43/EC relating to the advertising and sponsorship of tobacco products, OJ 1998 L 213/9, see *supra* at 1.1.

357 Case C-376/98 *Germany v Parliament and Council ('Tobacco Advertising')* [2000] ECR I-8419 at 98 and 111.

358 Cf. Article 3(1) of Directive 98/43.

fills this gap and is aimed at harmonising national rules on tobacco advertising in printed media, radio broadcasting and information society services, as well as those on sponsorship of events with cross-border effects with the aim of promoting tobacco products. The validity of Directive has been challenged anew by Germany.[359]

In the field of television broadcasts the Television Directive prohibits all forms of television advertising and teleshopping for cigarettes and other tobacco products.[360]

Directive 2001/37

Directive 2001/37 distinguishes between labelling, which the consumer is directly confronted with, and further product information, which is supposed to reach the consumer via dissemination by the Member States.

According to Article 5, the tar, nicotine and carbon monoxide yields of cigarettes have to be printed in a precisely determined size on one side of the cigarette packet in the official language or languages of the Member State where the product is placed on the market. Moreover, each unit packet of tobacco products, except for tobacco for oral use and other smokeless tobacco products, must carry two types of warning: the general warning 'Smoking kills/Smoking can kill' or 'Smoking seriously harms you and others around you' and an additional (similarly drastic) warning taken from the list in the annex of the Directive. It must be guaranteed that the warnings are most visible. The Member States can require additional warnings in the form of colour photographs.[361] The Directive provides for further detailed rules as regards the size, appearance, and durability of the labelling.

According to Article 6, manufacturers and importers of tobacco products have to submit to the Member States a list of all ingredients, and quantities thereof, used in the manufacture of those tobacco products by brand name and type. The Member States then have to ensure the dissemination of the provided information by any appropriate means, with a view to informing consumers.

Directive 2003/33

Directive 2003/33 generally prohibits tobacco advertising within in its scope of application.[362] Advertising is widely defined as 'any form of commercial

---

[359] Case C-380/03 *Germany v Parliament and Council*, Action brought on 10 September 2003, OJ 2003 C 275/31. For considerations on the validity of Directive 2003/33, see Görlitz, (2003) 14 *EuZW* 485.

[360] See *supra* at 2.5.2.1.

[361] This is further regulated in Commission Decision 2003/641/EC on the use of colour photographs or other illustrations as health warnings on tobacco packages, OJ 2003 L 226/24.

[362] That is to say with regard to printed media, radio broadcasting and information society services, as well as sponsorship of events with cross-border effects with the aim of promoting tobacco products. The prohibition is thus much more restricted than the universal prohibition in the annulled Directive 98/43.

communications with the aim or direct or indirect effect of promoting a tobacco product' (Article 2). Advertising in the press and other printed publications is prohibited, except for publications intended exclusively for professionals in the tobacco trade and publications which are printed and published in third countries, where those publications are not principally intended for the Community market. Advertising which is not permitted in the press and other printed publications is neither permitted in information society services (Article 3). Parallel to the Television Directive, which bans television advertising for tobacco products, Directive 2003/33 bans all forms of radio advertising for tobacco products (Article 4).[363] Not only is the sponsorship of events or activities involving or taking place in several Member States or otherwise having cross-border effects prohibited, but also any free distribution of tobacco products in the context of the sponsorship of those events (Article 5).

2.5.3.5 Consumer Credit

Directive 87/102

Directive 87/102 deals with credit agreements, which can be considered to be a type of financial service of chief importance to consumers.[364] According to its recitals, the Directive aims at establishing a Common Market in consumer credit and at reducing the differences of law and practice which result in unequal consumer protection in the field of consumer credit from one Member State to another.

Article 3 of Directive 87/102 is the only advertising provision. It requires a statement of the annual percentage rate of charge (by means of a representative example) to be included in any advertisement, or any offer which is displayed at business premises, in which a person offers credit or offers to arrange a credit agreement and in which a rate of interest or any figures relating to the cost of the credit are indicated. The obvious goal is to provide a transparent means to consumers enabling them to compare the costs of offered credits as accurately and easily as possible. Consequently, the calculation method of the annual percentage rate of charge and the determination of the total cost of the credit to the consumer are further aspects of main emphasis of the Directive.

---

363 In Case C-380/03 (see footnote 359) Germany claims that the Court should annul Articles 3 and 4 of the Directive. The main argument is that the contested provisions almost exclusively govern factual situations with no cross-border effect so that there are neither actual impediments to trade nor discernible distortions of competition as required by the Court in *Tobacco Advertising* for harmonisation based on Article 95. It is claimed moreover that the total ban expressed in Articles 3 and 4 of the Directive are disproportionate to the aim pursued.

364 Directive 87/102/EEC concerning consumer credit, OJ 1987 L 42/48, amended by Directive 90/88/EEC, OJ 1990 L 61/14, and Directive 98/7/EC, OJ 1998 L 101/17.

Article 3 is to prevent misleading and unfair advertising. It is a unique provision in that it states that it applies without prejudice to Directive 84/450 'and to the rules and principles applicable to unfair advertising'. It does not give further explanation on what these rules and principles of unfair advertising should be, but given that they are cited along with Directive 84/450 it can legitimately be assumed that they are supposed to be Community rules and principles and not national ones. Although this is not a direct reference to one general principle, one gets the impression that the Community legislator seemed to be quite aware of the fact that all the single rules in secondary law relating to unfair advertising establish or are guided by some kind of underlying principle of fair advertising, although it has never been written down as such.

Credit agreements are to be made in writing, and the consumers must receive a copy of it. With a view to protecting consumers against unfair credit terms and to enabling them to have full knowledge of the terms of the future performance,[365] Article 4 provides that, besides the essential terms of the contract, an agreement must state the annual percentage rate of charge and the conditions under which it may be amended as well as further information which could have a bearing on the implications of the borrower's undertaking. However, these information duties are of a contractual or even post-contractual nature. Where credit is granted in the form of an advance on a current account, the consumer is to be informed in writing, at or before the time the agreement is concluded of the credit limit, of the annual rate of interest and the charges applicable, and of the procedure for terminating the agreement. Any change in the annual rate of interest or in the relevant charges, during the period of the agreement, must be notified to the consumer at the time it occurs.

Proposal for a new Directive on consumer credit

The financial services sector faces rapid and drastic changes, and new types of services emerge continuously. The Community may not have been able to follow this pace, but with the adoption of the Directive on distance marketing of consumer financial services, which approaches the issue from the means-of-communication point of view, one gap has been filled. Due to the Consumer Credit Directive's minimum harmonisation approach and the far-reaching developments in the consumer credit sector, however, there still are enormous differences between the laws of the various Member States.[366] Therefore, the Commission has recognised that the Directive does no longer reflect the current situation on the consumer credit market and, after a long consultation process,[367] proposed its revision in 2002,[368] and later presented an amended

---

365 Case C-208/98 *Berliner Kindl Brauerei AG v Andreas Siepert* [2000] ECR I-1741 at 21.

366 Blaurock, (1999) 54 *JZ* 801 at 808.

367 See for the background of the Proposal Kaiser, (2002) 17 *VuR* 385.

368 COM (2002) 443 final, OJ 2002 C 331 E/200.

proposal in 2004.[369] The proposed Directive is to regulate consumer credit agreements much more comprehensively and pursues maximum harmonisation.

Article 4 of the proposed Directive concerns 'standard information' on the cost of credit, which any advertising concerning credit agreements must include in a given order and in a clear, concise and prominent way through a representative example. This information concerns basically:[370]

- the total amount of credit,
- the annual percentage rate of charge,
- the duration of the credit agreement,
- the number and amount of monthly payments and any kind of fees in connection with the credit agreement in conformity with the terms thereof and which are known to the creditor.

With its concept of 'responsible lending' in Article 9 the Proposal significantly extends the pre-contractual information duties. In good time before the consumer is bound by a credit agreement or any offer, the creditor and, where applicable, the credit intermediary must provide, on paper or on another durable medium, the necessary and essential information needed for the conclusion of the credit agreement under consideration. The information considered necessary for the consumers to make their choice in full knowledge of the facts must refer to:[371]

- the sureties and insurance required,
- the duration of the credit agreement,
- the amount, number and frequency of payments to be made,
- the costs of maintaining an account recording both payment transactions and credit transactions, the costs of using a card or another means of payment for both payment transactions and draw downs, and the costs relating to payment transactions in general,
- the total amount of credit and the conditions governing the drawdown of the credit,
- the borrowing rate, the conditions governing the application of this rate and any index, where available, or reference rate applicable to the initial borrowing rate, as well as the periods, conditions and procedures for varying the borrowing rate,
- the annual percentage rate of charge and the total cost of credit, by means of a representative example, and all the financial data and assumptions used for calculating this rate,
- costs payable by the consumer on conclusion of the credit agreement to

[369] COM (2004) 747 final.

[370] This is a simplified overview.

[371] Certain types of agreements are submitted to 'light regimes' with less strict information requirements.

persons other than the creditor or the credit intermediary,
- the existence or absence of the right of withdrawal, the period during which that right of withdrawal may be exercised, and the procedure for the exercise of that right,
- the right to be informed of the result of a database consultation for the assessment of the creditworthiness,
- the right of early repayment, and, where applicable, the costs arising there from, indicating the amount or the calculation method,
- the interests in the case of overdue payments as applicable at the time when the information according to this provision is given and the arrangements for their adjustment, and the charges for defaulting.

The concept of 'responsible lending' implies furthermore that the creditor shall seek to establish, among the credit agreements they usually offer or arrange, the most appropriate type and total amount of credit taking into account the financial situation of the consumer, the advantages and disadvantages associated with the product proposed, and the purpose of the credit. This means that next to the information particulars required in general it is considered necessary that consumers be provided with information according to their personal needs, i.e. with subjectively necessary information.

Finally, the Proposal introduces a right of withdrawal in Article 11. Consumer shall have a period of fourteen calendar days to withdraw their acceptance of the credit agreement without giving any reason. The modalities are to be aligned with Directive 2002/65 concerning the distance marketing of consumer financial services.

2.5.3.6 Investment services

Although the legislation regarding investment services is not mainly aiming at consumer protection it also contains fair-trading rules, where those rules apply to individual users of investment services.

Directive 2004/39

The recently adopted Directive 2004/39[372] has repealed Directive 93/22,[373] because the latter had proven not to provide an effective framework for cross-border investment business anymore in the fast-changing financial market.

Directive 93/22 was adopted with the main purpose to protect investors and the stability of the financial system by setting up a system of authorisation for firms that provide the investment services covered by the Directive (i.e. providing a European 'passport')[374] and by establishing several operating conditions. It

372 Directive 2004/39/EC on markets in financial instruments, OJ 2004 L 145/1.

373 Directive 93/22/EEC on investment services in the securities field, OJ 1993 L 141/27.

374 See Moloney, *EC Securities*, p. 359 et seq.

thus sought to translate Treaty freedoms into practice by establishing the conditions in which authorised investment firms could provide specified services in other Member States on the basis of home-country authorisation and supervision (which is still central to the new Directive 2004/39). Its Article 11 obliged the Member States to draw up rules of conduct which investment firms had to observe at all times.[375] They had to implement certain minimum principles, which had to be applied in such a way as to take account of the professional nature of the person for whom the service was provided. The information to be given had to relate to the product on the one hand and its suitability for the particular client on the other.[376] The Member States had to ensure, *inter alia*, that an investment firm

- acts honestly and fairly in conducting its business activities in the best interests of its clients and the integrity of the market,
- acts with due skill, care and diligence, in the best interests of its clients and the integrity of the market,
- makes adequate disclosure of relevant material information in its dealings with its clients.

The requirements of honest and fair business activities and the disclosure of relevant material information made Directive 93/22 a model for the stipulation of general fair trading principles. However, the rules of conduct provided for in Article 11 of Directive 93/22 have been considered particularly unclear and ambiguous,[377] which can be explained by the fact that the general principles were not accompanied by more detailed interpretation guidelines.

Article 19 of the new Directive 2004/39 now provides for more detailed conduct of business obligations when providing investment services to clients.[378] According to the new general rule, when providing investment services to clients, an investment firm must act honestly, fairly and professionally in accordance with the best interests of its clients. Furthermore, it must comply with the following principles:

- Marketing communications must be clearly identifiable as such, fair, clear and not misleading.
- Appropriate information must be provided in a comprehensible form to clients or potential clients about:
  - › the investment firm and its services,

[375] See also Commission Communication on the application of conduct-of-business rules under Article 11 of Directive 93/22/EEC, COM (2000) 772 final.

[376] Grundmann, (2002) 39 *CML Rev.* 269 at 274.

[377] The provision on the conduct-of-business rules has especially caused difficulties with regard to the Directive's structure of home-/host-State control, see Moloney, *EC Securities*, p. 398 et seq.

[378] The reformulated principles are to take full account of the standards for investor protection as adopted by the Committee of European Securities Regulators (CESR).

› financial instruments and proposed investment strategies,
› execution venues, and
› costs and associated charges,

so that they are reasonably able to understand the nature and risks of the investment service and of the specific type of financial instrument that is being offered and, consequently, to take investment decisions on an informed basis.

- When providing investment advice or portfolio management the investment firm must obtain the necessary information regarding the client's or potential client's knowledge and experience in the investment field relevant to the specific type of product or service, his financial situation and his investment objectives so as to enable the firm to recommend to the client or potential client the investment services and financial instruments that are suitable for him.
- In case the investment firm considers, on the basis of the information received, that the product or service is not appropriate to the client or potential client, the investment firm shall warn the client or potential client. It shall also warn the client if the client or potential client elects not to provide the information needed to determine whether the service or product envisaged is appropriate for him.

Directive 2004/39 has thus considerably expanded the information duties of the old Directive 93/22. Not only does it provide more precisely which information particulars have to be disclosed, but it has further developed the subjective aspect of the necessary information. It recognises that not every client needs the same information in order to make a transactional decision. Rather, in order to be able to make a choice in full knowledge of the facts, clients have to be advised and informed according to their knowledge and experience in the field.

Directive 85/611

Directive 85/611[379] applies to undertakings for collective investment in transferable securities (UCITS), i.e. undertakings whose sole object is the collective investment in transferable securities of capital raised from the public and the units of which are, at the request of the holders, repurchased or redeemed out of the undertakings' assets. The Directive mainly concerns the authorisation and structure of UCITS as well as obligations concerning the investment policies of UCITS. The section on obligations concerning information to be supplied to unit-holders (Articles 27 et seq.)[380] requires UCITS to publish, *inter alia*, a

379 Directive 85/611/EEC relating to undertakings for collective investment in transferable securities (UCITS), OJ 1985 L 375/3.

380 As amended by Directive 2001/107/EC amending Directive 85/611/EEC relating to undertakings for collective investment in transferable securities (UCITS) with a view to regulating management companies and simplified prospectuses, OJ 2002 L 41/20.

simplified and a full prospectus. As a general principle under Article 28(1) both the simplified and the full prospectuses

> 'must include the information necessary for investors to be able to make an informed judgement of the investment proposed to them, and, in particular, of the risks attached thereto'.

The simplified prospectus must furthermore be 'structured and written in such a way that it can be easily understood by the average investor' (Article 28(3)). The simplified prospectus is not only considered the principal marketing tool, but it must be offered to subscribers free of charge before the conclusion of the contract. The actual information included in the full and simplified prospectuses is defined in detail in the Directive's annex.

Directive 2003/71

The recently adopted Prospectus Directive[381] has coordinated and updated the Community requirements for the drawing up, approval and distribution of the prospectus to be published when securities are offered to the public or admitted to trading on a regulated market situated or operating within a Member State. It is based on the view that information is a key factor in investor protection (recital 21).

As a general rule, Article 5(1) of the Directive requires the prospectus (where there is an obligation to draw one up) to

> 'contain all information which, according to the particular nature of the issuer and of the securities offered to the public or admitted to trading on a regulated market, is necessary to enable investors to make an informed assessment of the assets and liabilities, financial position, profit and losses, and prospects of the issuer and of any guarantor, and of the rights attaching to such securities. This information shall be presented in an easily analysable and comprehensible form'.

Apart from information concerning the issuer and the securities to be offered to the public or to be admitted to trading, it must include a summary, which, in a brief manner and in non-technical language, conveys the essential characteristics and risks associated with the issuer, any guarantor and the securities, in the language in which the prospectus was originally drawn up (Article 5(2)). For particular types of securities specific rules may apply.

[381] Directive 2003/71/EC on the prospectus to be published when securities are offered to the public or admitted to trading and amending Directive 2001/34/EC, OJ 2003 L 345/64. See also Commission Regulation 809/2004/EC implementing Directive 2003/71/EC as regards information contained in prospectuses as well as the format, incorporation by reference and publication of such prospectuses and dissemination of advertisements, OJ 2004 L 149/1.

Detailed rules for minimum information requirements are to be adopted by the Commission according to a specified second-level procedure (Article 7(1), the Directive's detailed indicative annexes set standards for this information). Information which cannot be included in the prospectus, because it is not available at the time when the prospectus is drafted (i.e. the final offering price and the number of shares that will be allotted to the public), must be substituted by the objective criteria according to which the final decision will be taken (Article 8). When the information has become available it must be published in a supplement to the original prospectus.

Advertising rules are provided for in Article 15. Where the issuer, the offeror or the person applying for admission to trading is required to draw up a prospectus, any type of advertisements relating either to an offer to the public of securities or to an admission to trading must observe the following principles:

- indication of publication of a prospectus and where investors are able to obtain it,
- clear recognisability as such,
- no inaccurate or misleading information,
- all information concerning the offer to the public or the admission to trading disclosed in an oral or written form, even if not for advertising purposes, must be consistent with that contained in the prospectus.

The compliance with these principles is to be controlled by the competent authority of the home Member State.

Article 19 deals with the language in which the prospectus must be drawn up and tries to strike a balance between facilitating cross-border offers or multiple trading and the protection of the investor. Therefore, the host or home Member State is only entitled to require a summary in its official language(s). For the prospectus itself Article 19 distinguishes between three situations in which an offer to the public is made or admission to trading is sought:

1) only in the home Member State,
2) in one or more Member States excluding the home Member State,
3) in more than one Member State including the home Member State.

In the first situation, the prospectus must be drawn up in a language accepted by the competent authority of the home Member State. In the second situation, the prospectus must be drawn up either in a language accepted by the competent authorities of the host Member States or in a language customary in the sphere of international finance. In the third situation the prospectus must be drawn up in a language accepted by the competent authority of the home Member State and must also be made available either in a language accepted by the competent authorities of each host Member State or in a language customary in the sphere of international finance. Given that investors often are internationally acting companies the requirement of a language customary in the sphere of international finance seems sufficient. Since the summary must comprise the most vital information, consumers will obtain this information in their own language (if their Member State's competent authority requires it to be drawn up in its official language(s)).

2.5.3.7 Insurance mediation

General remarks

The insurance sector has seen much legislative activity in the past, the core of which are three generations of life- and non-life insurance directives. As insurance services are usually accompanied by complicated contract terms and involve a long-term relationship, which is to provide consumers with security, disclosure of information plays an important part in the directives in order to allow consumers to make autonomous choices.[382] However, given the current complexity of the legislative framework concerning insurances, which cannot possibly be fully considered in the present context, this sector shall rather be represented by the legislation relating to insurance intermediaries. Insurance intermediaries constitute an essential link in the process of selling insurance products, and in practice, these are the institutions consumers get directly in touch with when they are interested in an insurance contract. As they can also assume a crucial role in protecting the interests of insurance customers by offering them advice and assistance and by analysing their specific needs, legislation relating to insurance intermediaries has to stress particularly the fair-trading aspect.

Directive 2002/92

Article 12 of Directive 2002/92 on insurance mediation provides for minimum information requirements prior to the conclusion of any initial insurance contract, or on amendment or renewal thereof.[383] The insurance intermediary has to provide the customer with information concerning his identity (including address and registration details), his relation to insurance undertakings (e.g. whether there is a contractual obligation to conduct insurance mediation business exclusively with one or more insurance undertakings) and the basis of the advice to be given (based on a 'fair analysis' or on the exclusive analysis of one or more particular insurance undertakings).

For 'advice given on the basis of a fair analysis' the insurance intermediary is obliged to give advice on the basis of an analysis of a sufficiently large number of insurance contracts available on the market, to enable him to make a recommendation, in accordance with professional criteria, regarding which insurance contract would be adequate to meet the customer's needs. The insurance inter-

---

382 Vriesendorp-van Seumeren, (2002) 8 *NTER* 183 at 183.

383 Directive 2002/92/EC on insurance mediation, OJ 2003 L 9/3.

mediary must specify the demands and the needs of that customer as well as the underlying reasons for any advice given to the customer on a given insurance product, prior to the conclusion of any specific contract.

According to Article 13, all information to be provided to customers in accordance with Article 12 must, as a matter of principle, be communicated on paper or on any other durable medium available and accessible to the customer. The information must furthermore be in a clear and accurate manner, comprehensible to the customer and in an official language of the Member State of the commitment or in any other language agreed by the parties.

2.5.3.8 Package travel

General remarks

The free movement of persons has made tourism much easier within the Community. The attraction of travelling and the growing importance of travelling-related services have demonstrated the need for consumer protection in this sector. Package tours are popular as they allow convenient all-inclusive arrangements for a usually low price. On the other hand, these arrangements often lack transparency, and due to the enormous competition in the tourism sector the consumer faces an increased risk of misleading advertising. Recurring insolvencies of travel organisers entailing the risk of unsure repatriation of the tourist have left no doubt regarding the need of protection in the package travel sector.

Although its name does not reveal it straight away, Directive 90/314[384] on package travel is specific (minimum) consumer protection legislation.[385] Its main goal is therefore to provide, in the context of Internal-Market harmonisation, a high level of consumer protection in the field of 'package' travel. The term has been interpreted broadly by the Court so that the Directive has a wide scope of application.[386] Although it does contain pre-contractual information requirements, most parts of the Directive are in fact of a contractual nature, which makes the Directive a landmark measure in an emerging European contract law.[387] The rules concern, *inter alia*, liability issues in case of non-performance or bad performance of the contract, which are of particular importance in this field.[388]

---

[384] Directive 90/314/EEC on package travel, package holidays and package tours, OJ 1990 L 158/59.

[385] Joined Cases C-178/94, C-179/94, C-188/94, C-189/94 and C-190/94 *Erich Dillenkofer et al. v Germany* [1996] ECR I-4845 at 39.

[386] Arrangements *à la carte* do not *per se* fall out of the scope of the Directive, Case C-400/00 *Club-Tour et al. v Alberto Carlos Lobo Gonçalves Garrido et al.* [2002] ECR I-4051.

[387] Cf. Howells/Wilhelmsson, *EC Consumer Law*, p. 231.

[388] This is also the field where most of the case law is to be found. See for the protection against the risk of the organiser's insolvency Case C-364/96 *Verein für Konsumenteninformation v Österreichische Kreditver-*

Substance

As a general rule, according to Article 3(1), any descriptive matter concerning a 'package'[389] and supplied by the organiser or the retailer to the consumer, the price of the package and any other conditions applying to the contract must not contain any misleading information.

When a brochure is made available to the consumer, it shall indicate, according to Article 3(2), in a legible, comprehensible and accurate manner both the price and adequate information concerning:

- the destination and the means of transportation,
- the accommodation,
- the meals,
- the itinerary,
- the passport and visa requirements,
- the timetable for payment,
- the deadline for informing the consumer in the event of cancellation.

Before the conclusion of the contract, consumers have to be provided in writing or another appropriate form with general information on passport and visa requirements and on health formalities. Further information must be given in good time before the journey (but after the conclusion of the contract). However, this information is not meant to enable consumers to make a reasonable choice for the contract, but to make them better prepared for the journey. All the terms of the contract must be set out in writing or such other form as is comprehensible and accessible to the consumers and must be communicated to them before the conclusion of the contract.

The prices stipulated in the contract may not be changed unless the contract expressly provides for the possibility and states precisely how the revised price is to be calculated. In such a case, only variations in transportation costs, dues, taxes or fees chargeable and exchange rates may be reflected in the price. If the organiser alters the contract significantly, the consumer may either withdraw from the contract without penalty or accept a rider to the contract.

---

sicherungs AG [1998] ECR I-2949, Case C-410/96 *André Ambry* [1998] ECR I-7875, Case C-140/97 *Renate Greindl et al. v Austria* [1999] ECR I-3499. See for the right to compensation for non-material damage Case C-168/00 *Simone Leitner v TUI Deutschland GmbH & Co. KG* [2002] ECR I-2631, noted by Roth, (2003) 40 *CML Rev.* 937. For the right to damages under the Directive in case of non-performance or bad performance of the contract, see Loos, (2002) 8 *NTER* 157.

[389] This is the collective term for package travel, package holidays and package tours as defined by the Directive.

2.5.3.9 Timesharing

General remarks

Timesharing, the purchase of the right to use one or more immoveable properties on a timeshare basis, bears several risks for consumers. As the property usually is abroad, consumers have difficulties of getting a clear picture of it and are particularly dependent on the information of the vendor. Consumers have also a special interest in being provided the exact terms of their right to use the property. Directive 94/47[390] covers aspects relating to (1) information on the constituent parts of the timeshare contract and the arrangements for the communication of that information and (2) the procedures for cancelling and withdrawing from the contract (Article 1). The determination of the legal nature of the timeshare rights vary widely among the Member States, and the Directive does not aim at harmonisation in this respect.

Substance

The vendor is required to provide any person requesting information on the immovable property or properties with a document which, in addition to a general description of the property or properties, provides at least brief and accurate information on various particulars (relating to the parties, the nature of the offered right, the property, the services offered, the price and other costs, etc.) and on how further information may be obtained (Article 3(1) in connection with the annex). This information forms an integral part of the contract (Article 3(2)), which is a perfect example of how the Community makes use of pre-contractual information duties in order to govern the contract as such. Any changes to that information must be communicated to the purchaser before the contract is concluded (Article 3(2)). Although advertising referring to the immovable property must not give the information directly, it must indicate the possibility of obtaining the document with this information and where it can be obtained (Article 3(3)).

The Directive takes care of the language problems that may arise, because of the most likely cross-border-contract situation. The idea is that it is guaranteed that the consumer understands the contract and the disclosed information. Therefore, the contract and the information document have to be drawn up in the language or one of the languages of the Member State in which the purchaser is resident or in the language or one of the languages of the Member State of which he is national (Article 4).

The consumer has a right to withdraw without giving any reason within ten calendar days of signing the contract (Article 5(1)). The *ratio* is to allow consumers to reconsider their engagement, which may have been forced by aggressive

---

390 Directive 94/47/EC on the protection of purchasers in respect of certain aspects of contracts relating to the purchase of the right to use immovable properties on a timeshare basis, OJ 1994 L 280/83.

selling techniques. The period extends for an additional three months, in case certain specified information is not included in the contract. The same applies to the credit agreement, if the price was fully or partly covered by credit.

2.5.4 Public interest as the leading object

The Community is engaged in a multitude of public-interest objectives, i.e. objectives which are considered to be of a general interest for the functioning of the social order and which often represent cultural values. Consumer protection itself is such a public interest, which moreover assumes this role under the rule of reason. There is a clear tendency to relate public-interest objectives closely to the Internal Market. Article 95 of the Treaty, the general legal basis for harmonisation aiming at the creation of a functioning Internal Market, which provides to take as a base a high level of consumer protection, is the perfect example of how consumer protection has become an integral component of the Internal Market policy.[391]

Data protection and anti-discrimination, the two public-interest objectives to be discussed here, may seem to be further away from the pure Internal Market policy, but they are indeed necessary for a homogenous framework for free movement in the Community. Therefore, it is not surprising that the relevant legislation has likewise been based on Article 95. Some aspects are relevant for fair trading.[392]

2.5.4.1 Data protection

General remarks

Trading is obviously linked to the exchange of information. Especially in distance-communication media consumers have to take an active role and are forced to give away personal data, if they want to take part in the communication process, which is inevitable for the conclusion of a contract. The danger is even higher as consumers are not, or factually cannot be, aware of what kind of information they are giving away (e.g. while surfing on a trader's website). Also from the perspective of businesses, the free flow of personal information is essential for the efficient conduct of almost any economic activity on an EU-wide basis. As the Court of Justice pointed out:

> 'the economic and social integration resulting from the establishment and functioning of the Internal Market will necessarily lead to a substantial increase

---

[391] See Chapter 4 at 2.1.3.1.

[392] The protection of minors as a public-interest objective has especially been realised in the context of television advertising and has been discussed *supra* at 2.5.2.1.

> in cross-border flows of personal data between all those involved in a private or public capacity in economic and social activity in the Member States'.[393]

Therefore, several Community provisions provide for protection in this respect, based on the double objective of removing legal obstacles to the free movement of data while ensuring a strong protection of the privacy of individuals.[394] While the European Convention on Human Rights[395] generally protects the right to respect for private and family life in its Article 8, the specific protection of personal data has been given added emphasis by its incorporation into Article 8 of the Charter of Fundamental Rights of the European Union.[396]

A number of data-protection aspects are covered by some of the Directives discussed above. Directive 95/46[397] (General Data Protection Directive) and Directive 2002/58[398] (for the electronic communications sector) are specifically created directives on data protection. The Court held that the provisions of Directive 95/46, in so far as they govern the processing of personal data liable to infringe fundamental freedoms, must necessarily be interpreted in the light of fundamental rights, which, according to settled case-law, form an integral part of the general principles of Community law.[399]

Data protection legislation has already become fairly dense. On the whole it concerns the acquisition, the processing and the storage of the data. Although all elements can play a role in the context of a commercial transaction, for the present purposes just the elements very closely related to pre-contractual commercial communication are to be examined.[400]

---

393 Case C-101/01 *Bodil Lindqvist* [2003] ECR I-nyr at 80.

394 Cf. Gasparinetti in Nihoul, *Telecommunications and broadcasting networks*, p. 205 at 207.

395 Convention for the Protection of Human Rights and Fundamental Freedoms, signed in Rome on 4 November 1950.

396 Charter of Fundamental Rights of the European Union, OJ 2000 C 364/1. Although the Charter does not formally produce legal effects, it is increasingly cited by Advocates General at least as confirming particular rights, see Eeckhoudt, (2002) 39 *CML Rev.* 945 at 947. Moreover, it has been incorporated into the Treaty establishing a Constitution for Europe as Part II.

397 Directive 95/46/EC on the protection of individuals with regard to the processing of personal data and on the free movement of such data, OJ 1995 L 281/31. The Commission has regretted the late, divers and sometimes incorrect national implementation of Directive 95/46, see the first report on the implementation of the Directive (COM (2003) 265 final), p. 17 et seq.

398 Directive 2002/58/EC concerning the processing of personal data and the protection of privacy in the electronic communications sector (Directive on privacy and electronic communications), OJ 2002 L 201/37. This Directive has repealed Directive 97/66/EC concerning the processing of personal data and the protection of privacy in the telecommunications sector, OJ 1997 L 24/1.

399 Joined Cases C-465/00, C-138/01 and C-139/01 *Neukomm et al.* [2003] ECR I-4989 at 68, see also Case C-101/01 *Bodil Lindqvist* [2003] ECR I-nyr at 87. See the case notes by Classen, (2004) 41 *CML Rev.* 1377 and by Coudray, (2004) 41 *CML Rev.* 1361

400 For a more detailed analysis, see Boulanger/de Terwangne/Léonard/Louveaux/Moreau/Poullet in Nihoul, *Telecommunications and broadcasting networks*, p. 131.

Directive 95/46

On the whole, Directive 95/46 provides for maximum harmonisation, although it allows the Member States a margin for manoeuvre in certain areas and authorises them to maintain or introduce particular rules for specific situations.[401]

According to the general principle of Article 6(1)(a), personal data must be processed fairly and lawfully.[402] Moreover, it may only be collected for specified, explicit and legitimate purposes and not further processed in a way incompatible with those purposes (Article 6(1)(b)). The data must be proportionate in relation to the purposes for which they are collected and/or further processed (Article 6(1)(c)),[403] and it must be kept in a form which permits identification of data subjects for no longer than is necessary for the purposes for which the data were collected or for which they are further processed.

The data may only be processed if the data subject has unambiguously given his or her consent, or if it is necessary for the performance of a contract to which the data subject is a party (Article 7(a) and (b)). As a matter of principle, particularly private personal data (e.g. concerning religious beliefs, health, or sex life) may not be processed at all (Article 8(1)). Article 10 of the Directive provides that in cases of data collection the data subject must receive information on the identity of the processor of the data, the purposes of the processing and further information (such as the recipients of the data) in so far this is necessary to guarantee fair processing in respect of the data subject.[404]

Directive 2002/58

According to Article 11 of Directive 2002/58 any subscriber to an electronic communication service[405] must be provided, free of charge and via a simple means, with the possibility to stop automatic call-forwarding by a third party to the subscriber's terminal.

---

[401] Case C-101/01 *Bodil Lindqvist* [2003] ECR I-nyr at 96 et seq.

[402] Cf. Article 8(2) of the Charter of Fundamental Rights of the European Union (see footnote 396).

[403] A national rule which is incompatible with Article 8 of the European Convention of Human Rights cannot be proportionate in the sense of Article 6(1)(c) and Article 7(c) or (e), Joined Cases C-465/00, C-138/01 and C-139/01 *Neukomm et al.* [2003] ECR I-4989 at 91.

[404] Article 10 of the Directive leads Misita in Wilhelmsson/Tuominen/Tuomola, *Information Society*, p. 263 at p. 273 to equate 'fairness' in the sense of the Directive with 'transparency'.

[405] The definition of an 'electronic communications service' is to be found in Article 2(c) of Directive 2002/21 (framework Directive on electronic communications), see footnote 246. According to the basic definition, it is 'a service normally provided for remuneration which consists wholly or mainly in the conveyance of signals on electronic communications networks, including telecommunications services and transmission services in networks used for broadcasting, but exclude services providing, or exercising editorial control over, content transmitted using electronic communications networks and services'.

Article 13 of the Directive deals with unsolicited communications. The use of automatic calling machines, fax or electronic mail for the purposes of direct marketing directed at natural persons may only be allowed on an opt-in basis. The Directive's broad definition of 'electronic mail'[406] includes other unsolicited communications for purposes of direct marketing, such as SMS- or MMS-messages into the opt-in regime.[407] If an electronic mail address has been obtained from a customer in the context of a previous sale it may be used for direct marketing of the trader's own similar products or services, provided that the customer clearly and distinctly is given the opportunity to object, free of charge and in an easy manner, to such use when the data is collected. Other cases of unsolicited communications for purposes of direct marketing must be submitted to either an opt-in or an opt-out regime, leaving the choice between these options to national legislation. In any event, the practice of sending electronic mail for purposes of direct marketing disguising or concealing the identity of the sender on whose behalf the communication is made, or without a valid address to which the recipient may send a request that such communications cease, is prohibited.

2.5.4.2 Anti-discrimination

General remarks

Article 12 of the Television Directive sets out fundamental principles of public interest standards with regard to television advertising, including human dignity and any kind of discrimination on grounds of race, sex, nationality, religious or political beliefs. It this provision can even be considered a prototype in combining public-interest issues with fair trading.[408]

Since the Treaty of Amsterdam, Article 13 of the EC Treaty enables the Community to take action to combat discrimination based on sex, racial or ethnic origin, religion or disbelief, disability, age or sexual orientation. On that legal basis the Community adopted Directive 2000/43[409] (discrimination based on race or ethnic origin) and Directive 2000/78[410] (equal treatment in employ-

---

[406] According to Article 2(h) it is 'any text, voice, sound or image message sent over a public communications network which can be stored in the network or in the recipient's terminal equipment until it is collected by the recipient'.

[407] See also recital 40 of the Directive.

[408] See *supra* at 2.5.2.1.

[409] Directive 2000/43/EC implementing the principle of equal treatment between persons irrespective of racial or ethnic origin, OJ 2000 L 180/22.

[410] Directive 2000/78/EC establishing a general framework for equal treatment in employment and occupation, OJ 2000 L 303/16.

ment and occupation).[411] Whereas the latter Directive is specifically designed for the field of employment and occupation, Directive 2000/43 is also related to aspects of trading.

Directive 2000/43

The purpose of Directive 2000/43 is to lay down a framework for combating discrimination on the grounds of racial or ethnic origin, with a view to putting into effect in the Member States the principle of equal treatment. For the purposes of the Directive, the principle of equal treatment means that there shall be no direct or indirect discrimination based on racial or ethnic origin. This broad concept indicates that, next to its welfare objective, the Directive may easily have an impact on trade practices where those happen in a discriminatory way. This assumption is perfectly confirmed with regard to the definition of the material scope in Article 3. In the line with various social matters the Directive provides that

> 'this Directive shall apply to all persons, as regards both the public and private sectors, including public bodies, in relation to: [...]
> (h) access to and supply of goods and services which are available to the public, including housing'.

In fact, this requirement of non-discrimination regarding the access of goods and services ultimately comprises all commercial communications practices and gives the Directive a market-orientated rationale.[412] At the same time it establishes non-discrimination as a standard for fair trading. The Member States shall take care that the provisions adopted pursuant to the Directive, together with the relevant provisions already in force, are brought to the attention of the persons concerned by all appropriate means throughout their territory.

2.6 Concluding remarks

The preceding analysis of secondary law has revealed a remarkable density and variety of fair trading rules at Community level. Alongside the prohibition of misleading advertising as a general and universally applicable concept, the pre-contractual disclosure of various information particulars is undoubtedly the most striking recurring characteristic. One of the functions of the examination conducted was to draw a picture of the regulatory patchwork of fair trading in secondary legislation. In that respect the analysis stands in its own right. In addition, and more importantly in the context of this study, the

[411] See also the Council Decision establishing a Community action programme to combat discrimination (2001 to 2006), OJ 2000 L 303/23.

[412] Cf. McInerney, (2000) 25 *E.L.Rev.* 317 at 322 with regard to the proposal of the Directive.

examination was designed to constitute the groundwork for the exposure of a general concept of fair trading in the *acquis communautaire*.[413] Such a general concept is going to be revealed in the following chapter in a synthesising manner on the basis of the findings regarding both primary and secondary law. It is in that context that the information duties established in this chapter will be further systemised.

---

[413] It has been argued *supra* at 1.6. that, despite its conceptual flaws, secondary law does indeed allow conclusions concerning an underlying general concept of fair trading.

CHAPTER 3

The Existence of a Principle of Fair Trading and its Signification

1 The substance of the framework set by Community law

In the previous chapters the Community's legal framework with regard to fair trading has been analytically portrayed. It has become evident that fair-trading rules can be found at each regulatory level. Although the Treaty remains silent as far as explicit provisions on fair trading are concerned, the collision of national fair-trading rules with the Treaty's system of free movement has resulted in a remarkable number of statements by the Court of Justice on the matter. At the same time, an overwhelming quantity of secondary law pertaining to fair trading has emerged. Given the amount of existing rules in this field, there can therefore not be much doubt that fair trading is one of the essential concerns of current Community law and provides a dense regulatory system.

It is also true, however, that the manifest regulatory density does not as such inevitably imply the existence of an underlying principle of fair trading which links all the specific rules. The examination of the present piecemeal situation has indeed revealed several substantive inconsistencies, and the scope of application of the rules has proved being far from uniform. On the other hand, the much more striking outcome of the analysis is that there clearly are recurring conceptual patterns in both the case law of the Court and Community legislation. This suggests quite strongly that the rules should not to be understood as co-existing merely accidentally, but that they are linked by a common aim, which can be expressed by one underlying concept. It is thus submitted that the *acquis communautaire* does indeed comprise a principle of fair trading, which can be articulated in concrete terms and to which the myriad single rules can be traced back.

In the following, a principle of fair trading will be suggested, its existence will be demonstrated, and its meaning will be elucidated. The components of the principle will be analysed separately and their manifestation in the *acquis communautaire* will be illustrated. Obviously, not all the detailed findings of the previous chapters will be or need to be reiterated for this purpose. The primary aim of this chapter is to expose the relationship between the specific fair-trading rules and their underlying general concept of fair trading. This is done by what may be considered a combined deductive/inductive approach: on the one hand, the previous findings are generalised for the development of the principle of fair trading; on the other hand, the meaning of this principle is explained and illustrated by just those findings. The substantive analysis conducted in the previous chapters thus has its own significance and should have been taken account of. It constitutes the basis for the synthesising approach in this chapter, which systematises the concept of fair trading and presents in a condensed way its key features.

2 The definition of the principle of fair trading

It is submitted that in the *acquis communautaire* a principle of fair trading exists, which can be defined as follows:

Consumers must be enabled to make their choice in full knowledge of the facts.

Except for a minor linguistic adaptation the phrase is literally taken from the case law of the Court of Justice interpreting the free movement of goods.[1] This may be taken as a first indication that fair trading, as it is expressed in the *acquis communautaire*, contains all the essential elements of a fully-developed principle of fair trading. Moreover, it shows that the Treaty as interpreted by the Court sets the fundamental framework for fair trading, while secondary law, with its numerous specific provisions, implements it in more detail.

The individual components of this general concept are very closely interwoven. Nevertheless, they will carefully be considered separately in order to examine their function for fair trading and their manifestation in Community law most accurately. The individual components are:

- consumers
- facts
- in full knowledge
- being enabled to make their choice.

3 The notion of the 'consumer'

Fair trading, as presently defined, concerns the pre-contractual or pre-transactional activities of business towards consumers. It provides market-behavioural norms addressed to business for the benefit of consumers.[2] While business is the addressee of the behavioural norms, consumers are the actual target of fair trading. This is not an astonishing finding, since the

---

1 See Case 193/80 *Commission v Italy ('Italian Vinegar')* [1981] ECR 3019 at 27, Case 178/84 *Commission v Germany ('German Beer')* [1987] ECR 1227 at 35, Case C-362/88 *GB-INNO-BM v Confédération du commerce luxembourgeois* [1990] ECR I-667 at 17, Case C-126/91 *Schutzverband gegen Unwesen in der Wirtschaft e.V. v Yves Rocher GmbH* [1993] ECR I-2361 at 17. A very similar formulation, however specifically related to foodstuffs, can be found in Article 8 of Regulation 178/2002.

2 Of course, the Community measures address the Member States, which, in the case of directives, have to implement them. It can be said, however, that business is the addressee of the substance of the Community measures, i.e. the behavioural norms.

research was limited to business-to-consumer relations in the first place.[3] However, it can be established that the suggested formula for a principle of fair trading has indeed been used by the Court exactly in that way only in the connection with consumers, which confirms its specific consumer-oriented rationale. In view of the consumer being the reference point for fair trading the consumer notion has to be elucidated. This has to be done in accordance with the twofold role the notion of the consumer plays. Firstly, the formal definition of the consumer determines the *sedes personae* of the principle of fair trading. Secondly, the image of the consumer constitutes the yardstick for fair trading.

3.1 The formal definition of the consumer

Although the notion of the 'consumer' appears a couple of times in the Treaty, a legal definition is not given. It has been pointed out, however, that in connection with the fundamental freedoms, the consumer notion has to be brought down to its very basic idea, which is that consumers 'consume' or 'use', and that they do this for private purposes. This has led to the definition of consumers as being persons acquiring goods or services in the Internal Market for private consumption.[4]

The situation is different in secondary law. Secondary law has frequently defined the consumer, but has provided varying definitions.[5] The latter phenomenon can be explained by the Community legislator's conception of consumers who are not only users of particular products, but part of a socio-economic system in which they assume functions linked to various factors (e.g. being citizens, workers, or professionals).[6] According to this view, the definition of the consumer depends on the purpose and scope of protection that is to be assured

---

3 See Introduction at 2.1.1. It should be reminded that not all directives are limited to consumer protection. The purpose of the horizontally harmonizing Directive 84/450, for instance, is to protect consumers, traders and the general public. In the electronic-communications sector a certain tendency can be observed to put business on an equal footing with consumers where both groups are considered to be in a similar situation. See e.g. the concept of 'end-users' in Directive 2002/22/EC on universal service and user's rights relating to electronic communications networks and services (Universal Services Directive), OJ 2002 L 108/51, who may have the same rights as consumers although they are professionals. Most of the information requirements of Directive 2000/31 on e-commerce also affect business-to-business relations.

4 For the concept of the consumer in primary law, see Chapter 1 at 3.1.

5 See for an examination of various consumer definitions Faber, (1998) 6 *ZEuP* 854.

6 The first consumer protection programme of 1975 (Council Resolution on a preliminary programme for a consumer protection and information policy, OJ 1975 C 92/1, the consumer protection programme is attached as annex) stated in its point 3 that '[t]he consumer is no longer seen merely as a purchaser and user of goods and services for personal, family or group purposes but also as a person concerned with the various facets of society which may affect him either directly or indirectly as a consumer'. See moreover, Bourgoignie, *Théorie du droit de la consommation*, p. 36 et seq.

and is preferable to a universal definition.[7] The consumer needing protection against health risks may be different from the one whose economic interests are to be protected, such as in the context of fair trading.[8]

But also within the single field of fair trading, the definitions provided in Community legislation are not homogenous. Nevertheless, there is a common core, according to which a consumer is 'any natural person who is acting for purposes which are outside his or her trade, business or profession'.[9] The Court has tended to favour an abstract interpretation of this definition of the consumer.[10] Although the business side is frequently defined as well (and given names as 'seller' or 'supplier'), the definition of the (ultimate)[11] consumer remains the decisive one, because the negative definition assumes an excluding function: a person who is acting for purposes which are inside his or her trade, business or profession rather belongs to the business side.[12]

---

7 See also Reich in Reich/Micklitz, *Verbraucherrecht*, at 1.38.

8 See Christianos/Picod, (1996) *Rép. communautaire Dalloz* at paragraph 45.

9 Literally Article 2(e) of Directive 2000/31. Almost literally Article 1(2)(a) of Directive 87/102, Article 2(2) of Directive 97/7, Article 2(d) of Directive 2002/65. Similarly in Article 2 of Directive 85/577, Article 2 of Directive 94/47, Article 2(2) of Directive 97/7, Article 2(e) of Directive 98/6. Article 2(4) of Directive 90/314 contains a very specific definition for the contractors of package travel, which is broader as it may include business travellers. See also Reich, (1994) 2 *ZEuP* 381 at 389. See furthermore Bernardeau, (2001) *REDC* 341 on the impact of the Court's emphasis of consumers being natural persons in Joined Cases C-541/99 and C-542/99 *Cape Snc v Idealservice Srl et al.* [2001] ECR I-9049.

10 In Case C-361/89 *Patrice Di Pinto* [1991] ECR I-1189 at 15, concerning the Doorstep-Selling Directive, the Court has emphasised that a trader may claim that the Directive is applicable only if the transaction in respect of which he is canvassed lies outside his trade or profession. Advocate General Mischo (at 22 et seq. of his Opinion), by contrast, proposed as a yardstick the concrete necessity of protection with regard to the transaction. Consequently, he advocated the recognition of traders as consumers in case they unexpectedly find themselves in the position of a consumer in so far as they are required to perform an act in which they probably would be involved only once in their lives (in the concrete case: the sale of the business). See to this Franzen, *Privatrechtsangleichung*, p. 467. See furthermore Case C-45/96 *Bayerische Hypotheken- und Wechselbank AG v Edgard Dietzinger* [1998] ECR I-1199 at 22.

11 The reference to the 'ultimate' or 'final' consumer is more often to be found in connection with foodstuffs (e.g. Article 1(1) of Directive 2000/13, Article 3(18) of Regulation 178/2002, Article 3(6) of Regulation 1830/2003). The meaning is practically the same, the only difference being that more importance is attached to the fact that the person will not further use the object of consumption for business activities (i.e. that it will be consumed by that person him- or herself), while the ordinary definition of the consumer attaches the importance to the acting outside business purposes. See also 'end consumer' in connection with medicinal products, e.g. Case C-322/01 *Deutscher Apothekerverband e.V. v 0800 DocMorris NV and Jacques Waterval* [2003] ECR I-nyr at 34, 61, 62, 70, 74, 102.

12 See e.g. Case C-361/89 *Patrice Di Pinto* [1991] ECR I-1189 at 16 et seq. Somebody is not a consumer whose actions are connected with the professional activity of a trader, even if such acts may bring the running of the business to an end. It does not matter that this person may find himself in an unprepared situation similar to that of a consumer.

The different consumer concepts in primary and secondary fair trading law do not lead, however, to a conflict in the personal scope of a principle of fair trading. The functional approach in secondary law tends to be wider than the consumption approach in the context of the fundamental freedoms. The functional understanding certainly comprises the much more basic aspect of consumers being 'users' of goods or services. Consequently, the fair trading concept elaborated in the context of primary law applies also to secondary law situations. This is forcefully confirmed by the Court's interpretation of the directives' fair trading provisions in the light of the fundamental freedoms.[13]

3.2 The image of the consumer as a yardstick for fair trading

Beside the formal definition of the consumer there is the dimension of the consumer as an assessment yardstick for fair trading, the so-called 'image of the consumer', which has been developed by the Court of Justice. Such a yardstick is necessary, since the effect of a commercial communication may differ substantially according to the person who receives it.[14] Therefore, the assessment whether a particular commercial communication is fair or not cannot possibly be decided independently of the recipient of the communication. A general fairness assessment of a commercial communication also requires a generalised consumer standard.

Like primary law, the directives remain silent as to explicit definitions of applicable consumer standards for measuring the fairness of commercial communication. The predominant role of information in secondary law certainly allows indirect conclusions regarding the underlying concept of the consumer, since it is apparently assumed that the consumer is intellectually able to deal with it and makes use of it. However, it has been left to the Court of Justice to define positively the concept of the average consumer, which it has largely done in the context of reviewing national rules' compatibility with the Treaty's free-movement provisions, while the case law relating to Community legislation rather assumes a complementary role.

The standard, which is an expression of the principle of proportionality,[15] has been developed mainly in connection with (alleged) misleading advertising but can be said to apply universally in the context of fair trading, since it always concerns the dealing with information. Its being an expression of the legal principle of proportionality, which is a normative concept, suggests that also the image of the consumer is a normative concept.[16] Of course, it has then

[13] Cf. Chapter 1 at 1.

[14] Cf. Puurunen, (2003) 11 *ZEuP* 789 at 808 et seq.

[15] Case C-220/98 *Estée Lauder Cosmetics GmbH & Co. OHG v Lancaster Group GmbH ('Lifting')* [2000] ECR I-117 at 27 and 28, see also Case C-358/01 *Commission v Spain* [2003] ECR I-nyr at 53.

[16] Cf. Dittmer, (1998) 21 *E.I.P.R.* 313 at 316.

to be applied to a factual situation,[17] just like every legal standard does not stand for its own, but must be related to a factual situation in order to be effective. It is therefore submitted, that the dispute whether the image of the consumer is a normative or factual/empirical concept construes a contradiction where there is none.[18] Both aspects play a role, which is reflected in the Court's reasoning and which can be translated into a two-stage test.

At the first stage, there is the basic standard of the 'presumed expectations of an average consumer who is reasonably well informed and reasonably observant and circumspect'.[19] This test represents an objective-abstract *ex ante* approach. It implies that consumers are in principle considered to have a reasonable understanding of reality, and that they are able to relate carefully the obtained information to this reality and thus are not easily deceived. However, this does not mean that the concept of an 'average consumer' is not receptive to the diversity of consumers.[20] The 'average consumer' refers to the average member of the group of consumers to which the advertising is addressed, i.e. the target group.[21] Among the different groups of consumers, different degrees of being 'well-informed' and being 'observant and circumspect' are 'reasonable' (e.g. a lower degree among children compared to adults). Moreover, the Court has emphasised that the diversity of the Internal Market comes along with a diversity of consumers.[22] Therefore, national legislation must not 'crystallize given

---

[17] See Schweizer, (2000) 102 *GRUR* 923 at 926 et seq.

[18] Similarly Ahrens, (2000) 46 *WRP* 812 at 813 et seq. This discussion is particularly intense in German literature, which can be explained by the fact that the German image of the consumer has until recently been quite contrary to the European one. See e.g. Deutsch, (1996) 98 GRUR 541, Sack, (1998) 44 *WRP* 264, Schweizer, (2000) 102 *GRUR* 923, Spätgens, (2000) 46 *WRP* 1023, Groeschke/Kiethe, (2001) 47 *WRP* 230, Seibt, (2002) 104 *GRUR* 465.

[19] Literally or similarly in e.g. Case C-470/93 *Verein gegen Unwesen in Handel und Gewerbe Köln e.V. v Mars GmbH* [1995] ECR I-1923 at 24, Case C-210/96 *Gut Springenheide GmbH and Rudolf Tusky v Oberkreis-direktor des Kreises Steinfurt – Amt für Lebensmittelüberwachung* [1998] ECR I-4657 at 31 and 37, Case C-303/97 *Verbraucherschutzverein e.V. v Sektkellerei G.C. Kessler GmbH und Co.* [1999] ECR I-513 at 36, Case C-220/98 *Estée Lauder Cosmetics GmbH & Co. OHG v Lancaster Group GmbH ('Lifting')* [2000] ECR I-117 at 27, Case C-465/98 *Verein gegen Unwesen in Handel und Gewerbe Köln e.V. v Adolf Darbo AG* [2000] ECR I-2297 at 20, Case C-3/99 *Cidrerie Ruwet SA v Cidre Stassen SA and HP Bulmer Ltd.* [2000] ECR I-8749 at 53, Case C-112/99 *Toshiba Europe GmbH v Katun Germany GmbH* [2001] ECR I-7945 at 52, Case C-44/01 *Pippig Augenoptik GmbH & Co. KG v Hartlauer Handelsgesellschaft mbH* [2003] ECR I-3095 at 55, Case C-99/01 *Criminal proceedings against Gottfried Linhart and Hans Biffl* [2002] ECR I-9375 at 31, Case C-358/01 *Commission v Spain* [2003] ECR I-nyr at 53.

[20] See e.g. Case 382/87 *R. Buet and Educational Business Services (EBS) v Ministère public* [1989] ECR 1235 at 13, Case C-373/90 *Criminal proceedings against X ('Nissan')* [1992] ECR I-131 at 13–15.

[21] See e.g. Case C-313/94 *Fratelli Graffione SNC v Ditta Fransa* [1996] ECR I-6039 at 26. See also Schulte-Nölke/Schulze/Jones, *Casebook*, p. 226.

[22] Cf. Case 178/84 *Commission v Germany ('German Beer')* [1987] ECR 1227 at 32.

consumer habits',[23] which is to be done in part by ensuring that the consumer is adequately informed.

The adaptation of the standard to the various groups of consumers blends into the second stage of the test, which is the actual application of the standard. Here, national socio-cultural parameters have to be taken into account.[24] Given that there is a diversity of consumers, in order 'to apply that test to the present case' it has to be determined in particular whether 'social, cultural or linguistic factors' may justify a restrictive rule.[25] The Court therefore often refers the case back to the national court to ascertain the circumstances of the particular case and to bear in mind the consumers to which the advertising is addressed.[26]

In conclusion, whether commercial communication enables consumers to make their choice in full knowledge of the facts within the meaning of the principle of fair trading has to be assessed against the backdrop of the presumed expectations of an average consumer who is reasonably well informed and reasonably observant and circumspect, the average member of the group of consumers to which the communication is addressed being decisive. The application of this standard has to take into account national socio-cultural factors. This assessment is ultimately to be made by the national courts.

4 Information as the fundamental instrument for (fair) trading

European consumer law is commonly described as being ruled by the 'information paradigm'.[27] Information definitely plays an important role in European consumer law in general, but there cannot be the slightest doubt that information is the ultimate leitmotif in Community fair-trading law and

---

23 Case 170/78 *Commission v United Kingdom ('Beer and Wine')* [1983] ECR 2265 at 8 (interlocutory judgment [1980] ECR 417 at 14).

24 Cf. Leible, (2003) 30 *ZLR* 63 at 73.

25 Case C-220/98 *Estée Lauder Cosmetics GmbH & Co. OHG v Lancaster Group GmbH ('Lifting')* [2000] ECR I-117 at 29, similarly Case C-313/94 *Fratelli Graffione SNC v Ditta Fransa* [1996] ECR I-6039 at 22. In subsequent judgments the Court has referred to the consumer standard of *Lifting* although it has not repeated the formula of 'social, cultural or linguistic factors', e.g. Case C-3/99 *Cidrerie Ruwet SA v Cidre Stassen SA and HP Bulmer Ltd.* [2000] ECR I-8749 at 53, Case C-99/01 *Criminal proceedings against Gottfried Linhart and Hans Biffl* [2002] ECR I-9375 at 31.

26 In practice, national courts will face huge difficulties in performing this assessment. The suggestion of the Court of Justice in *Lifting* at 31 that the national court 'may consider it necessary to commission an expert opinion or a survey of public opinion in order to clarify whether or not a promotional description or statement is misleading' seems far from realistic to implement for a national court of first instance.

27 Howells/Wilhelmsson, (2003) 28 *E.L.Rev.* 370 at 380 et seq., Reich, *Bürgerrechte*, p. 280, Reich in Reich/Micklitz, *Verbraucherrecht*, at 1.10.

consequently governs the principle of fair trading. In fact, as will be demonstrated throughout this chapter, every aspect of fair trading can be explained by the availability and the processing of information, which makes fair trading a principle of market communication.[28]

The element of information is reflected in the principle of fair trading by the term 'facts'. If consumers must be enabled to make their choice in full knowledge of the 'facts', this means that information is the decisive basis for their choice. It should be noted that other language versions of the judgments incorporating the formula which is suggested here as the principle of fair trading are slightly less focussed on facts, but may be understood as hinting more generally at 'circumstances'.[29] It is submitted, however, that this linguistic subtlety does not alter the assessment of information being the basis for consumer choice, but rather shows how strongly the elements of the principle of fair trading are intertwined. In particular the element of 'knowledge', which reappears in the other language versions, comprises the concept of information, since knowledge is ultimately composed of information. Besides, some judgments use the expression 'to enable consumers to make an informed choice'[30] for expressing the idea of 'enabling them to make their choice in full knowledge of the facts'.

4.1 The indispensability of information exchange for an operational market

It is certainly not exaggerated to claim that the exchange of information – that is to say communication – is the essence of every market which is based on the exchange of performances. A transaction is inconceivable without the exchange of minimum information, concerning at least the mutual performances and the contractual parties.[31] The exchange of information comprises not only facts actively provided, but the whole set of details which is naturally transmitted and perceived in the factual context, e.g. by just seeing a product or the contractual party. Without communication, supply and demand side would simply not be able to deal with each other, and the assessment of different performances would not be possible.

---

28 Cf. Micklitz/Keßler, (2003) 49 *WRP* 919 at 921.

29 French: 'en toute connaissance de cause' (*Italian Vinegar, German Beer, GB-INNO-BM*), 'en pleine connaissance de cause' (*Yves Rocher*). German: 'in Kenntnis aller Umstände' (*Italian Vinegar, German Beer, GB-INNO-BM*), 'in voller Kenntnis der Sachlage' (*Yves Rocher*), the latter translation being closer to the English version. Dutch: 'met volle kennis van zaken' (*Italian Vinegar, German Beer, GB-INNO-BM, Yves Rocher*). For the exact references of the judgments, see *supra* footnote 1.

30 Cf. Case C-161/02 *Commission v France* [2003] ECR I-6567 at 2, Case C-74/02 *Commission v Germany* [2003] ECR I-9877 at 3, see also Case T-19/91 *Société d'Hygiène Dermatologique de Vichy v Commission* [1992] ECR II-415 at 98.

31 Cf. Junod Moser, *Conditions générales*, p. 46 et seq.

The communication process begins long before the conclusion of a contract. In fact, pre-contractual communication assumes a most decisive role, since it determines whether a contract will be concluded in the first place. Fair trading concerns this pre-contractual phase, the phase which leads consumers to their economic choice. Without information such a choice cannot possibly be made. Accordingly, 'advertising is an important element of the competitive situation on any given market, since it provides a better picture of the merits of each of the operators, the quality of their services and their fees'.[32] In Community legislation this idea is perfectly reflected by the notion 'commercial communication', which is the central point of reference in the E-Commerce Directive.[33] It comprises 'any form of communication' (i.e. also non-verbal) which is designed for sales promotion (i.e. in the pre-contractual sphere).

Information exchange does not only take place between suppliers and consumers. A competitive market requires that suppliers observe and react to the behaviour of their competitors, the prerequisite of which is the exchange of information. Competition is thus likewise inconceivable without information and could be described as a communicative process of information transfer.[34]

4.2 Is the role of information in the Internal Market the same as in a domestic market?

Economic theory usually refers to domestic markets. Doubts may arise as to whether conventional market theory and its assessment of the role of information applies in the same way to the Internal Market with its unique nature. Yet, the Internal Market, as far as it ultimately implies the idea of a single united market with conditions similar to those of a domestic market,[35] essentially obeys the same economic principles as any other economic market. The theoretical foundations of the economic role of information in the Internal Market can therefore be considered equal to that in economic markets in general. Despite the fact that the Internal Market still has a setting that differs from a domestic market, for an assessment of the structural function of information in the Internal Market the discussion whether and to what extent the Internal Market has actually fully been accomplished is not profitable at all. From the perspective of cross-border active consumers in the sense of *GB-INNO*[36] it is a

---

[32] Case T-144/99 *Institute of Professional Representatives before the European Patent Office v Commission* [2001] ECR II-1087 at 72.

[33] Art. 2(f) of Directive 2000/31. See Chapter 2 at 2.5.2.2.

[34] Keßler/Micklitz, *Harmonisierung des Lauterkeitsrechts*, p. 17 et seq. Similarly Alexandridou in Krämer/Micklitz/Tonner, *Law and diffuse interests*, p. 409 at p. 409 et seq. and at p. 421 with regard to advertising.

[35] Cf. Case 26/76 *Metro SB-Großmärkte GmbH & Co. KG v Commission* [1977] ECR 1875 at 20, Case 270/80 *Polydor Ltd. et al. v Harlequin Records Shops Ltd. et al.* [1982] ECR 329 at 16 and 18.

[36] Case C-362/88 *GB-INNO-BM v Confédération du commerce luxembourgeois* [1990] ECR I-667.

market just as realistic as their national markets, and it confronts them with the same informational environment, to which they are receptive. The same applies analogously to commercial market participants.

Consequently, the general information model can very well be applied to the Internal Market, i.e. also in the Internal Market, the exchange of information is the fundamental prerequisite for trading. Communication is the basic instrument for any market action. It therefore seems logical that governing market behaviour in the sense of creating a framework for fair trading necessarily involves rules concerning information.

5 Having full knowledge

In the definition of the principle of fair trading, according to which consumers must be enabled to make their choice in full knowledge of the facts, the component of 'in full knowledge' assumes the leading role. Most of the specific rules can be attributed to this component. Besides, the element of 'knowledge' reaffirms the role of information, since information is the basis of knowledge. This aspect of the definition thus aims at putting the consumer in a state to make an 'informed' choice.

The idea of having full knowledge can be said to comprise the guarantee of access to information, the obligation to disclose information where necessary (positive information duties), the obligation not to mislead (negative information duties), and the approval of disclosing correct information as a matter of principle (comparative advertising).

5.1 Access to information

The idea that consumers have to have information at their disposal in order to make an informed choice does not imply that all relevant information must necessarily be provided actively. As a logical preliminary stage the simple access as such to information must be guaranteed.

Access to information as a fundamental right?

Article 10(1) of the European Convention on Human Rights (to be respected by the Union under Article 6(2) EU) and Article 11(1) of the Charter of Fundamental Rights of the European Union both highlight the right of everybody to receive information. Serious doubts must be raised, however, as to whether the information referred to in those provisions is similar to information in the context of fair trading. As a matter of fact, the information concerned is considered to be a component of the freedom of expression. The right to receive information is therefore supposed to be a prerequisite to hold and express opinions rather than to be the basis for making informed purchase choices.

Access to information as a right deriving from Article 153 of the Treaty?

The right of consumers to information is furthermore an issue to be found in Article 153(1) of the Treaty. It may certainly be questioned whether the provision itself can be construed as a subjective right which can directly be evoked by consumers, but it does recognise quite clearly the existence of a right of consumers to information, albeit its origin is not further indicated.[37] The more crucial question in the present context is, however, whether the information referred to in Article 153(1) is equal to that playing a role in the context of fair trading.

Article 153(1) assigns the duty on the Community to promote the interests of consumers and to ensure a high level of consumer protection. In order to do so, the Community shall follow two strategies: it shall contribute

> 'to protecting the health, safety and economic interests of consumers,
> *as well as*
> to promoting their right to information, education and to organise themselves in order to safeguard their interests'.[38]

It is striking that the acknowledged right to information is connected to the right to education and self-organisation, while it is not included in the first group of objectives together with the economic interests of consumers. The systematic interpretation of Article 153(1) thus hints at the right of information being rather of an educational or social nature than of an economic one.[39] On the other hand, a link between education and the right to information may be established, if a good education is understood as the prerequisite for acting as an

[37] Reich, (1999) 14 *VuR* 3 at 7 et seq. recognises a 'negative direct effect' (unjustified or excessive restrictions to the access to information) but rejects a 'positive horizontal direct effect' (positive right to information) due to lack of sufficient precision of Article 153(1). He assigns the provision a supporting function to secondary law where the latter includes precise and unconditional information rights.

[38] Emphasis added.

[39] Reich in Reich/Micklitz, *Verbraucherrecht*, at 1.15 also underlines the close connection between the right to information and the right to education, the latter extending the first. The Commission, by contrast, seemingly takes a different view when it considers the right to information of Article 153(1) to require general obligations on pre-contractual information disclosure in its Green Paper on European Union Consumer Protection, COM (2001) 531 final at point 4.4.

[40] Stuyck, (2000) 37 *CML Rev.* 367 at 384 et seq. also understands the right to information to be economically related. In his view this does not clash with the right to education at all, because, 'consumer education in school is certainly an important element in the process of arming consumers against undue influence which may be exercised by advertisers and sellers and to help them to make well-considered consumption decisions'. Indeed, good education is certainly most beneficial for people acting as self-responsible consumers; see also De Nayer in Wilhelmsson/Tuominen/Tuomola, *Information Society*, p. 117 at p. 123. It is submitted, however, that, at least in practice, such kind of economic self-responsibility is a side effect of education in school rather than its main concern. Education in Article 153 seems therefore more likely to be meant in a more traditional sense.

informed and self-responsible consumer.[40] One could also think of an obligation on the Community to guarantee the information of consumers about their rights.[41]

Information in the context of fair trading, in any case, is clearly related to the economic interests of consumers. It is connected to their actual economic activity, since it constitutes the basis for their purchase choice and since the exchange of information is part of the transaction itself.[42] By contrast, it is very unclear what the right to information in Article 153(1) actually comprises. It is at least doubtful whether it concerns economic information in the same meaning and to the same extent as implied in the principle of fair trading.

Access to information as an Internal Market necessity

However, the doubts regarding the meaning of information in Article 153(1) in no way weakens the authority of the concept of the consumers' right to information and the implied necessity to access information. As has been demonstrated before, this right is deeply rooted in the proper functioning of a market anyway, since trading without the exchange of information is unfeasible.[43] Therefore, the right to information in an economic context and the implied necessity to access information are inseparably associated with the very concept of the Internal Market.

This interpretation is reflected in the free movement case law. In *GB-INNO*, for instance, the Court pointed out that the provision of information to the consumer was considered one of the principal requirements in Community law, and that national legislation denying the consumer access to certain kinds of information might not be justified by mandatory requirements concerning consumer protection in the context of Article 28.[44] In *Alpine Investments*, the Court took a similar view in the context of the free movement of services. One of the reasons why the Dutch ban on cold calling for financial services was justified

41 This seems to be correlated with the principle of transparency and access to documents which is described by Lenaerts, (2004) 41 *CML Rev.* 317 at 318 et seq. as a general principle of Community law aimed at consolidating the trust which individuals should place in Union governance.

42 Cf. Case C-303/97 *Verbraucherschutzverein e.V. v Sektkellerei G.C. Kessler GmbH und Co.* [1999] ECR I-513 at 28 and 33. For information to be within the realm of fair trading the economic context is crucial, see e.g. Case C-159/90 *The Society for the Protection of Unborn Children Ireland Ltd v Stephen Grogan and others* [1991] ECR I-4685. The Court rejected to consider the information in Ireland on the identity and location of clinics abroad where abortions are performed under Article 49. Abortion was straightforwardly regarded as a service, and the related information provision by clinics (i.e. the service providers) would also have been protected under Article 49. However, the information at issue was provided by student associations with no link to the clinics in other Member States. Therefore, it was not commercial communication, but rather a matter of free expression.

43 See *supra* at 4.

44 Case C-362/88 *GB-INNO-BM v Confédération du commerce luxembourgeois* [1990] ECR I-667 at 18.

was that the consumer was not in a position to compare the quality and price of the caller's services with competitors' offers.[45] This trade practice thus was not only particularly aggressive, but it restricted sufficient access to information for consumers (and consequently impaired their freedom of choice).

Access to information in Community legislation

In view of the interconnection between access to information, the right to information and the functioning of the Internal Market, the aspect of access to information is reflected in Community legislation mainly implicitly. Access to information is dealt with in connection with duties of information disclosure and the related standards for the recognisability and comprehensibility of information. These facets are to be examined separately.[46]

By contrast, an example of a more direct protection of the access to commercial information can be found in Article 3(h) of Directive 2000/43 combating discrimination on the grounds of racial or ethnic origin. This provision demands the non-discriminatory access to goods, which inevitably implies the access to information on those goods.

5.2 The duty to disclose information

The idea that consumers must be enabled to make their choice 'in full knowledge of the facts' is probably best reflected by the myriad information duties to be found in secondary law. In principle, actively providing consumers with information is most useful for them to make an informed purchase decision. It seems less clear, at first sight, whether the Court of Justice derives in its case law a positive duty to inform directly from the Treaty's free-movement provisions. This uncertainty mainly results from the negative-integration approach, which removes obstacles rather than to impose duties. However, the unambiguous confession of the Internal Market functioning on the basis of access to and exchange of information can hardly rule out a duty to inform, where information cannot be acquired in another way.[47]

Another reason for the prevalence of positive information duties is to be found in their close connection to the omnipresent principle of proportionality.[48] The Court has highlighted repeatedly that restrictions of the marketing of goods

---

45 Case C-384/93 *Alpine Investments BV v Minister van Financiën* [1995] ECR I-1141 at 46.

46 See *infra* at 5.2, 5.2.1 and 5.2.3.

47 See *supra* at 5.1 and at 4.

48 Cf. Weatherill, (1994) 2 *Consum.L.J.* 49 at 50 et seq., Weatherill in Micklitz, *Rechtseinheit oder Rechtsvielfalt*, p. 423 at 430.

were not proportionate to the aim of consumer protection and fair trading where the disclosure of information would achieve the same results.[49] The disclosure of information supports consumer-sovereignty, because it provides the basis for autonomous decision-making, whereas this is undermined by prohibitions.[50]

Positive information duties are governed by four basic ideas: recognisability, correctness, comprehensiveness, and comprehensibility. This reflects requirements as regards the quantity and the quality of information, the emphasis being on the quality of information.[51]

5.2.1 Recognisability

The recognisability of information may be considered most related to the aspect of information 'disclosure', since it requires concealed or obscure information to be revealed. Hence, it constitutes a central part of the general requirement of transparency which governs fair-trading law. Article 4(2) of Directive 97/7 and Article 3(2) of Directive 2002/65 express two aspects of recognisability, which can be generalised. Firstly, the information must be provided in a clear manner (informational recognisability),[52] and, secondly, the commercial purpose of the information must be made clear to the consumer (commercial recognisability).

The necessity of information to be provided in a clear manner is self-evident, if it is supposed to be recognised by the recipient. This is all the more the case in connection with positive information duties concerning information which the consumer would not gather in a natural way in the factual context.[53]

---

49 See e.g. Case 120/78 *Rewe-Zentral AG v Bundesmonopolverwaltung für Branntwein ('Cassis de Dijon')*, [1979] ECR 649 at 13, Case 178/84 *Commission v Germany ('German Beer')* [1987] ECR 1227 at 35, Case 216/84 *Commission v France ('Milk substitutes')* [1988] ECR 793 at 10, Case 407/85 *3 Glocken GmbH and Gertraud Kritzinger v USL Centro-Sud and Provincia autonoma di Bolzano* [1988] ECR 4233 at 16 and 18, Case C-362/88 *GB-INNO-BM v Confédération du commerce luxembourgeois* [1990] ECR I-667 at 17, Case C-366/98 *Yannick Geffroy and Casino France SNC* [2000] ECR I-6579 at 23, Case C-448/98 *Criminal proceedings against Jean-Pierre Guimont* [2000] ECR I-10663 at 31, Case C-12/00 *Commission v Spain* [2003] ECR I-459 at 86, Case C-14/00 *Commission v Italy* [2003] ECR I-513 at 81.

50 See Grundmann, (2002) 39 *CML Rev.* 269 at 280 et seq. and Grundmann/Kerber/Weatherill in Grundmann/Kerber/Weatherill, *Party Autonomy*, p. 3 at p. 7, whose considerations in the context of party autonomy can be understood as pointing out that (mandatory) information requirements are always proportionate.

51 Micklitz/Keßler, (2003) 49 *WRP* 919 at 922 stress the importance of the quality of information for a functioning process of market communication.

52 For comprehensibility (as different from recognisability), see *infra* at 5.2.4.

53 Obligations concerning clearly provided information ('easily visible', 'clearly legible' etc.) can be found in all of the labelling directives, which concern information that is not obvious by itself, e.g. the ingredients of pre-packaged foodstuffs.

The requirement to unveil the commercial purpose of the information results from modern communication means, which allow quite a blurred transition between editorial and commercial communication. Such an approach may unduly influence consumers, as the inability to identify the nature of the information may lead them to wrong conclusions.[54] Consequently, the Television Directive gives fairly detailed guidelines throughout its provisions in order to assure the distinction of promotional broadcasts from other television broadcasts, e.g. keeping commercials separate from other parts of the programme by optical and/or acoustic means, and assigning quotas for advertising emissions. Moreover, it prohibits subliminal techniques and surreptitious advertising. The E-Commerce Directive persistently repeats in Article 6 that commercial communication must be clearly identifiable as such and presented clearly and unambiguously.

The category of recognisability also comprises rules which require information to be communicated or confirmed on a durable medium. The purpose of these rules is to compensate the transitory nature of non-physical communication means, like modern means of distance communication. As these rules mainly take effect after the conclusion of the contract, they seem somewhat outside of the concept of fair trading, since the consumer's choice has already been made. However, this post-contractual information complements the right of withdrawal, which is likewise provided for in distance-communication legislation as a remedy for the lack of pre-contractual information, i.e. a situation of pre-contractual information asymmetry.[55] With all the information physically at hand consumers are enabled to reassess the deal post-contractually, and it serves them as a reference when revoking their choice.

5.2.2 Correctness

Making a choice in 'full knowledge of the facts' logically implies that the disclosed information is correct, because otherwise the facts are not fully known. Yet, the aspect of correctness in information disclosure is hardly ever expressed as a positive obligation. As an exception, Article 3(4) of Directive 2002/65 explicitly requires that the information communicated during the pre-contractual phase be in conformity with the contractual obligations of the potentially later concluded contract. In general, it is considered as a matter of course that a duty to disclose a fact means the disclosure of the correct fact.[56]

---

54 See Wilhelmsson in Wilhelmsson/Tuominen/Tuomola, *Information Society*, p. 367 at p. 375.

55 See *infra* at 5.2.3.1.

56 If, for instance, the disclosure of the identity of the seller is required, there is no need to add that the 'correct' identity of the seller is meant, since every other information would just not be the identity of the seller.

The correctness of information is tackled implicitly via misleading and comparative advertising.[57] In the case of misleading advertising, information is prohibited which creates a misconception in the mind of the consumer, because the facts are incorrect, or for other reasons. The prohibition of misleading information thus involves simultaneously that disclosed information must be correct. The function of comparative advertising for the correctness of facts is best represented by the Court's judgment in *Yves Rocher*, where it held that correct information (comparisons of correct prices in the case) might not be prohibited in the name of fair trading. On the contrary, the disclosure of correct information supports fair trading as it helps consumers to make their choice in full knowledge of the facts.[58]

5.2.3 Comprehensiveness

The idea of 'full' knowledge of the facts implies a certain comprehensiveness of the information. Consumers must have all the information they 'need' to make their choice. What consumers 'need' or what is 'relevant' for them can be determined from both an objective and a subjective point of view.

5.2.3.1 Objectively necessary information

It already follows from the free-movement case law that consumers have to be provided with the 'necessary' information.[59] This case law remains rather vague as to which information particulars belong to the necessary information. In an attempt to be somewhat more explicit, the Court of Justice pointed out in *Belgian Notification Numbers* that the basic facts consumers must know are those 'enabling them to decide whether or not they should consume the product and, if they do consume it, in what quantities'.[60] Without actually further identifying these 'facts' the Court thus assumes that the consumer's decision whether or not and in which quantity to buy a product depends on a number of indispensable details. From an objective point of view, this implies the knowledge of a given set of particulars which have to be known for a particular product. Just as a contract can only be made if an agreement is reached on the elements which are indispensable for the validity of the contract (*essen-*

[57] See in detail *infra* at 5.3 and at 5.4.

[58] Case C-126/91 *Schutzverband gegen Unwesen in der Wirtschaft e.V. v Yves Rocher GmbH* [1993] ECR I-2361 at 17.

[59] E.g. Case C-448/98 *Criminal proceedings against Jean-Pierre Guimont* [2000] ECR I-10663 at 31. See also Case C-12/00 *Commission v Spain* [2003] ECR I-459 at 86, Case C-14/00 *Commission v Italy* [2003] ECR I-513 at 81.

[60] Case C-217/99 *Commission v Belgium ('Belgian Notification Numbers')* [2000] ECR I-10251 at 26. See moreover Chapter 1 at 5.2.6.

tialia negotii), too, the choice to buy a product – which invariably leads to the conclusion of a contract – requires a necessary set of information. This objective approach implicitly recognises that, just like different types of contracts, different types of choices require different facts to constitute a valid decision-making basis. The case law itself has not explicitly established such a differentiated system. However, in *Belgian Notification Numbers*, the Court found it necessary to consider 'in particular', whether the notification number provided consumers with any information enabling them to adapt their consumption in such a way as to take precautionary measures for the protection of their health. Since health is probably the most vital consumer interest, it can be concluded that information disclosure must always take into account the consumers' health.

The more specific content of the necessary information is actually outlined in Community legislation, which gives concrete shape to the abstract case law requirements.

The availability of information from the context and structural information asymmetries as the yardstick for amount and content of positive information duties

It is striking that the amount and the content of positive information duties differs considerably among the various directives. This raises the question whether Community legislation recognises a particular and commonly applicable set of objectively necessary information, or whether this is individually determined according to each sector. The answer to this question depends on the understanding of the reasons for the variations in the required information density. It can easily be observed that the information duties increase in particular with regard to distance selling methods,[61] and with regard to products involving an increased personal risk[62] or being of a fundamental nature for consumption.[63] In particular, the latter categories allude to a connection between an increased need for protection and the amount of information to be provided.

However, this is not the only possible understanding. It is suggested that positive information duties have to be seen in connection with the availability of information from the context (i.e. naturally conveyed information) or structural information asymmetries. The active disclosure of information about the seller and the product in a distance-selling situation is required, because the consumer physically has no possibility (or only at excessive cost) of acquiring the information by himself. In addition, Article 6 of the Distance-Selling Directive bestows on the consumer a right of withdrawal. Yet, the motivation

[61] This concerns especially Directive 97/7, Directive 2000/31 and Directive 2002/65.

[62] These risks may concern health (e.g. cosmetic products, medicinal products, tobacco products), they may be financial risks (financial services in general), or they may be a danger for privacy (data protection).

[63] The products of a fundamental nature for consumption are mainly foodstuffs, which may involve health risks as well.

for this right is not the surprise effect as in the context of doorstep selling,[64] but it is to compensate for the impossibility of (physically) assessing the quality of the performance prior to the conclusion of the contract.[65] It is thus to remedy an environment of incomplete or asymmetric information which is caused by the distant nature of the transaction.[66] In a direct-selling situation, by contrast, consumers have immediate contact with the contracting party and the product and can use this automatically conveyed information to make their choice. The disclosure thus happens by a natural and manifest transmission of the information and does not have to be imposed by the law.[67]

This assumption serves as a general explanation model. More information on services has to be disclosed, for instance, since, being immaterial, less information is communicated in a self-evident way as is the case with goods. Goods, on the other hand, may also differ a lot in their natural information transmission. In the case of ingredients in foodstuffs or the contents of medicinal products, for example, the consumer is likewise unable to perceive lots of information particulars in a natural way, so that they must be provided actively. In the case of categories, such as medicinal products, which require a fairly educated or scientific background, the information asymmetry is of an even much more serious structural nature. The greater risk to human health is, in this particular context, more of a side-effect which draws additional attention to the interest of having and the necessity of providing information.[68] The actual necessity of information disclosure, however, is rooted in the information deficiency.

It is thus submitted that positive information duties mainly compensate for the lack of naturally available information, i.e. information apparent from the context. Structural information asymmetries could be understood as a sub-cate-

---

64 For the cancellation right regarding doorstep selling, see *infra* at 6.2.1 and at 6.2.2.

65 It must be admitted that this compensatory function of the right of withdrawal is very much dependent on the nature of the performance. It may in particular be much less effective in the case of services, which are immaterial anyway. In practice, it matters whether the consumer will be able to assess adequately the performance within the granted time for exercising the right of withdrawal, i.e. the cooling-off period. This is, however, a question of a sufficiently long cooling-off period, and it does not change the basic idea that the purpose of the right of withdrawal is to compensate for information asymmetries. Therefore, the fourteen-day period for financial services or the ten-day period for timeshare contracts may be seen as problematic, because they may be too short, cf. Rekaiti/Van den Bergh, (2000) 23 *JCP* 371 at 391.

66 Rekaiti/Van den Bergh, (2000) 23 *JCP* 371 at 379 et seq., Mota Pinto in Schulze/Ebers/Grigoleit, *Informationspflichten*, p. 157 at 159.

67 The perception of this information by consumers often happens subconsciously. It is this aspect of subconscious and passive information perception, which subliminal advertising techniques take advantage of, cf. Kroeber-Riel/Weinberg, *Konsumentenverhalten*, p. 253 et seq.

68 The risk aspect (e.g. also in financial services) is rather coped with by the quality of the information, i.e. its comprehensibility, see *infra* at 5.2.4.

gory of this concept.[69] As a consequence, the existence of explicit information duties in specific sectors does not automatically mean that these information particulars would play no role in contexts where their disclosure is not legally required. On the contrary, positive information duties existing in only some sectors are all the more to be understood as a general indicator of which information the legislator deems necessary for consumers to make their choice – that is to say the only reason why they are not made mandatory in other sectors is that there the information is already or more easily available from the context. This approach thus allows to establish a general system of information which is objectively necessary in a fair-trading environment by taking into consideration common positive information duties.[70]

Categories of objectively necessary information

It has been suggested that the information duties as classified in Article 3(1) of Directive 2002/65 ('supplier', 'financial service', 'distance contract', 'redress') serve as a model for a general framework of information duties.[71] Indeed, the physical absence of the contractual parties and the immateriality of the product make the legislation on the distance marketing of consumer financial services a perfect prototype of positive information duties which reflect universally valid information necessities. The groups as defined in the Directive can be generalised as 'contractual party', 'performance', 'contract', and 'remedies'. In the Directive, price and additional charges are associated with the performance. Given the existing quasi-horizontal harmonisation on cost transparency,[72] it seems justified to consider 'costs' to be an individual category under Community law.[73] All in all, these categories represent the consumers' economic interests, and any related information can influence them in their economic behaviour.

Contractual party

The main concern in this respect is the unveiled identity of the supplier or his representatives, including their geographical address. Consumers must

---

69 The idea of information asymmetries is taken up again in Chapter 4 at 2.2.2.2.

70 It seems that the presently proposed system largely comes to similar results as the concept of 'legitimate expectations' as suggested by Micklitz, see Micklitz in Krämer/Micklitz/Tonner, *Law and diffuse interests*, p. 245 at p. 267 et seq, Micklitz, (1999/2000) 19 *YEL* 167 at 192 et seq., Micklitz, (2002) 13 *EBLR* 583 at 591 et seq. The present system is freed, however, from its social justice implication and represents a market-oriented approach, specifically designed for the purposes of fair trading. The concept of 'legitimate expectations' is much broader, as it is supposed to be a general principle of social justice in European private law.

71 Ebers in Schulze/Ebers/Grigoleit, *Informationspflichten*, p. 171 at 176.

72 See Chapter 2 at 2.4.

73 Wilhelmsson in Schulze/Ebers/Grigoleit, *Informationspflichten*, p. 245 at p. 250 uses very similar categories.

know who their future contractual partner will be, because they may not want to contract with everybody. A second function of the disclosed identity is certainly to make sure that consumers know whom they can hold responsible in case of a dispute. The less obvious the identity of the supplier the higher the requirements for disclosure. Given that the Internet conceals the person in the background of the communication more than any other means of distance communication, the E-Commerce Directive requires that the information relating to the identity of the information-society service provider must be easily, directly and permanently accessible,[74] i.e. throughout the whole communication contact. There are further details, such as registration or authorisation by a supervisory authority, which have to be disclosed, where this is relevant.

The category of the contractual party shows once more why Community law addresses this issue specifically for distance-selling situations. Given that under direct-contact circumstances the identity and address of the other party is obvious from the factual context, positive information disclosure is not required in the same manner.[75] Yet, these particulars are considered necessary information in all other sales situations as well.

Performance

As a general rule, the main characteristics of the performance must be described. Depending on the nature of the performance the information to be disclosed may thus differ considerably. It has been demonstrated before that the gravity of information asymmetries is often very closely connected to the performance. The performance has a strong influence on which, how much, and in which manner information has to be disclosed.[76] For instance, much more detailed (and simplified) information has to be provided with regard to medicinal products than with regard to most other products. As a matter of fact, public health is an interest which has always to be taken into account in the disclosure of information.[77] The degree of danger for health will usually be linked to the type of the performance. In general, the conducted analysis of the legislation concerning the various product sectors reflects the variety of information disclosure.[78]

---

[74] Article 5 of Directive 2000/31.

[75] Of course, in a direct-selling situation the personal identity and address of the seller is not known under normal circumstances. But in a shop, as the ultimate prototype of a direct-selling situation, it is clear which business the seller represents and where this shop is geographically located.

[76] The aspect of 'in which manner' information has to be disclosed is illustrated with regard to comprehensibility *infra* at 5.2.4.

[77] Cf. Case C-217/99 *Commission v Belgium ('Belgian Notification Numbers')* [2000] ECR I-10251 at 26, see Chapter 1 at 5.2.6.

[78] See Chapter 2 at 2.5.3.

Costs

Unsurprisingly, price is considered to be a most decisive factor for consumer choice. Given that in synallagmatic contracts the amount of money paid is the consumer's exchange for the performance to be received, an agreement on the price will be an indispensable element of the contract itself. However, in practice, the consumer will not only be interested in the price of the performance itself, but in all the additional charges that come with the purchase of the performance, such as various taxes or delivery costs. The protection of making a decision 'in full knowledge of the facts' must therefore not be limited to guaranteeing price transparency, but it must concern cost transparency.

Community legislation clearly pursues this objective of cost transparency in virtually all of the examined directives. The fact that the costs accompanying the actual performance price vary considerably according to the respective sector and the purchase situation partly explains the vertical harmonisation approach. The quasi-horizontally harmonising Directive 98/6 (Unit Prices Directive) is an exception in this respect, which proves the importance attached to price. Directive 98/6 illustrates furthermore that the costs must not only be transparent, but that their indication has to serve comparison in the best possible way. This may be done by specifying 'selling price' and the 'unit price', as required by the Unit Prices Directive, or, in the case of the Consumer Credit Directive, by indicating the 'annual percentage rate of charge' and the 'total cost'. A choice made 'in full knowledge of the facts' does not only mean that the facts with regard to the respective performance are known, but that the entire deal has been assessed in the context of other possible deals.[79] Fair-trading legislation cannot accomplish this assessment,[80] but it aims at preparing it by facilitating comparison.

Contract

Similarly to the performance category, the information to be disclosed about the contract varies considerably according to different contracts. It may go so far that all the contractual terms and conditions have to be communicated before the consumer is bound the contract or offer.[81]

The extent to which Community-law pre-contractual information-duties influence the actual content of the contract, which is initially nationally determined, varies as well. The sometimes fairly dense information relating to essential elements of the contract (e.g. the performance) required prior to contract conclusion hardly leaves the content of the contract unaffected. As a matter

79 This is why, as a matter of principle, comparative advertising must not be prohibited. See *infra* at 5.4.

80 Although advisory duties, as required, for instance, in the insurance-mediation sector, come very close to assessing the deal for the consumer. See also *infra* at 5.2.3.2 regarding subjectively necessary information.

81 See Article 5(1) of Directive 2002/65.

of fact, the requirement of pre-contractual information can be regarded as a technique of the Community to govern the contract as such (in addition to the principal objective to enable consumers to make their choice in full knowledge of the facts). Article 3(2) of Directive 94/47 makes this concept very clear by stating explicitly that certain pre-contractual information 'forms an integral part of the contract'.

Besides, the existing information duties are closely related to the regulated marketing and communication method. The E-Commerce Directive, for instance, establishes information requirements relating to the different technical steps necessary for concluding a contract and relating to the technical means for identifying and correcting input errors prior to the placing of the order.[82]

Finally, ancillary information that comes with the performance of a contract, such as information relating to the processing of the consumer's personal data, must also be disclosed to the consumer. Information relating to the consumers' privacy is thus also recognised to potentially influence their economic choice.

Remedies

To this category belongs information on contractual remedies, such as the existence of a right of withdrawal, as well as information on the existence of judicial or out-of-court complaint and redress mechanisms. Although enforcement is far less developed in Community legislation than the substantive rules which are to be enforced, basic information about existing enforcement possibilities is usually required.

5.2.3.2 Subjectively necessary information

Of course, there is also a subjective point of view with regard to 'necessary' information. *Belgian Notification Numbers*, which has been cited as a confirmation of objectively necessary information, applies equally to the subjective aspect. If the basic facts consumers must know are those which enable them to make a qualified decision for or against a product and to decide in which quantity they wish to consume this product,[83] this might differ from consumer to consumer. Not every consumer will base their choice on the same facts, or, at least, different consumers may attach different importance to the various facts. The reasons for this may vary from simple personal preferences to varying individual capacities. The Court has recognised in *German Beer* that personal preferences could be decisive in determining what information was necessary to make a 'choice in full knowledge of the facts'. It has acknowledged that it was legitimate to seek to enable consumers who attribute specific qualities to beers manufactured from particular raw materials to make their choice in the light

[82] Article 10 of Directive 2000/31.

[83] Case C-217/99 *Commission v Belgium ('Belgian Notification Numbers')* [2000] ECR I-10251 at 26.

of that consideration.[84] However, that information was considered to be of an additional nature. The provision of the relevant information was not obligatory, but optional.

That the amount and quality of the subjectively necessary information is flexible and depends on external factors can be seen in *Buet*. The Court not only held that the necessity of the degree of protection may vary according to the situation consumers find themselves in (doorstep selling in the case), but that the consequences of the contractual engagement could influence the need for protection.[85] The consequences of a contract, however, may vary for each individual consumer so that prior information must also individually be adapted. However, for a generally applicable concept, not every potential individual consequence can be taken into account. This problem is solved by the adaptation of the consumer yardstick. If particular groups of consumers are concerned by the commercial communication the average member of this group has to be taken into account.[86]

In secondary law, subjectively necessary information is likewise recognised and mainly reflected by advisory duties in the sectors of investment services and insurance mediation.[87] The idea is also incorporated in the Proposal for a new directive on consumer credit.

According to Article 19 of the new Directive 2004/39 on investment services, when providing investment services to clients, an investment firm must act honestly, fairly and professionally in accordance with the best interests of its clients.[88] This obligation plainly hints at the fact that the relevance of the information to be disclosed is determined (also) from the subjective point of view of the clients. Otherwise it would not be in their interest. The Directive provides more precisely that the investment firm must obtain the necessary information regarding the clients' knowledge and experience in the investment field relevant to the specific type of product or service, their financial situation and their investment objectives so as to enable the firm to recommend to the clients the investment services and financial instruments that are suitable for them. In case the investment firm considers, on the basis of the information received,

---

84 Case 178/84 *Commission v Germany ('German Beer')* [1987] ECR 1227 at 35.

85 Case 382/87 *R. Buet and Educational Business Services (EBS) v Ministère public* [1989] ECR 1235 at 14. According to the Court, the purchase of unsuitable or low-quality educational material could compromise the consumers' chances of obtaining further training and thus consolidating their position on the labour market.

86 In *Buet* at 13 the standard was a 'category of people who, for one reason or another, are behind with their education and are seeking to catch up'.

87 Case C-322/01 *Deutscher Apothekerverband e.V. v 0800 DocMorris NV and Jacques Waterval* [2003] ECR I-nyr at 106, 113 recognises, as a matter of principle, a need for individual advice also in connection with medicinal products.

88 See Chapter 2 at 2.5.3.6. See furthermore Grundmann, (2003) 14 *EBLR* 237 at 251 et seq.

that the product or service is not appropriate to the clients, the investment firm has to warn them. It must also warn the clients if they decide not to provide the information needed to determine whether the service or product envisaged is appropriate for them.

Article 12 of Directive 2002/92 on insurance mediation specifies that for 'advice given on the basis of a fair analysis' the insurance intermediary is obliged to give advice which insurance contract would be adequate to meet the customer's needs.[89] The insurance intermediary must specify the demands and the needs of that customer as well as the underlying reasons for any advice given to the customer on a given insurance product, prior to the conclusion of any specific contract. However, the sector of insurance mediation shows that subjectively necessary information is related to the performance itself. The performance in insurance mediation is not the provision of a (standard) insurance, but it is a service which consists in finding the best suitable insurance for the consumer. This is impossible without taking into account the personal preferences and providing information which is related to them.

The concept of 'responsible lending' of Article 9 of the Proposal for a new Directive on consumer credit implies that the creditor shall seek to establish, among the credit agreements they usually offer or arrange, the most appropriate type and total amount of credit taking into account the financial situation of the consumer, the advantages and disadvantages associated with the product proposed, and the purpose of the credit.[90] This means that next to the information particulars required in general it is considered necessary that consumers be provided with information according to their personal needs.

In conclusion, there is a recognition of subjectively necessary information which must be disclosed, however this is less developed than duties regarding objectively necessary information. The reason for this is that individual choices can be based on objectively necessary information. The idea that objectively necessary information must comprise everything which enables consumers to make their choice in full knowledge of the facts implies that it provides consumers with the facts they need for their personal choice. The choice itself is subjective of course, but the consumers are free to disregard some objectively necessary particulars, while they take others more into account. This becomes evident with regard to the food sector, where the personal preferences usually differ tremendously. The idea is to provide for a high level of information disclosure in general, which meets the various conceivable personal information necessities, but which can then be processed according to individual preferences. Consumers who attribute specific qualities to certain products are then enabled to make their choice in the light of that consideration.[91] It is therefore an objective neces-

89 See Chapter 2 at 2.5.3.7.

90 See Chapter 2 at 2.5.3.5.

91 Cf. Case C-51/94 *Commission v Germany ('Sauce hollandaise')* [1995] ECR I-3599 at 36, Case 407/85 *3 Glocken GmbH and Gertraud Kritzinger v USL Centro-Sud and Provincia autonoma di Bolzano* [1988] ECR 4233 at 16.

sity to identify genetically modified food as such, independent of whether this is a subjective necessity for every individual consumer. It is sufficient that individual consumers are enabled to use objectively necessary information in order to relate it to their subjective preferences. Moreover, this approach meets the necessities of the functioning of a mass-production market, which cannot adapt the information for each product for each individual consumer.

5.2.3.3 Unnecessary information

It has been demonstrated that the idea of 'full' knowledge of the facts implies that consumers must have all the information at their disposal which they objectively, and in part subjectively, 'need' to make their choice. On the other hand, an overflow of information can be counterproductive for making a choice, since too much or irrelevant information can considerably hamper the recognition and processing of the necessary facts.[92] Due to limited capacities of processing information and selective perception, the flow of information can only be handled to a certain extent.[93] It could be said that too much information is equal to too little or no information.

Community law, however, does not address this problem from the point of view of amount of information. The directives containing information duties actually do not set limits to the disclosure of information, neither in quantity nor in quality. As minimum harmonisation directives they even allow Member States to exceed their requirements, certainly regarding quantity. Yet, the idea that not every piece of information is useful for making a choice, or that it can even be counterproductive, is not totally ignored. Rather it is approached from different viewpoints. First, the overflow of information makes it more complex and less comprehensible. Therefore simplification of information is required.[94] Second, where too much and/or unnecessary information hinders the processing of the relevant information consumers are not 'enabled' to make their choice.[95]

5.2.4 Comprehensibility

'Full knowledge' implies not only 'full amount of (necessary) information', but also the 'full understanding' of it. Therefore, the information must be provided in a clear and comprehensible manner, appropriate to the

[92] See Niemöller, *Verbraucherleitbild*, p. 16, who adds that consumers tend to make choices without too high a cognitive effort, i.e. they are deliberately doing without information in exchange for a simplified and efficient decision-making process. Cf. also Micklitz/Keßler (2002) 51 *GRUR Int.* 885 at 890.

[93] See Noah, (1994) 11 *YJR* 293 at 374 et seq. with regard to the overuse of warnings on labels.

[94] See *infra* at 5.2.4.1.

[95] See *infra* at 6.

means of communication used.[96] Article 4(2) of Directive 97/7 and Article 3(2) of Directive 2002/65 additionally require the disclosure of the information to respect the 'principles of good faith in commercial transactions', which alludes to a flexible understanding of what might be necessary for comprehension in different contexts.

Information simplification is the first aspect of achieving comprehensibility to be examined. Secondly, language requirements will be analysed. This analysis will demonstrate that language is considered to be just one of many conceivable means to convey information. Information comprehensibility is actually in itself the ultimate objective.

5.2.4.1 Information simplification

The achievement of utmost comprehensibility works in two ways, namely taking into account the quality of the information on the one hand, and the characteristics of the recipient on the other hand. The latter aspect, however, is more related to intellectual capabilities of certain types of consumers (e.g. minors) and how they can be 'enabled' to make their choice; it will therefore be discussed separately.[97]

The more complicated information is, the more simplification it needs so that it can be absorbed best by the consumer, i.e. that the latter can really acquire the necessary 'knowledge'. Research concerning labels has shown that consumers are more likely to read and understand labels that are clear and concise, while too detailed a product information may lead consumers to disregard the label completely, or at least cause them much difficulties to sort the information according to importance.[98] While aspects of information simplification can be found in various directives, the Unit Prices Directive and the Consumer Credit Directive are suited best for an illustration.[99] By requiring the indication of the 'selling price' and the 'unit price' the Unit Prices Directive groups a multitude of information details into an easily comprehensible statement on which consumers can base their decision. The Consumer Credit Directive does the same with the requirement of the indication of the 'annual percentage rate of charge' and the 'total cost'.[100] These examples show that information comprehensibility is not only for the benefit of the individual product it refers to, but its further merit is that it enables consumers to compare the product with others of the same type.

---

96 E.g. Article 3(2) of Directive 90/314, Article 4(2) of Directive 97/7, Article 10(1) of Directive 2000/31, Article 56 of Directive 2001/83, Article 3(2) of Directive 2002/65, Article 13 of Directive 2002/92.

97 See *infra* at 6.4. This is an example of how strongly interwoven the elements of the general principle of fair trading are and how dense this principle is.

98 Golan/Kuchler/Mitchell/Greene/Jessup, (2001) 24 *JCP* 117 at 139 et seq.

99 See Chapter 2 at 2.4 and at 2.5.3.5.

100 See also Grundmann, (2002) 39 *CML Rev.* 269 at 287.

5.2.4.2 Language

The language used for transmitting the information may be one of the first things that come to one's mind when thinking about the comprehensibility of information. It is all the more striking that secondary law rarely deals with this aspect and regards it as a matter for the Member States, as is expressed by the eighth recital of Directive 97/7.[101]

On the other hand, as an exception several of the product-sector instruments do address language, such as the General Foodstuffs Labelling Directive 2000/13. Its Article 16(1) requires the Member States to ensure that the sale of foodstuffs is prohibited where the particulars do not appear in a language easily understood by the consumer, unless the consumer is in fact informed by means of other measures as regards one or more labelling particulars. On the basis of the Foodstuffs Directive the Court has developed its *Piageme* case law.[102] This case law is fairly restrictive regarding a right of consumers to their own language.[103] According to the *Piageme* doctrine the comprehensibility of information is not understood as being linked to the language used, but it can be achieved by other effective measures taken to convey the information (e.g. designs, symbols or pictograms). The Court has applied the *Piageme* doctrine analogously in the context of Directive 76/768 on the labelling of cosmetic products, which also deals with the language aspect.[104]

The crucial idea remains that consumers must be enabled to make their choice in full knowledge of the facts. Full knowledge requires comprehensible information. It is thus decisive for fair trading that comprehensibility is achieved, but it does not matter by which means. The use of language, and in particular the use of the consumer's own language, is just one of many conceivable means of transmission of comprehensible information.[105]

At first sight, other directives might seem to clash with the aforesaid. Directive 2001/83 relating to medicinal products for human use requires many particulars for labelling to appear in the official language or languages of the Member State where the product is placed on the market (Article 63). Contrary to the sectors of foodstuffs and cosmetic products symbols or pictograms may only assume a supplementary function (Article 62). Directive 2001/37 concerning the manufacture, presentation and sale of tobacco products requires health

---

[101] See also Kraus in Schulze/Ebers/Grigoleit, *Informationspflichten*, p. 29 at 41 et seq., Micklitz, (2003) 11 *ZEuP* 635 at 640 et seq.

[102] Case C-369/89 *Piageme and others v BVBA Peeters* [1991] ECR I-2971 and Case C-85/94 *Piageme and others v Peeters NV* [1995] ECR I-2955. For a broad analysis including related and subsequent case law, see Chapter 2 at 2.5.3.1.

[103] See Micklitz, (2003) 11 *ZEuP* 635 at 644 et seq.

[104] See Case C-169/99 *Hans Schwarzkopf GmbH & Co. KG v Zentrale zur Bekämpfung unlauteren Wettbewerbs e.V.* [2001] ECR I-5901.

[105] In the same way Rott, (1999) 98 *ZVglRWiss* 382 at 403.

warnings to be printed in the official language or languages of the Member State where the product is placed on the market (Article 5). Directive 2002/92 on insurance mediation provides that the information has to be given to the customer in an official language of the Member State of the commitment or in any other language agreed by the parties (Article 13). Timeshare contracts and the related information document have to be drawn up in the language or one of the languages of the Member State in which the purchaser is resident or in the language or one of the languages of the Member State of which he is national, according to Article 4 of Directive 94/47.[106] Under Directive 2003/71 the summary of the prospectus to be published when securities are offered may have to be drawn up in the official language of the Member State where the consumer resides (Article 19).

However, also these rules feature comprehensibility as the guiding fundamental principle. It has simply been deemed that this can only be sufficiently achieved by the use of a particular language, because other means are not able to convey the same information effectively. The obligation of the use of a particular language thus reflects the judgment of the legislator that this is the only means in certain circumstances which can guarantee sufficient comprehensibility. The Court has confirmed this prerogative of the legislator to determine the means for comprehensibility in *Meyhui*. Where the information is not easily discernible for the average consumer it is necessary for him to be given the clearest information possible as to what he is buying (it may be added that the same applies to the information relating to under which terms he is buying it). In the case the prescription of the language to use was therefore not considered disproportionate to the goal pursued.[107]

5.3 The duty not to mislead

It is obvious that consumers are not enabled to make their choice in full knowledge of the facts, if they are provided with untrue information, or if other circumstances cause a misconception which would be the basis for their decision. The obligation not to provide the consumer with incorrect information or not to create a misconception in another way is therefore a core element of the Community concept of fair trading. In addition to the positive concept of providing the consumer with 'adequate information' there is thus the complementing negative concept requiring the consumer not to be provided with 'inadequate information'.[108]

[106] Directive 1999/44/EC on certain aspects of the sale of consumer goods and associated guarantees, OJ 1999 L 171/12 features a similar requirement in Article 6 concerning guarantees.

[107] Case C-51/93 *Meyhui NV v Schott Zwiesel Glaswerke AG* [1994] ECR I-3879 at 18–20. The case concerned the compatibility of Directive 69/493 relating to crystal glass with Article 28 of the Treaty.

[108] See Bernitz in Balate, *Unfair advertising*, p. 53 at p. 63 for the use of the terms 'adequate information' and 'inadequate information'.

In fact, the prohibition of misleading advertising is a sub-principle to the principle of fair trading. The vast majority of practices hindering consumers to make their choice in full knowledge of the facts come under this category. It has also been pronounced by Community law as a general concept in Directive 84/450, which is an instrument of horizontal harmonisation and undoubtedly the central measure protecting from misleading advertising.[109]

Article 2 of Directive 84/450 prohibits 'advertising which in any way, including its presentation, deceives or is likely to deceive the persons to whom it is addressed or whom it reaches and which, by reason of its deceptive nature, is likely to affect their economic behaviour'. The prohibition of misleading advertising has been repeated in sectoral harmonisation directives.[110]

As advertising is regarded as a device for the cross-border promotion of goods and services, a general prohibition of a particular way of advertising may seriously impede free movement. Therefore, the Court has interpreted misleading advertising restrictively. In *Nissan* the Court moreover underlined that the potential influence of the communication on the consumer's economic behaviour was necessary for advertising to be considered misleading.[111] This confirms that the ban on misleading advertising aims at protecting consumers from being wrongfully influenced in making their economic choice in full knowledge of the facts. The Court has pointed out in the same judgment that the disclosure of true facts may not in itself be misleading.[112] This analysis coincides with the Court's view adopted in free-movement case law. In response to the German fair-trading legislation, according to which 'eye-catching' price comparisons were supposed to bear the risk of misleading consumers, the Court held in *Yves Rocher* that the disclosure of correct information could not be misleading by definition, but rather was of considerable use in that it enabled consumers to make their choice in full knowledge of the facts.[113]

5.4 The approval of disclosing correct information

The obligation to disclose objectively and subjectively necessary information on the one hand, and the obligation not to mislead in disclosing information on the other hand, are complemented by the general approval to disclose information as long as it is correct. This third line is represented by the rules on comparative advertising.

---

109 See the detailed analysis in Chapter 2 at 2.3.

110 Cf. e.g. Article 6(3) of Directive 76/768, Article 3 of Directive 87/102, Article 3(1) of Directive 90/314, Article 2 of Directive 2000/13, Article 87 of Directive 2001/83.

111 Case C-373/90 *Criminal proceedings against X ('Nissan')* [1992] ECR I-131 at 16. See also Chapter 1 at 5.3.3.

112 *Nissan* at 17.

113 Case C-126/91 *Schutzverband gegen Unwesen in der Wirtschaft e.V. v Yves Rocher GmbH* [1993] ECR I-2361 at 17.

Directive 84/450 as amended by Directive 97/55 is the central Community instrument to set the framework for comparative advertising on the basis of maximum harmonisation.[114] The basic idea is that comparative advertising must be permitted as long as it is based on correct facts.[115] These facts constitute the source for consumers to make an informed choice and therefore enable them to make the best possible use of the Internal Market.[116] Comparative advertising does not mean that the advertising itself has to compare, but it suffices if it provides the facts for the consumer to compare, as the Court held in *Toshiba*.[117] This has also been expressed in free-movement case law. In *Yves Rocher* the Court held that correct (price) comparisons may not be prohibited in the name of fair trading as being misleading, because they actually were useful for the consumer to make an informed choice.[118] The disclosure of correct information thus enables consumers to make their choice in full knowledge of the facts.

6 Being enabled to make a choice

It has been argued that the concentration of Community consumer-protection law on information has only been possible because the underlying image of the consumer is that of a 'strong' one, while national laws fill the gap and also protect the 'weak' consumer.[119] It is true that it is assumed at Community level that consumers are, in principle, able to deal with information. However, it is submitted, that this results from the very nature of the human being as communicative creature. Also 'vulnerable' consumers ultimately base their economic decisions on information. The crucial question is therefore rather whether and to what extent Community law creates the framework for consumers to be able to cope with the information they are faced with.[120] This implies that quality standards have to be applied to the information and to the circumstances in which it is disclosed. In this respect it can be established that the Community does not only enable strong consumers to make their choices, but it does very well take care of weaker types of consumers as well, in that it aims at ensuring that information can be understood and adequately processed by them.

---

114 See the detailed analysis in Chapter 2 at 2.3. Cf. also Case C-44/01 *Pippig Augenoptik GmbH & Co. KG v Hartlauer Handelsgesellschaft mbH* [2003] ECR I-3095 at 44.

115 Restrictions to comparative advertising are made e.g. where it creates confusion or results in denigration. See the requirements for comparative advertising as defined in Article 3a(1) of Directive 84/450.

116 *Pippig Augenoptik* at 64.

117 Case C-112/99 *Toshiba Europe GmbH v Katun Germany GmbH* [2001] ECR I-7945 at 39 et seq.

118 Case C-126/91 *Schutzverband gegen Unwesen in der Wirtschaft e.V. v Yves Rocher GmbH* [1993] ECR I-2361 at 17. See Evrard, (1993) 1 *JTDE* 11 at 11.

119 Howells/Wilhelmsson, (2003) 28 *E.L.Rev.* 370 at 382.

120 Cf. also Micklitz in Krämer/Micklitz/Tonner, *Law and diffuse interests*, p. 245 at p. 264.

6.1 Rationality of the information

Whether consumers are enabled to make their choice in full knowledge of the facts largely depends on the facts themselves. This aspect has earlier been captured under 'recognisability', 'correctness' and 'comprehensiveness' of the information.[121] Those qualities of the information are mainly responsible for providing the consumer with 'full knowledge'. There is, however, another aspect to the nature of the information – the rationality of information – which is more responsible for 'enabling consumers to make their choice'. The idea is that consumers are only able to process adequately the information they are given, if the information does not distract them by irrational content.

This approach allows the explanation of public-interest motivated provisions by an information-oriented rationale. The prototype of such a rule is Article 12 of the Television Directive, according to which advertising shall not

'(a) prejudice respect for human dignity;
(b) include any discrimination on grounds of race, sex or nationality;
(c) be offensive to religious or political beliefs;
(d) encourage behaviour prejudicial to health or to safety;
(e) encourage behaviour prejudicial to the protection of the environment'.

It has been suggested that this concerns 'unwanted' trading in the name of public interest, rather than a restriction of consumers' abilities to act autonomously.[122] However, irrational commercial communication which disrespects values and addresses emotions also has the effect of distracting consumers from making their choice, instead of enabling them to do so. This kind of irrational information distorts the perception of decisive rational information and thereby causes intransparency.[123] Bearing in mind that the creation of optimal circumstances for consumer choice is at the centre of fair trading,[124] rules banning distracting commercial communication can be understood as economically motivated and relating to fair trading.

This approach is confirmed by Article 15 of the Television Directive, which deals with alcohol advertising. Alcohol advertising on television is not prohibited, but it must comply with certain criteria, such as not linking the consumption of alcohol to enhanced physical performance or sexual success. These

---

[121] See *supra* at 5.2.

[122] Keßler/Micklitz, *Harmonisierung des Lauterkeitsrechts*, p. 70 et seq, Micklitz/Keßler, (2003) 49 *WRP* 919 at 922, who admit, however, that the exact delimitation of 'unwanted' from 'unfair' trading is not always possible.

[123] See Kroeber-Riel/Weinberg, *Konsumentenverhalten*, p. 238 et seq. for how emotions can determine consumer behaviour.

[124] On the Community goal of consumer choice by informing consumers, see also Reich, (1994) 2 *ZEuP* 381 at 387.

and other criteria are to avoid any distraction from the objective information on the alcoholic product, since the consumer would otherwise be influenced or hindered in the rational processing of the information. The rules on alcohol advertising are thus strongly related to the information-based fair-trading reasoning, which supersedes a possible public-interest motivation.

On the other hand, it must be pointed out that there are clearly limits to a purely information-based explanation of public-interest rules. Claiming that, for instance, the prohibition of any discrimination on grounds of race, sex or nationality was solely aimed at not distracting consumers from making economic choices would reduce the obviously represented ethical values to a purely economic meaning.[125] This would be incompatible with the values professed in Article 13 of the Treaty and with other clear statements in this regard.[126] It can therefore be concluded that the category of public-interest related rules is of a hybrid nature, serving objectives of both fair and 'unwanted' trading.

The category of 'unwanted' trading does certainly fit the prohibition of tobacco advertising in certain media. Tobacco advertising is prohibited in television under the Television Directive and in printed media, radio broadcasting and information society services under Directive 2003/33.[127] The prohibition of tobacco advertising (in specific sectors) adds nothing to enable or not to enable consumers to make a choice in full knowledge of the facts. It rather conceals facts which could be the basis for a consumer choice. It thus falls outside the system of fair trading as ascertained here. Tobacco advertising could, however, be considered 'unwanted' trading in the name of health protection. The same holds true for large-scales lotteries, if their prohibition is understood as unwanted for the 'maintenance of order in society'.[128] In the end, total prohibitions of commercial communication can hardly be in line with the concept of (fair) trading in general, but rather serve other interests.

---

125 Accordingly, Howells/Wilhelmsson, (1997) 17 *YEL* 207 at 258 understand Article 12 of the Television Directive to 'concern the effects of advertising on the development of our social values in general'.

126 E.g. Council Recommendation on the development of the competitiveness of the European audiovisual and information services industry by promoting national frameworks aimed at achieving a comparable and effective level of protection of minors and human dignity (98/560/EC), OJ 1998 L 270/48. See also the Second Evaluation Report on the application of Council Recommendation of 24 September 1998 concerning the protection of minors and human dignity, COM (2003) 776 final.

127 At this point the discussion on the legality of the prohibitions need not be reiterated. It should be remembered, however, that total prohibitions in the name of promoting the functioning of the Internal Market are problematic. Cf. Case C-376/98 *Germany v Parliament and Council ('Tobacco Advertising')* [2000] ECR I-8419 at 95 et seq.

128 See Chapter 1 at 5.2.7.

6.2 Adequate decision-making circumstances

6.2.1 Neutrality of the situation of information disclosure

For the consumer being able to make an informed choice, not only must the information be objective, but also the situation in which the information is disclosed should be as neutral as possible.[129] Unlike misleading advertising, which can also be caused by a misleading situation, what is meant by neutrality of the situation is not dependent on a misconception in the consumer's mind, but rather consists in the prevention of uncomfortable or inadequate decision-making circumstances. The less uncomfortable those circumstances are, the less disturbed the consumer will be in processing the information. This is necessary for consumers to make a decision according to their preferences, otherwise their behaviour would be irrational.[130]

Illustration: the right of cancellation in Directive 85/577

Community law does not positively prescribe such a neutral situation, but with the right of cancellation as realised in the Doorstep-Selling Directive it has introduced a concept which is to remedy an inadequate decision-making situation. The reasons for the right of cancellation, which is definitely the focal point of Directive 85/577, are alluded to in its fourth recital. There it is stated that in the context of doorstep-selling the consumer is unprepared and unable to compare the quality and price of the offer with other offers. Also the mental pressure resulting from somebody intruding into the consumers' private sphere and persuading them to enter into a contract at the doorstep has been mentioned.[131]

The lack of choice is an obvious problem of information deficiency. Analogous to the situation in cold calling, consumers face a restriction in comparing other offers, which hinders them to make a choice in full knowledge of the facts.[132] The right of cancellation allows consumers to compare other offers afterwards and be released from the contractual bond, if they have found an offer that better matches their preferences.

However, economically speaking and taking into account that the Directive is an instrument adopted in the name of the Internal Market, the protection of consumers of being caught unawares or put under mental pressure is less likely a purpose of the Directive, at least it can be expressed differently. The crucial issue in these situations (and thus the actually underlying purpose of

---

[129] For context-dependence in legal decision making, see Kelman/Rottenstreich/Tversky in Sunstein, *Behavioral Law*, p. 61.

[130] Cf. Rekaiti/Van den Bergh, (2000) 23 *JCP* 371 at 375.

[131] Howells/Wilhelmsson, *Consumer Law*, p. 167.

[132] See Case C-384/93 *Alpine Investments BV v Minister van Financiën* [1995] ECR I-1141 at 46.

protection) is that consumers do not find themselves in circumstances which are adequate for making a choice in full knowledge of the facts, because in an uncomfortable situation they cannot properly process the information they are faced with and may therefore come to wrong conclusions.[133] The right of cancellation is to enable consumers to correct the consequences of their potentially wrong conclusions.[134] The system does only work properly, of course, if it is guaranteed that the consumers are informed about their right of cancellation and that its execution is not attached to obstacles. This is why the Directive stresses the giving notice of the right of cancellation and the Court defends a simple method of execution.[135]

Consequently, the right of cancellation guaranteed in the Doorstep-Selling Directive can entirely be explained as a remedy for inadequate circumstances for information processing.[136] The right of cancellation is adequate to cure such a failure, since it allows the consumer to be released from any obligations under the contract.

6.2.2 Sufficient deliberation time

It is obvious that consumers must have sufficient time to consider the received information adequately and to compare it to their preferences in order to be able to make their choice. Community law offers solutions prior to the conclusion of the contract and subsequent to the conclusion of the contract.

Proactive approach

This particular aspect of 'enabling' consumers to make their choice is mentioned in Article 4(1) of Directive 97/7, which requires detailed information consumers have to be provided with in 'good time prior to the conclusion of the contract'. The same idea is laid down in Article 3(1) and Article 5(1) of Directive 2002/65, where the communication of the information has to happen in 'good time before the consumer is bound by any distance contract or offer'.

---

[133] That is to say the consumers may be unable to see all the implications of their act, Case C-45/96 *Bayerische Hypotheken- und Wechselbank AG v Edgard Dietzinger* [1998] ECR I-1199 at 19.

[134] Schwintowski, (2001) 12 *EWS* 201 at 208 legitimately draws attention to the fact that the right of cancellation can be misused by somebody to withdraw from his contractual obligation although he was perfectly able to make his choice in full knowledge of the facts in the concrete doorstep-selling situation. However, this argument rather concerns the efficacy of the right of cancellation (as the reactive approach as such) in relation to the goal pursued. The motivation for the right of cancellation – to remedy a situation which did not enable consumers to make their choice in full knowledge of the facts – remains valid.

[135] Case C-423/97 *Travel Vac SL v Manuel José Antelm Sanchis* [1999] ECR I-2195 at 50 et seq.

[136] The right of withdrawal in the Distance-Selling Directive is less aimed at curing inadequate circumstances for information processing than insufficient availability of information, see *supra* at 5.2.3.1.

The reason why the temporal aspect of enabling consumers to make their decision is explicitly regulated for distance-selling situations is to be found in the communication media used or in the moment the contract is concluded. The Internet allows consumers to be trapped in a binding contract by just a (accidental) click on a button, and confronting them with significant information when it is too late.[137] This is why Directive 2000/31 requires certain information to be shown even throughout the whole communication contact. But also in traditional mail-order business facts may not have been available in 'good time prior to the conclusion of the contract'. This is the case where a contract is concluded by the (distant) acceptance of an order made by the consumer, the latter later being bound by contractual terms he could not fully assess, because prior information was lacking.

Reactive approach

The Doorstep-Selling Directive, as a model piece of legislation for direct-communication situations, features a reactive solution. The acknowledged surprise effect of doorstep canvassing not only implies psychologically inadequate decision-making circumstances,[138] but also that the consumer lacks sufficient time to consider the information in a pressure situation before making a decision.[139] The right of cancellation is to remedy this situation by enabling consumers to free themselves from obligations which they could not consider sufficiently.

6.3 Preservation of consumer sovereignty

Fair trading requires that consumers remain the sovereign of the transactional decision making-process. Otherwise, they are not 'enabled' to make an autonomous choice but rather a choice is forced upon them. Although there is some overlapping with the aspect of adequate decision-making circumstances the preservation of consumer sovereignty forms a separate group of fair-trading components, since it not only indirectly influences the decision-making process by provoking irrational choices, but it directly interferes with the consumers' capacity to decide autonomously.

---

137 Cf. Salaün in Nihoul, *Telecommunications and broadcasting networks*, p. 103 at p. 113.

138 See *supra* at 6.2.1.

139 Cf. Loos (2003) 19 *TvC* 6 at 9. Loos seems to consider cooling-off periods in general as motivated by providing sufficient deliberation time. It is submitted, however, that the additional deliberation time is not always the reason for rights of withdrawal. As has been demonstrated *supra* at 5.2.3.1 the right of withdrawal in the context of distance selling is to compensate the impossibility to (physically) assess the quality of the performance prior to the conclusion of the contract, i.e. to remedy an environment of incomplete or asymmetric information which is caused by the distant nature of the transaction. The fact that the consumer is moreover given additional deliberation time is a welcome side-effect.

Inertia selling

The prohibition of unsolicited supply of goods or services (inertia selling) serves the preservation of consumer sovereignty. According to Article 9 of Directive 97/7 and Article 9 of Directive 2002/65, this practice is prohibited where the supply involves a demand for payment. This is to prevent the consumer from being put into a position of having made a choice (i.e. ordering a good or service), where such a choice has actually not been made. The rule is reinforced at the contract-law level, since the consumer has to be exempted from the provision of any consideration in cases of unsolicited supply, the absence of a response not constituting consent.

Unsolicited communication

Also the various opt-in and opt-out rules to be found in the context of unsolicited (and intrusive) communication (such as cold calling or email spamming)[140] can be explained by the objective to preserve consumer sovereignty. By the use of automated techniques the supplier may impose information on consumers at relatively low cost, which they have not chosen for. The imposed information may easily come along with imposed economic decisions, if the consumer is faced with persuasive selling techniques. Providing the consumer with the right to opt in or to opt out, the ultimate decision power is handed back to the consumer.

6.4 Capacity of the consumer to process the information

As a matter of principle, in Community law the consumer is deemed to be able to process information. This can be inferred from the multitude of information rules in secondary law and from the Court's general concept of the average consumer who is reasonably well informed and reasonably observant and circumspect.[141] This consumer image is actually a consequence of the structural conception of the Internal Market, in which consumers are allocated a decisive role, since they determine market action by their consumption choices.[142] This implies, in turn, that consumers must be in possession of the necessary information, and that they are able to deal with it.

Community law also takes account of the fact that not every consumer has the same intellectual capacity to process information in the same way. In the consumer image this aspect is taken into account by the fact that it is the average member of the commercial communication's target group who is taken as a reference. Minors are the prime example of consumers who are less capable of processing information and of making rational decisions.

---

[140] See Article 10 of Directive 97/7, Article 10 of Directive 2002/65, Article 7 of Directive 2000/31, Article 13 of Directive 2002/58.

[141] See *supra* at 3.2 for a more differentiated picture.

[142] Keßler/Micklitz, *Harmonisierung des Lauterkeitsrechts*, p. 45.

Generally speaking, secondary law has not much dealt with the aspect of consumer innate information processing capacity in its fair trading legislation. The Television Directive, however, has taken care of the particular group of minors and, as a matter of fact, thereby takes an exceptional position in Community legislation.[143] As a consequence the advertising provision concerning minors (Article 16 of the Television Directive) prohibits, *inter alia*, advertising which exploits the minors' inexperience or credulity. This and other rules are thus to 'enable' minors to make their choice by ensuring that the information they are confronted with takes account of their limited information processing capacity.

However, the fact that explicit rules on this aspect are scarce does not mean that less capable consumers would be more in danger of unfair trading. As a matter of fact, the basic principle that consumers must be enabled to make their choice in full knowledge of the facts, as well as its subcomponents (e.g. recognisability or comprehensibility of information), are always to be seen in connection with the image of the consumer. This assures that in the case of less capable consumers the requirements are always adapted to the average member of this group.

7 Concluding remarks

It has been demonstrated that the *acquis communautaire* includes a fully-fledged principle of fair trading, which requires that consumers must be enabled to make their choice in full knowledge of the facts. It is submitted that this principle, which has been developed by the Court of Justice in its free-movement case law, is the conceptual foundation of Community fair trading law as a whole.

The objective of the principle of fair trading is to guarantee autonomous consumer choice. The means to achieve this is the adequate availability and processing of information. This is the pivotal point of this principle and the explanatory key to fair trading with consumers. The crucial role of information is linked to the fact that market activity is a communicative process. The principle has to be seen in connection with the image of the consumer as developed by the European Court of Justice, which assumes the function of the necessary yardstick for the relation between information and information recipients. Although it contains negative elements, such as the prohibition of misleading advertising, the principle itself establishes a positive obligation, namely to adopt fair market behaviour.

[143] Article 90 of Directive 2001/83, which prohibits the advertising of medicinal products for human use directed exclusively or principally at children, is indeed another exceptional rule taking into account the incapacity of children to deal with complex information.

The ambit of the principle of fair trading will be examined separately in the following chapter. This will build the bridge between the principle's substantive link to market activity and its field of application in the Internal Market.

CHAPTER 4

The Ambit of the Principle of Fair Trading

1 Fair trading – a general principle of Community law?

1.1 Aligning the principle's substantive universality with the field of application

It has been demonstrated that the *acquis communautaire* comprises a general concept of fair trading – a principle of fair trading. According to the principle's substance, consumers must be enabled to make their choice in full knowledge of the facts. It has furthermore been illustrated that this principle underpins a wide variety of specific rules, which can be regarded as concrete expressions of this principle.

At the level of Community legislation a multitude of rules can be related to the principle of fair trading. This seems to create a very dense system of specific fair-trading rules, all linked by one principle. This density is misleading, however, as it concerns only the substance of the principle. The scope, by contrast, is most diffuse, given that the scopes of application of all these single secondary-law rules (linked to the scopes of the directives which comprise them) differ considerably.

In view of this, it is of major interest to establish to what extent the principle of fair trading is not only coherent and universal in its substance but also in its field of application. It is therefore to be examined whether and to what extent the universality of the principle's substance comes along with a universality in its scope of application. The question will therefore be asked whether the 'principle' of fair trading could be regarded as a 'general principle' of fair trading within the scope of Community law.

The answer to this question is not only of doctrinal interest. The particular significance of identifying the principle of fair trading as a 'general principle' within the sphere of Community law is rooted in the fact that as a general principle of law it is itself a source of law.[1] This implies consequences for the possibilities of invoking the principle of fair trading and the legality and interpretation of (future) legislation.

Bringing up the notion of a 'general principle of fair trading' in a Community law context raises the question whether and to what extent such a principle could rank as what is commonly known as a 'general principle of Community law'. Therefore the examination of the ambit of the principle of fair trading will start with casting some light on the notion of general principles of Community law and discussing whether and to what extent the principle of fair trading fits to this notion.

---

1 See Hartley, *Foundations*, p. 131, Kapteyn/VerLoren van Themaat, *Law of the European Communities*, 3rd ed., p. 79.

1.2 The notion of general principles of Community law

Definition of general principles of Community law

General principles of law are not defined as such in the EC Treaty. However, the Treaty expressly recognises general principles as a source of law in Article 288(2) in the context of the non-contractual liability of the Community. General principles of law are more obviously mentioned at Union level. According to Article 6(1) EU, the 'Union is founded on the principles of liberty, democracy, respect for human rights and fundamental freedoms, and the rule of law, principles which are common to the Member States'. The wording suggests that the named principles not only pre-existed this provision, but the Union itself. Article 6(2) EU requires the *Union* to respect fundamental rights, as guaranteed by the European Convention on Human Rights and as they result from the constitutional traditions common to the Member States, as general principles of *Community* law.

A universally valid definition of general principles of Community law is not obvious.[2] It is suggested that they are principles constituting the groundwork of the Community's legal order and incorporating fundamental values of the Community, which bind the Community and the Member States in the areas covered by Community law.[3] As a consequence, they assume a 'constitutional' rank and are a separate source of Community law, i.e. they belong to the 'law', the observation of which is to be ensured by the Court of Justice according to Article 220.[4] Where they are not explicitly to be found in the Treaty,[5] they come to life as soon as they are identified by the Court of Justice.[6] Although the Court has not always been very explanatory why principles are considered a general principle of Community law and where they are derived from,[7] it did point out

---

2 Brown/Jacobs/Kennedy, *Court of Justice*, p. 345.

3 See Tridimas, *General Principles*, p. 23.

4 Cf. Hartley, *Foundations*, p. 131, Tridimas, *General Principles*, p. 9 et seq.

5 On *lacunae* in the Treaty, see Herdegen in Bernitz/Nergelius, *General Principles*, p. 3 at p. 4 et seq. Some general principles of Community law have been incorporated in the Treaty after they had been recognised by the Court of Justice, such as proportionality in Article 5(3). Subsidiarity, by contrast, is a general principle of Community law, which has been created by its incorporation into the EC Treaty (by the Treaty of Maastricht).

6 Already the Court of Justice of the European Coal and Steel Community filled *lacunae*. In Joined Cases 7/56 and 3/57–7/57 *Algera et al. v Assembly* [1957] ECR 39 the Court was confronted with the question whether certain decisions of the Assembly of the ECSC could be revoked. As the Community legal order did not contain a coherent set of rules of administrative law, the Court resolved the problem by referring to the national legal systems of the Member States and extracting the generally accepted principles on that issue.

7 See e.g. Case 29/69 *Erich Stauder v City of Ulm - Sozialamt* [1969] ECR 419 at 7, where the Court took it for granted without further explanation that fundamental human rights are enshrined in the general principles of Community law, which are protected by the Court.

that it relies on them on the basis of its general judicial mandate under Article 220.[8]

Classifications of general principles of Community law

In the course of time various general principles of Community law have been spelled out by the Court in a pragmatic and eclectic way.[9] Different approaches have been taken by doctrine to classify them and thereby delineate the notion of general principles of Community law. One common way is to classify them according to their origin, another according to their subject matter.

The sources of general principles of Community law can effectively be traced down to two main origins:[10]

- principles common to the laws of the Member States (e.g. fundamental rights, legal certainty),[11]
- principles which derive from the distinct characteristics of the Community legal order (e.g. supremacy, direct effect, non-discrimination on grounds of nationality).

This shows that general principles of Community law can emerge from both the national and the Community level.[12] These are, as a matter of fact, all relevant spheres of law, which makes the source itself not a very helpful indicator whether a principle can be considered a general principle of Community law.[13]

---

8 E.g. Joined Cases C-46/93 and C-48/93 *Brasserie du Pêcheur SA v Germany and R. v Secretary of State for Transport, ex parte: Factortame Ltd et al.* [1996] ECR I-1029 at 27, see Herdegen in Bernitz/Nergelius, *General Principles*, p. 3 at p. 15.

9 Simon, *Système juridique*, p. 247.

10 See e.g. Arnull, *Court of Justice*, p. 190 et seq., Simon, *Système juridique*, p. 247 et seq., Tridimas, *General Principles*, p. 3.

11 Allusions to this category of principles can be found in Article 288(2) EC and Article 6(1) EU. It should be added that the Court not only examines the Member States' national laws but takes into account sources of international law to which the Member States adhere (such as the European Convention on Human Rights) in order to identify general principles of law. However, international treaties are considered as an expression of the general principles of law common to the laws of the Member States rather than a separate source. The situation is different, of course, if a principle of international law itself is to be identified, such as *pacta sunt servanda*, see Case C-162/96 *Racke v Hauptzollamt Mainz* [1998] ECR I-3655 at 46.

12 It should be noted that principles derived from those common to the Member States are then construed within the framework of the structure and objectives of the Community, Case 11/70 *Internationale Handelsgesellschaft mbH v Einfuhr- und Vorratsstelle für Getreide und Futtermittel* [1970] ECR 1125 at 4, see also Case 4/73 *J. Nold, Kohlen- und Baustoffgroßhandlung v Commission* [1974] ECR 491 at 14 and Case C-370/88 *Procurator Fiscal v Andrew Marshall* [1990] ECR I-4071 at 27.

13 Van Gerven, (2004) 41 *CML Rev.* 505 at 518 points out that general principles are in fact 'the result of a dialectical interaction, and cross-fertilization, between national laws and Community law'.

With Tridimas three types of general principles of Community law can be distinguished according to their subject matter:[14]

- principles which underlie the constitutional structure of the Community (i.e. principles which refer to the relationship between the Community and the Member States, such as the principle of primacy, the attribution of competences and subsidiarity),
- principles which derive from the rule of law and concern primarily the relationship between the individual and the Community or national authorities (such as equality and proportionality),
- principles of substantive Community law (such as those underlying the fundamental freedoms or specific Community policies).

1.3 Assessing the principle of fair trading

From a formalistic point of view, the question whether the principle of fair trading is a general principle of Community law might quite promptly be answered in the negative. The reason for this is that it is neither spelled out as one in the Treaty, nor has the Court yet recognised it as one. It is submitted, however, that such a formalistic approach ignores the actual impact of the principle of fair trading. The question must therefore more precisely be asked whether and to what extent the principle of fair trading assumes a role which factually puts it into the rank of a general principle of Community law.

As far as the source of the principle is concerned, the principle of fair trading could certainly assume the role of a general principle of Community law, since both the laws common to the Member States and Community law itself are recognised sources. As a matter of fact, however, the laws of the Member States can be ruled out as a (direct) source. Although it is true that fair trading is a principle which is one way or another recognised in all of the Member States,[15] the Court has not provided any signs of taking national laws as source of what it has developed as the principle of fair trading. It has rather used them as a starting point of its reasoning, but referred to concepts of Community law in order to establish the principle of fair trading as it did.[16]

Regarding the subject matter, fair trading is neither a concept which underlies the constitutional structure of the Community nor one which derives from the rule of law. It is submitted that, according to Tridimas' classification, fair trading is a principle of substantive law. It is in fact the elucidation of its relation

---

14 Tridimas, *General Principles*, p. 3.

15 It is suggested that even in legal systems which have no general clause an underlying principle of fair trading could be established following an inductive analysis of specific fair trading rules.

16 See *infra* at 2.1.2. Moreover the Court's conclusions on fair trading are usually quite different from those of the Member State.

to substantive law which allows to delineate the ambit of the principle of fair trading further.

Fair trading, by its very nature, concerns 'trading'. Trading, in turn, relates to economic activities, i.e. market actions. It is the concern of fair trading to provide a framework for fair market actions or fair market behaviour. This connection with market behaviour makes fair trading a principle relating to the Internal Market,[17] which is the central playing field for economic activities in the Community context.[18] It is therefore suggested that fair trading cannot play a role in matters not related to the Internal Market. This does not mean that fair trading may not at all concern non-economic areas. For instance, public health is – in principle – a non-economic issue. However, when it comes to the marketing of medicinal products fair trading comes into play (e.g. in the form of labelling rules). In such a case, where consumer choice is involved, there is a clear overlapping of the non-economic policy with the Internal Market.[19] It is in this sense that it can be maintained that in the Community context fair trading is always related to some extent to the Internal Market.

Having established this inherent link of fair trading to market activities, it becomes evident that the potential field of application of the principle of fair trading in the sphere of Community law is limited and necessarily related to the Internal Market. Considering the principle of fair trading in the context of general principles of Community law as a whole does not take into account this structurally limited relevance of fair trading. It seems therefore more reasonable to question whether and to what extent fair trading is a general principle of the Internal Market, since this is the area where it can conceptually play a role. In order to answer this question the relationship between fair trading and the Internal Market will be further examined.

2 Fair trading – a general principle of Internal Market law

It is submitted that the principle of fair trading is a general principle of Internal Market law. Its field of application thus matches that of Internal Market law itself. The validity of this suggestion will be demonstrated

17 See Chapter 3 at 4 and in particular at 4.2 for the link to the Internal Market from the substantive point of view.

18 Other major areas of economic activities are competition policy and international trade, which are outside the scope of this study.

19 It must be pointed out that public health is nowadays so tightly linked to economic activities that it has clearly been caught by Internal Market law in many respects. See e.g. Davies, (2002) 29 *LIEI* 27 on the relationship between healthcare systems and the free movement of services. Fair trading is thus just one facet of how actually non-economic interests are related to the Internal Market.

by legal considerations and by conceptual considerations relating to the function of the Internal Market.

2.1 Legal considerations

The general applicability of the principle of fair trading within the sphere of the Internal Market can be derived from indications in the case law of the Court and from indications in the Treaty.

2.1.1 The relevant legal sources

The scope of the principle of fair trading within Community law is inseparably linked to the scope of the legal source it is derived from. It must therefore be determined which legal sources can be taken into account in order to ascertain a general principle of fair trading in the Internal Market.

In the foregoing analysis, primary law and secondary law have been analysed together with the related case law of the Court in order to extract a substantive meaning of fair trading. In the context of primary law, the case law of the Court was in fact the predominant source. The scopes of application of these legal sources vary enormously. The general scope of application of the Treaty, 'the basic constitutional Charter'[20] of the European Community, is beyond doubt. The Court of Justice is charged by Article 220 to 'ensure that in the interpretation and application of this Treaty the law is observed'. The case law of the Court interpreting the Treaty must therefore be considered to be as influential as the Treaty itself, since it is an expression of the Treaty.[21] The situation is completely different as regards secondary law. Measures of secondary law have a limited scope of application. This results from the fact that the Community competence for adopting secondary law is limited (Article 5(1)) and that the legislature itself restricts the scope of application of the legislative measure.

The piecemeal approach in secondary fair-trading law perfectly reflects this phenomenon. The analysis has shown that the legal instruments concern a multitude of different sectors, i.e. they have very different scopes of application. For identifying the substance of the principle of fair trading this did not pose any problems. All the various provisions of Community legislation could be explained by the principle of fair trading, which has turned out to be the underlying general concept for them. At the same time the specific rules have given a concrete meaning to the general concept. More precisely, they have helped to understand the concrete facets of fair trading inherent in the principle which

---

[20] Case 294/83 *Parti écologiste 'Les Verts' v European Parliament* [1986] ECR 1339 at 23, see also Opinion 1/91 [1991] ECR I-6079 at 1.

[21] Even if the Court acts as a policy maker, it still bases its considerations on the Treaty, i.e. it gives expression to the Treaty. See Chapter 1 at 4.1.

are expressed by these rules. However, while all these rules complement each other at the substantive level, they do of course not add up to a universal scope of application. Legally speaking, the fact that the specific rules are expressions of one and the same underlying principle does obviously not denote that this principle multiplies their scopes of application. Each rule contained in a directive is only applicable within the scope of that directive.[22] It may be argued that the situation is slightly different in the case of the horizontally applicable Directive 84/450 and the quasi-horizontally applicable Directive 98/6. Indeed, the prohibition of misleading advertising, the approval of comparative advertising, and cost transparency can be regarded as widely applicable sub-concepts of the principle of fair trading. However, compared to the source of primary law also their scope is limited.

As a consequence, in order to determine how far the principle of fair trading reaches within Community law, it is the Treaty and the case law interpreting the Treaty that have to be taken into account. Secondary law cannot legally exceed the boundaries of primary law, neither in substance nor in scope.

As with the analysis regarding the substance of the principle of fair trading, the examination begins with the case law of the Court. It has developed the principle of fair trading, which is not explicitly to be found in the Treaty, and it is the best indicator for fair trading being a legal principle of the Internal Market. It is then to be considered which conclusions can be drawn from the Treaty as far as the ambit of the principle of fair trading is concerned.

2.1.2 Indications in the case law of the Court

The principle of fair trading as identified in its substance in the foregoing analysis has been developed by the Court of Justice in its free movement case law. Tracing the methodology of the Court's reasoning helps to draw conclusions as to the principle's scope according to the Court.

2.1.2.1 Starting point: fair trading as a national interest

Fair trading has been introduced by the Court as a legitimate mandatory requirement of public interest (usually as a set together with consumer protection), which can justify an obstacle to free movement under the

[22] This may be illustrated by the following example. Although the right of withdrawal in doorstep-sales can be explained by the general principle of fair trading in the same way as can the language requirements for the labelling of medicinal products, this signifies by no means that there is always a right of withdrawal in connection with the sale of medicinal products, or that doorstep sales must happen in the official language of the Member State where the doorstep is located. Nevertheless, both rules are implied substantively in the principle of fair trading and enable consumers to make their choice in full knowledge of the facts.

rule of reason. The Court thus acknowledges fair trading to be an interest which can legitimately impede free movement, which is the leading principle in the Internal Market according to Article 14(2). This implies that, from the Community law point of view, fair trading is regarded as an interest which is in principle equivalent to that of free movement. Of course, it depends on the outcome of the proportionality test which of the two interests prevails in the specific case. Nevertheless, it may be assumed that the interests which the Court puts on the scales are basically equivalent.

It might be tempting to conclude directly from the mere fact of the Court declaring fair trading a public interest which can justify derogations from the principle of free movement that fair trading is also, just like free movement itself, a general value of Community law. Although this reasoning may seem conclusive on the surface, it fails to take into account that, as a starting point, it is a national interest of fair trading which the Court accepts to obstruct free movement. Fair trading is considered a public interest, but one of national origin. Therefore, at first instance, two interests originating from different legal spheres are weighed against each other: the Community law interest of free movement and the national law interest of fair trading. At the very outset, it is therefore submitted, fair trading is not dealt with as a principle of Community law but as a national concept.

2.1.2.2 Fair trading redefined as a Community interest

As a second step, however, the national concept of fair trading has to meet the requirements of the Community law yardstick of proportionality in order to derogate free movement successfully.[23] Proportionality can thus be understood to serve as a catalyst by the help of which the concept of fair trading is elevated from the national to the Community level.[24] This suggestion is supported by two considerations.

The result of the proportionality test is spelled out narrowly and concretely

The first consideration accepts that, as a matter of principle, the interest of fair trading is dealt with by the Court as a national interest, which, however, is redefined at Community level. This happens by the application of the general principle of proportionality, according to which the national measure must be suitable for securing the attainment of the pursued objective and must not go beyond what is necessary in order to attain it.[25] In the case of fair trading, proportionality is spelled out as a very concrete condition, which is that consum-

---

[23] See also Chapter 1 at 4.2.2.

[24] Cf. in a broader context Amtenbrink in Nordhausen, *Entwicklungen*, p. 53 at 59.

[25] See Case C-55/94 *Reinhard Gebhard v Consiglio dell'Ordine degli Avvocati e Procuratori di Milano* [1995] ECR I-4165 at 37.

ers must be enabled to make their choice in full knowledge of the facts. National measures which do not meet this requirement are not justifiable. This requirement, which has been identified in the present study as the content of the principle of fair trading, is complemented by the yardstick of the consumer who is reasonably well informed and reasonably observant and circumspect, which results likewise from the application of the proportionality test.[26] It can be said that the Court thus specifies the conditions which the national measure must obey so concretely and narrowly that not much leeway is actually left where the national concept falls into the realm of Community law.[27]

This analysis is reinforced by the observation that the Court tends to go beyond its assigned function to decide on questions of law[28] and decides on questions of fact.[29] *Mars* serves as a good example here.[30] The Court brought up the yardstick of the reasonably circumspect consumer, according to which it had to be decided whether ice-cream bars bearing a "+10%" marking, which occupied more than 10% of the total surface area of the wrapping, were misleading in that the increase of the bars' substance was larger than that represented. This yardstick, which derives directly from the principle of proportionality, is to be understood as a normative standard against which a factual situation has to be measured.[31] However, it should be the national court which applies the legal standard to the facts of the individual case and decides whether reasonably circumspect consumers are misled. The Court of Justice did not allow this, but decided itself that reasonably circumspect consumers were not misled by the labelling in question.[32] It is obvious that, consequently, the national court's discretion is reduced to zero in such a case.[33]

In order for the originally national interest of fair trading to prevail over the Community interest of free movement, the margins are so tightly set by Community law that it actually defines fair trading in the sense of a proper Community interest.

---

26 Case C-220/98 *Estée Lauder Cosmetics GmbH & Co. OHG v Lancaster Group GmbH ('Lifting')* [2000] ECR I-117 at 28.

27 See also Gormley, (2001) 4 *Cam. YBELS* 167 at 168 note 7.

28 According to Article 220(1) of the Treaty, the Court is to ensure that the law is observed.

29 On this phenomenon Davies, *Nationality Discrimination*, p. 36 et seq.

30 Case C-470/93 *Verein gegen Unwesen in Handel und Gewerbe Köln e.V. v Mars GmbH* [1995] ECR I-1923. See Chapter 1 at 5.3.3.

31 See Chapter 3 at 3.2.

32 *Mars* at 24.

33 See the compelling reasoning of Davies, *Nationality Discrimination*, p. 38 that taking the division of jurisdiction on law and fact seriously would leave it open to the national judge to reject the Court's view on the facts without defying the supremacy of Community law.

The national interest is reconciled with the market integration objective

According to the second consideration, the weighing of free movement and fair trading against each other should not be reduced to a conflict of interests which results into one interest prevailing to the detriment of the other. Through the mechanism of proportionality the national interest of fair trading is rather translated into the respective Community interest by refining it with free-movement considerations. In case a national fair-trading measure is considered a justified obstacle to free movement, this does not mean that the purely national interest overcomes the Community interest. It actually means that the interest is compatible with the Community interest itself.[34] This redefinition of the interest of fair trading by the help of proportionality then makes it compatible with the market integration objective of Community law, an objective not taken account of in the original national interest.[35] The Court thus gives fair trading a Community law meaning and ultimately turns it into a Community concept which reflects an interest inherent in the Internal Market.

2.1.2.3 Comparison with the Court's reasoning regarding fundamental rights

It follows from the preceding reasoning that the Court accepts the derogation of free movement – a principle of substantive Community law – by fair trading – another principle of substantive Community law, namely of Internal Market law. Although this analysis may seem to depart from the traditional understanding that it is an overriding national interest which may justify obstacles to free movement, a comparison with the Court's reasoning regarding free movement and fundamental rights in *Familiapress* confirms that an originally national interest can coincide with a principle of Community law.[36]

According to Austrian law, the sale of periodicals inviting consumers to take part in prize draws was prohibited. Obviously, this was an obstacle to the free movement of periodicals legally marketed in other Member States (Germany in the case). The Court acknowledged, as it was argued by the Austrian Government, that the maintenance of press diversity constituted an overriding requirement justifying a restriction on free movement of goods. In the context of the proportionality test, the Court then emphasised that overriding requirements which are to justify obstacles to the free movement of goods must be interpreted in the light of the general principles of law and in particular of fundamental rights, freedom of expression as enshrined in Article 10 of the European

[34] Similarly Weatherill, *Consumer Law and Policy*, p. 41.

[35] On the function of proportionality to balance domestic interests with market integration, see Davies, (2003) 3 *ERA-Forum* 55 at 64.

[36] Case C-368/95 *Vereinigte Familiapress Zeitungsverlags- und vertriebs GmbH v Heinrich Bauer Verlag* [1997] ECR I-3689.

Convention on Human Rights being the relevant fundamental right.[37] What is actually remarkable about the judgment is that the Court pointed out at the same time with the acknowledgment of press diversity as a mandatory requirement of public interest, that is to say before the proportionality test, that

> '[s]uch diversity helps to safeguard freedom of expression, as protected by Article 10 of the European Convention on Human Rights and Fundamental Freedoms, which is one of the fundamental rights guaranteed by the Community legal order'.[38]

It is suggested that, right from the start, the Court has thus considered the public interest of maintenance of press diversity to be a direct constituent of freedom of expression as a general principle of Community law, rather than being a purely national interest. Consequently, it was a Community law interest which could justify derogations of another Community law interest.

Transferring this conclusion to the principle of fair trading, it can be established that it is perfectly compatible with the case law of the Court to regard fair trading as a Community law interest which can justify obstacles to free movement, which is another Community law interest.

2.1.3 Indications in the Treaty

Although the Treaty does not provide direct indications regarding the position of fair trading within Community law, conclusions can be drawn from the interrelationship between the Internal Market and consumer protection as set out in the Treaty.

In order to be able to establish a connection between the Internal Market and fair trading, it is furthermore necessary to shed light upon the interrelationship between fair trading and consumer protection. The latter relationship is not to be found in the Treaty, but it is set up by the Court interpreting the Treaty. The suggested reasoning is the following: if the Treaty relates consumer protection to the Internal Market (section 2.1.3.1), and if the Court, in its interpretation of the Treaty, relates fair trading to consumer protection (section 2.1.3.2), then fair trading is related to the Internal Market (section 2.1.3.3). The Court's definition of the relationship between fair trading and consumer protection thus replaces the missing (direct) link in the Treaty.

---

37 *Familiapress* at 24 et seq. See earlier Case C-260/89 *Elliniki Radiophonia Tiléorassi AE et al. v Dimotiki Etairia Pliroforissis et al. ('ERT')* [1991] ECR I-2925 at 43 et seq.

38 *Familiapress* at 18 with reference to Case C-353/89 *Commission v Netherlands* [1991] ECR I-4069 at 30 and Case C-148/91 *Vereniging Veronica Omroep Organisatie v Commissariaat voor de Media* [1993] ECR I-487 at 10.

2.1.3.1 Consumer protection inherent in the objective of the Internal Market

Article 3(1)(t), which provides that the activities of the Community shall include 'a contribution to the strengthening of consumer protection', does not suggest that great importance is attached to consumer protection compared to other objectives of the Treaty. In fact, consumer protection is not even labelled a Community 'policy' in Article 3.[39] However, Title XIV concerning consumer protection (which contains only Article 153) belongs to Part Three of the Treaty headed 'Community policies', which implies that consumer protection is indeed a Community policy.[40]

A closer look at the relevant legal bases for Community measures relating to consumer protection reveals an overlapping between the interest of consumer protection and that of the establishment and functioning of the Internal Market.[41] Fair trading is situated exactly in this overlapping area.

Article 95

In Article 95(1) the Treaty provides a general legal basis for the adoption of harmonisation measures which have as their object the establishment and functioning of the Internal Market. This legal competence is complemented by Article 95(3), which requires the Commission to take as a base a high level of protection in its proposals concerning certain public interests, among them consumer protection.[42]

As far as its function as a legal basis is concerned, Article 95 does not itself enlighten very much the relationship between the Internal Market objective and the public interest objectives. The question in this context is to what extent harmonisation measures with public interest objectives in the sense of Article 93(3) must aim at the establishment and functioning of the Internal Market in the sense of Article 93(1). The Court's judgment in *Tobacco Advertising* suggests a hierarchy among the objectives.[43] Accordingly, a measure to be

---

39 The issue of the environment, by contrast, which is often compared to that of consumer protection, is a Community 'policy', according to Article 3(1)(l). See in this context Wilhelmsson, (1998) 21 *JCP* 45, who suggests that the relationship between consumer protection and environmental protection is one conflict rather than one of harmony.

40 See Weatherill, *Consumer Law and Policy*, p. 36 on how the law of market integration is itself a form of (indirect) consumer policy .

41 See also Reich, (1999) 14 *VuR* 3 at 4 et seq.

42 Weatherill, *Consumer Law and Policy*, p. 18 draws attention to the textual limitations of Article 95(3). First, it is addressed to the Commission and not to the Council and the Parliament. Second, taking a high level of protection 'as a base' implies that the level may be lowered in the course of the legislation process. However, this does not change anything with regard to the relationship between the Internal Market and consumer protection as a matter of principle, which can be inferred from Article 95(3).

43 See the discussion in Chapter 2 at 1.1.

adopted under Article 95 may fulfil a public interest objective in the sense of Article 95(3) only as far as it serves the establishment and the functioning of the Internal Market.[44]

However, for the present purpose of determining the Treaty's general conception of the relationship between consumer protection and the Internal Market Article 95 is entirely clear. Article 95(3) is an unambiguous indication that, as a matter of principle, consumer protection and the Internal Market are objectives which overlap to some extent, albeit it is not explained to what extent or which issues exactly are covered by both objectives at the same time.[45] It can therefore be concluded that the Treaty recognises that the objective of the establishment and functioning of the Internal Market and the objective of consumer protection are at least partly congruent.

Although this is only an indicator for an overlapping of the Internal Market and consumer protection in the Treaty and not itself an evidence, it should be noted that, indeed, Community legislation concerning consumer protection in general and fair trading in particular is almost exclusively based on Article 95 (or, before, on Article 94 with its similar concept of the Common Market).[46] Moreover, in the Directives, consumer protection is frequently mentioned as a separate objective alongside that of the functioning of the Internal Market.

Article 153

Article 153 features consumer protection as a separate Community policy, providing an individual legal basis for Community measures for the attainment of consumer protection in Article 153(3)(b) in order to support, supplement or monitor the Member States' policies. As far as consumer protection 'in the context of the completion of the internal market' is concerned, however, Article 153(3)(a) refers to Article 95 as a legal basis for the adoption of harmonisation measures. The principal function of Article 153(3)(a) is thus to confirm that the interests of consumers are taken into account in the process of harmonisation in view of the Internal Market.[47] It is not clear whether Article 153(3)(a) and Article 153(3)(b) exclude each other, or whether they have overlapping scopes.[48] For

---

44 Cf. Case C-376/98 *Germany v Parliament and Council ('Tobacco Advertising')* [2000] ECR I-8419 at 88, see also Amtenbrink in Nordhausen, *Entwicklungen*, p. 53 at 65 and 67.

45 According to Reich in Wilhelmsson, *Critical Contract Law*, p. 55 at p. 64 'every rule on consumer protection has some, at least indirect or potential, connection with the functioning of the internal market'.

46 It is an indicator and not an evidence, because the legislation could be based on the wrong legal basis and be illegal. See also Chapter 2 at 1.1. See moreover Askham in Vaughan, *Law of the European Communities*, at paragraph 73 et seq.

47 Simon in Constantinesco/Kovar/Simon, *Traité*, p. 385 et seq.

48 In fact, measures based on either Article 153(3)(a)/Article 95 or on Article 153(3)(b) are to be adopted according to the co-decision procedure under Article 251. However, measures based on Article 153(3)(b) may be minimum harmonisation only (Article 153(5)), measures based on Article 95 may be derogated under Article 95(4), (5), (6), (10). See also Weatherill, *Consumer Law and Policy*, p. 27.

the present purposes it is sufficient, however, to ascertain that Article 153(3)(a) clearly relates consumer protection, at least partly, to the Internal Market.[49]

Besides, Article 153(2) provides that requirements of consumer protection must be taken into account in defining and implementing other Community policies and activities. Not only does Article 153(2) thus provide that consumer protection is to form a constituent part of the Internal Market as one of the principal Community policies, it actually associates consumer protection with the entire realm of Community law.[50]

Conclusion

It can be concluded that the Treaty establishes a close link between the Internal Market and consumer protection. Article 95(3) and Article 153(3)(a) indicate that consumer protection is regarded at least partly as a sub-concept of a functioning Internal Market. Moreover, Article 153(2) extends the objective of consumer protection to the Internal Market policy, and beyond that to other Community policies and activities.

2.1.3.2 Fair trading inherent in the objective of consumer protection

Given the link between the Internal Market and consumer protection, the establishment of a link between fair trading and consumer protection, as an intermediary step, would make it finally possible to confirm the connection between fair trading and the Internal Market. The Treaty does not provide this link explicitly. However, in Article 153(1) the protection of the economic interests of consumers is regarded as one of the means to ensure a high level of consumer protection. This allows to associate fair trading, which safeguards consumers' interests in their economic activities, with consumer protection in the sense of the Treaty.

Moreover, the link between fair trading and consumer protection can easily be inferred from the Court's line of reasoning in the interpretation of the Treaty's free movement provisions. It has been pointed out earlier that, in its review of national rules, the Court of Justice predominantly refers to fair trading and consumer protection as one common set of mandatory requirements of public interest when it comes to a possible justification of the national rule.[51] It is under

49 The interrelationship is also recognised by Weatherill in Grundmann/Kerber/Weatherill, *Party Autonomy*, p. 173 at p. 189, who points out, however, that, from a constitutional point of view, it is important that the two alternatives are demarcated from each other.

50 For a critical view on this provision, which in German is graphically called *Querschnittsklausel* (cross-section clause), see Dreher, (1997) 52 *JZ* 167 at 176, who condemns it for allocating too important a role to consumer protection in comparison with other Community policies.

51 See Chapter 1 at 4.2.1.

this common set of grounds of justification, sometimes under the ground of consumer protection alone, that the Court has developed, by means of the mechanism of proportionality, the concept that has been suggested as principle of fair trading. National rules which are found to restrict the free movement of goods and services can be justified, if they enable consumers to make their choice in full knowledge of the facts.[52] Fair trading is thus related to consumer protection. The difference to the national law concepts of consumer protection is, however, that the Community law concept of consumer protection is underpinned by a market-integration rationale.[53] This is the result of reconciling the national law interest with the Community law interest.

2.1.3.3 Consequence: fair trading inherent in the objective of the Internal Market

It has been demonstrated that the Treaty suggests an inseparable relationship between the objective of a functioning Internal Market and the objective of consumer protection on the one hand, and between fair trading and consumer protection on the other hand. This finally allows to establish a positive link between the objective of a functioning Internal Market and fair trading. According to the Treaty and the case law of the Court of Justice interpreting the Treaty, fair trading is a concept inherent in the objective of a properly functioning Internal Market.

It can be said that fair trading constitutes the intersection of the objectives of a functioning Internal Market and consumer protection. Both objectives are wider than fair trading. A properly functioning Internal Market requires a comprehensive elimination of trade barriers. The protection of consumers involves also non-economic aspects. Fair trading is situated where both objectives meet. It constitutes the market behavioural law directed towards consumers for the purpose of the proper functioning of the Internal Market.[54]

2.2 Conceptual considerations

In order to determine the scope of the principle of fair trading, a look at the conceptual foundation and the resulting function of fair trading within the Internal Market is indispensable. The role of fair trading as a guarantee of information exchange and its function as a legal remedy against

---

[52] The vast majority of the national measures the Court dealt with, however, did rather prevent the consumers from making their choice in full knowledge of the facts instead of enabling them to do so, see the case law analysis in Chapter 1. See also Gormley in Micklitz, *Rechtseinheit oder Rechtsvielfalt*, p. 473 at 475.

[53] See *supra* at 2.1.2.2.

[54] Cf. Micklitz, (2002) 13 *EBLR* 583 at 588.

the consequences of market failures shows that fair trading is a principle which is connected to the very functioning of the Internal Market. Without a principle of fair trading, it is suggested, the Internal Market would not function properly. This assigns fair trading a central role in achieving the objective of a properly functioning Internal Market.

2.2.1 Fair trading as a guarantee of information exchange

It has been demonstrated earlier that communication is the absolute basis for the functioning of a market in general and the Internal Market in particular.[55] Trading is inconceivable without the exchange of information. Therefore, it was argued that information is the logical reference object of fair-trading rules and the underlying principle of fair trading in order to induce fair market behaviour. Interfering into the market in order to establish fairness in market action can only take place by regulating information exchange. This is exactly what a principle does, according to which consumers must be enabled to make their choice in full knowledge of the facts.

This line of argument can be taken further. Since communication is the basis for a functioning Internal Market, it can be claimed that fair trading is just as well the basis for a functioning Internal Market. The reason for this is that it is the very purpose of fair trading to guarantee the exchange of information, which is hampered in situations not in accordance with the principle of fair trading as defined. Fair trading is thus inseparably linked to a functioning Internal Market.

In order to illustrate this view observations from a law-and-economics perspective are constructive, which shed light on the function of fair trading as a legal remedy against consequences of market failures. Given that modern economic theory is complex and sophisticated,[56] a comprehensive discussion of the law-and-economics approach to information is clearly beyond the framework and purpose of the present study. The observations will therefore be strictly limited to what seems beneficial for the comprehension of the concept of fair trading in the Internal Market.

2.2.2 Fair trading as a legal remedy against consequences of market failures

It is a key characteristic of an efficient market that supply corresponds to demand. This is why the ultimate goal of production is consumption. In a properly functioning market consumers are therefore able to purchase the products according to their preferences. However, consumers are not able to do

---

[55] See Chapter 3 at 4.

[56] See Hadfield/Howse/Trebilcock, (1998) 21 *JCP* 131 at 135 with further references.

so if they lack the information they need in order to compare their preferences with the offer.[57] This can happen structurally as a result of imperfect competition and information asymmetries. Both are realities in the Internal Market.

2.2.2.1 Imperfect competition

EC competition-law rules aim at combating restrictions of competition, thereby attempting to create the framework for undistorted and effective competition to take place. Article 3(1)(g) makes clear that the system of ensuring undistorted competition forms part of the Internal Market,[58] which is also recognised by the Court of Justice.[59]

It is commonly accepted that competition, through generating greater efficiency,[60] leads to a higher level of consumer welfare.[61] Competition law, being an instrument for creating and maintaining competition, thus serves as a means for maximising consumer welfare.[62] Undistorted competition must therefore be seen as the principal basis for market transparency, which satisfies the consumers' needs.[63] In the end, the interests of all market actors are 'symbiotic'.[64] A situation of perfect competition would imply perfect disclosure of information concerning all relevant variables, since this would perfectly satisfy the demand

---

57 Rekaiti/Van den Bergh, (2000) 23 *JCP* 371 at 374. See also Hartlief, (2004) 27 *JCP* 253 at 261.

58 For a critical view, see Gormley, (2002) 13 *EBLR* 517 at 518.

59 Case C-300/89 *Commission v Council ('Titanium Dioxide')* [1991] ECR I-2867 at 23, Case C-376/98 *Germany v Parliament and Council ('Tobacco Advertising')* [2000] ECR I-8419 at 106. See also Introduction at 2.2.2.

60 Cf. Nihoul, (1998) 22 *Telecom. Pol.* 207 at 208, who argues furthermore that the approach taken by the EC authorities in implementing competition law may actually be counter-productive for efficiency (in particular at 212 et seq.). See moreover Monti, (2002) 39 *CML Rev.* 1057 at 1063 et seq.

61 That is to say the advantages of competition for the consumer cannot prevail where competition is weakened, e.g. because one or a few companies dominate the market, see Nihoul, *Concurrence*, p. 23.

62 See e.g. Bishop/Walker, *Economics*, at 2.01 and 2.22, who suggest that EC competition law values consumer welfare above producer welfare (both being part of the general concept of social welfare). They illustrate their assumption by the possibility to grant exemptions under Article 81(3) for agreements which, *inter alia*, allow consumers a fair share of the resulting benefit. See moreover Stuyck in Krämer/Micklitz/Tonner, *Law and diffuse interests*, p. 279 at p. 280 and comprehensively on the relationship between competition policy and consumer interest Reich in Reich/Micklitz, *Verbraucherrecht*, at § 4. See also Joined Cases 46/87 and 227/88 *Hoechst AG v Commission* [1989] ECR I-2859 at 25.

63 Stuyck (2002) 18 *TvC* 154 at 160 calls competition law the 'corner stone of consumer law'. Cf. also Askham in Vaughan, *Law of the European Communities*, at paragraph 96.

64 Fox, (2003) 26 *WoCo* 149 at 156.

side, which is an incentive for the supply side, and which in the end means the most efficient use of resources.[65]

However, a situation of perfect competition remains theory.[66] What can be achieved in reality has been described as 'workable competition'.[67] In the context of EC competition law it is understood as an efficient and competitive market, responding to consumer demand and without insurmountable entry barriers.[68] The imperfection thus requires specific action for consumers to be able to make informative consumption choices in order to keep the market as competitive as possible.[69] The Court has defined workable competition in *Metro I* as

> 'the degree of competition necessary to ensure the observance of the basic requirements and the attainment of the objectives of the Treaty, in particular the creation of a single market achieving conditions similar to those of a domestic market'.[70]

According to the Court, the concept of competition in the Internal Market is thus strongly interwoven with the objectives of the Treaty. This conception builds the bridge to fair trading. Not only is consumer protection an objective of the Treaty according to Article 3(t), but provisions like Article 95(3) and Article 153 leave no doubt that the Community legal order is not underpinned by a purely liberal understanding of the market, but rather opts for an active consumer-oriented market policy.[71]

---

65 It has been argued – e.g. by the Chicago School of Law and Economics – that competition can protect itself far better than can the legislator. According to this view, perfect competition would exist without a legal framework, see references in Jones/Sufrin, *EC Competition Law*, p. 21. Cf. also Gerber, *Law and Competition*, p. 56.

66 It is true that 'virtually any government measure in the economic or social sphere may have some impact on the conditions of competition', Douglas-Scott, *Constitutional Law*, p. 164 et seq. See also Alpa in Collins, *Directive on Unfair Commercial Practices*, p. 91 at p. 99.

67 For the dogmatic background to this concept, see Vedder, *Competition Law*, p. 27 et seq.

68 Hildebrand, *Economic Analysis*, p. 210.

69 Tunney, (2002) 25 *JCP* 329 at 339 et seq. argues that the over-emphasis of information transparency in the name of consumer protection can impede competition and ultimately worsen the position of the consumers. Tunney illustrates his point by referring to price lists to consumers, where competitors can signal prospective prices. This facilitates price-fixing and consequently is an opportunity for collusive behaviour. It must be countered, however, that, firstly, it is not the information, which *per se* causes the collusion, but rather the (implicit) agreement of the competitors, and, secondly, it is exactly the purpose of competition law to prevent such a collusive behaviour. In fact, this confirms that competition law and fair-trading law are complementary to each other.

70 Case 26/76 *Metro SB-Großmärkte GmbH & Co. KG v Commission* [1977] ECR 1875 at 20. The market-integration function is a particularity of EC competition law.

71 Cf. Drexl, (2002) 13 *EBLR* 557 at 566. See also Micklitz/Weatherill, (1993) 16 *JCP* 285 at 285, who argue that the consumer was the ultimate beneficiary of the Treaty's economic objectives even before the introduction of explicit references to consumers.

Fair-trading law is necessary in order to pursue the Treaty's objectives of consumer protection and a functioning Internal Market, which, according to *Metro I*, are inherent in the objective of workable competition as well. Both these functions concern not only the flow of information as such, but also relate to the quality of the information. These two aspects are equally important for consumers to make informed decisions. In that sense, by promoting consumer-oriented market transparency, fair-trading rules reinforce the idea of competition. Competition law and fair-trading law are therefore complementary and ultimately directed towards the same end, namely consumer welfare through market transparency.[72] The EC legal system, like national legal systems, consequently tackles market intransparency from two sides, namely via both competition law and fair-trading law.[73]

2.2.2.2 Information asymmetries

Information asymmetries can have various reasons. Those resulting from particular (distance) selling and communication techniques or from particular types of products have been named in an earlier context.[74] Also imperfect competition entails information asymmetries, as has just been suggested.[75] There are, however, information asymmetries of a more structural nature. At the outset of a transaction, the seller of a product inevitably knows more about the product than the buyer, regardless of the state of perfection of competition.[76] This knowledge may concern very basic details, such as the origin or the composition of the product, or it may be more complex, relating e.g. to the functioning of the product or to potential risks connected to it,[77] or to the contractual terms that are going to apply to the contract.[78] As a matter of fact, there is thus a structural information asymmetry between the supplier side and the consumption side, which may have various degrees, but which necessarily

---

72 Drexl, (2002) 13 *EBLR* 557 at 574 rightly includes contract law as well. According to him, 'contract law, trade practices law and competition law serve the same objectives, namely of promoting informed decisions of individual market participants in a competitive internal market'. On the relationship between market-order law and consumer law, see also Keßler, (1999) 14 *VuR* 415 at 416.

73 See also Keßler/Micklitz, *Harmonisierung des Lauterkeitsrechts*, p. 24 et seq.

74 See Chapter 3 at 5.2.3.1.

75 See also Gómez in Collins, *Directive on Unfair Commercial Practices*, p. 187 at p. 198 et seq.

76 Akerlof, (1970) 84 *QJ Econ.* 488 at 489 et seq.

77 There are cases, of course, where the consumer's knowledge may exceed that of the seller (e.g. regarding the functioning of the product). However, the seller always is ahead of the consumer regarding certain details, like from where and for which price he has acquired the product, or other facts concerning 'the past' of the product, which may be of relevance for the consumer's preferences. See also Ulen in Grundmann/Kerber/Weatherill, *Party Autonomy*, p. 98 at p. 102 et seq.

78 Junod Moser, *Conditions générales*, p. 159.

exists prior to a prospective transaction.[79] Although asymmetric information distribution does not *per se* constitute a market failure, it does so where it cannot be overcome by one side (i.e. usually the consumption side), or where it can only be overcome at excessive costs.[80]

Disclosure of information in order to counteract given information asymmetries is therefore closely connected with the objective of a properly functioning market.[81] Market transparency is an indispensable prerequisite for the active participation of consumers in the market by making autonomous choices.[82] The principle of fair trading, which sets the framework for consumers to make an informed choice, can consequently be regarded as inherent in the functioning of the Internal Market.

2.2.3 Fair trading as a principle of Internal Market law

It has been demonstrated that fair trading is related to the Internal Market not only under legal considerations, but that it is a conceptual foundation for its proper functioning. The objective of fair trading is to enable consumers to make their choice in full knowledge of the facts, in order to let them participate actively in the Internal Market. It is an indispensable necessity of an efficiently functioning Internal Market that the consumption side can fully participate in that market. This conceptual and economic analysis is confirmed by the free movement case law of the Court, which acknowledges the active and decisive role of consumers that they are allocated by the Internal Market.[83] However, consumers can only fully assume this role, if they are enabled to make informed choices.

These conceptual considerations do support the idea of fair trading being a legal principle. Internal Market law aims at fulfilling the objective of a properly functioning market by the legal instruments of negative and positive integration. Fair trading is inseparably related to this objective. The legal instruments therefore have to take into account the principle of fair trading, do they want

79 The existence of unavoidable information asymmetries can be considered essentially undisputed and can also be explained by cost analysis. Grundmann, (2002) 39 *CML Rev.* 269 at 275 et seq. illustrates this with an example concerning standard term contracts: it is much more costly for a consumer concluding a standard term contract only once to gather information than for a company that uses the same contract for all its transactions and therefore innumerably divides its costs. For the time aspect of information acquisition, see Howells in Wilhelmsson, *Critical Contract Law*, p. 327 at p. 329.

80 Cf. Grundmann, (2002) 39 *CML Rev.* 269 at 279.

81 Cf. Strassner, *Verbraucherinformationsrecht*, p. 127 et seq, Twigg-Flesner/Weatherill/Willett, (2002) 25 *JCP* 291 at 291, Weatherill in Grundmann/Kerber/Weatherill, *Party Autonomy*, p. 173 at p. 181.

82 Micklitz/Keßler, (2003) 49 *WRP* 919 at 922.

83 See the case law analysis in Chapter 1, in particular at 5.2.4.

to achieve their objective. The principle of fair trading is thus forming part of Internal Market law.

3 Consequences of the ambit

It follows from the foregoing analysis that the principle of fair trading is a general principle of Internal Market law. This implies that it applies wherever Community Internal Market law applies. It is a source of law in the sense that the entire Internal Market law must be interpreted in the light of and in compatibility with the principle of fair trading. This concerns the Treaty freedoms, Internal Market Community legislation and national rules which are within the scope of Internal Market law. As a matter of fact, this is exactly what happens.

The Treaty freedoms are most certainly interpreted in the light of the principle of fair trading, given that it has been developed on their basis. The ability of consumers to make their choice in full knowledge of the facts has been inferred from the concept that there must be no restrictions to intra-Community trade. Rules which do not obey this principle are unjustified and disproportionate restrictions of free movement. Moreover, the Court's doctrine to interpret Community legislation in the light of the Treaty freedoms entails that the principle of fair trading is also taken into account in secondary law.

Also national law being within the scope of Internal Market law must be interpreted in the light of the principle of fair trading, just like any national law must be interpreted in the light of Community law, where it affects the scope of Community law. This duty is reinforced by the principle in Article 10 of the Treaty.[84] It is the national judge who has to perform this task.

The limits to the scope of the principle of fair trading are likewise linked to the limits of Internal Market law. Ultimately, this concerns only situations which are not covered by secondary fair-trading law and which fall outside the scope of free movement due to the *Keck* doctrine.[85]

The question whether and to what extent there are enforcement possibilities for fair trading is indirectly related to the ambit of the principle of fair trading, rather than a direct consequence of it. The issue of enforcement has been explicitly excluded from the scope of this book, because the principle of fair trading cannot itself be enforced.[86] Its function is that of an authoritative source of interpretation for specific enforceable rights, it does not constitute itself an enforceable right. However, the clear awareness of the ambit of the principle

84 Cf. also Gormley in Bernitz/Nergelius, *General Principles*, p. 113 and Weatherill, *Law and Integration*, p. 116 et seq.

85 For the detailed examination of the scope and impact of the *Keck* doctrine, see Chapter 1 at 5.4.

86 See Introduction at 2.2.4.

of fair trading is a necessary prerequisite for the examination of enforcement possibilities. It follows from fair trading being a general principle of Internal Market law that all Internal Market rules containing enforceable rights must be interpreted in the light of this principle.

CHAPTER 5

Towards a General Legislative Framework for Fair Trading

1 Assessing current legislative initiatives in the light of the principle of fair trading

It has been demonstrated in the previous chapters that the current *acquis communautaire* comprises a comprehensive general concept of fair trading, which must moreover be regarded as a general principle of Internal Market law. This is the fundamental finding of this study, which is to be concluded by examining in the light of the established principle of fair trading the future legislative scenario in the field, which is presently in the pipeline.

Of late, the Commission has resuscitated earlier plans for the creation of a general legislative framework for fair trading;[1] this has resulted in concrete legislative proposals. While the proper functioning of the Internal Market is the leading argument for the necessity of creating a general legislative framework, the question whether and to what extent the Internal Market already knows a general and homogenous legal concept of fair trading has been totally neglected in the preparatory legislative process. Tacitly, it seems, the Commission assumes that currently such a general concept of fair trading does not yet exist. However, this assumption is in stark contrast to the findings of this study. The relationship between the existing principle and the envisaged legislative framework must therefore be elucidated.

In principle, two proposals play a role in this context: the proposal for a regulation concerning sales promotions and the proposal for a directive concerning unfair commercial practices. However, it is actually just the latter initiative which aims at introducing something like a general concept of fair trading into Community legislation. Its discussion will therefore be central to this chapter. Beforehand, a brief overview will be given of the proposal for a regulation concerning sales promotions.

2 The proposal for a regulation concerning sales promotions

In 2001 the Commission published a proposal for a regulation concerning sales promotions, of which it presented an amended version in 2002.[2] The objective and the content of this proposal prove it to be another patch

---

1 See Chapter 2 at 2.1 for the historical background of fair trading legislation.

2 Proposal for a Regulation concerning sales promotions in the Internal Market, COM (2001) 546 final, OJ 2002 C 75 E/11. Amended proposal for a Regulation concerning sales promotions in the Internal Market, COM (2002) 585 final. The roots of the Proposal are to be found in the 1996 Green Paper on Commercial Communications in the Internal Market, COM (96) 192 final, and the 1998 Follow-up to the Green paper, COM (98) 121 final.

in the existing legislative patchwork, rather than an attempt for introducing a general fair trading concept.

2.1 The objective and the content of the proposed regulation

According to Article 1 of the proposed regulation, its objective is to establish rules concerning the use and commercial communication of sales promotions in order to ensure the proper functioning of the Internal Market and a high level of consumer protection. The legal instrument of a regulation implies maximum harmonisation and direct applicability.

The central idea of the proposed regulation is to remove national restrictions on the use or commercial communication of sales promotions (Article 3(1)), and to submit them to requirements under Community law, mainly relating to transparency.[3] The regulation is not intended as specific consumer legislation. This is connected with the fact that fair trading is not its only underlying objective, but that it seemingly aims at guaranteeing the free movement of the service of 'sales promotion' as such, and the free establishment of business which provides this service, i.e. the so-called 'promoters', such as advertising agencies. The recipients of the sales promotions are the 'customers', i.e. companies, organisations or individuals who purchase the goods or services promoted by the 'promoters'.

The regulation defines 'sales promotion' as the offer of a discount, a free gift, a premium or an opportunity to participate in a promotional contest or game (Article 2(b)).[4] The proposed regulation thus covers just a limited number of marketing practices. Remaining national restrictions relating to sales promotions which are not covered by the regulation (except for national provisions governing sales or resales below cost) have to be mutually accepted (Article 3(2)). This is in line with the general approach of home State control prevailing.

The key condition for sales promotions is transparency. In addition to other information requirements deriving from Community law, the regulation sets out particular information requirements in the annex; these must be provided in a clear and unambiguous manner (Article 4). While the single types of sales promotion must additionally obey to specific information requirements,[5] all types of sales promotion must provide the following information (point 1.1. of the annex):

- the price (inclusive of taxes) of the promoted good or service and any additional costs associated with freight, delivery or postage,
- the promoter's name and address,

---

[3] See Göhre, (2002) 48 *WRP* 36 at 39 et seq. with regard to the first proposal.

[4] These types of sales promotions are further defined in the proposed regulation.

[5] It is distinguished between obligatory information ('information to be provided in the commercial communication') and information on request ('information to be made available on request unconditional on purchase of the promoted product or service').

- the duration of the offer including the start date and either the end date or the quantity of stock available,
- where the offer is subject to conditions, an indication of where these conditions or any other information can be obtained,
- an indication of how the terms and conditions governing the sales promotion can be obtained.

The regulation specifically addresses minors in Article 5. In this context, the public-interest reasoning indeed prevails over the purely information-oriented approach that characterises the rest of the regulation. When making a sales promotion, their personal data must not be collected without the consent of the minors' legal guardian. A minor must not be provided a free gift or a premium or a service, if it is of a nature that could in any way harm his or her health. The provision of free gifts to minors in the form of a product the sale of which to minors is prohibited, in particular alcoholic beverages to individuals under the age of 18, is prohibited.

Redress is addressed in Article 6. The burden of proof as to the accuracy of the information provided is placed on the 'promoters'. Furthermore the contact details of the promoter must be indicated and the handling of complaints must fulfil certain standards (e.g. response in writing).

2.2 Assessment of the proposal with regard to a general legislative framework for fair trading

The proposal undeniably relates to the principle of fair trading as defined earlier in this work. The various transparency requirements improve the ability of consumers to make an informed choice. It is submitted that the content of the proposed regulation does not conflict with the principle of fair trading.

However, what is more important in the present context is that the regulation does not in any way replace the existing Internal Market law principle of fair trading. It is yet another contribution to the piecemeal approach. As with other sectoral legislation, its rules can largely be explained by the principle of fair trading as the underlying concept, but the proposed regulation does not itself establish a general concept. As a matter of fact, it does not even aim to do so.

The (initial) proposal for the regulation on sales promotions has been published on the same day as the Green Paper on consumer protection,[6] which eventually led to a proposal for a directive on unfair commercial practices, the latter being the actual candidate for a general legislative framework for fair trading. The reason for the fact that two legislative initiatives with clearly overlapping scopes have been launched simultaneously seems to be indeed that two

[6] See *infra* at 3.1.

different Directorates General of the Commission are dealing with fair trading.[7] From the very beginning, the Commission has noted that the two proposals were complementary and would co-exist in the legislation process.[8] However, justifying the co-existence with the mere argument that the proposed regulation represents a targeted action in the field of sales promotions whereas the proposed directive has a framework character is less than wholly convincing. Although the framework directive is supposed to co-exist with legislation already in force and with possible future sectoral legislation, the presentation at the same time of a general legislative framework and a specifically targeted measure remains peculiar.[9]

It would have been possible to integrate the liberalisation and transparency ideas of the proposed regulation into the proposed framework directive. Alternatively, given that the proposed regulation deals with sales promotions, such as premiums, which are suitable for concealing the actual costs of a good or service, it would have been a reasonable option to amend the Unit Prices Directive in order to transform it into a general directive on cost transparency.[10]

The future of the proposal is currently still uncertain.[11] However, it should be pointed out that if the regulation on sales promotions will finally be adopted, it will certainly not constitute a 'general legislative framework' for fair trading nor be part of such. Rather, as the Commission rightly states, it represents a targeted action in the field of sales promotions, which would have to submit to a possible future general legislative framework and/or the existing principle of fair trading. In this respect, it is therefore not to be seen as a particularly ground-breaking development with regard to a principle of fair trading in EC law.

---

7 The Green Paper on commercial communications and the related proposal on sales promotions stem from DG Internal Market, the Green Paper on consumer protection and the related proposal for a directive on unfair commercial practices have been drafted under the responsibility of DG Health and Consumer Protection. See also de Vrey (2004) 20 *TvC* 2 at 4, and Glöckner, (2004) 50 *WRP* 936 at 937 on the repeated mutual blocking of the two Directorates General.

8 COM (2001) 531 final, p. 11 and COM (2001) 546 final, p. 3. Reiterated in COM (2003) 356 final at paragraph 45.

9 Also, this practice seems hardly compatible with the repeated confessions on better law-making, see e.g. the Interinstitutional Agreement on better law-making, OJ 2003 C 321/1.

10 On the Unit Prices Directive, see Chapter 2 at 2.4. For the relationship between free gifts and price transparency, see Case 286/81 *Oosthoek's Uitgeversmaatschappij B.V.* [1982] ECR 4575 at 18.

11 There is actually quite some negative response among many Member States with regard to the proposal, but the Council is still reflecting on a compromise solution which could be accepted by a qualified majority. See also Lettl, (2004) 50 *WRP* 1079 at 1081, 1085.

3 The initiative for a Directive concerning unfair commercial practices

It has been noted earlier that the efforts to create a general legislative framework for fair trading date back to the very early years of the Community itself.[12] The legislative culmination of these efforts is Directive 84/450 as amended relating to misleading and comparative advertising. Apart from this horizontally harmonising Directive, the efforts led to the piecemeal situation as it has been portrayed. In its consumer policy Action Plan 1999-2001,[13] the Commission revitalised the project of a general legislative framework for fair trading.[14]

3.1 The way to the Council's Common Position

The consultation was formally launched by the 2001 Green Paper on consumer protection.[15] Despite its broad title the Green Paper did not concern consumer protection in general but focussed very closely on the reform of the harmonisation concerning fair commercial practices.[16] According to the Commission, the reform could be pursued on the basis of the existing 'specific approach' or a suggested 'mixed approach', which was clearly favoured. The core of this approach was the adoption of a comprehensive framework directive harmonising national fairness rules for business-to-consumer commercial practices, which would co-exist with existing and future sector-specific directives and assume the role of a 'safety net' for cross-border restrictions which fall outside the coordinated fields of the sector-specific directives. For reasons of legal certainty it was proposed that the framework directive should be providing more than merely a general concept, but it should address the main differences in national rules on commercial practices which affect the operation of the Internal Market.

The Green Paper on consumer protection received a wide response, and in 2002 the Commission published a follow-up Communication,[17] calling for further consultation before presenting a legislative proposal. It named the following main features of a framework directive:

---

[12] See Chapter 2 at 2.1.

[13] COM (98) 696 final.

[14] For this purpose three studies were commissioned which were to prepare a consultation process: Bultmann/Howells/Keßler/Micklitz/Radeideh/Reich/Stuyck/Voigt, *Fair Trading Vol. I-III*, PriceWaterhouseCoopers/University of Utrecht/University of Tilburg, *Consumer Law and the Information Society*, Lex Fori, *Normes juridiques "douces".*

[15] Green Paper on European Union Consumer Protection, COM (2001) 531 final.

[16] In expert circles the Green Paper was therefore considered to be a good example of 'misleading advertising'.

[17] Follow-up Communication to the Green Paper on EU Consumer Protection, COM (2002) 289 final.

- only covering business-to-consumer relationships
- maximum harmonisation
- simplification
- application of the principle of 'mutual recognition' and 'control by the country of origin'
- balance between legal certainty and adaptability to market circumstances
- scope based on the wider concept of 'fair commercial practices', phrased in terms of an obligation not to trade unfairly, rather than a duty to trade fairly
- general clause consisting of (1) the unfairness of the practice and (2) a 'consumer detriment test'
- a number of specific rules in order to substantiate the general clause.

Although it was thought that some provisions of existing consumer protection directives could be repealed and incorporated into the framework directive, the latter should coexist with legislation in force, which would be reformed at a later stage. The establishment of an expert group and further consultation on national fairness notions were announced in order to prepare a proposal for a directive.[18]

In 2003 the Commission finally adopted a proposal for an 'Unfair Commercial Practices Directive',[19] which mostly implemented the objectives set out in the follow-up Communication to the Green Paper.[20] The Explanatory Memorandum reiterated the steps of the consultation process and reconfirmed the need for reform for the sake of eliminating significant barriers to the functioning of the Internal Market, given that unfair commercial practices impaired the consumers' ability to make informed and therefore efficient choices.[21]

In accordance with the procedure of Article 251 of the Treaty,[22] after the opinion of the European Economic and Social Committee[23] and the opinion with

---

18 See the study coordinated by Schulze/Schulte-Nölke, *Analysis of National Fairness Laws*. See furthermore GFA, *Ex-ante Impact Assessment*.

19 Proposal for a Directive concerning unfair business-to-consumer commercial practices in the Internal Market and amending directives 84/450/EEC, 97/7/EC and 98/27/EC (the Unfair Commercial Practices Directive), COM (2003) 356 final. Together with the proposal an Extended Impact Assessment has been published.

20 The consultation process produced furthermore the Proposal for a Regulation on cooperation between national authorities responsible for the enforcement of consumer protection laws ("the regulation on consumer protection cooperation"), COM (2003) 443 final. The Regulation was adopted by the Council in October 2004.

21 COM (2003) 356 final at paragraph 16.

22 The legal basis chosen for the proposed Directive is Article 95 only.

23 OJ 2004 C 108/81.

amendments by the European Parliament in first reading,[24] the Council adopted a Common Position by qualified majority in November 2004.[25] Although it is at present not certain whether the text of the Common Position will remain unchanged, the adoption of an Unfair Commercial Practices Directive at the end of the legislation process is definitely more likely than ever before.

3.2 The structure of the Directive and the criteria for analysis

The Common Position of the Council with a view of the adoption of an Unfair Commercial Practices Directive is divided into four 'chapters'.[26] The first chapter comprises 'general provisions' and determines the purpose and the scope of the Directive, and provides definitions. The second chapter is headed 'unfair commercial practices' and contains a general clause prohibiting unfair commercial practices and a general test for determining the unfairness of commercial practices. The chapter is further divided into two sections, one on 'misleading commercial practices', and one on 'aggressive commercial practices'. Both sections apply the conditions of the general test in these two areas of unfair trading. The third chapter, which consists of only one article, relates to 'codes of conduct'.[27] The fourth chapter contains 'final provisions', which deal with enforcement in a broad sense, amendments of existing legislation, and the review of the Directive. Finally, a first annex contains a blacklist of unfair commercial practices, and a second annex contains a non-exhaustive list of Community law provisions setting out rules for advertising and commercial communication.

The intention to present a comprehensive legislative framework for fair trading which meets a high standard of legal certainty has entailed as a consequence that the Directive will be a fairly dense piece of legislation. Next to a general unfairness concept it contains quite a lot of detailed rules (especially in the annex), which are to ensure a uniform application of the general clause. It is not the aim to analyse the Directive in its entirety and to comment on all of its content and its implications. The focus is clearly put on the general concept that the Directive establishes, which will be analysed in the light of the currently

---

24 European Parliament Report A5-0188/2004 of 18 March 2004, adopted on 20 April 2004.

25 Council document 11630/04 CONSOM 63 MI 215 CODEC 929 of 9 November 2004, adopted on 15 November 2004 (Interinstitutional File: 2003/0134 (COD)). The Commission approved the Common Position on 16 November 2004, COM (2004) 753 final. For the failures in the past due to the requirement of unanimity vote under Article 94, see Chapter 2 at 2.1. See also Beater, (2003) 11 *ZEuP* 11 at 12 et seq.

26 The text of the Common Position is reproduced in the Annex at the end of this book. In the following, the text of the Common Position is referred to as 'the Directive', in order to facilitate the reading.

27 Codes of conduct for commercial practices have a long tradition in several Member States, for instance in the Netherlands, see Radeideh/de Vrey in Micklitz/Keßler, *Marketing Practices*, p. 237 at p. 240 et seq.

existing Internal Market principle of fair trading as established earlier in this work. The contemplation of specific rules is certainly useful and necessary for the understanding of the general concept they are meant to embody. However, a clear understanding of which general concept is intended to be introduced by the Directive requires one not to get lost in minutiae.[28]

An integrated method of analysis will be pursued in the sense that the findings concerning the Directive will immediately be compared to the general Internal Market principle of fair trading. In addition, the *acquis communautaire* principle of fair trading and the Directive's concept of the prohibition of unfair commercial practices are afterwards directly compared with each other.[29] The text of the original Commission proposal will be taken into account, where it deviates substantially from the text of the Common Position.

3.3 General considerations

3.3.1 Purpose

The purpose of the Directive, according to Article 1, is to contribute to the proper functioning of the Internal Market and to achieve a high level of consumer protection by approximating the laws, regulations and administrative provisions of the Member States on unfair commercial practices harming consumers' economic interests.

Article 1 already hints at the negative approach taken: it is not the national legal frameworks concerning 'fair' commercial practices that are to be harmonised, but those on 'unfair' commercial practices harming consumers' economic interests. The second recital, by contrast, states that the development of 'fair' commercial practices within the area without internal frontiers is vital for the promotion of the development of cross-border activities. However, this does not have to be a contradiction. The Green Paper had already pointed out that it was the intention to feature a framework directive based on a legal model such as 'fair commercial practices', which would imply a general test not to engage in 'unfair commercial practices'.[30] The negative test of 'unfair commercial practices' may thus very well be based on the positive concept of 'fair trading'. The crucial question is therefore, whether the negative test amounts to the same comprehensiveness as the positive principle of 'fair trading'.[31]

The definition of the purpose reveals furthermore a conceptual double foundation for harmonisation, namely the contribution to the proper functioning of

---

[28] In particular, the blacklist of unfair commercial practices of the first annex of the Directive will not be discussed in detail.

[29] See *infra* at 3.6.

[30] COM (2001) 531 final, p. 13.

[31] This will be further discussed *infra* at 3.6.

the Internal Market and the achievement of a high level of consumer protection. It seems that consumer protection refers to the aspect of 'harming consumers' economic interests'. As has been explained earlier, the functioning of the Internal Market itself is based on the respect of the consumers' economic interests in that they are enabled to assume their role as active market participants by making informed choices.[32] It can therefore be argued that this actually makes consumer protection as an individual goal superfluous. Accordingly, the legal basis chosen is solely Article 95, not even in combination with Article 153.

It should be borne in mind moreover that, besides harmonisation of not yet harmonised rules, another objective of the Directive is to establish a coherent conceptual framework for the currently existing piecemeal legislation.

3.3.2 Definitions

Article 2 provides the definitions of twelve terms for the purposes of the Directive. Many definitions are very closely related to specific provisions of the Directive, sometimes they concern terms which appear only once. Hence, they will be dealt with in the particular context. 'Consumer', 'commercial practices', and 'product', however, are fundamental terms, which appear throughout the Directive.

The (average) consumer

The 'consumer' is defined as 'any natural person who [...] is acting for purposes which are outside his trade, business, craft or profession', which is the standard definition to be found in most consumer legislation.[33] The Common Position does no longer feature a positive definition of the 'average consumer' as did the original proposal, according to which it was the 'the consumer who is reasonably well informed and reasonably observant and circumspect'. This was clearly meant as the codification of the standard developed by the Court of Justice. However, it was an incomplete definition as it failed to include the socio-cultural parameters that have to be taken into account in the actual application of the test.[34] The omission of the definition in the Common Position was due to concerns that this would prevent the concept from evolving in line with the Court's case law. The Directive still does refer to the concept of the 'average consumer' in its single provisions though. This notion is then meant to be identical with the one developed by the Court of Justice.[35]

---

[32] See Chapter 4 at 2.1.3.1 and at 2.2.

[33] See Chapter 3 at 3.1.

[34] See Chapter 1 at 5.3 and Chapter 3 at 3.2 for the consumer image as developed by the Court of Justice with further references to case law.

[35] For an important deviation from this concept due to Article 5(3) of the Directive, see *infra* at 3.4.2.1.

Commercial practices

The definition of 'business-to-consumer commercial practices', or just 'commercial practices', is certainly a most decisive one for the scope of application of the Directive. It is submitted, however, that the definition is hardly satisfactory. The collective reference to the terms 'act', 'omission', 'course of conduct', 'representation', 'commercial communication', 'advertising', and 'marketing' actually appears to be more confusing than enlightening, in particular, because many of the terms have overlapping connotations; they are differently used in existing legislation, and they require further definition themselves.

It is obvious that the legislator wants to include any conceivable means used by a trader which is 'directly connected with the promotion, sale or supply of a product to consumers'. It would have been preferable, however, to stick to the notion of 'commercial communication', which, in the sense of the E-Commerce Directive, already includes 'any form of communication'.

Product

It should finally be noted that 'product' is used in the Directive as meaning 'any good or service including immovable property, rights and obligations'.[36] The Directive is thus applicable with regard to a maximum of contractual performances relevant for consumers.

3.3.3 Scope

It results from Article 1 that the Directive is only concerned with practices harming consumers' economic interests. The definition of the (average) consumer has already been commented on. Pure business-to-business issues are not covered by the Directive.

The aspect of economic interests implies furthermore that only the economic dimension of commercial practices is concerned. Matters of taste, decency and social responsibility, for instance, are not covered as such.[37] They are covered, however, if they do affect the consumers' economic interests in the sense of the unfairness test.

According to Article 3(1), the Directive is applicable 'to unfair business-to-consumer commercial practices, as laid down in Article 5, before, during and after a commercial transaction in relation to a product.' Although it is obvious that the intention by Article 3(1) is to make sure, in particular, that also after-sales practices are covered by the Directive, it can actually be said to have merely a clarifying function. As will be demonstrated, the general test in Article 5 for the unfairness of a commercial practice requires, *inter alia*, that the practice causes or is likely to cause the consumer to take a transactional decision that

---

36 The use of the term 'product' unfortunately varies considerably in Community legislation.

37 See COM (2003) 356 final at 39.

he would not have taken otherwise.[38] Together with the broad definition of a 'transactional decision' in Article 2(k), which already refers to decisions to be taken before, during and after a commercial transaction, there can hardly be any doubt that the Directive applies comprehensively to commercial practices which influence the consumers' transactional decision-making, irrespective of the point in time.

The rest of Article 3 is mainly concerned with clarifying what is excluded from the Directive's scope. Contract law is outside the scope, in particular with regard to the rules on the validity, formation or effect of a contract. It is also pointed out that the Directive does not affect Community or national rules relating to the health and safety aspects of products. However, health claims, for instance, which are 'directly connected with the promotion, sale or supply of a product to consumers' in the sense of the definition of 'commercial practices' would clearly fall under the Directive. The Directive is moreover without prejudice to the rules determining the jurisdiction of the courts.

The Directive's scope of application is furthermore restricted in an indirect way by three characteristics, at which a closer look should be taken: its design as a framework directive, the derogation of its maximum harmonisation approach, and the absence of the country of origin principle.

The framework character of the Directive entails that it applies only in case that no other Community rules govern specific aspects of unfair commercial practices (Article 3(4)). This has two consequences. On the one hand, it means that where in sectoral legislation certain aspects have been left open they are caught by the framework directive which assumes a complementary role ('safety-net'). This mechanism is to be welcomed, since it guarantees that issues, which were not regulated before, are caught by an explicit fair trading concept. On the other hand, the continuing existence of the sectoral directives signifies that the incoherence of fair trading legislation actually will persist. A real improvement of the currently poor legislative situation, however, would require a general legislative framework which replaces piecemeal legislation rather than merely complementing it.[39] Unfortunately, this is currently not intended.

Article 3(5) contains a (temporary) derogation from the maximum harmonisation approach of the Directive, which was not provided for in the original Commission proposal. For a period of effectively eight years (which may even be prolonged) the Member States will be able to apply more restrictive national provisions which implement directives containing minimum harmonisation clauses, as long as they are proportionate to the aim of adequately protecting

---

[38] See *infra* at 3.4.2.

[39] See the examples concerning information duties given by Schulte-Nölke/Busch, (2004) 12 *ZEuP* 99 at 112 et seq. demonstrating how the incoherence of Community fair trading law as a whole may even be enhanced as a consequence of the adoption of the Directive as another regulatory layer for fair trading. See moreover Glöckner, (2004) 50 *WRP* 936 at 942 et seq.

consumers against unfair commercial practices. This minimum harmonisation clause limits the integrative impact of the Directive and (temporarily) undermines the goal of a more coherent fair trading law in Europe. According to Article 3(9), the Member States may impose more restrictive requirements without temporal limits in relation to 'financial services' within the meaning of Directive 2002/65.[40]

Article 4 of the Directive in the version of the Common Position has been deprived of the effect it would have had in the wording of the original Commission proposal. There, Article 4 established a firm country of origin principle, which did not allow for any derogation. Traders were only to comply with the national provisions falling within the field approximated by the Directive of the Member State in which they were established (Article 4(1) of the original proposal). It was this Member State, which had to ensure the compliance with its laws, i.e. a true system of home State control was established. What has been left in the text of the Common Position is the originally second paragraph, which provides that the receiving Member States must not restrict the free movement of goods or services for reasons falling within field approximated by the Directive. However, this alone, it is submitted, merely states the obvious. It does not prohibit the host Member State to add a secondary control, as long as it constitutes an implementation of the Directive.[41] Given that, at least in the first years, the Directive actually only provides for minimum harmonisation for large parts of its scope of application, commercial practices will still have to obey different national requirements. On the other hand, this means that consumers will usually only be confronted with their home State legal order, in which they usually have more confidence, while the scenario of foreign laws applying usually constitutes a deterrent for cross-border shopping.[42]

3.4 Unfair commercial practices

The second chapter of the Directive, headed 'unfair commercial practices', contains a general clause prohibiting unfair commercial practices and a general test for determining unfairness (Article 5). Additionally, the chapter comprises one section on misleading commercial practices (Articles 6 and 7),

---

40 Cf. the permission of Article 4(2) of Directive 2002/65 to allow more stringent requirements for information of the consumer prior to the conclusion of the distance contract than provided for in the Directive.

41 The prohibition of a secondary control as established by the Court in Joined Cases C-34/95, C-35/95 and C-36/95 *Konsumentombudsmannen (KO) v De Agostini (Svenska) Förlag AB and TV-Shop i Sverige AB* [1997] ECR I-3843 at 34 and 61 in the context of the Television Directive is not applicable here, given the lack of a provision which requires the sole exercise of control by the home State.

42 Cf. Henning-Bodewig (2004) 53 *GRUR Int.* 183 at 193 and de Vrey (2004) 20 *TvC* 2 at 7.

and one section on aggressive commercial practices (Articles 8 and 9). Misleading and aggressive commercial practices are types of practices which are regarded as unfair 'in particular'. Finally, the first annex contains a list of misleading and aggressive commercial practices which are regarded as unfair 'in all circumstances'.

In accordance with the principal aim of this work, the main focus is on examining which principle is expressed in the general clause and the general unfairness test.

3.4.1 The general prohibition of unfair commercial practices

The central provision is the general clause in Article 5 of the Directive.[43] A general clause containing open legal notions which need to be translated into concrete rules is far from new in European consumer legislation.[44] Article 3 of Directive 93/13 on unfair terms in consumer contracts can be considered the prototype of a general clause based on fairness considerations, which in the specific case was expressed under the label of 'good faith'.[45] More specifically concerning fair-trading legislation, the prohibition of misleading advertising in Directive 84/450 was a first step towards a general clause, however merely covering one particular aspect of fair trading. The novelty of Article 5 of the Directive on unfair commercial practices is, however, that the general clause containing the open legal notion is complemented by multi-stage test in order to give it a concrete meaning and to assure a uniform application.

The core of Article 5, the actual general clause, is the prohibition of unfair commercial practices in the very brief paragraph 1. It thus does not provide a duty to trade fairly, but rather a duty not to trade unfairly. Whether this negative approach has the same impact as the existing principle of fair trading inherent in Internal Market law depends on the actual shape of the unfairness notion. In any event, the fact that the general clause formulates a prohibition does not mean that the underlying concept would not be a positive one, that is to say a concept of 'fair trading'. On the contrary, the Commission pointed out already in the Green Paper that it understands the general clause as being based on legal models such 'fair commercial practices' or 'good market behaviour', but which would imply a general test not to engage in unfair commercial practices.

---

43 On the necessity of a general clause for a 'serious' harmonisation of fair trading law, see Beater, (2003) 11 *ZEuP* 11 at 44 et seq. See also Schricker/Henning-Bodewig, (2001) 47 *WRP* 1367 at 1378 et seq.

44 Franzen, *Privatrechtsangleichung*, p. 536 rightly points out that this commonly accepted understanding of general clauses is fairly vague, given that in principle every legal notion requires interpretation and concretisation.

45 Already Directive 86/653/EEC relating to self-employed commercial agents, OJ 1986 L 382/17 contains a general clause in Article 3 and Article 4, according to which the commercial agent and the principal must 'act dutifully and in good faith' in their relations with each other.

3.4.2 The general test for determining unfairness

Given the vagueness of the notion 'unfair', the rest of the Article – and, in fact, almost the rest of the Directive – concerns the definition of 'unfair', or rather paraphrases what 'unfair' signifies. Article 5 provides such a definition at three levels. These levels are characterised by a gradation from general to specific, and from most to least discretion.

The structure of the unfairness definition

At the first level, a general test is provided. According to this test, a commercial practice shall be regarded as unfair if

- it is contrary to the requirements of professional diligence, and
- it materially distorts or is likely to materially distort the economic behaviour with regard to the product of the average consumer whom it reaches or to whom it is addressed, or of the average member of the group when a commercial practice is specifically directed to a particular group of consumers.

At the second level, two types of commercial practices are highlighted, which shall be regarded as unfair 'in particular'. Both types are further defined in the Directive and dedicated own sections. These are

- misleading practices, or
- aggressive practices.

At the third level, a reference is made to the first annex, which contains a list of misleading and aggressive commercial practices which are regarded as unfair 'in all circumstances'.

Contemplating the structure from the reverse direction (i.e. third level to first level), it becomes apparent that the framework Directive actually microscopically reflects the character of Community fair-trading law as a whole: very specific rules which can be found in sectoral legislation, sub-general concepts which exist e.g. in the Misleading Advertising Directive, and an underlying general concept, which appears in the case law of the Court of Justice and which is a general principle of Internal Market law. This entire structure is thus mirrored in Article 5 itself.

The two conditions of the general unfairness test

Article 5(2) sets out two conditions which have to be met cumulatively. It is peculiar that the condition of professional diligence precedes that of the material distortion of the consumers' economic behaviour. It is relatively obvious that the latter condition is the actual general concept, while the first condition is rather a limitation of that concept. Therefore, the examination starts with the condition of the material distortion of consumers' economic behaviour.

3.4.2.1 The material distortion of the consumers' economic behaviour

One of the two conditions for a commercial practice to be unfair is that

> 'it materially distorts or is likely to materially distort the economic behaviour with regard to the product of the average consumer whom it reaches or to whom it is addressed'.

Since the concept of material distortion of the consumers' economic behaviour needs further clarification, it is explained in Article 2(e) that

> '"to materially distort the economic behaviour of consumers" means using a commercial practice to appreciably impair the consumer's ability to make an informed decision, thereby causing the consumer to take a transactional decision that he would not have taken otherwise'.

Finally, the text of the Common Position defines the term 'transactional decision', which was not legally defined in the original Commission proposal. According to Article 2(k),

> '"transactional decision" means any decision taken by a consumer concerning whether, how and on what terms to purchase, make payment in whole or in part for, retain or dispose of a product or to exercise a contractual right in relation to the product, whether the consumer decides to act or to refrain from acting'.

It is not clear why this somewhat awkward regulatory mechanism has been chosen. Unlike the term 'transactional decision', which is reasonable to define universally for all the provisions of the Directive, the notion of 'material distortion of the consumers' economic behaviour' does not appear elsewhere in the Directive than in Article 5. Although it would have been possible to base the definitions of 'misleading' and 'aggressive' commercial practices on the concept of materially distorting the economic behaviour of consumers, the relevant Articles of the Directive use a separate definition for these categories (although derived from the same idea). Defining the concept beforehand in Article 2 thus loses its logic if the notion only reappears once. It would have seemed more sensible to do without the separate definition of 'material distortion of the consumers' economic behaviour' and instead to incorporate the definition into Article 5 directly, which would have made the underlying concept of 'unfairness' more apparent. This has been done in the sections on misleading and aggressive commercial practices. Thus, reformulating the condition, a commercial practice is regarded as unfair if

> with regard to the average consumer whom it reaches or to whom it is addressed, it appreciably impairs or is likely to appreciably impair the consumer's ability to make an informed decision and thereby causing or being likely to cause the consumer to take a transactional decision with regard to the product that he would not have taken otherwise.

The elements of this test could then be recapitulated as follows:

- the practice must impair the consumer's ability to make an informed decision, this must at least be likely
- the impairment must be appreciable
- as a consequence (causality) the consumer takes a transactional decision concerning the product that he would not have taken otherwise, this must at least be likely
- benchmark is the average consumer (who is reached by the practice, i.e. not only the consumer who is addressed).

The impairment of the consumers' ability to make an informed choice

The pivotal point is the ability of the consumer to make an informed choice. It is the essence of the test to ensure the integrity of this ability and its economic effects. In this respect, the first item of the test is already a fairly close negative reflection of the principle of fair trading as a general principle of Internal Market law. Fair trading means that consumers must be enabled to make their choice in full knowledge of the facts. Accordingly, unfair trading is characterised by impairing the consumers' ability to make such an informed choice.

The aspect of 'likelihood' assumes the function of a threshold in two ways. On the one hand, the likelihood of impairing the consumers' ability to make a choice is sufficient, which guarantees the preventive effect of the provision (otherwise, it would have to be proven that a commercial practice has actually impaired at least one average consumer's ability to make an informed decision). On the other hand, the likelihood of impairing the consumers' ability to make a choice is necessary, as it guarantees that not everything is regarded as an impairment. This mechanism is well-known from Article 2(2) of Directive 84/450 on misleading advertising ('likely to deceive') and the case law of the Court, which requires the risk of misleading consumers to be 'sufficiently serious'.[46] However, the problem remains what is 'likely'. The Directive has no obvious answer to this.

'Appreciability' and the causality of taking a transactional decision that the consumer would not have taken otherwise

Since the idea of impairing the consumer's ability to make an informed decision is the essential foundation of the test, it remains to be examined whether

[46] Case C-313/94 *Fratelli Graffione SNC v Ditta Fransa* [1996] ECR I-6039 at 24.

and to what extent the test's additional elements complement the basic course of expressing a general concept of fair trading in a negative way.

The impairment of the consumer's ability to make an informed decision must be appreciable, and as a consequence the consumer has to take or must be likely to take a transactional decision that he would not have taken otherwise. It follows from Article 2(e) that it is the impairment which has to happen appreciably, not the effect of this impairment, i.e. causing the consumer to take a transactional decision that he would not have taken otherwise.[47] Indeed, both aspects are closely connected. It is suggested that, reasonably viewed, the impairment of the consumer's ability to make an informed decision can only be considered appreciable, if it causes him to take a transactional decision that he would not have taken otherwise. An inappreciable impairment would simply have no effect on the consumer's economic behaviour. It can thus be argued that the condition of 'appreciability' is superfluous in combination with that of an impact on the transactional decision. Of course, the argument works the other way around as well: the condition of an impact on the transactional decision can be regarded as superfluous in combination with that of 'appreciability'. There is, in any case, a redundancy of the conditions.[48] The basic idea is thus that the impairment of the average consumers' ability to make an informed decision affects or is likely to affect their economic behaviour in a way that would not have occurred without this impairment.

The principle of fair trading of Internal Market law requires that consumers are enabled to make their choice in full knowledge of the facts. Though less obvious, this principle also comprises the element of 'affecting the consumer's economic behaviour'. Due to the positive approach it is implied in the ability to make a (economic) choice. If consumers are enabled to make their choice, this choice made represents economic behaviour, which ideally meets their preferences. Of course, the choice not to make a transaction is also economic behaviour. The negative approach requires a clarification, because a mere impairment of the ability to take a transactional decision may very well result in the same transactional decision that would have been taken without the impairment. The decisive factor is the degree of impairment, the highest degree being that the consumer is 'disabled' from taking a transactional decision. This would be the exact contrast to being 'enabled' as understood from the positive principle of fair trading.

The condition of affecting or being likely to affect the consumer's economic behaviour thus assumes the function of the threshold from which a mere

[47] The Commission, it seems, had a different understanding with regard to the old notion of 'significance' in the original proposal, see COM (2003) 356 final at 54.

[48] Accordingly, in the definitions of 'misleading' (Articles 6 and 7) and 'aggressive' (Article 8) commercial practices, the element of appreciability is left aside, while that of 'taking a transactional decision that would not have been taken otherwise' is included.

impairment of the decision ability becomes relevant, i.e. 'appreciable' in the sense of the Directive. Such a threshold in the form of a risk assessment is necessary for a codified fair trading principle to be proportionate. This is likewise known from Article 2(2) of Directive 84/450 on misleading advertising, which requires that the deceptive advertising 'is likely to affect [the recipients'] economic behaviour'.[49] More generally, the Court has held that misconceptions which are not liable to influence the decision-making process of the consumer in any reasonable respect are irrelevant.[50]

The benchmark for the test

The benchmark for the test is the average consumer in the meaning of the case law of the Court of Justice, which is analogous to the Internal Market principle of fair trading.[51] As a matter of principle, the test applies to every consumer whom the commercial practice reaches, not only to specifically addressed consumers. In order to adapt the standard with regard to commercial practices specifically directed to a particular group of consumers, according to Article 5(2)(b), the standard is the average member of that group.

Article 5(3) was inserted into the text of the Common Position and was not featured in the original proposal. Although the obvious motivation to protect vulnerable consumers (in particular children)[52], which takes into account the differing capacities of consumers to process information,[53] may be considered an honourable one, this provision is hardly satisfactory. Commercial practices which reach the generality of consumers, but are likely to materially distort the economic behaviour only of a group of consumers who are particularly vulnerable to the practice or the underlying product shall be assessed from the perspective of the average member of that group. The difference to Article 5(2)(b) is that this provision concerns commercial practices which *reach* the generality of consumers, while Article 5(2)(b) requires that the commercial practices be *directed* to a particular group. One could say, however, that commercial practices which are likely to materially distort the economic behaviour only of a group of consumers are typically directed to that group, so that Article 5(2)(b) would apply anyway. Otherwise, Article 5(3) implies that the benchmark for commercial practices which reach the generality of consumers is, as a matter of principle, the average vulnerable consumer, since it is always likely that this type of consumer is affected in his capacity to make an informed choice. It must be doubted that this implication was intended by the legislator, since this would entail the vulnerable consumer as the *de facto* standard benchmark.

---

49 See also Case C-373/90 *Criminal proceedings against X ('Nissan')* [1992] ECR I-131 at 16.

50 See Chapter 1 at 5.3.3.

51 See *supra* at 3.3.2.

52 Cf. also COM (2003) 356 final at 30

53 See Chapter 3 at 6.4.

That this is not intended can be seen by the addition that Article 5(3) 'is without prejudice to the common and legitimate advertising practice of making exaggerated statements or statements which are not meant to be taken literally'. However, this condition must be considered a complete failure. It is absolutely contrary to the general purpose of the Directive, not to allow commercial practices which impair the consumer's ability to make an informed decision on the one hand, but to allow 'exaggerated statements or statements which are not meant to be taken literally' and to consider them 'legitimate' on the other hand. These kinds of statements are usually the ones which prevent consumers from making an informed decision, because they make the decisions based on wrong facts. It makes also no sense to exclude statements which are not meant to be taken literally, because this implies that it is left to the discretion of the trader, whether a commercial practice is unfair or not, while it must be the impact on the recipient, which is decisive. It is moreover questionable to include such an exemption into a rule, the very purpose of which is to protect vulnerable consumers in particular.

Conclusion

For an understanding of the Directive's general concept of unfair practices, which underlies the more specific rules, it is important to be aware of the fundamental elements which actually constitute the concept. The 'material distortion of the consumers' economic behaviour' is one of the two conditions of the general test for unfair commercial practices which are named by Article 5. It consists itself of two elements: the (likely) impairment of the consumer's ability to make an informed decision and, as a causality of the impairment, the consumers' (likely) taking a transactional decision that they would not have taken otherwise.[54] As will be demonstrated hereafter, these two elements already comprise the full substance of the unfairness notion.

3.4.2.2 The requirements of professional diligence

The condition that, according to Article 5(2)(a) the commercial practice must, in addition, be contrary to the requirements of professional diligence in order to be unfair and prohibited appears peculiar and problematic in a number of aspects in the present context.[55]

Article 2(h) defines 'professional diligence' as

---

54 In order to facilitate the reading the following refrains from mentioning each time that the likelihood of the conditions is sufficient/necessary.

55 See also the critical remarks by Köhler/Lettl, (2003) 49 *WRP* 1019 at 1036 et seq. and Glöckner, (2004) 50 *WRP* 936 at 939, 942.

'the standard of special skill and care which a trader may reasonably be expected to exercise towards consumers, commensurate with honest market practice and/or the general principle of good faith in the trader's field of activity'.

The points of reference for the skill and care which a trader may reasonably be expected to exercise are thus 'honest market practice and/or the general principle of good faith in the trader's field of activity'. The Common Position thus modified the original proposal, which used the trader's 'normal market practice' as a standard, and which was even less suitable.

The requirement of 'honest market practice and/or the general principle of good faith in the trader's field of activity' in the sense of Article 2(h) implies that professional custom and usage varies according to different economic branches. A problem could arise in fields where market practice also varies between Member States. Some branches may use selling techniques, which are accepted in some Member States as being in conformance with good business conduct or similar concepts while others consider them illegal.[56] Taking such a national perspective for the assessment of 'honest market practice and/or the general principle of good faith in the trader's field of activity' would certainly undermine the harmonising effect of the Directive.

This national understanding of 'normal market practice' could be countered by the settled case law of the Court of Justice, according to which:

'The need for a uniform application of Community law and the principle of equality require that the terms of a provision of Community law which makes no express reference to the law of the Member States for the purpose of determining its meaning and scope must normally be given an independent and uniform interpretation throughout the Community'.[57]

The problem with the present concept is, however, that where the national assessments of the meaning of an 'honest market practice and/or the general principle of good faith in the trader's field of activity' differ, there can hardly

---

56 An example is the technique of multi-level marketing, which is popular in certain branches (e.g. in the cosmetics sector), but which is judged very differently in the Member States, i.e. from still being an 'honest market practice' to being an 'unfair practice'. See Micklitz/Monazzahian/Rößler, *Multilevel Marketing, Vol. II*, p. 140 et seq. There is a consensus, however, on the unfairness of pyramid promotional schemes, which are included in the Directive's blacklist of unfair commercial practices (no. 13 in the first annex).

57 Case 327/82 *Ekro BV Vee- en Vleeshandel v Produktschap voor Vee en Vlees* [1984] ECR 107 at 11. Subsequently, see Case C-287/98 *Luxemburg v Berthe Linster et al.* [2000] ECR I-6917 at 43, Case C-357/98 *R. v Secretary of State for the Home Department, ex parte Nana Yaa Konadu Yiadom* [2000] ECR I-9265 at 26, Case C-151/02 *Landeshauptstadt Kiel v Norbert Jaeger* [2003] ECR I-8389 at 58, Case C-236/01 *Monsanto Agricoltura Italia SpA et al. v Presidenza del Consiglio dei Ministri et al.* [2003] ECR I-8105 at 72.

have evolved a Community 'honest' practice. The practices may have been legal in some countries and illegal and therefore unexercised in others. As the 'trader's fields of activity' are thus currently characterised by a nationally heterogeneous legal or professional assessment, they could not develop into a Community-wide practice with a common European legal or professional assessment. This renders the introduction of a concept of professional diligence in the present shape quite ineffectual.

The Commission justified the concept of 'professional diligence' in the original proposal, claiming it was 'necessary to ensure that normal business practices which are in conformity with custom and usage, such as advertising based on brand recognition or product placement, will not be caught by the Directive even if they are capable of influencing consumers' economic behaviour'.[58] This is a somewhat deficient reasoning, since it implies that the main purpose of the 'material distortion' condition is to avoid that consumers are influenced in their economic behaviour. This is far from true. It can safely be claimed that the basic purpose of all advertising is to influence the consumers' economic behaviour in order to make them buy a particular good or service. This is just what advertising is about. The decisive point is that the consumer's economic behaviour results from an autonomous and informed decision. Therefore consumers must be enabled to make their choice in full knowledge of the facts or, in the negative terms of the general test, the consumers' ability to make an informed decision must not be impaired. It is thus not the influence as such of the consumer's economic behaviour, but the method by which this is achieved, which can make a commercial practice unfair.

In this respect, the requirements of professional diligence are not very helpful as an additional condition to the non-impairment of the consumer's ability to make an informed decision. On the contrary, it actually allows the use of commercial practices which indeed do impair the consumer's ability to make an informed decision, provided that they are regarded as an 'honest practice' in the trader's field of activity. It is true that recital 6 sentence 5 of the proposal suggests that this is not intended:

> 'Further, this Directive does not affect accepted advertising and marketing practices, such as legitimate product placement, brand differentiation or the offering of incentives which may legitimately affect consumers' perceptions of products and influence their behaviour without impairing the consumer's ability to make an informed decision'.

However, if those practices do not impair the consumers' ability to make an informed decision, they would not be unfair under the general clause anyway.

---

58 COM (2003) 356 final at 53.

As a matter of fact, the condition of 'professional diligence' bears the risk of crystallising existing commercial practices, which would be unfair under the crucial condition of 'material distortion of the consumers' economic behaviour', but which are still considered an accepted practice in the trader's fields of activity. This condition thus could undermine the general test for unfair commercial practices, since a commercial practice can never be unfair, if it is not considered contrary to the requirements of professional diligence. If, for political reasons, it is desired that particular practices should not be considered unfair although they would fulfil the general unfairness test (e.g. because advertising based on brand recognition or product placement uses subliminal techniques and thus impairs the consumer to make an informed decision), they should be exempted explicitly. Introducing a complementary general test to the actual unfairness condition, in addition runs the risk that unexpected practices are not covered by the prohibition, although they do impair the consumer's ability to make an informed decision.

It is hardly necessary to point out that the condition of being contrary to the requirements of professional diligence has no counterpart in the existing Internal Market law principle of fair trading.

3.5 Misleading and aggressive commercial practices as particular sub-categories

According to Article 5(4), misleading and aggressive commercial practices are practices which are considered to be unfair 'in particular'. Indeed, these types of commercial practices, as defined in the Directive, are specific expressions of what is regarded as unfair according to the general test. Both types put a slightly different emphasis on the components of the general test.

In the previous section, two fundamental pillars have been exposed which carry the general test for unfair commercial practices:

1) the impairment of the consumer's ability to make an informed decision
2) the consumer's taking a transactional decision that he would not have taken otherwise as a consequence of the impairment.

It has then been submitted that the idea of an 'appreciable' impairment is embodied by the requirement of the consequential effect of taking a transactional decision which would not have been taken otherwise. It has finally been argued that the concept of being contrary to 'professional diligence' is either superfluous or a conceptual paradox. As a consequence, the two conditions listed above can be regarded as the ultimate core of the unfairness test. Although, the provisions on misleading and aggressive commercial practices do not avail themselves of the 'material distortion' notion, the two conditions underlying 'unfairness' can be rediscovered in the respective definitions of misleading and aggressive commercial practices.

Misleading commercial practices are characterised by the fact that a deceptive act or omission creates a misrepresentation in the minds of consumers, which leads to a deviation of their economic behaviour. Misleading commercial practices thus concern the first pillar, particularly emphasising the impairment of the consumers' ability to make an *informed* decision.

Aggressive commercial practices are characterised by the use of harassment, coercion and undue influence. Here, the first pillar is similarly concerned, but the emphasis rests upon the impairment of the consumers' *ability* to make an informed decision. In addition, this type of commercial practice concerns the second pillar in that it may directly affect the consumer's freedom of conduct.

3.5.1 Misleading commercial practices

Misleading practices are considered to constitute the largest part of unfair commercial practices, which is reflected by the density of their regulation in the Directive. There has always been a certain ambivalence in the understanding of the relationship between misleading and unfair practices, which can be traced in the Misleading Advertising Directive. On the one hand, unfair advertising was excluded from the original proposal at the time of the adoption of the Directive. On the other hand, the Directive clearly acknowledges a close relationship, since its defined purpose is to 'protect [...] against misleading advertising and the unfair consequences thereof' (Article 1).[59] Besides, the Court has never hesitated to consider misleading practices under the mandatory interest justification of fair trading.

The Directive distinguishes between misleading actions (Article 6) and misleading omissions (Article 7). As recital 14 indicates, this distinction is to follow the laws and practices of the Member States. As will be demonstrated later, misleading omissions are often merely a reflection of misleading actions. The Directive makes use of this concept, however, to introduce some basic information duties.

3.5.1.1 Misleading actions

The definition of misleading commercial practices is essentially based on that given in Directive 84/450 on misleading and comparative advertising.[60] The underlying idea is, once more, that the average consumer must not be caused to take a transactional decision which he would not have taken otherwise by being impaired from making an informed decision, no matter whether the

---

59 See Chapter 2 at 2.1 and at 2.3.

60 As far as misleading advertising is concerned, according to Article 14, the scope of application of Directive 84/450 is going to be confined to protecting traders.

information provided is false or factually correct. As far as misleading actions are concerned, this impairment can happen by a deception (Article 6(1)) or in a 'factual context' (Article 6(2)).

Misleading by deception

The items named in relation to which commercial practices can be misleading by deception are largely taken from the Misleading Advertising Directive and have further been complemented. Although product-related characteristics dominate, other features are characteristics of the trader (i.e. the contractual party), the price, the proper execution of the contract, and rights and risks of the consumers. The Common Position deleted the provision contained in the original proposal which, in connection with claims made about a product, reversed the burden of proof. A trader making such a claim was required to substantiate it. The current text of the Directive thus abandoned the idea to turn into a rule a possibility which exists in Article 6 of the Misleading Advertising Directive and takes account of the fact that consumers usually are in no or at least in a far worse position to prove that a claim is untrue.

Misleading in a factual context

The concept of being misleading in a 'factual context' (Article 6(2)) is not further explained. The intention is apparently to catch all other situations, which may not be covered by 'deception'. Yet, since the deception can happen 'in any way, including overall presentation', and the factual context is to take 'account of all [the commercial practice's] features and circumstances', some overlapping can be assumed. What is yet again decisive is that the practice causes or is likely to cause the average consumer to take a transactional decision that he would not have taken otherwise, because he is impaired to make an informed decision. That the concept of being misled in a 'factual context' is of a broad nature can be seen by the fact that misleading omissions are basically captured by the same concept according to Article 7(1).

The commercial practices being misleading in a 'factual context' are related to two situations. Firstly, the marketing of a product may create confusion with products or distinguishing marks of a competitor. Secondly, the trader does not comply with provisions of a code of conduct by which he has undertaken to be bound. This provision tries to strike a balance between the fact that codes of conduct are voluntary on the one hand and that the consumers rely on the commitments contained in such codes. Therefore, further conditions are attached to the non-compliance.

3.5.1.2 Misleading omissions

The category of misleading omissions does not as such appear in the Misleading Advertising Directive. However, there is no reason to suppose that in Article 7 the Unfair Commercial Practices Directive introduces a totally new concept regarding misleading commercial communication. Depending on the definition of misleading actions, omissions are likewise covered.[61]

Omissions as a negative reflection of actions

It can easily be argued that presentations which are 'in any way' deceptive and, in particular misleading 'factual contexts' in the sense of Article 6, can happen by omissions as well, the decisive factor being that by impairing the consumers' ability to make an informed choice they cause them to take a transactional decision which they would not have taken otherwise. Although in *Nissan*, concerning the parallel import of undriven but previously registered cars, the Court ultimately came to the conclusion that the advertising was not misleading in the sense of the Misleading Advertising Directive, it did consider it possible that advertising the cars as 'new' could be misleading insofar as this sought to conceal the fact of the previous registration (which was for the national court to ascertain in the light of the circumstances of the particular case).[62] This example illustrates that misleading action (advertising as 'new') and misleading omission (not indicating the previous registration) are indeed very closely related and, as a matter of fact, are exchangeable, basically depending on the point of view from which the phenomenon is described.

The actual function of the concept of misleading omissions

The real magnitude of the concept of misleading omissions is to be seen in the fact that it partly derogates from the essential course of the Directive, which is to prohibit unfair commercial practices, and is used as a tool to incorporate some basic positive information duties.[63] This duty is set out at three levels, and is linked to the threshold of an 'invitation to purchase' for determining at which stage of the business-to-consumer contact the information must be provided.

As a general rule, Article 7(1) equates with a misleading action the omission of

> 'material information that the average consumer needs, according to the context, to take an informed transactional decision and thereby causes or is likely to cause the average consumer to take a transactional decision that he would not have taken otherwise'.

---

61 Cf. also Henning-Bodewig (2004) 53 *GRUR Int.* 183 at 191.

62 Case C-373/90 *Criminal proceedings against X ('Nissan')* [1992] ECR I-131 at 15. See Chapter 2 at 2.3.

63 Schulte-Nölke/Busch, (2004) 12 *ZEuP* 99 at 104 et seq. even consider the concept of pre-contractual information disclosure in Article 7 to be the actual focus of the Directive. The regrets expressed by de Vrey (2004) 20 *TvC* 2 at 8 et seq. and at 11 that positive information obligations are not given enough attention in the Directive seem to be unfounded, especially if one takes into account that the non-disclosure of information will be covered by the general clause as being unfair, if the consumer's ability to make an informed choice is impaired without the disclosure of this information. Cf. also *infra* at 3.6.2.

More concretely, it is a misleading omission, according to Article 7(2),

> 'when a trader hides or provides in an unclear, unintelligible, ambiguous or untimely manner such material information as referred to in paragraph 1 or fails to identify the commercial intent of the commercial practice if not already apparent from the context'.

Article 7(3) clarifies that limitations of the communication medium and any measures taken by the trader to make the information available to consumers by other means shall be taken into account in deciding whether information has been omitted.

Finally, Article 7(4) defines certain details as material, i.e. they must be provided if they are not already apparent from the context. The required information items relate to the product, the trader, the costs (i.e. the price including additional charges), the main contractual terms (i.e. 'arrangements' for payment, delivery, performance, complaint handling), and possible remedies (right of withdrawal).

The rules governing misleading omissions closely resemble the Internal Market law principle of fair trading. At the first level, the general idea is that consumers must be enabled to make their choice in full knowledge of the facts. Accordingly, they have to be provided with the information they need to make an informed decision. At the second level, the manner of information disclosure must meet the standards of comprehensibility and economic recognisability. At the third level, substantive information duties are assigned to the trader, which belong exactly to the categories which have been identified as objectively necessary in the context of the principle of fair trading in the *acquis communautaire*.[64] What matters is that the information is available to the consumer. Information apparent from the context is therefore not required to be disclosed actively.

According to Article 7(5), information requirements established by Community law in relation to commercial communication are to be regarded as 'material' in the sense of Article 7. Given that the specific directives continue to apply anyway, the main consequence of this incorporation is to be seen in the fact that the information requirements of the specific directives are submitted to the enforcement scheme of the general Directive.[65]

The concept of the 'invitation to purchase'

The concept of the 'invitation to purchase' calls for more attention. The intention is clear: not every commercial communication should fulfil the same requirements, no matter how far it is from the possible conclusion of a contract.

---

64 See Chapter 3 at 5.2.3.1.

65 Likewise Schulte-Nölke/Busch, (2004) 12 *ZEuP* 99 at 108 et seq., who moreover reject the idea that Article 7(5) turns the minimum information standards of the specific directives into maximum standards.

The underlying idea is that the business-to-consumer contact prior to contract conclusion does not only know a pre-contractual phase, but also a phase even before that, which is not yet dense enough to relate it to fair-trading obligations, and which may never even reach that density.[66] In principle, this approach has to be welcomed. However, problems arise due to the definition of an 'invitation to purchase'. According to Article 2(i) this

> 'means a commercial communication which indicates characteristics of the product and the price in a way appropriate to the means of the commercial communication used and thereby enables the consumer to make a purchase'.

A commercial practice has thus reached the status of an 'invitation to purchase' only if it indicates characteristics of the product and the price. The text of the Common Position has deleted the requirement that 'the main' characteristics have to be indicated for a commercial practice to be an invitation to purchase. This is certainly an improvement in the wording, since it was incoherent with Article 7(4), which requires the indication of, *inter alia*, the main characteristics of the product and the price for invitations to purchase. According to the Commission proposal's definition, these items were, however, already an integral component of an 'invitation to purchase'. Still, it must be doubted that the wording has actually changed the substance of this concept. An invitation to purchase requires the indication of the price – which is a main characteristic of the contract – and the indication of characteristics of the product which enable the consumer to make a purchase – these will be most probably at least the main characteristics of the product.

This incoherence may be explained by the fact that the definition of an 'invitation to purchase' refers to a concept of contract law, which in German law is known as *invitatio ad offerendum*, and the purpose of which is to distinguish a legally binding contractual offer from the mere invitation to the other party to make such a contractual offer. In both situations the 'offer' encompasses all the necessary elements of a valid contract (*essentialia negotii*), however, the *invitatio ad offerendum* lacks the desire to create a legal bond. While a contractual offer is therefore legally binding and just needs acceptance, the *invitatio ad offerendum* has no contractual consequence.[67] The concept can be rediscovered in Article 14

[66] The Commission wanted to exclude general brand or product awareness marketing in its original proposal, see COM (2003) 356 final at 64.

[67] This concept permits the trader to display products in shop windows or in catalogues without being contractually liable, if the number of purchase requests exceeds the quantity of products in stock. Moreover, the trader can choose his contractual parties according to their financial reliability. It should be noted that other countries have chosen different solutions. According to French law, for instance, the offer to a broad public of a trader is legally binding in the first instance, but the acceptance of this offer can be refused, if there is a legitimate interest. See Schlesinger, *Formation of Contracts*, p. 77 et seq., Youngs, *Comparative Law*, p. 344 et seq., Zweigert/Kötz, *Comparative Law*, p. 356 et seq.

of the CISG.[68] This provision distinguishes between a proposal for concluding a contract which is sufficiently definite and indicates the intention of the offeror to be bound in case of acceptance, and a mere invitation to make offers.[69]

Fair-trading law, however, requires an approach which is different from that of a purely contractual perspective, which is moreover excluded from the scope of the Directive according to Article 3(2).[70] Making fair-trading law applicable only to invitations to purchase which indicate (the main) characteristics of the product and other fundamental components of the future contract is senseless, since it is precisely the task of fair-trading law to submit commercial communication which does not enable the consumers to make an informed choice to requirements which do enable them to make that choice.[71] What does matter, though, is whether the commercial contact is close and targeted enough that it can influence the consumers' decision-making process and can cause them to take a transactional decision. This quite necessary threshold, however, should be linked to the very notion of 'commercial practice', and indeed is done so in Article 2(d). It is pointed out that the commercial communication must be 'directly connected with the promotion, sale or supply of a product to consumers'. Although a clearer definition might be desirable, it can be inferred from the element of 'direct connection' that there must be close and targeted enough a commercial contact between business and consumers for the fair-trading rules to apply. This is thus the genuine underlying threshold, and not whether (the main) characteristics of the product and the price are indicated.

It is submitted that the idea of a certain density of the contact between trader and consumer is inherent in the Internal Market law principle of fair trading. The concept that consumers must be enabled to make their choice in full knowledge of the facts logically applies only where there such a choice is at issue in the first place. This, however, requires a certain density in the pre-contractual sphere. Before this density has been reached there is no choice to be made.

---

68 United Nations Convention on Contracts for the International Sale of Goods, signed on 11 April 1980 in Vienna.

69 Article 2:201 of the Principles of European Contract Law also requires an intention for a legal bond. In the case of a proposal to supply goods or services at stated prices to the public, this is presumed to be an offer to sell or supply at that price until the stock of goods, or the supplier's capacity to supply the service, is exhausted. See Lando/Beale, *Principles of European contract law.*

70 Henning-Bodewig (2004) 53 *GRUR Int.* 183 at 192. Schulte-Nölke/Busch, (2004) 12 *ZEuP* 99 at 106 also point out that the 'invitation to purchase' must be understood in a specific fair-trading law sense rather than in a contract-law sense.

71 The desire to create a legal bond is not a yardstick which is incorporated in the Directive. This can also be seen with regard to point 5 of the first annex, which considers 'bait advertising' as a commercial practice which is in all circumstances considered unfair (while, from the contractual point of view, the concept of the *invitatio ad offerendum* would not consider these offers as legally binding, e.g. when the trader runs out of stock).

3.5.2 Aggressive commercial practices

According to the Directive's eleventh recital, aggressive commercial practices are currently not regulated at Community level. This is far from true. Although they have received much less attention than misleading practices indeed, certain aspects have definitely been regulated, the rules on inertia selling and those concerning various types of unsolicited commercial communication being prime examples.

In accordance with what has earlier been illustrated, aggressive commercial practices are characterised by the impairment of the consumers' freedom of choice or conduct, which affects their transactional decision.[72] Article 8 names the use of harassment, coercion, including the use of physical force, and undue influence as the recognised means by which the impairment can be executed. Although all notions are similarly vague, 'undue influence' is the only term which is further defined in Article 2(j), according to which it 'means exploiting a position of power in relation to the consumer so as to apply pressure, even without using or threatening to use physical force'. Article 9 names several criteria of which account shall be taken in determining whether a commercial practice uses harassment, coercion or undue influence. The dominating element is the threat, other aspects being persistence, the exploitation of specific circumstances of the consumer, and non-contractual barriers. Concrete situations of prohibited aggressive commercial practices are described in the blacklist of the first annex.

Aggressive commercial practices are far less problematic than misleading commercial practices as far as their qualification as unfair is concerned. The impairment of the consumers' ability to make an informed choice is usually much stronger, the emphasis resting on the 'ability'. The consumer is no longer sovereign over his decision-making process, and he is disabled from making an autonomous choice. This is absolutely in line with the general unfairness test, and it is also reflected in the Internal Market law principle of fair trading, according to which consumers must be enabled to make their choice in full knowledge of the facts.

3.6 Comparison of the established principle of fair trading with the concept of the Directive

During the analysis of the Directive, the various rules have already been mirrored against the principle of fair trading which has been identified as a general principle of Internal Market law. In the following, both basic concepts are to be confronted with each other directly.

---

[72] See *supra* at 3.5.

3.6.1 The concepts

The original concepts

The Internal Market law principle of fair trading implies the following:

> Consumers must be enabled to make their choice in full knowledge of the facts.

It is suggested that, when the various definitions at different places are merged into one, the general clause of the Directive essentially states the following:

> A commercial practice is prohibited, if, with regard to the average consumer whom it reaches or to whom it is addressed, it appreciably impairs or is likely to appreciably impair the consumer's ability to make an informed decision, thereby causing or being likely to cause the consumer to take a transactional decision concerning the product that he would not have taken otherwise, and if it is contrary to the requirements of professional diligence.

A refinement of the general clause of the Directive

It has been argued that the condition of being contrary to the requirements of professional diligence is either superfluous or a conceptual paradox.[73] It is a restriction of the general concept, which seems to be politically motivated. The comparison with the Internal Market law principle of fair trading shows that the condition has no counterpart in that principle.

Moreover, it has been suggested that the element of 'appreciability' has no added value, since an inappreciable impairment would not have the required consequence of taking or being likely to take a transactional decision that the consumer would not have taken otherwise.

It is suggested that the general clause can be further simplified to the following essence:

> A commercial practice is prohibited, if it impairs or is likely to impair the average consumer's ability to make an informed decision and thereby causes or is likely to cause the consumer to take a transactional decision that he would not have taken otherwise.

The essential two elements of unfairness are thus

1) the (likely) impairment of the average consumer's ability to make an informed decision
2) the consumer's (likely) taking of a transactional decision that he would not have taken otherwise as a consequence of the impairment.

---

[73] See *supra* at 3.4.2.2.

3.6.2 Comparison

Basic similarity

The refinement of the general clause shows that its core is very similar to the Internal Market law principle of fair trading. The wording of one as a negative concept and of the other one as a positive concept must not mislead as to the similarity in substance. In fact this most obvious difference of the concepts in appearance is at the same time their closest similarity in substance.

It is submitted that, as a matter of principle, everything can be expressed in either a positive way or in a negative way while conveying the same meaning. Permitting only fair trading is the same as prohibiting unfair trading. Requiring that consumers must be enabled to make their choice in full knowledge of the facts is the same as prohibiting that consumers are not enabled to make their choice in full knowledge of the facts, i.e. impairing their ability to make an informed decision.

For instance, the positive wording of the Internal Market law principle of fair trading seems to suggest that it is more likely to imply positive duties of information disclosure than the negative wording in the general clause of the Directive. This is not the case. That consumers must be enabled to make their choice in full knowledge of the facts implies, indeed, that they are provided with the necessary information where this information is not available otherwise (e.g. from the context). However, the same holds true for a concept which requires that commercial communication must not impair the consumer's ability to make an informed decision. If the information at hand is not sufficient to make an informed decision, then the consumer's ability to make an informed decision is impaired. This can only be cured by disclosing the necessary information. This is moreover perfectly illustrated by the Directive's concept of misleading omissions, which is introduced as a sub-principle of the general clause.

The argument works the other way around as well. If, for example, the negative concept prohibits misleading advertising or aggressive advertising, because this would impair the consumers' ability to make an informed decision, this is also reflected in the positive principle. The Internal Market law principle of fair trading prohibits misleading and aggressive advertising because consumers would then not be enabled to make their choice in full knowledge of the facts.

Differences?

The question of differences is more crucial regarding the fact that the general clause in the Directive requires the causality between the impaired decision-making ability and the taking of a transactional decision and that it contains the element of 'likelihood'. Both elements seem to be absent in the Internal Market law principle of fair trading. However, this does not cause a conflict between the concepts.

The causality criterion, it is submitted, is necessary in a negatively worded concept, which is to be proportionate and compatible with the requirements of trading reality. Prohibiting any impairment of the consumers' ability to make an informed choice, however slight it may be, without this impairment materialising or being likely to materialise in a difference of economic behaviour would ultimately amount to a prohibition of any commercial communication, since the impairment as such cannot not be ruled out. The principle that consumers must be enabled to make their choice in full knowledge of the facts, can be said to comprise this causal element. It concerns 'their' choice. It is not supposed to mean that consumers must be enabled to make 'a' choice whether it materialises or not. That it concerns 'their' choice means that the decision-making process must be related to a particular transactional decision that they are about to take and that the principle of fair trading is only infringed, if the defect in enabling them to make their choice in full knowledge of the facts causes economic behaviour that would not have been caused otherwise.

The likelihood of the impairment of the consumer's ability to make an informed decision assumes the function of a threshold in two ways, in that it marks what is sufficient on the one hand and what is necessary on the other hand. The sufficiency of likelihood guarantees the preventive effect of the prohibition in that an impairment does not need to have actually occurred (and does not need to be proven). In a positive wording of the concept this must not be included. The concept that consumers must be enabled to make their choice in full knowledge of the facts is preventive from the start. The likelihood as a necessity rules out that every commercial communication could be regarded as an impairment. However, this seems a less crucial function, due to the causality requirement concerning the transactional decision. Also in this case, a positive wording does not need the aspect of likelihood. Where the Internal Market law principle occurs in its negative function as the prohibition of misleading advertising, secondary law and case law also include this aspect of likelihood.[74] The same holds true for the aspect of likelihood in affecting the consumer's economic behaviour.

On the other hand, some differences can be seen between the two concepts with regard to the consumer yardstick applied. The Directive's notion of the 'average consumer' was meant to reflect the consumer image of the Court of Justice. By deleting the definition of this concept in the text of the Common Position it was furthermore intended to leave the notion open for development in line with future case law of the Court. However, by the insertion of Article 5(3), the Directive actually goes its own way. Commercial practices which reach the generality of consumers, but are likely to materially distort the economic behaviour only of a group of consumers who are particularly vulnerable to the practice or the underlying product shall be assessed from the

[74] See *supra* at 3.4.2.1. See also Chapter 3 at 5.3.

perspective of the average member of that group. This could be said to entail that the benchmark for commercial practices which reach the generality of consumers is, as a matter of principle, the average vulnerable consumer, since it is always likely that this type of consumer is affected in his capacity to make an informed choice. It should be remembered that commercial practices which are *directed* to a specific group of consumers will be measured according to the average member for that group under Article 5(2) anyway. Article 5(3), however, introduces the *de facto* standard yardstick of the (average) vulnerable consumer for commercial practices which *reach* the generality of consumers. This may not have been intended by the legislator,[75] but it is implied in the provision. If this provision continues to be part of the Directive, it would remain to be seen whether the Court would find an interpretation that brings it in line with the general consumer standard developed by the Court.

3.6.3 Conclusion

The Internal Market law principle of fair trading and the underlying concept of the general clause of the Directive display a remarkable similarity, provided that the general clause is freed from the unfortunate condition of requirements of professional diligence and further simplified in its wording.

In particular, the seemingly biggest difference, that is the positively worded concept of the Internal Market principle of fair trading and the negatively worded concept of the general clause, does not lead to a discrepancy in meaning. It is suggested that the idea of fair trading can equally be expressed as a duty to trade fairly or a duty not to trade unfairly. This view is based on the assumption that there is nothing in-between fair or unfair trading. Trading which is not fair is unfair and vice versa.

The disparities of the concepts, because of the required causality between the impaired decision-making ability and the taking of a transactional decision in the general clause, and because it contains the element of 'likelihood', can be explained by its negative wording. It does not appear to influence the basic congruence of the two concepts.

The applicable consumer yardstick could, however, be seen as a distinguishing feature between the two concepts, if Article 5(3) is not understood as just a clarifying provision for the protection of vulnerable consumers, but as a general rule for taking the vulnerable consumer as the basic yardstick. Although the latter interpretation may not have been intended, the wording of the Directive allows it.

---

75 Lettl, (2004) 50 *WRP* 1079 at 1098 assumes that different nuances were not intended by the use of the terms 'reach' and 'direct'.

4 The future of the Directive

The Common Position with a view to the adoption of a Directive against unfair commercial practices represents a crucial step in the legislative procedure. Having cleared this hurdle, it seems quite improbable that the Directive will not be adopted. Possible modifications of the text should be minor.

Yet, there are two questions that are appropriate to be asked with regard to the future of the Directive. The first is: can the Directive be legally adopted? The second: do we need the Directive, if we already have a general principle of fair trading in the *acquis communautaire*?

4.1 Can the Directive be legally adopted?

The question is imprecise insofar as the Directive would come into force in any case, if it were adopted. An illegal Directive would not be void, but it would be voidable and could be challenged before the Court of Justice. The legality of the adoption of the Directive should therefore briefly be examined.[76]

4.1.1 Legal basis

The Directive is going to be based on Article 95. In order to be covered by Article 95 the prohibition of unfair commercial practices must aim at the establishment and functioning of the Internal Market and must observe the limits of the Community competence as interpreted by the Court of Justice.[77]

The Internal Market objective of the prohibition of unfair commercial practices

It has been argued at various places in this study that fair trading is linked to the Internal Market.[78] It has moreover been demonstrated that the prohibition of unfair trading and the obligation of fair trading are equivalent. There can be no reasonable doubt that the subject matter of the Directive is of Internal Market relevance.

It has been submitted by some writers that Article 95 cannot provide a legal basis for the harmonisation of rules which come under the *Keck* doctrine.[79] The underlying idea is that the exclusion of rules concerning certain selling arrangements (which do not meet the conditions of the *Keck* proviso) from the scope

---

[76] The considerations only relate to the prohibition of unfair commercial practices and not to other aspects of the Directive, such as enforcement provisions.

[77] See also the considerations on the legal basis for harmonisation of fair trading law in Chapter 2 at 1.1.

[78] See e.g. Chapter 3 at 4. and Chapter 4 in general.

[79] Mortelmans (1994) 42 *SEW* 236 at 244, Mortelmans/van Ooik, (2001) 50 *Ars Aequi* 114 at 125 et seq., Mortelmans (2002) 39 *CML Rev.* 1303 at 1326. See also Bogdandy/Bast (2002) 39 *CML Rev.* 227 at 245, Davies, *Nationality Discrimination*, p. 64 note 39.

of the free movement of goods implies that they do not constitute restrictions on trade and are not taken into account regarding the Internal Market objective. Given that rules on commercial practices may indeed fall under the *Keck* doctrine,[80] this would raise doubts on the legality of the Directive. However, this view must be rejected. The Court has clearly not taken up this doctrinal line of reasoning, although it had the opportunity to do so. In *Tobacco Advertising*,[81] where the Court dealt with the legality of a Directive (partly) concerning selling arrangements, the *Keck* argument did not even appear.[82] Moreover, positive integration and negative integration are two different issues. It can be said that 'the concept of "establishment and functioning of the internal Market" embraces more than the lifting of the Community's internal frontiers',[83] it closes gaps which have been created by the removal of trade barriers. This understanding of the differing functions of positive and negative is also confirmed by the Court's competition reasoning in the context of Internal Market harmonisation. Contrary to the definition of the Internal Market in Article 14(2) of the Treaty, which refers solely to free movement, the Court has repeatedly established the objective of removing (appreciable) distortions of competition as being conducive to the attainment of the Internal Market and thus to fall within the scope of Article 95.[84] Although it may be disputed that obstacles to free movement and distortions of competition are separable from each other, the reasoning of the Court demonstrates, that it considers the creation of an Internal Market by means of positive integration to be a broader concept than by means of negative integration.

The Court of Justice criteria for Article 95

Although it basically takes a generous approach as to what is covered by the Internal Market objective of Article 95, the Court has made clear that the legislature must obey certain rules in order to legally pursue this objective the sense of Article 95. It has thus established in *Tobacco Advertising* that a measure adopted on the basis of Article 95 must genuinely have as its object the improvement of the conditions for the establishment and functioning of the Internal Market, i.e. the mere finding of disparities between national rules and of the abstract risk of

---

80 It has been demonstrated, however, that the dominance of good-related rules and of the *Keck* proviso entail that less national rules come under *Keck* than one might expect, see Chapter 1 at 5.4.

81 Case C-376/98 *Germany v Parliament and Council ('Tobacco Advertising')* [2000] ECR I-8419.

82 Although Mortelmans/van Ooik, (2001) 50 *Ars Aequi* 114 at 126 find hints in the Court' reasoning in line with their hypothesis, they acknowledge that the Court did not actually address the *Keck* issue.

83 Kapteyn/VerLoren van Themaat, *Law of the European Communities*, 3rd ed., p. 785. Similarly, with reference to the vital element of breeding consumer confidence, Weatherill in Craig/de Búrca, *EU Law*, p. 693 at 718.

84 Case C-300/89 *Commission v Council ('Titanium Dioxide')* [1991] ECR I-2867 at 23, *Tobacco Advertising* at 106.

obstacles is not sufficient.[85] The Court's reasoning can be translated into a three-stage test.[86] Firstly, there have to exist obstacles to free movement or appreciable distortions of competition (*de minimis* requirement). Secondly, the legal measure actually has to contribute to eliminating obstacles to free movement or to removing appreciable distortions of competition.[87] Thirdly, as an additional requirement Article 95 may not be used to circumvent the limits on other Treaty provisions,[88] which is, however, not problematic here.

According to the studies commissioned by the Commission during the consultation process, there are indeed currently obstacles to free movement and appreciable distortions of competition resulting from the differences of the national laws concerning unfair commercial practices.[89] It is a point on which virtually all stakeholders seem to agree. Whether the proposed concept of a prohibition of unfair commercial practices actually contributes to eliminating the obstacles to free movement or to removing appreciable distortions of competition in the view of the Court is less obvious. The test suggested by the Court is not clear, because it introduces vague concepts itself.[90]

It is suggested that the adoption of the Directive would meet the criteria.[91] The high amount of fair trading related cases that the Court of Justice had to decide in the light of free movement suggests that at least the obstacles to trade are an undeniable reality. By harmonising the law of fair trading, which is known to all Member States, but regulated differently, the barriers for cross-border trade faced by businesses are certainly reduced. The adoption of the proposal would confront them with the same (un)fairness concept throughout the Community, which allows them to use the same marketing practices Europe-wide and to access the national markets under the same legal conditions as those of their home country. The fact that Internal Market law already knows a principle of fair trading does not affect this reasoning, since it can only eliminate barriers (on a case by case basis), but does not create a homogenous legal framework for fair trading in the Internal Market. Moreover, it poses no problem that the general clause is worded as a prohibition. It does not have the effect that commercial communication would be totally banned, which would be incompatible with the Internal Market objective.[92] The prohibition affects only a very

---

85 *Tobacco Advertising* at 84.

86 Weatherill, (2004) 15 *EBLR* 23 at 26 et seq. reflects on whether the building of consumer confidence is an additional route (next to that of market-building) to assessing the validity of harmonisation measures, however, leaving the question open.

87 *Tobacco Advertising* at 108.

88 *Tobacco Advertising* at 79.

89 The main results can be found in the Extended Impact Assessment published together with the June 2003 proposal for a Directive on unfair commercial practices.

90 E.g. when is distortion 'appreciable'? See Weatherill, (2002) 13 *EBLR* 497 at 506 et seq.

91 More pessimistically, Wiebe, (2002) 48 *WRP* 283 at 289.

92 Cf. *Tobacco Advertising* at 101 et seq.

specific part of commercial communication (i.e. the unfair one) and is actually equivalent to a duty to trade fairly.[93] Finally, and most importantly, the proposed system of prohibition of unfair commercial practices contributes to the consumers' ability to make informed economic choices, in that it bans practices which obstruct them to do so. Consumers, who play a vital role in the functioning of the Internal Market, would thus be supported in making use of their active cross-border function.

4.1.2 Proportionality and subsidiarity

In the context of the determination of the competence or legislative capacity of the Community and its institutions 'the principle of proportionality requires that measures taken by the Community institutions should be appropriate to achieve the objective pursued without going beyond what is necessary to that end'.[94] This formula reappears in No. 1 of the Protocol on proportionality and subsidiarity annexed by the Treaty of Amsterdam to the EC Treaty.

It is the objective of the Directive to contribute to the proper functioning of the Internal Market and to achieve a high level of consumer protection. The harmonisation of fair trading is an appropriate means to achieve this objective, given its necessity for the proper functioning of the Internal Market and the interrelationship between the Internal Market and consumer protection.[95] The Directive does not go beyond what is necessary to achieve this objective. It contains a similar fair trading concept to the one which is a general principle of Internal Market law.[96] Its effect is mainly restricted to making coherent the present incoherence in secondary law and to extending the scope of the general concept to situations which are not currently covered by Internal Market law.[97] Moreover, a framework directive has been chosen instead of a detailed measure in the sense of No. 6 of the Protocol on proportionality and subsidiarity.

According to the principle of subsidiarity as enshrined in Article 5(2) of the Treaty, in areas of shared competence, the Community must take action only if and insofar as the objectives of the proposed action cannot be sufficiently achieved by the Member States. The past has proven that in the area of unfair commercial practices the objective of a functioning Internal Market cannot sufficiently be achieved at national level. It is precisely the current national heterogeneity which is responsible for the obstacles to free movement and distortions of competition.[98] Therefore, action at Community level would

---

93 See *supra* at 3.6.2.

94 E.g. Case C-359/92 *Germany v Council* [1994] ECR I-3681 at 44 referring to settled case law, in particular Case C-174/89 *Hoche* [1990] ECR I-2681 at 19.

95 See Chapter 4 at 2.1.3.1 and at 2.2.

96 See *supra* at 3.6.

97 See *infra* at 4.2.

98 This results from the studies commissioned by the Commission. Cf. footnote 89.

produce clear benefits compared with action at the level of the Member States.[99] This reasoning matches that of the Court in *British American Tobacco*, where it held that

> 'the principle of subsidiarity applies where the Community legislature makes use of Article 95 EC, inasmuch as that provision does not give it exclusive competence to regulate economic activity on the Internal Market, but only a certain competence for the purpose of improving the conditions for its establishment and functioning, by eliminating barriers to the free movement of goods and the freedom to provide services or by removing distortions of competition'.[100]

4.1.3 Compatibility with the existing principle of fair trading

The principle of fair trading has been identified in this study as a general principle of Internal Market law.[101] This entails that the principle of fair trading is an overriding rule of law which invalidates actions taken in the sphere of Internal Market law which are contrary to this principle.[102]

The comparison of the Internal Market law principle of fair trading and the concept of unfair trading of the Directive revealed a high degree of similarity.[103] However, this similarity is only achieved if the condition of 'requirements of professional diligence' is ignored. This condition, indeed, is hardly compatible with the principle of fair trading if it was understood as allowing to impair the consumer's ability to make an informed decision and thereby causing him to take a transactional decision that he would not have taken otherwise, just because this is in conformity with accepted business conduct. The Directive is not sufficiently clear whether there is a conflict and how it is to be resolved. As a consequence of this ambiguity the general concept of the Directive would not violate the Internal Market law principle of fair trading, but would rather need to be interpreted in the light of it. A practice which impairs the consumer's ability to make an informed decision and thereby causes him to take a transactional decision that he would not have taken otherwise, would therefore be prohibited, irrespective of the role this practice assumes in accepted business conduct. The same applies to the consumer yardstick. Since it remains unclear whether Article 5(3) of the Directive actually deviates from the general consumer yardstick,

---

99 Cf. No. 5 of the Protocol on proportionality and subsidiarity.

100 Case C-491/01 *R. v Secretary of State for Health, ex parte British American Tobacco (Investments) Ltd and Imperial Tobacco Ltd.* [2002] ECR I-11453 at 179, dealing with the validity of Directive 2001/37/EC concerning the manufacture, presentation and sale of tobacco products.

101 See Chapter 4.

102 Cf. Temple Lang in Bernitz/Nergelius, *General Principles*, p. 163 with regard to general principles of Community law.

103 See *supra* at 3.6.

the provision would have to be interpreted in the light of the Internal Market law principle of fair trading. This would mean that the vulnerable consumer would not become the standard benchmark, but only if a commercial practice is directed at a group of vulnerable consumers.

4.2 Do we need the Directive?

The principal objective of the study was to find out whether there is a principle of fair trading in the *acquis communautaire*. Such a principle could indeed be exposed and defined. It is a general principle of Internal Market law that consumers must be enabled to make their choice in full knowledge of the facts. Therefore, the question arises inevitably: do we actually need the Directive when a general principle of fair trading is already existent? The suggested answer is threefold: we do not necessarily need it, but we should have it, albeit not in its present form.[104] This opinion reconciles the position that a fully fledged principle of fair trading currently exists with the view that the codification of a general fair trading concept bears advantages, provided that it is well-drafted.

We do not necessarily need it

The focus of the assertion that the Directive is not necessarily needed is on the content of the Internal Market law principle of fair trading. The concept that consumers must be enabled to make their choice in full knowledge of the facts is a fully fledged and homogenous concept of fair business conduct towards consumers in the Internal Market. It is a universal principle, suitable for all present and future trading situations. Moreover, it has a wide ambit, since it underlies the entire realm of Internal Market law. From this perspective, the adoption of a framework directive is therefore dispensable. The Directive would not provide something which was non-existent before.

But we should have it

On the other hand, although the ambit of the existing principle of fair trading is wide indeed, it does not match the universality and perfection of the principle's content. Its boundaries are those of the legal range of the Internal Market. In practice this means that a situation for which currently no secondary law exists and which is beyond the reach of negative integration is not covered by the existing principle of fair trading. Where there is no harmonisation and where Article 28 fails to apply because of *Keck* (in spite of the limits to the impact of the *Keck* doctrine), the principle of fair trading is ineffective. This vacuum could and should indeed be filled by a general clause in secondary law.

---

[104] Again the considerations refer only to the concept of fair trading of the Directive, not its other content, such as enforcement rules, which certainly imply advantages to the present situation.

The coherence of the Internal Market principle of fair trading is clearly disturbed by the myriad rules in secondary law with different scopes of application and differing rules. It is true that, in the end, it is possible to bring them down to the principle of fair trading that has been suggested. However, this does not change anything to the legislative piecemeal situation. The power of the Internal Market principle of fair trading is therefore restricted to eliminating barriers on a case by case basis. It does not, however, create itself a homogenous legal framework for fair trading in the Internal Market. This makes it therefore desirable to introduce a general legislative framework for fair trading.

The Directive would always have to be interpreted in the light of the existing principle of fair trading, the Internal Market principle of fair trading would not be sacrificed to the introduction of a general clause in secondary law. There is therefore little risk that it would decrease the present standard, but it would complement it with more legal certainty and market-participant confidence. It can safely be assumed that there is currently hardly any awareness of the existence of a general principle of fair trading in Internal Market law. The uncertainty created by the current piecemeal situation in secondary law and the somewhat unpredictable ambit of the principle of fair trading could be overcome by a clear codification in secondary law. This would encourage trading confidence in both traders and consumers and support the integrity and functioning of the Internal Market.

Albeit not in its present form

The current text of the Directive is not to be condemned in its entirety. On the contrary, its combination of a general clause with more concrete rules which implement this clause is to be welcomed. It is a pity, however, that the original idea of maximum harmonisation has been watered down by some kind of temporary minimum harmonisation solution.

According to the suggested interpretation, the substance of the general clause is largely equal with the Internal Market principle. However, the requirement of professional diligence is out of place in this context and should be eliminated. It appears sensible to introduce a general clause which is identical in wording to the Internal Market principle of fair trading, i.e. which provides that consumers must be enabled to make their choice in full knowledge of the facts. It has been demonstrated throughout this work that this phrasing comprises the concept of fair trading in its entirety.

Moreover, in order for the Directive to constitute a real legislative framework it should replace existing legislation rather than merely complementing it. The Directive does catch situations which are currently not regulated, and it does provide a conceptual framework for fair trading legislation. As a matter of fact, it does not, however, solve the piecemeal situation in secondary law, as long as the current legislation continues to exist. If it is to be prevented that the vagueness of a general clause could lead to different interpretations and applications (which is a realistic risk), one could think of establishing a 'Community code on fair trading' with a general clause and coherent specific rules. This would mean to follow the successful paths that have been taken in order to make legislation coherent by establishing codes, such as in the field of medicinal products or customs. Improving the consistency among specific legislation by the adoption of general legislation without repealing the specific one (i.e. which continues to take precedence) is certainly a futile attempt.

Finally, a fair trading directive should be better-drafted than the current Common Position. The definitions (in particular the definition of commercial practices) and the dubious interrelationships between the various definitions are quite confusing, not to say misleading. Also the consumer yardstick remains ambiguous. It is submitted that also the text of a directive on unfair commercial practices contains 'material information', which should not be provided 'in an unclear, unintelligible, ambiguous or untimely manner'.[105]

[105] Article 7(2) of the Common Position.

Annex

Common Position adopted by the Council with a view to the adoption of a

DIRECTIVE OF THE EUROPEAN PARLIAMENT AND OF THE COUNCIL*

concerning unfair business-to-consumer commercial practices in the Internal Market and amending Council Directive 84/450/EEC, Directives 97/7/EC, 98/27/EC and 2002/65/EC of the European Parliament and of the Council and Regulation (EC) No /2004 of the European Parliament and of the Council ("Unfair Commercial Practices Directive")

THE EUROPEAN PARLIAMENT AND THE COUNCIL OF THE EUROPEAN UNION,

Having regard to the Treaty establishing the European Community, and in particular Article 95 thereof,

Having regard to the proposal from the Commission,

Having regard to the Opinion of the European Economic and Social Committee,

Acting in accordance with the procedure laid down in Article 251 of the Treaty,

Whereas:

(1) Article 153(1) and (3)(a) of the Treaty provides that the Community is to contribute to the attainment of a high level of consumer protection by the measures it adopts pursuant to Article 95 thereof.

(2) In accordance with Article 14(2) of the Treaty, the internal market comprises an area without internal frontiers in which the free movement of goods and services and freedom of establishment are ensured. The development of fair commercial practices within the area without internal frontiers is vital for the promotion of the development of cross-border activities.

(3) The laws of the Member States relating to unfair commercial practices show marked differences which can generate appreciable distortions of competition and obstacles to the smooth functioning of the internal market. In the field of advertising, Council Directive 84/450/EEC of 10 September 1984 concerning misleading and comparative advertising establishes minimum criteria for harmonising legislation on misleading advertising, but does not prevent the Member States from retaining or adopting measures which provide more extensive protection for consumers. As a result, Member States' provisions on misleading advertising diverge significantly.

---

* Source: Council document 11630/04 CONSOM 63 MI 215 CODEC 929 of 9 November 2004, adopted on 15 November 2004 (Interinstitutional File: 2003/0134 (COD)). The footnotes in the Common Position have been omitted.

(4) These disparities cause uncertainty as to which national rules apply to unfair commercial practices harming consumers' economic interests and create many barriers affecting business and consumers. These barriers increase the cost to business of exercising internal market freedoms, in particular when businesses wish to engage in cross border marketing, advertising campaigns and sales promotions. Such barriers also make consumers uncertain of their rights and undermine their confidence in the internal market.

(5) In the absence of uniform rules at Community level, obstacles to the free movement of services and goods across borders or the freedom of establishment could be justified in the light of the case-law of the Court of Justice of the European Communities as long as they seek to protect recognised public interest objectives and are proportionate to those objectives. In view of the Community's objectives, as set out in the provisions of the Treaty and in secondary Community law relating to freedom of movement, and in accordance with the Commission's policy on commercial communications as indicated in the Communication from the Commission entitled "The follow-up to the Green Paper on Commercial Communications in the Internal Market", such obstacles should be eliminated. These obstacles can only be eliminated by establishing uniform rules at Community level which establish a high level of consumer protection and by clarifying certain legal concepts at Community level to the extent necessary for the proper functioning of the internal market and to meet the requirement of legal certainty.

(6) This Directive therefore approximates the laws of the Member States on unfair commercial practices, including unfair advertising, which directly harm consumers' economic interests and thereby indirectly harm the economic interests of legitimate competitors. In line with the principle of proportionality, this Directive protects consumers from the consequences of such unfair commercial practices where they are material but recognises that in some cases the impact on consumers may be negligible. It neither covers nor affects the national laws on unfair commercial practices which harm only competitors' economic interests or which relate to a transaction between traders; taking full account of the principle of subsidiarity, Member States will continue to be able to regulate such practices, in conformity with Community law, if they choose to do so. Nor does this Directive cover or affect the provisions of Directive 84/450/EEC on advertising which misleads business but which is not misleading for consumers and on comparative advertising. Further, this Directive does not affect accepted advertising and marketing practices, such as legitimate product placement, brand differentiation or the offering of incentives which may legitimately affect consumers' perceptions of products and influence their behaviour without impairing the consumer's ability to make an informed decision.

(7) This Directive addresses commercial practices directly related to influencing consumers' transactional decisions in relation to products. It does not address commercial practices carried out primarily for other purposes, including for example commercial communication aimed at investors, such as annual reports and corporate promotional literature. It does not address legal requirements related to taste and decency which vary widely among the Member

States. Commercial practices such as, for example, commercial solicitation in the streets, may be undesirable in Member States for cultural reasons. Member States should accordingly be able to continue to ban commercial practices in their territory, in conformity with Community law, for reasons of taste and decency even where such practices do not limit consumers' freedom of choice.

(8) This Directive directly protects consumer economic interests from unfair business-to-consumer commercial practices. Thereby, it also indirectly protects legitimate businesses from their competitors who do not play by the rules in this Directive and thus guarantees fair competition in fields coordinated by it. It is understood that there are other commercial practices which, although not harming consumers, may hurt competitors and business customers. The Commission should carefully examine the need for Community action in the field of unfair competition beyond the remit of this Directive and, if necessary, make a legislative proposal to cover these other aspects of unfair competition.

(9) This Directive is without prejudice to individual actions brought by those who have been harmed by an unfair commercial practice. It is also without prejudice to Community and national rules on contract law, on intellectual property rights, on the health and safety aspects of products, on conditions of establishment and authorisation regimes, including those rules which, in conformity with Community law, relate to gambling activities, and to Community competition rules and the national provisions implementing them. The Member States will thus be able to retain or introduce restrictions and prohibitions of commercial practices on grounds of the protection of the health and safety of consumers in their territory wherever the trader is based, for example in relation to alcohol, tobacco or pharmaceuticals. Financial services and immovable property, by reason of their complexity and inherent serious risks, necessitate detailed requirements, including positive obligations on traders. For this reason, in the field of financial services and immovable property, this Directive is without prejudice to the right of Member States to go beyond its provisions to protect the economic interests of consumers. It is not appropriate to regulate here the certification and indication of the standard of fineness of articles of precious metal.

(10) It is necessary to ensure that the relationship between this Directive and existing Community law is coherent, particularly where detailed provisions on unfair commercial practices apply to specific sectors. This Directive therefore amends Directive 84/450/EEC, Directive 97/7/EC of the European Parliament and of the Council of 20 May 1997 on the protection of consumers in respect of distance contracts, Directive 98/27/EC of the European Parliament and of the Council of 19 May 1998 on injunctions for the protection of consumers' interests and Directive 2002/65/EC of the European Parliament and of the Council of 23 September 2002 concerning the distance marketing of consumer financial services. This Directive accordingly applies only in so far as there are no specific Community law provisions regulating specific aspects of unfair commercial practices, such as information requirements and rules on the way the information is presented to the consumer. It provides protection for consumers where there is no specific sectoral legislation at Community level and prohib-

its traders from creating a false impression of the nature of products. This is particularly important for complex products with high levels of risk to consumers, such as certain financial services products. This Directive consequently complements the Community acquis, which is applicable to commercial practices harming consumers' economic interests.

(11) The high level of convergence achieved by the approximation of national provisions through this Directive creates a high common level of consumer protection. This Directive establishes a single general prohibition of those unfair commercial practices distorting consumers' economic behaviour. It also sets rules on aggressive commercial practices, which are currently not regulated at Community level.

(12) Harmonisation will considerably increase legal certainty for both consumers and business. Both consumers and business will be able to rely on a single regulatory framework based on clearly defined legal concepts regulating all aspects of unfair commercial practices across the EU. The effect will be to eliminate the barriers stemming from the fragmentation of the rules on unfair commercial practices harming consumer economic interests and to enable the internal market to be achieved in this area.

(13) In order to achieve the Community's objectives through the removal of internal market barriers, it is necessary to replace Member States' existing, divergent general clauses and legal principles. The single, common general prohibition established by this Directive therefore covers unfair commercial practices distorting consumers' economic behaviour. In order to support consumer confidence the general prohibition should apply equally to unfair commercial practices which occur outside any contractual relationship between a trader and a consumer or following the conclusion of a contract and during its execution. The general prohibition is elaborated by rules on the two types of commercial practices which are by far the most common, namely misleading commercial practices and aggressive commercial practices.

(14) It is desirable that misleading commercial practices cover those practices, including misleading advertising, which by deceiving the consumer prevent him from making an informed and thus efficient choice. In conformity with the laws and practices of Member States on misleading advertising, this Directive classifies misleading practices into misleading actions and misleading omissions. In respect of omissions, this Directive sets out a limited number of key items of information which the consumer needs to make an informed transactional decision. Such information will not have to be disclosed in all advertisements, but only where the trader makes an invitation to purchase, which is a concept clearly defined in this Directive. The full harmonisation approach adopted in this Directive does not preclude the Member States from specifying in national law the main characteristics of particular products such as, for example, collectors' items or electrical goods, the omission of which would be material when an invitation to purchase is made. It is not the intention of this Directive to reduce consumer choice by prohibiting the promotion of products which look similar to other products unless this similarity confuses consumers as to the commercial origin of the product and is therefore misleading. This Directive should be without prejudice to existing

Community law which expressly affords Member States the choice between several regulatory options for the protection of consumers in the field of commercial practices. In particular, this Directive should be without prejudice to Article 13(3) of Directive 2002/58/EC of the European Parliament and of the Council of 12 July 2002 concerning the processing of personal data and the protection of privacy in the electronic communications sector.

(15) Where Community law sets out information requirements in relation to commercial communication, advertising and marketing that information is considered as material under this Directive. Member States will be able to retain or add information requirements relating to contract law and having contract law consequences where this is allowed by the minimum clauses in the existing Community law instruments. A non-exhaustive list of such information requirements in the acquis is contained in Annex II. Given the full harmonisation introduced by this Directive only the information required in Community law is considered as material for the purpose of Article 7(5) thereof. Where Member States have introduced information requirements over and above what is specified in Community law, on the basis of minimum clauses, the omission of that extra information will not constitute a misleading omission under this Directive. By contrast Member States will be able, when allowed by the minimum clauses in Community law, to maintain or introduce more stringent provisions in conformity with Community law so as to ensure a higher level of protection of consumers' individual contractual rights.

(16) The provisions on aggressive commercial practices should cover those practices which significantly impair the consumer's freedom of choice. Those are practices using harassment, coercion, including the use of physical force, and undue influence.

(17) It is desirable that those commercial practices which are in all circumstances unfair be identified to provide greater legal certainty. Annex I therefore contains the full list of all such practices. These are the only commercial practices which can be deemed to be unfair without a case-by-case assessment against the provisions of Articles 5 to 9.

(18) It is appropriate to protect all consumers from unfair commercial practices; however the Court of Justice has found it necessary in adjudicating on advertising cases since the enactment of Directive 84/450/EEC to examine the effect on a notional, typical consumer. In line with the principle of proportionality, and to permit the effective application of the protections contained in it, this Directive takes as a benchmark the average consumer as interpreted by the Court of Justice but also contains provisions aimed at preventing the exploitation of consumers whose characteristics make them particularly vulnerable to unfair commercial practices. Where a commercial practice is specifically aimed at a particular group of consumers, such as children, it is desirable that the impact of the commercial practice be assessed from the perspective of the average member of that group. The average consumer test is not a statistical test. National courts and authorities will have to exercise their own faculty of judgement, having regard to the case-law of the Court of Justice, to determine the typical reaction of the average consumer in a given case.

(19) Where certain characteristics such as age, physical or mental infirmity or credulity make consumers particularly susceptible to a commercial practice or to the underlying product and the economic behaviour only of such consumers is likely to be distorted by the practice in a way that the trader can reasonably foresee, it is appropriate to ensure that they are adequately protected by assessing the practice from the perspective of the average member of that group.

(20) It is appropriate to provide a role for codes of conduct, which enable traders to apply the principles of this Directive effectively in specific economic fields. In sectors where there are specific mandatory requirements regulating the behaviour of traders, it is appropriate that these will also provide evidence as to the requirements of professional diligence in that sector. The control exercised by code owners at national or Community level to eliminate unfair commercial practices may avoid the need for recourse to administrative or judicial action and should therefore be encouraged. With the aim of pursuing a high level of consumer protection, consumers' organisations could be informed and involved in the drafting of codes of conduct.

(21) Persons or organisations regarded under national law as having a legitimate interest in the mater must have legal remedies for initiating proceedings against unfair commercial practices, either before a court or before an administrative authority which is competent to decide upon complaints or to initiate appropriate legal proceedings. While it is for national law to determine the burden of proof, it is appropriate to enable courts and administrative authorities to require traders to produce evidence as to the accuracy of factual claims they have made.

(22) It is necessary that Member States lay down penalties for infringements of the provisions of this Directive and they must ensure that these are enforced. The penalties must be effective, proportionate and dissuasive.

(23) Since the objectives of this Directive, namely to eliminate the barriers to the functioning of the internal market represented by national laws on unfair commercial practices and to provide a high common level of consumer protection, by approximating the laws, regulations and administrative provisions of the Member States on unfair commercial practices, cannot be sufficiently achieved by the Member States and can therefore be better achieved at Community level, the Community may adopt measures, in accordance with the principle of subsidiarity as set out in Article 5 of the Treaty. In accordance with the principle of proportionality, as set out in that Article, this Directive does not go beyond what is necessary in order to eliminate the internal market barriers and achieve a high common level of consumer protection.

(24) It is appropriate to review this Directive to ensure that barriers to the internal market have been addressed and a high level of consumer protection achieved. The review could lead to a Commission proposal to amend this Directive, which may include a limited extension to the derogation in Article 3(5), and/or amendments to other consumer protection legislation reflecting the Commission's Consumer Policy Strategy commitment to review the existing acquis in order to achieve a high, common level of consumer protection.

(25) This Directive respects the fundamental rights and observes the principles recognised in particular by the Charter of Fundamental Rights of the European Union,

HAVE ADOPTED THIS DIRECTIVE:

CHAPTER 1: GENERAL PROVISIONS

Article 1
Purpose
The purpose of this Directive is to contribute to the proper functioning of the internal market and achieve a high level of consumer protection by approximating the laws, regulations and administrative provisions of the Member States on unfair commercial practices harming consumers' economic interests.

Article 2
Definitions
For the purposes of this Directive:
(a) "consumer" means any natural person who, in commercial practices covered by this Directive, is acting for purposes which are outside his trade, business, craft or profession;
(b) "trader" means any natural or legal person who, in commercial practices covered by this Directive, is acting for purposes relating to his trade, business, craft or profession and anyone acting in the name of or on behalf of a trader;
(c) "product" means any good or service including immovable property, rights and obligations;
(d) "business-to-consumer commercial practices" (hereinafter also referred to as "commercial practices") means any act, omission, course of conduct or representation, commercial communication including advertising and marketing, by a trader, directly connected with the promotion, sale or supply of a product to consumers;
(e) "to materially distort the economic behaviour of consumers" means using a commercial practice to appreciably impair the consumer's ability to make an informed decision, thereby causing the consumer to take a transactional decision that he would not have taken otherwise;
(f) "code of conduct" means an agreement or set of rules not imposed by law, regulation or administrative provision of a Member State which defines the behaviour of traders who undertake to be bound by the code in relation to one or more particular commercial practices or business sectors;
(g) "code owner" means any entity, including a trader or group of traders, which is responsible for the formulation and revision of a code of conduct and/or for monitoring compliance with the code by those who have undertaken to be bound by it;
(h) "professional diligence" means the standard of special skill and care which a trader may reasonably be expected to exercise towards consumers, commensurate with honest market practice and/or the general principle of good faith in the trader's field of activity;

(i) "invitation to purchase" means a commercial communication which indicates characteristics of the product and the price in a way appropriate to the means of the commercial communication used and thereby enables the consumer to make a purchase;
(j) "undue influence" means exploiting a position of power in relation to the consumer so as to apply pressure, even without using or threatening to use physical force, in a way which significantly limits the consumer's ability to make an informed decision;
(k) "transactional decision" means any decision taken by a consumer concerning whether, how and on what terms to purchase, make payment in whole or in part for, retain or dispose of a product or to exercise a contractual right in relation to the product, whether the consumer decides to act or to refrain from acting;
(l) "regulated profession" means a professional activity or a group of professional activities, access to which or the pursuit of which, or one of the modes of pursuing which, is conditional, directly or indirectly, upon possession of specific professional qualifications, pursuant to laws, regulations or administrative provisions.

Article 3
Scope
1. This Directive shall apply to unfair business-to-consumer commercial practices, as laid down in Article 5, before, during and after a commercial transaction in relation to a product.
2. This Directive is without prejudice to contract law and, in particular, to the rules on the validity, formation or effect of a contract.
3. This Directive is without prejudice to Community or national rules relating to the health and safety aspects of products.
4. In the case of conflict between the provisions of this Directive and other Community rules regulating specific aspects of unfair commercial practices, the later shall prevail and apply to those specific aspects.
5. For a period of six years from [24 months after the entry into force of this Directive], Member States shall be able to apply national provisions within the field approximated by this Directive which are more restrictive or prescriptive than this Directive and which implement directives containing minimum harmonisation clauses. These measures must be essential to ensure that consumers are adequately protected against unfair commercial practices and must be proportionate to the attainment of this objective. The review referred to in Article 18 may, if considered appropriate, include a proposal to prolong this derogation for a further limited period.
6. Member States shall notify the Commission without delay of any national provisions applied on the basis of paragraph 5.
7. This Directive is without prejudice to the rules determining the jurisdiction of the courts.
8. This Directive is without prejudice to any conditions of establishment or of authorisation regimes, or to the deontological codes of conduct or other specific rules governing regulated professions in order to uphold high standards of integrity on the part of the professional, which Member States may, in conformity with Community law, impose on professionals.

9. In relation to "financial services", as defined in Directive 2002/65/EC, and immovable property, Member States may impose requirements which are more restrictive or prescriptive than this Directive in the field which it approximates.
10. This Directive shall not apply to the application of the laws, regulations and administrative provisions of Member States relating to the certification and indication of the standard of fineness of articles of precious metal.

Article 4
Internal market
Member States shall neither restrict the freedom to provide services nor restrict the free movement of goods for reasons falling within the field approximated by this Directive.

CHAPTER 2: UNFAIR COMMERCIAL PRACTICES

Article 5
Prohibition of unfair commercial practices
1. Unfair commercial practices shall be prohibited.
2. A commercial practice shall be unfair if:
(a) it is contrary to the requirements of professional diligence, and
(b) it materially distorts or is likely to materially distort the economic behaviour with regard to the product of the average consumer whom it reaches or to whom it is addressed, or of the average member of the group when a commercial practice is directed to a particular group of consumers.
3. Commercial practices which reach the generality of consumers, but are likely to materially distort the economic behaviour only of a group of consumers who are particularly vulnerable to the practice or the underlying product because of their mental or physical infirmity, age or credulity in a way which the trader could reasonably be expected to foresee, shall be assessed from the perspective of the average member of that group. This is without prejudice to the common and legitimate advertising practice of making exaggerated statements or statements which are not meant to be taken literally.
4. In particular, commercial practices shall be unfair which:
(a) are misleading as set out in Articles 6 and 7, or
(b) are aggressive as set out in Articles 8 and 9.
5. Annex I contains the list of those commercial practices which shall in all circumstances be regarded as unfair.

Section 1: Misleading Commercial Practices

Article 6
Misleading actions
1. A commercial practice shall be regarded as misleading if it contains false information and is therefore untruthful or in any way, including overall presentation, deceives or is likely to deceive the average consumer, even if the information is factually correct, in relation to one

or more of the following elements, and in either case causes or is likely to cause him to take a transactional decision that he would not have taken otherwise:

(a) the existence or nature of the product;

(b) the main characteristics of the product, such as its availability, benefits, risks, execution, composition, accessories, after-sale customer assistance and complaint handling, method and date of manufacture or provision, delivery, fitness for purpose, usage, quantity, specification, geographical or commercial origin or the results to be expected from its use, or the results and material features of tests or checks carried out on the product;

(c) the extent of the trader's commitments, the motives for the commercial practice and the nature of the sales process, any statement or symbol in relation to direct or indirect sponsorship or approval of the trader or the product;

(d) the price or the manner in which the price is calculated, or the existence of a specific price advantage;

(e) the need for a service, part, replacement or repair;

(f) the nature, attributes and rights of the trader or his agent, such as his identity and assets, his qualifications, status, approval, affiliation or connection and ownership of industrial, commercial or intellectual property rights or his awards and distinctions;

(g) the consumer's rights or the risks he may face.

2. A commercial practice shall also be regarded as misleading where, in its factual context, taking account of all its features and circumstances, it thereby causes or is likely to cause the average consumer to take a transactional decision that he would not have taken otherwise, and it involves:

(a) any marketing of a product, including comparative advertising, which creates confusion with any products, trade marks, trade names and other distinguishing marks of a competitor;

(b) non-compliance by the trader with commitments contained in codes of conduct by which the trader has undertaken to be bound, where:

(i) the commitment is not aspirational but is firm and is capable of being verified, and

(ii) the trader indicates in a commercial practice that he is bound by the code.

Article 7

Misleading omissions

1. A commercial practice shall be regarded as misleading which, in its factual context, taking account of all its features and circumstances and the limitations of the communication medium, omits material information that the average consumer needs, according to the context, to take an informed transactional decision and thereby causes or is likely to cause the average consumer to take a transactional decision that he would not have taken otherwise.

2. It shall also be regarded as a misleading omission when a trader hides or provides in an unclear, unintelligible, ambiguous or untimely manner such material information as referred to in paragraph 1 or fails to identify the commercial intent of the commercial practice if not already apparent from the context.

3. Where the medium used to communicate the commercial practice imposes limitations of space or time, these limitations and any measures taken by the trader to make the informa-

tion available to consumers by other means shall be taken into account in deciding whether information has been omitted.

4. In the case of an invitation to purchase, the following information shall be regarded as material, if not already apparent from the context:

(a) the main characteristics of the product, to an extent appropriate to the medium and the product;

(b) the geographical address and the identity of the trader, such as his trading name and, where applicable, the geographical address and the identity of the trader on whose behalf he is acting;

(c) the price inclusive of taxes, or where the nature of the product means that the price cannot reasonably be calculated in advance, the manner in which the price is calculated, as well as, where appropriate, all additional freight, delivery or postal charges or, where these charges cannot reasonably be calculated in advance, the fact that such additional charges may be payable;

(d) the arrangements for payment, delivery, performance and the complaint handling policy, if they depart from the requirements of professional diligence;

(e) for products and transactions involving a right of withdrawal or cancellation, the existence of such a right.

5. Information requirements established by Community law in relation to commercial communication including advertising or marketing, a non-exhaustive list of which is contained in Annex II, shall be regarded as material.

Section 2: Aggressive Commercial Practices

Article 8

Aggressive commercial practices

A commercial practice shall be regarded as aggressive if, in its factual context, taking account of all its features and circumstances, by harassment, coercion, including the use of physical force, or undue influence, it significantly impairs or is likely to significantly impair the average consumer's freedom of choice or conduct with regard to the product and thereby causes him or is likely to cause him to take a transactional decision that he would not have taken otherwise.

Article 9

Use of harassment, coercion and undue influence

In determining whether a commercial practice uses harassment, coercion, including the use of physical force, or undue influence, account shall be taken of:

(a) its timing, location, nature or persistence;

(b) the use of threatening or abusive language or behaviour;

(c) the exploitation by the trader of any specific misfortune or circumstance of such gravity as to impair the consumer's judgement, of which the trader is aware, to influence the consumer's decision with regard to the product;

(d) any onerous or disproportionate non-contractual barriers imposed by the trader where a consumer wishes to exercise rights under the contract, including rights to terminate a contract or to switch to another product or another trader;
(e) any threat to take any action that cannot legally be taken.

CHAPTER 3: CODES OF CONDUCT

Article 10
Codes of conduct
This Directive does not exclude the control, which Member States may encourage, of unfair commercial practices by code owners and recourse to such bodies by the persons or organisations referred to in Article 11 if proceedings before such bodies are in addition to the court or administrative proceedings referred to in that Article.

CHAPTER 4: FINAL PROVISIONS

Article 11
Enforcement
1. Member States shall ensure that adequate and effective means exist to combat unfair commercial practices and for compliance with the provisions of this Directive in the interest of consumers.

Such means shall include legal provisions under which persons or organisations regarded under national law as having a legitimate interest in combating unfair commercial practices, including competitors, may:
– take legal action against such unfair commercial practices; and/or
– bring such unfair commercial practices before an administrative authority competent either to decide on complaints or to initiate appropriate legal proceedings.

It shall be for each Member State to decide which of these facilities shall be available and whether to enable the courts or administrative authorities to require prior recourse to other established means of dealing with complaints, including those referred to in Article 10. These facilities shall be available regardless of whether the consumers affected are in the territory of the Member State where the trader is located or in another Member State.

It shall be for each Member State to decide:
– whether these legal facilities may be directed separately or jointly against a number of traders from the same economic sector; and
– whether these legal facilities may be directed against a code owner where the relevant code promotes non-compliance with legal requirements.

2. Under the legal provisions referred to in paragraph 1, Member States shall confer upon the courts or administrative authorities powers enabling them, in cases where they deem such measures to be necessary taking into account all the interests involved and in particular the public interest:
– to order the cessation of, or to institute appropriate legal proceedings for an order for the cessation of, unfair commercial practices, or

– if the unfair commercial practice has not yet been carried out but is imminent, to order the prohibition of the practice, or to institute appropriate legal proceedings for an order for the prohibition of the practice,

even without proof of actual loss or damage or of intention or negligence on the part of the trader.

Member States shall also make provision for the measures referred to in the first subparagraph to be taken under an accelerated procedure:

– either with interim effect, or
– with definitive effect,

on the understanding that it is for each Member State to decide which of the two options to select.

Furthermore, Member States may confer upon the courts or administrative authorities powers enabling them, with a view to eliminating the continuing effects of unfair commercial practices the cessation of which has been ordered by a final decision:

– to require publication of that decision in full or in part and in such form as they deem adequate,
– to require in addition the publication of a corrective statement.

3. The administrative authorities referred to in paragraph 1 must:

(a) be composed so as not to cast doubt on their impartiality;

(b) have adequate powers, where they decide on complaints, to monitor and enforce the observance of their decisions effectively;

(c) normally give reasons for their decisions.

Where the powers referred to in paragraph 2 are exercised exclusively by an administrative authority, reasons for its decisions shall always be given. Furthermore, in this case, provision must be made for procedures whereby improper or unreasonable exercise of its powers by the administrative authority or improper or unreasonable failure to exercise the said powers can be the subject of judicial review.

Article 12

Courts and administrative authorities: substantiation of claims

Member States shall confer upon the courts or administrative authorities powers enabling them in the civil or administrative proceedings provided for in Article 11:

(a) to require the trader to furnish evidence as to the accuracy of factual claims in relation to a commercial practice if, taking into account the legitimate interest of the trader and any other party to the proceedings, such a requirement appears appropriate on the basis of the circumstances of the particular case; and

(b) to consider factual claims as inaccurate if the evidence demanded in accordance with (a) is not furnished or is deemed insufficient by the court or administrative authority.

Article 13

Penalties

Member States shall lay down penalties for infringements of national provisions adopted in application of this Directive and shall take all necessary measures to ensure that these are enforced. These penalties must be effective, proportionate and dissuasive.

Article 14

Amendments to Directive 1984/450/EEC

Directive 84/450/EEC is hereby amended as follows:

1) Article 1 shall be replaced by the following:

"Article 1

The purpose of this Directive is to protect traders against misleading advertising and the unfair consequences thereof and to lay down the conditions under which comparative advertising is permitted.";

2) In Article 2:

– Point 3 shall be replaced by the following:

3. "trader" means any natural or legal person who is acting for purposes relating to his trade, craft, business or profession and any one acting in the name of or on behalf of a trader."

– The following point shall be added:

4. "code owner" means any entity, including a trader or group of traders, which is responsible for the formulation and revision of a code of conduct and/or for monitoring compliance with the code by those who have undertaken to be bound by it.".

3) Article 3a shall be replaced by the following:

"Article 3a

1. Comparative advertising shall, as far as the comparison is concerned, be permitted when the following conditions are met:

(a) it is not misleading according to Articles 2(2), 3 and 7(1) of this Directive or Articles 6 and 7 of Directive 2004/.../EC of the European Parliament and of the Council of ...... concerning unfair business-to-consumer commercial practices in the internal market;

(b) it compares goods or services meeting the same needs or intended for the same purpose;

(c) it objectively compares one or more material, relevant, verifiable and representative features of those goods and services, which may include price;

(d) it does not discredit or denigrate the trade marks, trade names, other distinguishing marks, goods, services, activities, or circumstances of a competitor;

(e) for products with designation of origin, it relates in each case to products with the same designation;

(f) it does not take unfair advantage of the reputation of a trade mark, trade name or other distinguishing marks of a competitor or of the designation of origin of competing products;

(g) it does not present goods or services as imitations or replicas of goods or services bearing a protected trade mark or trade name;

(h) it does not create confusion among traders, between the advertiser and a competitor or between the advertiser's trade marks, trade names, other distinguishing marks, goods or services and those of a competitor.

4) Article 4(1) shall be replaced by the following:

"1. Member States shall ensure that adequate and effective means exist to combat misleading advertising and for compliance with the provisions on comparative advertising in the interest of traders and competitors. Such means shall include legal provisions under which persons or organisations regarded under national law as having a legitimate interest in combating misleading advertising or regulating comparative advertising may:

(a) take legal action against such advertising; or
(b) bring such advertising before an administrative authority competent either to decide on complaints or to initiate appropriate legal proceedings.
It shall be for each Member State to decide which of these facilities shall be available and whether to enable the courts or administrative authorities to require prior recourse to other established means of dealing with complaints, including those referred to in Article 5.
It shall be for each Member State to decide:
(a) whether these legal facilities may be directed separately or jointly against a number of traders from the same economic sector; and
(b) whether these legal facilities may be directed against a code owner where the relevant code promotes non-compliance with legal requirements."
5) Article 7(1) shall be replaced by the following:
"1. This Directive shall not preclude Member States from retaining or adopting provisions with a view to ensuring more extensive protection, with regard to misleading advertising, for traders and competitors".

Article 15
Amendments to Directives 97/7/EC and 2002/65/EC
1) Article 9 of Directive 97/7/EC shall be replaced by the following:
"Article 9
Inertia selling
Given the prohibition of inertia selling practices laid down in Directive 2004/.../EC of the European Parliament and of the Council of ...... concerning unfair business-to-consumer commercial practices in the internal market, Member States shall take the measures necessary to exempt the consumer from the provision of any consideration in cases of unsolicited supply, the absence of a response not constituting consent."
2) Article 9 of Directive 2002/65/EC shall be replaced by the following:
"Article 9
Given the prohibition of inertia selling practices laid down in Directive 2004/.../EC of the European Parliament and of the Council of ...... concerning unfair business-to-consumer commercial practices in the internal market and without prejudice to the provisions of Member States' legislation on the tacit renewal of distance contracts, when such rules permit tacit renewal, Member States shall take measures to exempt the consumer from any obligation in the event of unsolicited supplies, the absence of a reply not constituting consent."

Article 16
Amendments to Directive 98/27/EC and Regulation (EC) No .../2004
1) In the Annex to Directive 98/27/EC, point 1 shall be replaced by the following:
"1. Directive 2004/.../EC of the European Parliament and of the Council of ...... concerning unfair business-to-consumer commercial practices in the internal market (OJ L ...)".
2) In the Annex to Regulation (EC) No .../2004 of the European Parliament and of the Council of ...... on cooperation between national authorities responsible for the enforcement of the consumer protection law ("the Regulation on consumer protection cooperation") the following point shall be added:

"15. Directive 2004/.../EC of the European Parliament and of the Council of ...... concerning unfair business-to-consumer commercial practices in the internal market (OJ L ..., p. ...)".

Article 17

Information

Member States shall take appropriate measures to inform the consumer of the national law transposing this Directive and shall, where appropriate, encourage traders and code owners to inform consumers of their codes of conduct.

Article 18

Review

1. The Commission shall not later than four years after [24 months after the entry into force of this Directive] submit to the European Parliament and the Council a comprehensive report on the application of this Directive, in particular of Article 4 and Annex I, on the scope for further harmonisation and simplification of Community law relating to consumer protection, and, having regard to Article 3(5), on any measures that need to be taken at Community level to ensure that appropriate levels of consumer protection are maintained. The report shall be accompanied, if necessary, by a proposal to revise this Directive or other relevant parts of Community law.

2. The European Parliament and the Council shall endeavour to act, in accordance with the Treaty, within two years of the presentation by the Commission of any proposal submitted under paragraph 1.

Article 19

Transposition

Member States shall adopt and publish the laws, regulations and administrative provisions necessary to comply with this Directive by [24 months after the entry into force of this Directive]. They shall forthwith inform the Commission thereof and inform the Commission of any subsequent amendments without delay.

They shall apply those measures by [30 months after the entry into force of this Directive]. When Member States adopt those measures, they shall contain a reference to this Directive or be accompanied by such a reference on the occasion of their official publication. Member States shall determine how such reference is to be made.

Article 20

Entry into force

This Directive shall enter into force on the day following that of its publication in the Official Journal of the European Union.

Article 21

Addressees

This Directive is addressed to the Member States.

Annex I: Commercial practices which are in all circumstances considered unfair

Misleading commercial practices

(1) Claiming to be a signatory to a code of conduct when the trader is not.

(2) Displaying a trust mark, quality mark or equivalent without having obtained the necessary authorisation.

(3) Claiming that a code of conduct has an endorsement from a public or other body which it does not have.

(4) Claiming that a product has been approved, endorsed or authorised by a public or private body when it has not or making such a claim without complying with the terms of the approval, endorsement or authorisation.

(5) Making an invitation to purchase products at a specified price without disclosing the existence of any reasonable grounds the trader may have for believing that he will not be able to offer for supply or to procure another trader to supply, those products or equivalent products at that price for a period that is, and in quantities that are, reasonable having regard to the product, the scale of advertising of the product and the price offered (bait advertising).

(6) Making an invitation to purchase products at a specified price and then:

a) refusing to show the advertised item to consumers, or

b) refusing to take orders for it or deliver it within a reasonable time, or

c) demonstrating a defective sample of it,

with the intention of promoting a different product (bait and switch).

(7) Falsely stating that the product will only be available for a very limited time in order to elicit an immediate decision and deprive consumers of sufficient opportunity or time to make an informed choice.

(8) Undertaking to provide after-sales service to consumers with whom the trader has communicated prior to a transaction in a language which is not an official language of the Member State where the trader is located and then making such service available only in another language without clearly disclosing this to the consumer before the consumer is committed to the transaction.

(9) Stating or otherwise creating the impression that a product can legally be sold when it cannot.

(10) Presenting rights given to consumers in law as a distinctive feature of the trader's offer.

(11) Using editorial content in the media to promote a product where a trader has paid for the promotion without making that clear in the content or by images or sounds clearly identifiable by the consumer (Advertorial). This is without prejudice to Council Directive 89/552/EEC.

(12) Making a materially inaccurate claim concerning the nature and extent of the risk to the personal security of the consumer or his family if the consumer does not purchase the product.

(13) Establishing, operating or promoting a pyramid promotional scheme where a consumer gives consideration for the opportunity to receive compensation that is derived primarily from the introduction of other consumers into the scheme rather than from the sale or consumption of products.

(14) Claiming that the trader is about to cease trading or move premises when he is not.

(15) Claiming that products are able to facilitate winning in games of chance.
(16) Falsely claiming that a product is able to cure illnesses, dysfunction or malformations.
(17) Passing on materially inaccurate information on market conditions or on the possibility of finding the product with the intention of inducing the consumer to acquire the product at conditions less favourable than normal market conditions.
(18) Claiming in a commercial practice to offer a competition or prize promotion without awarding the prizes described or a reasonable equivalent.
(19) Describing a product as "gratis", "free", "without charge" or similar if the consumer has to pay anything other than the unavoidable cost of responding to the commercial practice and collecting or paying for delivery of the item.
(20) Including in marketing material an invoice or similar document seeking payment which gives the consumer the impression that he has already ordered the marketed product when he has not.

Aggressive commercial practices
(21) Creating the impression that the consumer cannot leave the premises until a contract is formed.
(22) Conducting personal visits to the consumer's home ignoring the consumer's request to leave or not to return except in circumstances and to the extent justified, under national law, to enforce a contractual obligation.
(23) Making persistent and unwanted solicitations by telephone, fax, e-mail or other remote media except in circumstances and to the extent justified under national law to enforce a contractual obligation. This is without prejudice to Article 10 of Directive 97/7/EC and Directives 95/46/EC and 2002/58/EC.
(24) Requiring a consumer who wishes to claim on an insurance policy to produce documents which could not reasonably be considered relevant as to whether the claim was valid, in order to dissuade the consumer from exercising his contractual rights.
(25) Including in an advertisement a direct appeal to children to persuade their parents or other adults to buy advertised products for them. This provision is without prejudice to Article 16 of Directive 89/552/EEC.
(26) Demanding immediate or deferred payment for or the return or safekeeping of products supplied by the trader, but not solicited by the consumer except where the product is a substitute supplied in conformity with Article 7(3) of Directive 97/7/EC (inertia selling).
(27) Explicitly informing the consumer that if he does not buy the product or service, the trader's job or livelihood will be in jeopardy.
(28) Creating the impression that the consumer has already won a prize without needing to make a purchase when in fact the opportunity to win the prize or the award of the prize are dependent on the consumer buying a product.

Annex II: Community law provisions setting out rules for advertising and commercial communication

Articles 4 and 5 of Directive 97/7/EC

Article 3 of Council Directive 90/314/EEC of 13 June 1990 on package travel, package holidays and package tours

Article 3(3) of Directive 94/47/EC of the European Parliament and of the Council of 26 October 1994 on the protection of purchasers in respect of certain aspects of contracts relating to the purchase of a right to use immovable properties on a timeshare basis

Article 3(4) of Directive 98/6/EC of the European Parliament and of the Council of 16 February 1998 on consumer protection in the indication of the prices of products offered to consumers

Articles 86 to 100 of Directive 2001/83/EC of the European Parliament and of the Council of 6 November 2001 on the Community code relating to medicinal products for human use

Articles 5 and 6 of Directive 2000/31/EC of the European Parliament and of the Council of 8 June 2000 on certain legal aspects of information society services, in particular electronic commerce, in the Internal Market ("Directive on electronic commerce")

Article 1(d) of Directive 98/7/EC of the European Parliament and of the Council of 16 February 1998 amending Directive 87/102/EEC for the approximation of the laws, regulations and administrative provisions of the Member States concerning consumer credit

Articles 3 and 4 of Directive 2002/65/EC

Article 1(9) of Directive 2001/107/EC of the European Parliament and of the Council of 21 January 2002 amending Council Directive 85/611/EEC on the coordination of laws, regulations and administrative provisions relating to undertakings for collective investment in transferable securities (UCITS) with a view to regulating management companies and simplified prospectuses

Articles 12 and 13 of Directive 2002/92/EC of the European Parliament and of the Council of 9 December 2002 on insurance mediation

Article 36 of Directive 2002/83/EC of the European Parliament and of the Council of 5 November 2002 concerning life assurance

Article 19 of Directive 2004/39/EC of the European Parliament and of the Council of 21 April 2004 on markets in financial instruments

Articles 31 and 43 of Council Directive 92/49/EEC of 18 June 1992 on the coordination of laws, regulations and administrative provisions relating to direct insurance other than life assurance 4 (third non-life insurance Directive)

Articles 5, 7 and 8 of Directive 2003/71/EC of the European Parliament and of the Council of 4 November 2003 on the prospectus to be published when securities are offered to the public or admitted to trading.

Bibliography

Ahlfeld, Martin, *Zwingende Erfordernisse im Sinne der Cassis-Rechtsprechung des Europäischen Gerichtshofs zu Art. 30 EGV* (Baden-Baden, Nomos Verlagsgesellschaft, 1997).

Ahrens, Hans-Jürgen, 'Verwirrtheiten juristischer Verkehrskreise zum Verbraucherleitbild einer „normativen" Verkehrsauffassung', (2000) 46 *Wettbewerb in Recht und Praxis* 812–816.

Akerlof, George A., 'The Market for "Lemons": Quality Uncertainty and the Market Mechanism', (1970) 84 *Quarterly Journal of Economics* 488–500.

Alexandridou, Elisa, 'Advertising in the Internal Market – A few remarks', in Krämer, Ludwig and Micklitz, Hans-W. and Tonner, Klaus (eds.), *Law and diffuse interests in the European legal order: Liber amicorum Norbert Reich* (Baden-Baden, Nomos Verlagsgesellschaft, 1997), pp. 409–428.

Alexandridou, Elisa, 'The Country of Origin Principle in E-Commerce Viewed from a Greek Perspective', in Wilhelmsson, Thomas / Tuominen, Salla / Tuomola, Heli (eds.), *Consumer Law in the Information Society* (The Hague, Kluwer Law International, 2001), pp. 103–116.

Alpa, Guido, 'Trading On-line and the Protection of the Consumer', (2001) 12 *European Business Law Review* 244–250.

Alpa, Guido, 'European Private Law: Results, Projects and Hopes', (2002) 14 *European Business Law Review* 379–403.

Alpa, Guido, 'Rules on Competition and Fair Trading', in Collins, Hugh (ed.), *The Forthcoming EC Directive on Unfair Commercial Practices* (The Hague, Kluwer Law International, 2004), pp. 91–110.

Amtenbrink, Fabian, 'Note on Case C-192/94 *El Corte Inglés SA v Cristina Blázquez Rivero*', (1996) 11 *Verbraucher und Recht* 286–290.

Amtenbrink, Fabian, 'Harmonisierungsmaßnahmen im Binnenmarkt im Lichte der Entscheidung des Europäischen Gerichtshofs zur Tabakwerberichtlinie', (2001) 16 *Verbraucher und Recht* 163–174.

Amtenbrink, Fabian, 'Öffentliche Interessen im Spannungsfeld von Grundfreiheiten und Harmonisierungsmaßnahmen', in Nordhausen, Annette, *Neue Entwicklungen in der Dienstleistungs- und Warenverkehrsfreiheit* (Baden-Baden, Nomos Verlagsgesellschaft, 2002), pp. 53–69.

Amtenbrink, Fabian and Schneider, Claudia, 'Europäische Vorgaben für ein neues Kaufrecht und deutsche Schuldrechtsreform', (1999) 14 *Verbraucher und Recht* 293–301.

Amtenbrink, Fabian and Appeldoorn, Jochen Friso, 'Is er leven na het Tabaksreclamearrest?', (2001) 49 *Sociaal-economische wetgeving* 413–420.

Antoniolli, Luisa, 'Consumer Protection, Fair Dealing in Marketing Contracts and European Contract Law – A uniform Law?', in Collins, Hugh (ed.), *The Forthcoming EC Directive on Unfair Commercial Practices* (The Hague, Kluwer Law International, 2004), pp. 241–294.

Arndt, Hans-Wolfgang and Köhler, Markus, 'Elektronischer Handel nach der E-Commerce-Richtlinie', (2001) 12 *Europäisches Wirtschafts- & Steuerrecht* 102–112.

Arnull, Anthony, *The European Union and its Court of Justice* (Oxford, Oxford University Press, 1999).

Askham, Tony, 'Part 7: Consumers', in Vaughan, David (ed.), *Law of the European Communities Service Vol. 2* (London, Butterworths, loose-leaf, supplement as of July 1998 [Issue 45]).

Barents, René, 'De tabaksrichtlijn in rook opgegaan', (2000) 6 *Nederlands tijdschrift voor Europees recht* 327–331.

Barnard, Catherine, 'Fitting the remaining pieces into the goods and persons jigsaw?', (2001) 26 *European Law Review* 35–59.

Beater, Axel, *Verbraucherschutz und Schutzzweckdenken im Wettbewerbsrecht* (Tübingen, Mohr Siebeck, 2000).

Beater, Axel, 'Europäisches Recht gegen unlauteren Wettbewerb – Ansatzpunkte, Grundlagen, Entwicklung, Erforderlichkeit', (2003) 11 *Zeitschrift für Europäisches Privatrecht* 11–50.

Benegoetxea, Joxerramon/MacCormick, Neil/Moral Soriano, Leonor, 'Integration and Integrity in the Legal Reasoning of the European Court of Justice', in de Búrca, Graínne/ Weiler, Joseph (eds.), *The European Court of Justice* (Oxford, Oxford University Press, 2001), pp. 41–85.

Bernardeau, Ludovic, 'La notion de consommateur en droit communautaire (à la suite de l'arrêt de la C.J.C.E. du 22 novembre 2001, *Idealservice*, aff. jointes C-541/99 et C-542/99)', (2001) *Revue européenne de droit de la consommation* 341–362.

Bernitz, Ulf, 'The legal concept of unfairness and the economic and social environment: fair trade, market law and the consumer interest', in Balate, Eric (ed.), *Unfair advertising and comparative advertising – Publicité déloyale et publicité comparative*, (Brussels, Story-Scientia, 1988), pp. 53–67.

Biondi, Andrea, 'Advertising alcohol and the free movement principle: the *Gourmet* decision', (2001) 26 *European Law Review* 616–622.

Bishop, Simon/Walker, Mike, *The Economics of EC Competition law: Concepts, Application and Measurement* (2nd ed., London, Sweet & Maxwell, 2002).

Blaurock, Uwe, 'Verbraucherkredit und Verbraucherleitbild in der Europäischen Union', (1999) 54 *Juristenzeitung* 801–809.

Boehme-Neßler, Volker, 'Europäisches Internetrecht', (2001) 12 *Europäisches Wirtschafts- & Steuerrecht* 149–156.

Bogdandy, Armin von and Bast, Jürgen, 'The European Union's Vertical Order of Competences: The Current Law and Proposals for its Reform', (2002) 39 *Common Market Law Review* 227–268.

Bouckaert, Jan/Waelbroeck, Denis, 'Les produits pharmaceutiques face à la libre circulation des marchandises – jurisprudence récente', (1993) 1 *Journal des Tribunaux – Droit européen* 8–11.

Boulanger, Marie-Hélène / de Terwangne, Cécile / Léonard, Thierry / Louveaux, Sophie / Moreau, Damien / Poullet, Yves, 'La protection des données à caractère personnel en droit communautaire', in Nihoul, Paul (ed.), *Telecommunications and broadcasting networks under EC law: the protection afforded to consumers and undertakings in the information society* (Köln, Bundesanzeiger Verlagsgesellschaft, 2000), pp. 131–181.

Bourgoignie, Thierry, *Éléments pour une théorie du droit de la consommation : au regard des développements du droit belge et du droit de la Communauté économique européenne*, (Bruxelles, Story Scientia, 1988).

Boyron, Sophie, 'In the name of European Law: the metric martyrs case', (2002) 27 *European Law Review* 771–779.

Brown, Lionel Neville/Jacobs, Francis Geoffrey/Kennedy, Tom, *The Court of Justice of the European Communities*, (London, Sweet & Maxwell, 2000).

Bultmann, Fritz A. / Howells, Geraint / Keßler, Jürgen / Micklitz, Hans-W. / Radeideh, Malek / Reich, Norbert / Stuyck, Jules / Voigt, Dennis, *The Feasibility of a General Legislative Framework on Fair Trading – Volume I–III, A Study commissioned by the European Commission*, (Berlin, November 2000, accessible via the website of the European Commission DG SANCO, http://europa.eu.int/comm/consumers/index_en.htm).

de Búrca, Graínne, 'Proportionality and Subsidiarity as General Principles of Law', in Bernitz, Ulf and Nergelius, Joakim (eds.), *General Principles of European Community Law*, (The Hague, Kluwer Law International, 2000), pp. 95–112.

Calais-Auloy, Jean, 'Le contrôle de la publicité déloyale en France', in Balate, Eric (ed.), *Unfair advertising and comparative advertising – Publicité déloyale et publicité comparative*, (Brussels, Story-Scientia, 1988), pp. 85–92.

Calliess, Gralf-Peter, 'Nach der Schuldrechtsreform: Perspektiven des deutschen, europäischen und internationalen Verbrauchervertragsrechts', (2003) 203 *Archiv für die civilistische Praxis* 575–602.

Christianos, Vassili and Picod, Fabrice, 'Consommateurs', *Encyclopédie juridique Dalloz : Répertoire droit communautaire* (2nd ed., Paris, Editeur Dalloz-Sirey, 'rubrique' dating from April 1996) 1–42.

Classen, Claus Dieter, 'Note on Joined Cases C-465/00, C-138/01 and C-139/01 *Neukomm et al*', (2004) 41 *Common Market Law Review* 1377–1385.

de Cock Buning, Madeleine/Hondius, Ewoud/Prins, Corien/de Vries, Marc, 'Consumer@Protection.EU. An Analysis of European Consumer Legislation in the Information Society', (2001) 24 *Journal of Consumer Policy* 287–338.

Collins, Hugh, 'EC Regulation of Unfair Commercial Practices', in Collins, Hugh (ed.), *The Forthcoming EC Directive on Unfair Commercial Practices* (The Hague, Kluwer Law International, 2004), pp. 1–42.

Constantinesco, Vlad/ Kovar, Robert/Simon, Denys, *Traité sur l'Union Européenne – Commentaire article par article* (Paris, Economica, 1995).

Constantinesco, Vlad, 'The ECJ as a Law-Maker: *Praeter aut Contra Legem?*', in O'Keeffe, David and Bavasso, Antonio (eds.), *Liber Amicorum in Honour of Lord Slynn of Hadley, Volume I, Judicial review in European Union Law* (The Hague, Kluwer Law International, 2000), pp. 73–79.

Coudray, Ludovic, 'Note on Case C-101/01 *Bodil Lindqvist*', (2004) 41 *Common Market Law Review* 1361–1376.

Craig, Paul/de Búrca, Graínne, *EU Law – Text, Cases and Materials*, (3rd ed., Oxford, Oxford University Press, 2003).

da Cruz Vilaça, José Luís, 'On the Application of *Keck* in the Field of Free Provision of Services' in Adenas, Mads and Roth, Wulf-Henning (eds.), *Services and Free Movement in EU Law* (Oxford, Oxford University Press, 2002), pp. 25–40.

Cseres, Katalin, 'Le Livre Vert de la Commission sur la protection des consommateurs : Don Quichotte contre les pratiques commerciales déloyales', (2001) *Revue européenne de droit de la consommation* 221–243.

Davies, Gareth, 'Welfare as a Service', (2002) 29 *Legal Issues of Economic Integration* 27–40.

Davies, Gareth, *Nationality Discrimination in the European Internal Market*, (The Hague, Kluwer Law International, 2003).

Davies, Gareth, *European Union Internal Market Law*, (2nd ed., London, Cavendish Publishing, 2003).

Davies, Gareth, 'Consumer Protection as an obstacle to the Free Movement of Goods', (2003) 3 *ERA-Forum* 55–66.

Deutsch, Volker, 'Der Einfluß des europäischen Rechts auf den Irreführungstatbestand des § 3 UWG', (1996) 98 *Gewerblicher Rechtsschutz und Urheberrecht* 541–547.

Deutsch, Volker, 'Noch einmal: Das Verbraucherleitbild des EuGH und das „Nissan"-Urteil', (1997) 99 *Gewerblicher Rechtsschutz und Urheberrecht* 44–45.

Dickie, John, 'Consumer Confidence and the EC Directive on Distance Contracts', (1998) 21 *Journal of Consumer Policy* 217–229.

Dittmer, Stefan, 'Misleading Advertising – An End to the "Cursory Average Consumer"?', (1998) 21 *European Intellectual Property Review* 313–317.

Dougan, Michael, 'Minimum Harmonisation and the Internal Market', (2000) 37 *Common Market Law Review* 853–885.

Douglas-Scott, Sionaidh, *Constitutional Law of the European Union* (Harlow, Longman, 2002).

Dreher, Meinrad, 'Der Verbraucher – Das Phantom in den opera des europäischen und deutschen Rechts?', (1997) 52 *Juristenzeitung* 167–178.

Drexl, Josef, 'Community Legislation Continued: Complete Harmonisation, Framework Legislation or Non-Binding Measures – Alternative Approaches to European Contract Law, Consumer Protection and Unfair Trade Practices', (2002) 13 *European Business Law Review* 557–582.

Drexl, Josef, 'Continuing Contract Law Harmonisation under the White Paper of 1985? – Between Minimum Harmonisation, Mutual Recognition, Conflict of Laws, and Uniform Law', in Grundmann, Stefan and Stuyck, Jules (eds.), *An Academic Green Paper on European Contract Law* (The Hague, Kluwer Law International, 2002), pp. 103–129.

Drijber, Berend Jan, 'The revised Television without frontiers Directive: Is it fit for the next Century?', (1999) 36 *Common Market Law Review* 87–122.

Dworkin, Ronald, *Taking Rights Seriously* (London, Duckworth, 1977).

Ebers, Martin, 'Informations- und Beratungspflichten bei Finanzdienstleistungen: Allgemeine und besondere Rechtsgrundsätze', in Schulze, Reiner/Ebers, Martin/Grigoleit, Hans Christoph (eds.), *Informationspflichten und Vertragsschluss im Acquis communautaire* (Tübingen, Mohr Siebeck, 2003), pp. 171–190.

Edelmann, Hervé, 'Zur Anwendbarkeit des Haustürwiderrufsgesetzes auf Bürgschaftsverträge – zugleich Besprechung des EuGH-Urteils vom 17.3.1998 – C-45/96', (1998) 13 *Verbraucher und Recht* 179–182.

Eeckhout, Piet, 'The EU Charter of Fundamental Rights and the Federal Question', (2002) 39 *Common Market Law Review* 945–994.

Eilmansberger, Thomas, 'The Relationship between Rights and Remedies in EC Law: In Search of the Missing Link', (2004) 41 *Common Market Law Review* 1999–1246.

Emiliou, Nicholas, *The Principle of Proportionality in European Law – A Comparative Study* (London, Kluwer Law International, 1996).

Enchelmaier, Stefan, 'Note on Case C-469/00 *Ravil SARL v Bellon import SARL and Biraghi SpA* and Case C-108/01 *Consorzio del Prosciutto di Parma et al. v Asda Stores Ltd et al*', (2004) 41 *Common Market Law Review* 825–838.

Evrard, Jean-J., 'Les articles 30 à 36 du traité CEE et les pratiques du commerce', (1993) 1 *Journal des Tribunaux – Droit européen* 11–12.

Fallon, Marc, 'Note on Joined Cases C-369/96 and C-376/96 *Jean-Claude Arblade & Fils SARL and Bernhard Leloup et al. SARL*', (2001) *Revue critique de droit international privé* 728–737.

Faber, Wolfgang, 'Elemente verschiedener Verbraucherbegriffe in EG-Richtlinien, zwischenstaatlichen Übereinkommen und nationalem Zivil- und Kollisionsrecht', (1998) 6 *Zeitschrift für Europäisches Privatrecht* 854–892.

Fezer, Karl-Heinz and Koos, Stefan, 'Das gemeinschaftsrechtliche Herkunftslandprinzip und die e-commerce-Richtlinie – Zur dringenden Notwendigkeit einer Harmonisierung des Wettbewerbsrechts in den Mitgliedstaaten der Europäischen Union als einer gemeinschaftsrechtlichen Aufgabe', (2000) 20 *Praxis des internationalen Privat- und Verfahrensrechts* 349–354.

Fezer, Karl-Heinz, 'Modernisierung des deutschen Rechts gegen den unlauteren Wettbewerb auf der Grundlage einer Europäisierung des Wettbewerbsrechts', (2001) 47 *Wettbewerb in Recht und Praxis* 989–1022.

Fischer, Nikolaj, 'Europäischer Verbraucherschutz im deutschen Privatrecht – Einige kritische Anmerkungen', (2003) 18 *Verbraucher und Recht* 20–25.

Fox, Eleanor M., '"We Protect Competition, You Protect Competitors"', (2003) 26 *World Competition* 149–165.

Franzen, Martin, *Privatrechtsangleichung durch die Europäische Gemeinschaft* (Berlin, de Gruyter, 1999).

Gasparinetti, Marco, 'Personal Data and Directive 95/46/EC: "The Great Wall of Europe", to Too Much Ado About Nothing?', in Nihoul, Paul (ed.), *Telecommunications and broadcasting networks under EC law: the protection afforded to consumers and undertakings in the information society* (Köln, Bundesanzeiger Verlagsgesellschaft, 2000), pp. 205–210.

Gauthronet, Serge and Drouard, Etienne, *Unsolicited Commercial Communications and Data Protection*, (January 2001, accessible via the website of the European Commission DG MARKT, http://www.europa.eu.int/comm/internal_market/privacy/studies_en.htm).

Gerber, David J., *Law and Competition in Twentieth Century Europe: Protecting Prometheus* (Oxford, Clarendon Press, 1998).

van Gerven, Walter, 'The ECJ Case-Law as a Means of Unification of Private Law?', in Hartkamp, Arthur et al. (eds.), *Towards a European Civil Code* (2nd ed., The Hague, Kluwer Law International, 1998), pp. 91–104.

van Gerven, Walter, 'Harmonization of Private Law: Do We Need It?', (2004) 41 *Common Market Law Review* 505–532.

GFA Management GmbH, *Ex-ante Impact Assessment of the options outlined in the Green Paper on EU Consumer Protection*, (November 2002, accessible via the website of the European Commission DG SANCO, http://europa.eu.int/comm/consumers/index_en.htm).

Glöckner, Jochen, 'Richtlinienvorschlag über unlautere Geschäftspraktiken, deutsches UWG oder die schwierige Umsetzung von europarechtlichen Generalklauseln', (2004) 50 *Wettbewerb in Recht und Praxis* 936–945.

Göhre, Stefan, 'Frischer Wind aus Brüssel? – Der Vorschlag der Europäischen Kommission für eine Verordnung über Verkaufsförderung im Binnenmarkt und das Grünbuch der Europäischen Kommission zum Verbraucherschutz in der Europäischen Union', (2002) 48 *Wettbewerb in Recht und Praxis* 36–47.

Golan, Elise/Kuchler, Fred/Mitchell, Lorraine/Greene, Cathy/Jessup, Amber, 'Economics of Food Labeling', (2001) 24 *Journal of Consumer Policy* 117–184.

Gómez, Fernando, 'EC Consumer Protection Law and EC Competition Law: How related are they? A Law and Economics Perspective', in Collins, Hugh (ed.), *The Forthcoming EC Directive on Unfair Commercial Practices* (The Hague, Kluwer Law International, 2004), pp. 187–208.

Görlitz, Niklas, 'EU-Binnenmarktkompetenzen und Tabakwerbeverbote – Kompetenzrechtliche Anmerkungen zur neuen Richtlinie über Werbung und Sponsoring zu Gunsten von Tabakerzeugnissen' (2003) 14 *Europäische Zeitschrift für Wirtschaftsrecht* 485–490.

Gormley, Laurence William, 'Cassis de Dijon and the Communication from the Commission', (1981) 6 *European Law Review* 454–459.

Gormley, Laurence William, *Prohibiting restrictions on trade within the EEC: The theory and application of Articles 30-36 of the EEC Treaty* (Amsterdam, North Holland, 1985).

Gormley, Laurence William, 'Some reflections on the internal market and free movement of goods', (1989) *Legal Issues of European Integration* 9–20.

Gormley, Laurence William, '"Actually or Potentially, Directly or Indirectly"? Obstacles to the Free Movement of Goods', (1989) 9 *Yearbook of European Law* 197–208.

Gormley, Laurence William, 'Note on Case C-145/88 *Torfaen Borough Council v B & Q PLC*', (1990) 27 *Common Market Law Review* 141–150.

Gormley, Laurence William, 'Recent Case Law on the Free Movement of Goods: Some Hot Potatoes', (1990) 27 *Common Market Law Review* 825–857.

Gormley, Laurence William, 'Reasoning Renounced? The Remarkable Judgment in *Keck & Mithouard*', (1994) 5 *European Business Law Review* 63–67.

Gormley, Laurence William, 'European Community Action on Good Manufacturing Practice: Consumer Protection and Product Liability', in Smit Sibinga, Cornelis Theodoor et al. (eds.), *Good Manufacturing Practice in Transfusion Medicine* (Dordrecht, Kluwer Academic Publishers, 1994), pp. 59–65.

Gormley, Laurence William, 'Pay your money and take your chance?', (1994) 19 *European Law Review* 644–653.

Gormley, Laurence William, 'Two Years after Keck', (1996) 19 *Fordham International Law Journal* 866–886.

Gormley, Laurence William, 'All that glitters is not gold?', (1996) 21 *European Law Review* 44–49.

Gormley, Laurence William, 'A Well-Tempered Consumer? Comments on Stephen Weatherill's Paper', in Micklitz, Hans-W. (ed.), *Rechtseinheit oder Rechtsvielfalt in Europa:*

Rolle des Verbraucherrechts in der EG und in den MOE-Staaten (Baden-Baden, Nomos Verlagsgesellschaft, 1996), pp. 473–476.
Gormley, Laurence William, 'Consolidation, Codification and Improving the Quality of Community Legislation – The Community Customs Code', in Emiliou, Nicholas and O'Keeffe, David (eds.), *The European Union and World Trade Law* (Chichester, John Wiley & Sons, 1996), pp. 124–135.
Gormley, Laurence William, 'Some Food for Thought?', (1997) *European Food Law Review* 1–10.
Gormley, Laurence William, 'Public Interest Litigation', in O'Keeffe, David and Bavasso, Antonio (eds.), *Liber Amicorum in Honour of Lord Slynn of Hadley, Volume I, Judicial review in European Union Law* (The Hague, Kluwer Law International, 2000), pp. 191–201.
Gormley, Laurence William, 'The Development of General Principles of Law Within Article 10 (ex Article 5) EC', in Bernitz, Ulf and Nergelius, Joakim (eds.), *General Principles of European Community Law* (The Hague, Kluwer Law International, 2000), pp. 113–118.
Gormley, Laurence William, 'Judicial review in EC and EU law – Some architectural malfunctions and design improvements?', (2001) 4 *The Cambridge Yearbook of European Legal Studies* 167–189.
Gormley, Laurence William, 'Competition and Free Movement: Is the Internal Market the Same as a Common Market?', (2002) 13 *European Business Law Review* 517–522.
Gorny, Dietrich, 'Der Abschied vom verständigen Durchschnittsverbraucher im Lebensmittel-Werberecht', (2003) 30 *Zeitschrift für das gesamte Lebensmittelrecht* 253–264.
Goyder, D. G., *EC Competition Law* (3rd ed., Oxford, Oxford University Press, 1998).
Greaves, Rosa, 'Advertising Restrictions and the Free Movement of Goods and Services', (1998) 23 *European Law Review* 305–319.
Groeschke, Peer and Kiethe, Kurt, 'Die Ubiquität des europäischen Verbraucherleitbildes – Der europäische Paß des informierten und verständigen Verbrauchers', (2001) 47 *Wettbewerb in Recht und Praxis* 230–238.
Grundmann, Stefan, *Europäisches Schuldvertragsrecht* (Berlin, de Gruyter, 1999).
Grundmann, Stefan/Kerber, Wolfgang/Weatherill, Stephen, 'Party Autonomy and the Role of Information in the Internal Market – an Overview, in Grundmann, Stefan/Kerber, Wolfgang/Weatherill, Stephen (eds.), *Party Autonomy and the Role of Information in the Internal Market* (Berlin, de Gruyter, 2001), pp. 3–38.
Grundmann, Stefan, 'Information, Party Autonomy and Economic Agents in European Contract Law', (2002) 39 *Common Market Law Review* 269–293.
Grundmann, Stefan, 'Das Internationale Privatrecht der E-Commerce-Richtlinie – was ist kategorial anders im Kollisionsrecht des Binnenmarkts und warum?', (2003) 67 *Rabels Zeitschrift* 246–297.
Grundmann, Stefan, 'Consumer Law, Commercial Law, Private Law: How can the Sales Directive and the Sales Convention be so Similar', (2003) 14 *European Business Law Review* 237–257.
Grundmann, Stefan, 'EC Consumer and EC Competition Law: How Related are they? Examining the Existing EC Contract Law Sources', in Collins, Hugh (ed.), *The Forthcoming*

EC Directive on Unfair Commercial Practices (The Hague, Kluwer Law International, 2004), pp. 209–222.

Günther, Eva, 'Verbraucherinformation – Mehr als Zugangsrechte', (2003) 18 *Verbraucher und Recht* 25–30.

Hadfield, Gillian K./Howse, Robert/Trebilcock, Michael J., 'Information-Based Principles for Rethinking Consumer Protection Policy', (1998) 21 *Journal of Consumer Policy* 131–169.

Härting, Niko and Schirmbacher, Martin 'Finanzdienstleistungen im Fernabsatz', (2002) *Computer und Recht* 809–817.

Harvey, Brian W. and Parry, Deborah L., *The Law of Consumer Protection and Fair Trading* (6th ed., London, Butterworths, 2000).

Hartley, Trevor Clayton, *The Foundations of European Community Law* (5th ed., Oxford, Oxford University Press, 2003).

Hartlief, Tom, 'Freedom and Protection in Contemporary Contract Law', (2004) 27 *Journal of Consumer Policy* 253–267.

Heermann, Peter W., 'Artikel 30 EGV im Lichte der „Keck"-Rechtsprechung: Anerkennung sonstiger Verkaufsmodalitäten und Einführung eines einheitlichen Rechtfertigungstatbesta nds', (1999) 48 *Gewerblicher Rechtsschutz und Urheberrecht, Internationaler Teil* 579–595.

Hellner, Michael, 'The Country of Origin Principle in the E-commerce Directive – A Conflict with Conflict of Laws?', (2004) 8 *European Review of Private Law* 193–213.

Henning-Bodewig, Frauke, 'E-Commerce und irreführende Werbung', (2001) 47 *Wettbewerb in Recht und Praxis* 771–777.

Henning-Bodewig, Frauke, 'Richtlinienvorschlag über unlautere Geschäftspraktiken und UWG-Reform', (2004) 53 *Gewerblicher Rechtsschutz und Urheberrecht, Internationaler Teil* 183–193.

Henning-Bodewig, Frauke and Schricker Gerhard, 'New Initiatives for the Harmonisation of Unfair Competition Law in Europe', (2002) 25 *European Intellectual Property Review* 271–276.

Herdegen, Matthias, 'The Origins and Development of the General Principles of Community Law', in Bernitz, Ulf and Nergelius (eds.), *General Principles of European Community Law* (The Hague, Kluwer Law International, 2000), pp. 3–23.

Hermann, A. H. and Jones, Colin, *Fair Trading in Europe* (London, Kluwer-Harrap Handbooks, 1977).

Hervey, Tamara K., 'Up in smoke? Community (anti)-tobacco law and policy', (2001) 26 *European Law Review* 101–125.

Hildebrand, Doris, *The Role of Economic Analysis in the EC Competition Rules,* (2nd ed., The Hague, Kluwer Law International, 2002).

Howells, Geraint, 'Contract Law: The Challenge for the Critical Consumer Lawyer', in Wilhelmsson, Thomas (ed.), *Perspectives of Critical Contract Law* (Aldershot, Dartmouth, 1993), p. 327–347.

Howells, Geraint, 'European Consumer Law – The Minimal and Maximal Harmonisation Debate and Pro Independent Consumer Law competence', in Grundmann, Stefan and Stuyck, Jules (eds.), *An Academic Green Paper on European Contract Law* (The Hague, Kluwer Law International, 2002), pp. 73–80.

Howells, Geraint and Weatherill, Stephen, *Consumer Protection Law* (Aldershot, Dartmouth, 1995).

Howells, Geraint and Wilhelmsson, Thomas, *EC Consumer Law* (Aldershot, Ashgate/Dartmouth, 1997).

Howells, Geraint and Wilhelmsson, Thomas, 'EC and US Approaches to Consumer Protection – Should the Gap Be Bridged?', (1997) 17 *Yearbook of European Law* 207–267.

Howells, Geraint and Wilhelmsson, Thomas, 'EC Consumer law: has it come of age?', (2003) 28 *European Law Review* 380–388.

Hultmark Ramberg, Christina, 'The E-Commerce Directive and formation of contract in a comparative perspective', (2001) 26 *European Law Review* 429–450.

Jacobs, Francis G., 'The Evolution of the European Legal Order', (2004) 41 *Common Market Law Review* 303–316.

Jarvis, Malcolm Andrew, *The Application of EC Law in National Courts: The Free Movement of Goods* (Oxford, Clarendon Press, 1998).

Jarvis, Malcolm Andrew, 'Note on Case C-325/00 *Commission v Germany*', (2003) 40 *Common Market Law Review* 715–728.

Joliet, René, 'Das Recht des unlauteren Wettbewerbs und der freie Warenverkehr – Die Rechtsprechung des Europäischen Gerichtshofs', (1994) 43 *Gewerblicher Rechtsschutz und Urheberrecht, Internationaler Teil* 1–14.

Joliet, René, 'Der freie Warenverkehr: Das Urteil Keck und Mithouard und die Neuorientierung der Rechtsprechung', (1994) 43 *Gewerblicher Rechtsschutz und Urheberrecht, Internationaler Teil* 979–987.

Jones, Alison and Sufrin, Brenda, *EC Competition Law* (Oxford, Oxford University Press, 2001).

Junod Moser, Dominique, *Les conditions générales à la croisée du droit de la concurrence et du droit de la consommation – Etude de droit suisse et de droit européen* (Bâle, Helbing & Lichtenhahn, 2001).

Kaiser, Sven, 'Vorschlag der EU-Kommission für eine Überarbeitung der Verbraucherkreditrichtlinie – Darstellung der wesentlichen Änderungen', (2002) 17 *Verbraucher und Recht* 385–390.

Kapteyn, Paul Joan George and VerLoren van Themaat, Pieter, *Introduction to the Law of the European Communities* (2nd ed., edited by Gormley, Laurence William, Deventer, Kluwer Law and Taxation, 1989).

Kapteyn, Paul Joan George and VerLoren van Themaat, Pieter, *Introduction to the Law of the European Communities* (3rd ed., edited by Gormley, Laurence William, London, Kluwer Law International, 1998).

Karsten, Jens and Sinai, Ali R., 'The Action Plan on European Contract Law: Perspectives for the Future of European Contract Law and EC Consumer Law', (2003) 26 *Journal of Consumer Policy* 159–195.

Katzenberger, Paul, 'Kollisionsrecht des unlauteren Wettbewerbs', in Schricker, Gerhard and Henning-Bodewig, Frauke (eds.), *Neuordnung des Wettbewerbsrechts* (Baden-Baden, Nomos Verlagsgesellschaft, 1998/99), pp. 218–230.

Kelman, Mark/Rottenstreich, Yuval/Tversky, Amos, 'Context-Dependence in Legal Decision Making', in Sunstein, Cass R. (ed.), *Behavioral Law and Economics* (Cambridge, Cambridge University Press, 2000), pp. 61–94.

Kemper, Rainer and Rosenow, Jörg, 'Der Irreführungsbegriff auf dem Weg nach Europa', (2001) 47 *Wettbewerb in Recht und Praxis* 370–378.

Kerber, Wolfgang/Vanberg, Viktor, 'Constitutional Aspects of Party Autonomy and Its Limits – The Perspective of Constitutional Economics', in Grundmann, Stefan/Kerber, Wolfgang/ Weatherill, Stephen (eds.), *Party Autonomy and the Role of Information in the Internal Market* (Berlin, de Gruyter, 2001), pp. 49–79.

Keßler, Jürgen, 'European Consumer Law – zu den dogmatischen Konzepten des europäischen Verbraucherrechts', (1999) 14 *Verbraucher und Recht* 415–422.

Keßler, Jürgen/Micklitz, Hans-W., *Die Harmonisierung des Lauterkeitsrechts in den Mitgliedstaaten der Europäischen Gemeinschaft und die Reform des UWG* (Baden-Baden, Nomos Verlagsgesellschaft, 2003).

Kieninger, Eva-Maria, 'Die Richtlinie über den Fernabsatz von Finanzdienstleistungen – Voll- oder Teilharmonisierung?', in Nordhausen, Annette, *Neue Entwicklungen in der Dienstleistungs- und Warenverkehrsfreiheit* (Baden-Baden, Nomos Verlagsgesellschaft, 2002), pp. 13–21.

Köhler, Helmut, 'Die neuen europäischen Begriffe und Grundsätze des Lebensmittelrechts', (2002) 104 *Gewerblicher Rechtsschutz und Urheberrecht* 844–853.

Köhler, Helmut and Lettl, Tobias, 'Das geltende europäische Lauterkeitsrecht, der Vorschlag für eine EG-Richtlinie über unlautere Geschäftspraktiken und die UWG-Reform', (2003) 49 *Wettbewerb in Recht und Praxis* 1019–1057.

Kötz, Hein, 'Precontractual Duties of Disclosure: A Comparative and Economic Perspective', (2000) 9 *European Journal of Law and Economics* 5–19.

Kotler, Philip / Armstrong, Gary / Saunders, John / Wong, Veronica, *Principles of Marketing* (3rd European ed., Harlow, Prentice Hall Europe, 2001).

Koutrakos, Panos, 'On groceries, alcohol and olive oil: more on free movement of goods after *Keck*', (2001) 26 *European Law Review* 391–407.

Kraus, Dieter, 'Zur verbraucherrechtlichen Rechtsprechung des Europäischen Gerichtshofs im Rahmen des Europäischen Privatrechts', in Schulze, Reiner/Ebers, Martin/Grigoleit, Hans Christoph (eds.), *Informationspflichten und Vertragsschluss im Acquis communautaire* (Tübingen, Mohr Siebeck, 2003), pp. 29–48.

Kroeber-Riel, Werner and Weinberg, Peter, *Konsumentenverhalten* (7th ed., München, Vahlen, 1999).

Kurcz, Bartlomiej, *Harmonisation by means of Directives – never-ending story?*, (2001) 12 *European Business Law Review* 287–307.

Kutscher, Hans, *Methods of interpretation as seen by a judge at the Court of Justice* (Luxemburg, Court of Justice of the European Communities, 1976).

Lando, Ole and Beale, Hugh, *The principles of European contract law* (The Hague, Kluwer Law International, 2000).

Landy, Laurence, 'Le consommateur européen : une notion éclatée', in Osman, Filali (ed.), *Vers un code européen de la consommation* (Bruxelles, Bruylant, 1998), pp. 57–71.

Lawson, Richard, 'The legal control of unfair advertising in the United Kingdom', in Balate, Eric (ed.), *Unfair advertising and comparative advertising – Publicité déloyale et publicité comparative*, (Brussels, Story-Scientia, 1988), pp. 69–84.

Le Berre, Nelly/Arnould, Joël/Derenne, Jacques, 'Le nouveaux droit communautaire du commerce électronique', (2002) 10 *Journal des Tribunaux – Droit européen* 113–117.

Leible, Stephan, 'Note on Case C-405/98 *Konsumentombudsmannen (KO) v Gourmet International Products AB (GIP)*', (2001) 12 *Europäische Zeitschrift für Wirtschaftsrecht* 253–255.

Leible, Stephan, 'Das Verbot des Apothekenversandhandels mit Arzneimitteln – Eine Verkaufsmodalität im Sinne der Keck-Rechtsprechung?', (2003) 14 *Europäische Zeitschrift für Wirtschaftsrecht* 37–44.

Leible, Stephan, 'Note on Case C-99/01 *Criminal proceedings against Gottfried Linhart and Hans Biffl*', (2003) 30 *Zeitschrift für das gesamte Lebensmittelrecht* 63–77.

Lenaerts, Koen, 'In The Union We Trust: Trust-Enhancing Principles of Community Law', (2004) 41 *Common Market Law Review* 317–343.

Lenz, Carl Otto, 'Unlauterer Wettbewerb und freier Warenverkehr in der Rechtsprechung des Europäischen Gerichtshofes', (1994) 2 *Zeitschrift für Europäisches Privatrecht* 624–647.

Lettl, Tobias, 'Gemeinschaftsrecht und neues UWG', (2004) 50 *Wettbewerb in Recht und Praxis* 1079–1132.

Lex Fori, *La meilleure pratique dans le recours à des normes juridiques "douces" et son application aux consommateurs au sein de l'Union Européenne*, (accessible via the website of the European Commission DG SANCO, http://europa.eu.int/comm/consumers/index_en.htm).

Loos, Marcus Bernardus Maria, 'Naar een gemeenschapsautonome interpretatie van het begrip 'schade': schadevergoeding voor immateriële schade bij pakketreizen', (2002) 8 *Nederlands tijdschrift voor Europees recht* 157–161.

Loos, Marcus Bernardus Maria, 'De effectiviteit van de bedenktijd als instrument van consumentenbescherming', (2003) 19 *Tijdschrift voor Consumentenrecht* 6–23.

Lopez-Tarruella, Aurelio, 'A European Community Regulatory Framework for Electronic Commerce?', (2001) 38 *Common Market Law Review* 1337–1384.

MacMaoláin, Caoimhín, 'The new genetically modified food labelling requirements: finally a lasting solution', (2003) 28 *European Law Review* 865–879.

Mankowski, Peter, 'Das Herkunftslandprinzip als Internationales Privatrecht der e-commerce-Richtlinie', (2001) 100 *Zeitschrift für vergleichende Rechtswissenschaft* 137–181.

McInerney, Siobhan, 'Equal Treatment between Persons irrespective of racial or ethnic Origin: a Comment', (2000) 25 *European Law Review* 317–323.

Mercer, David, *Marketing: The Encyclopaedic Dictionary* (Oxford, Blackwell Publishers, 1999).

Meyer, Andreas, 'Produktspezifische Werberegelungen im Europäischen Gemeinschaftsrecht', in Schricker, Gerhard and Henning-Bodewig, Frauke (eds.), *Neuordnung des Wettbewerbsrechts* (Baden-Baden, Nomos Verlagsgesellschaft, 1998/99), pp. 93–111.

Micklitz, Hans-W., 'Legitime Erwartungen als Gerechtigkeitsprinzip des europäischen Privatrechts', in Krämer, Ludwig and Micklitz, Hans-W. and Tonner, Klaus (eds.), *Law and diffuse interests in the European legal order: Liber amicorum Norbert Reich* (Baden-Baden, Nomos Verlagsgesellschaft, 1997), pp. 245–277.

Micklitz, Hans-W., 'Umweltwerbung und Verbraucherleitbild in der EG', in Reich, Norbert and Heine-Mernik, Renate (eds.), *Umweltverfassung und nachhaltige Entwicklung in der Europäischen Union* (Baden-Baden, Nomos Verlagsgesellschaft, 1997), pp. 65–88.

Micklitz, Hans-W., 'Case C-45/96 *Bayerische Hypotheken- und Wechselbank AG v Edgard Dietzinger*', (1998) 9 *Europäische Zeitschrift für Wirtschaftsrecht* 253–254.

Micklitz, Hans-W., 'Perspektiven eines Europäischen Privatrechts – Ius commune praeter legem?', (1998) 6 *Zeitschrift für Europäisches Privatrecht* 253–276.

Micklitz, Hans-W., 'Principles of Social Justice in European Private Law', (1999/2000) 19 *Yearbook of European Law* 167–204.

Micklitz, Hans-W. in Grabitz, Eberhard and Hilf, Meinhard (eds.), *Das Recht der Europäischen Union* (München, Verlag C.H. Beck, loose-leaf, supplement as of January 2000).

Micklitz, Hans-W., 'Fernabsatz und E-Commerce im Schuldrechtsmodernisierungsgesetz', (2001) 12 *Europäische Zeitschrift für Wirtschaftsrecht* 133–143.

Micklitz, Hans-W., 'Vertragsschlussmodalitäten im Diskussionsentwurf eines Schuldrechtsmodernisierungsgesetzes', (2001) 16 *Verbraucher und Recht* 71–78.

Micklitz, Hans-W., 'A Comment on Party Autonomy and Consumer Regulation in the European Community – A Plea for Consistency', in Grundmann, Stefan/Kerber, Wolfgang/Weatherill, Stephen (eds.), *Party Autonomy and the Role of Information in the Internal Market* (Berlin, de Gruyter, 2001), pp. 197–204.

Micklitz, Hans-W., 'An Expanded and Systematized Community Consumer Law as Alternative or Complement?', (2002) 13 *European Business Law Review* 583–598.

Micklitz, Hans-W., 'Zum Recht des Verbrauchers auf die eigene Sprache', (2003) 11 *Zeitschrift für Europäisches Privatrecht* 635–655.

Micklitz, Hans-W., 'Zur Notwendigkeit eines neuen Konzepts für die Fortentwicklung des Verbraucherrechts in der EU', (2003) 18 *Verbraucher und Recht* 2–12.

Micklitz, Hans-W., 'A General Framework Directive on Fair Trading', in Collins, Hugh (ed.), *The Forthcoming EC Directive on Unfair Commercial Practices* (The Hague, Kluwer Law International, 2004), pp. 43–89.

Micklitz, Hans-W. and Weatherill, Stephen, 'Consumer Policy in the European Community: Before and After Maastricht', (1993) 16 *Journal of Consumer Policy* 285–321.

Micklitz, Hans-W./Monazzahian, Bettina/Rößler, Christina, *Door to Door Selling – Pyramid Selling – Multilevel Marketing – Volume I–II, A Study commissioned by the European Commission,* (Berlin, November 1999, accessible via the website of the European Commission DG SANCO, http://europa.eu.int/comm/consumers/index_en.htm).

Micklitz, Hans-W. and Keßler, Jürgen, 'Europäisches Lauterkeitsrecht – Dogmatische und ökonomische Aspekte einer Harmonisierung des Wettbewerbsverhaltensrechts im europäischen Binnenmarkt', (2002) 51 *Gewerblicher Rechtsschutz und Urheberrecht, Internationaler Teil* 885–901.

Micklitz, Hans-W. and Keßler, Jürgen (eds.), *Marketing Practices Regulation and Consumer Protection in the EC Member States and the US* (Baden-Baden, Nomos Verlagsgesellschaft, 2002).

Micklitz, Hans-W. and Keßler, Jürgen, 'Funktionswandel des UWG', (2003) 49 *Wettbewerb in Recht und Praxis* 919–936.

Micklitz, Hans-W. and Radeideh, Malek, 'CLAB Europa – Die europäische Datenbank missbräuchlicher Klauseln in Verbraucherverträgen', (2003) 11 *Zeitschrift für Europäisches Privatrecht* 85–113.

Micklitz, Hans-W. and Schirmbacher, Martin, 'Duties to inform contained in Directive 2002/65/EC concerning the distance marketing of consumer financial services', (2003) 3 *European Banking and Financial Law Journal* 457–486.

Misita, Nevenko, 'The Protection of Privacy: A Consumer Perspective', in Wilhelmsson, Thomas / Tuominen, Salla / Tuomola, Heli (eds.), *Consumer Law in the Information Society* (The Hague, Kluwer Law International, 2001), pp. 263–291.

Moloney, Niamh, *EC Securities Regulation* (Oxford, Oxford University Press, 2002).

Monti, Giorgio, 'Article 81 EC and Public Policy', (2002) 39 *Common Market Law Review* 1057–1099.

Mortelmans, Kamiel Jan Maria, 'De interne markt en het facettenbeleid na het Keck-arrest : nationaal beleid, vrij verkeer of harmonisatie', (1994) 42 *Sociaal-economische wetgeving* 236–250.

Mortelmans, Kamiel Jan Maria, 'The Common Market, the Internal Market and the Single Market, what's in a Market?', (1998) 35 *Common Market Law Review* 101–136.

Mortelmans, Kamiel Jan Maria and van Ooik, Ronald Hendrik, 'Het Europese verbod op tabaksreclame: verbetering van de interne markt of bescherming van de volksgezondheid?', (2001) 50 *Ars Aequi* 114–130.

Mortelmans, Kamiel Jan Maria, 'The Relationship between the Treaty Rules and Community Measures for the Establishment and Functioning of the Internal Market – Towards a Concordance Rule', (2002) 39 *Common Market Law Review* 1303–1346.

Möstl, Markus, 'Grenzen der Rechtsangleichung im europäischen Binnenmarkt – Kompetenzielle, grundfreiheitliche und grundrechtliche Schranken des Gemeinschaftsgesetzgebers', (2002) *Europarecht* 318–350.

Mota Pinto, Paulo, 'Grundsätze von Informationspflichten im Fernabsatz nach geltendem EU-Vertragsrecht', in Schulze, Reiner/Ebers, Martin/Grigoleit, Hans Christoph (eds.), *Informationspflichten und Vertragsschluss im Acquis communautaire* (Tübingen, Mohr Siebeck, 2003), pp. 157–170.

Niemöller, Stefan, *Das Verbraucherleitbild in der deutschen und europäischen Rechtsprechung* (München, Beck Verlag, 1999).

Nihoul, Paul, 'L'interdiction d'ouvrir les magasins le dimanche est-elle contraire à la libre circulation des marchandises?', (1993) 1 *Journal des Tribunaux – Droit européen* 12–13.

Nihoul, Paul, 'Competition or regulation for multimedia', (1998) 22 *Telecommunications Policy* 207–218.

Nihoul, Paul, *La concurrence et le droit* (Colombelles, Éditions EMS, 2001).

Nihoul, Paul/Rodford, Peter B., *EU Electronic Communications Law – Competition and Regulation in the European Telecommunications Market* (Oxford, Oxford University Press, 2004).

Noah, Lars, 'The Imperative to Warn: Disentangling the "Right to Know" from the "Need to Know" About Consumer Product Hazards', (1994) 11 *Yale Journal on Regulation* 293–400.

Noll, Jürgen, 'European Community & E-commerce: Fostering Consumer Confidence', (2002) 9 *Electronic Communication Law Review* 207–219.

Nourissat, Cyril, 'Droit communautaire et forclusion biennale: l'étrange effet utile de l'esprit de la directive «clause abusive»!', (2003) 179 *Recueil Dalloz de doctrine, de jurisprudence et de la législation : Cahier droit des affaires* 486–490.

De Nayer, Benoît, 'The Consumer in Electronic Commerce: Beyond Confidence', in Wilhelmsson, Thomas / Tuominen, Salla / Tuomola, Heli (eds.), *Consumer Law in the Information Society* (The Hague, Kluwer Law International, 2001), pp. 117–125.

Ohly, Ansgar, *Richterrecht und Generalklausel im Recht des unlauteren Wettbewerbs* (Köln, Carl Heymanns Verlag, 1997).

Ohly, Ansgar, 'Die Bemühungen um eine Rechtsvereinheitlichung auf EU-Ebene von den Anfängen bis zur Richtlinie über irreführende Werbung von 1984', in Schricker, Gerhard and Henning-Bodewig, Frauke (eds.), *Neuordnung des Wettbewerbsrechts* (Baden-Baden, Nomos Verlagsgesellschaft, 1998/99), pp. 69–80.

Ohly, Ansgar, 'Herkunftslandprinzip und Kollisionsrecht', (2001) 50 *Gewerblicher Rechtsschutz und Urheberrecht, Internationaler Teil* 899–908.

Oliver, Peter and Roth, Wulf-Henning, 'The Internal Market and the Four Freedoms', (2004) 41 *Common Market Law Review* 407–441.

O'Rourke, Raymond, *European Food Law* (2nd ed., Bembridge/Isle of Wight, Palladian Law Publishing, 2001).

O'Shaughnessy, John, *Competitive Marketing: A Strategic Approach* (3rd ed., London/New York, Routledge, 1995).

Oughton, David/Willett Chris, 'Quality Regulation in European Private Law', (2002) 25 *Journal of Consumer Policy* 299–328.

Paefgen, Walter G., 'Kollisionsrechtlicher Verbraucherschutz im Internationalen Vertragsrecht und europäisches Gemeinschaftsrecht', (2003) 11 *Zeitschrift für Europäisches Privatrecht* 266–294.

Perau, Guido, *Werbeverbote im Gemeinschaftsrecht: Gemeinschaftsrechtliche Grenzen nationaler und gemeinschaftsrechtlicher Werbebeschränkungen* (Baden-Baden, Nomos Verlagsgesellschaft, 1997).

Picod, Fabrice, 'Les fondements juridiques de la politique communautaire de protection des consommateurs', in Osman, Filali (ed.), *Vers un code européen de la consommation* (Bruxelles, Bruylant, 1998), pp. 73–85.

Pfeiffer, Thomas, 'Der Vertragsschluss im Gemeinschaftsrecht', in Schulze, Reiner/Ebers, Martin/Grigoleit, Hans Christoph (eds.), *Informationspflichten und Vertragsschluss im Acquis communautaire* (Tübingen, Mohr Siebeck, 2003), pp. 103–115.

Polanski, Paul Przemyslaw, 'A New Approach to Regulating Internet Commerce: Custom as a Source of Electronic Commerce Law', (2002) 9 *Electronic Communication Law Review* 165–205.

PriceWaterhouseCoopers/University of Utrecht/University of Tilburg, *Consumer Law and the Information Society*, (Amsterdam, August 2000, accessible via the website of the European Commission DG SANCO, http://europa.eu.int/comm/consumers/index_en.htm).
Pützhoven, Andreas, 'Harmonisierung des europäischen Verbraucherschutzrechts', (1999) 10 *Europäisches Wirtschafts- & Steuerrecht* 447–453.
Puurunen, Tapio, 'Choice of Law in European Business-To-Consumer Electronic Commerce – A Trail Out of a Political Impasse', (2003) 11 *Zeitschrift für Europäisches Privatrecht* 789–816.
Radeideh, Malek/Franck, Jérôme, 'France', in Micklitz, Hans-W./Keßler, Jürgen (eds.), *Marketing Practices Regulation and Consumer Protection in the EC Member States and the US* (Baden-Baden, Nomos Verlagsgesellschaft, 2002), pp. 76–95.
Radeideh, Malek/de Vrey, Rogier, 'Netherlands', in Micklitz, Hans-W./Keßler, Jürgen (eds.), *Marketing Practices Regulation and Consumer Protection in the EC Member States and the US* (Baden-Baden, Nomos Verlagsgesellschaft, 2002), pp. 237–266.
Rasmussen, Hjalte, *On Law and Policy in the European Court of Justice* (Dordrecht, Martinus Nijhoff Publishers, 1986).
Rasmussen, Hjalte, *The European Court of Justice* (Copenhagen, GradJura Publishers, 1998).
Reich, Norbert, 'From Contract to Trade Practices Law: Protection of Consumers' Economic Interests by the EC', in Wilhelmsson, Thomas (ed.), *Perspectives of Critical Contract Law* (Aldershot, Dartmouth, 1993), p. 55–105.
Reich, Norbert, 'The "November Revolution" of the European Court of Justice: Keck, Meng and Audi Revisited', (1994) 31 *Common Market Law Review* 459–492.
Reich, Norbert, 'Zur Theorie des Europäischen Verbraucherrechtes', (1994) 2 *Zeitschrift für Europäisches Privatrecht* 381–407.
Reich, Norbert, 'Competition Law and the Consumer', in Gormley, Laurence William (ed.), *Current and Future Perspectives on EC Competition Law* (The Hague, Kluwer Law International, 1997), pp. 127–137.
Reich, Norbert, *Bürgerrechte in der Europäischen Union* (Baden-Baden, Nomos Verlagsgesellschaft, 1999).
Reich, Norbert, 'Verbraucherpolitik und Verbraucherschutz im Vertrag von Amsterdam', (1999) 14 *Verbraucher und Recht* 3–10.
Reich, Norbert, 'Book review: Stefan Niemöller, Das Verbraucherleitbild in der deutschen und europäischen Rechtsprechung', (2000) 164 *Zeitschrift für das gesamte Handelsrecht und Wirtschaftsrecht* 433–438.
Reich, Norbert, 'Rechtsangleichung im Binnenmarkt – Marktöffnung oder Sozialschutz', (2001) 16 *Verbraucher und Recht* 203–206.
Reich, Norbert, 'Die Vorlagepflicht auf teilharmonisierten Rechtsgebieten am Beispiel der Richtlinien zum Verbraucherschutz', (2002) 66 *Rabels Zeitschrift* 531–552.
Reich, Norbert and Rörig, Ursula, 'Note on Case C-481/99 *Georg and Helga Heininger v Bayerische Hypo- und Vereinsbank AG*', (2002) 13 *Europäische Zeitschrift für Wirtschaftsrecht* 87–89.
Reich, Norbert and Micklitz, Hans-W., *Europäisches Verbraucherrecht* (4th ed., Baden-Baden, Nomos Verlagsgesellschaft, 2003).

Rekaiti, Pamaria and Van den Bergh, Roger, 'Cooling-Off Periods in the Consumer Laws of the EC Member States. A Comparative Law and Economics Approach', (2000) 23 *Journal of Consumer Policy* 371–407.

Rösler, Hannes, 'Europäische Integration durch Verbraucherschutz: Entwicklungsursachen und Beschränkungen', (2003) 18 *Verbraucher und Recht* 12–20.

Roth, Wulf-Henning, 'Note on Joined Cases C-267/91 and C-268/91 *Bernard Keck and Daniel Mithouard*', (1994) 31 *Common Market Law Review* 845–855.

Roth, Wulf-Henning, 'Transposing "Pointillist" EC Guidelines into Systematic National Codes – Problems and Consequences', (2002) 6 *European Review of Private Law* 761–776.

Roth, Wulf-Henning, 'The European Court of Justice's Case Law on Freedom to Provide Services: Is *Keck* Relevant?' in Adenas, Mads and Roth, Wulf-Henning (eds.), *Services and Free Movement in EU Law* (Oxford, Oxford University Press, 2002), pp. 1–24.

Roth, Wulf-Henning, 'Note on Case C-168/00 *Simone Leitner v TUI Deutschland GmbH & Co. KG*', (2003) 40 *Common Market Law Review* 937–951.

Rott, Peter, 'Informationspflichten in Fernabsatzverträgen in Fernabsatzverträgen als Paradigma für die Sprachenproblematik im Vertragsrecht', (1998) 98 *Zeitschrift für vergleichende Rechtswissenschaft* 382–409.

Rott, Peter, *Die Umsetzung der Haustürwiderrufsrichtlinie in den Mitgliedstaaten* (Baden-Baden, Nomos Verlagsgesellschaft, 2000).

Rott, Peter, 'Widerruf und Rückabwicklung nach der Umsetzung der Fernabsatzrichtlinie und dem Entwurf eines Schuldrechtsmodernisierungsgesetzes', (2001) 16 *Verbraucher und Recht* 78–87.

Rott, Peter, 'Minimum harmonisation for the completion of the Internal Market? The example of consumer sales law', (2003) 40 *Common Market Law Review* 1107–1135.

Sack, Rolf, 'Das Verbraucherleitbild und das Unternehmerleitbild im europäischen und deutschen Wettbewerbsrecht', (1998) 44 *Wettbewerb in Recht und Praxis* 264–269.

Sack, Rolf, 'Die Toshiba-Entscheidung des EuGH zur vergleichenden Werbung', (2002) 48 *Wettbewerb in Recht und Praxis* 363–367.

Salaün, Anne, 'Les transactions commerciales sur Internet', in Nihoul, Paul (ed.), *Telecommunications and broadcasting networks under EC law: the protection afforded to consumers and undertakings in the information society* (Köln, Bundesanzeiger Verlagsgesellschaft, 2000), pp. 103–129.

Scherer, Inge, '"Cold Calling" in der europäischen Rechtsvereinheitlichung', (2001) 47 *Wettbewerb in Recht und Praxis* 1255–1260.

Schlesinger, Rudolf B. (ed.), *Formation of Contracts – A Study of the Common Core of Legal Systems, Vol. I* (Dobbs Ferry, Oceana Publications, 1968).

Schmid, Gregor, *Freier Dienstleistungsverkehr und Recht des unlauteren Wettbewerbs, dargestellt am Beispiel der Telefonwerbung* (Köln, Carl Heymanns Verlag, 2000).

Schmitz, Bob, 'Advertising and Commercial Communications – Towards a Coherent and Effective EC Policy', (1993) 16 *Journal of Consumer Policy* 387–410.

Schotthöfer, Peter (ed.), *Handbuch des Werberechts in den EU-Staaten einschließlich Norwegen, Schweiz, Liechtenstein und USA* (2nd ed., Köln, Schmidt Verlag, 1997).

Schricker, Gerhard (ed.), *Recht der Werbung in Europa* (Baden-Baden, Nomos Verlagsgesellschaft, 1995, loose-leaf).

Schricker, Gerhard and Henning-Bodewig, 'Elemente einer Harmonisierung des Rechts des unlauteren Wettbewerbs in der europäischen Union', (2001) 47 *Wettbewerb in Recht und Praxis* 1367–1407.

Schroeder, Werner, 'Vom Brüsseler Kampf gegen den Tabakrauch – 2. Teil', (2001) 12 *Europäische Zeitschrift für Wirtschaftsrecht* 489–495.

Schulte-Nölke, Hans, 'Functions of Contracts in EC Private Law', in Schulze, Reiner/Ebers, Martin/Grigoleit, Hans Christoph (eds.), *Informationspflichten und Vertragsschluss im Acquis communautaire* (Tübingen, Mohr Siebeck, 2003), pp. 85–101.

Schulte-Nölke, Hans and Busch, Christoph W., 'Der Vorschlag der Kommission für eine Richtlinie über unlautere Geschäftspraktiken KOM (2003) 356 endg.', (2004) 12 *Zeitschrift für Europäisches Privatrecht* 99–117.

Schulze, Rainer / Schulte-Nölke, Hans / Jones Jackie (eds.), *A Casebook on European Consumer Law* (Oxford, Hart Publishing, 2002).

Schulze, Rainer and Schulte-Nölke, Hans, *Analysis of National Fairness Laws Aimed at Protecting Consumers in Relation to Commercial Practices*, (June 2003, accessible via the website of the European Commission DG SANCO, http://europa.eu.int/comm/consumers/index_en.htm).

Schweizer, Robert, 'Die „normative Verkehrsauffassung" – ein doppeltes Mißverständnis – Konsequenzen für das Leitbild des „durchschnittlich informierten, verständigen und aufmerksamen Durchschnittsverbrauchers', (2000) 102 *Gewerblicher Rechtsschutz und Urheberrecht* 923–933.

Schwintowski, Hans-Peter, 'Vertragsschluss für Waren und Dienstleistungen im europäischen Verbraucherrecht: Form- und Inhaltsbindungen kontra Privatautonomie', (2001) 12 *Europäisches Wirtschafts- & Steuerrecht* 201–208.

Schwintowski, Hans-Peter, 'Informationspflichten und effet utile', in Schulze, Reiner/Ebers, Martin/Grigoleit, Hans Christoph (eds.), *Informationspflichten und Vertragsschluss im Acquis communautaire* (Tübingen, Mohr Siebeck, 2003), pp. 267–290.

Segnana, Olivier, 'Le contentieux de la base juridique – A propos de l'annulation par la Cour de justice des C.E. de la directive relative à la publicité pour le tabac', (2001) 9 *Journal des Tribunaux – Droit européen* 9–15.

Seibt, Katrin, 'Das europäische Verbraucherleitbild – ein Abschied von der Verwechslungsgefahr als Rechtsfrage?', (2002) 104 *Gewerblicher Rechtsschutz und Urheberrecht* 465–472.

Simon, Denys, *Le système juridique communautaire* (2nd ed., Paris, Presses Universitaires de France, 1998).

Slot, Piet Jan, 'A Contribution to the Constitutional Debate in the EU in the Light of the Tobacco Judgment', (2002) 13 *European Business Law Review* 1–27.

Snell, Jukka, *Goods and Services in EC Law – A study of the Relationship Between the Freedoms* (Oxford, Oxford University Press, 2002).

Snell, Jukka and Adenas, Mads, 'Exploring the Outer Limits: Restrictions on the Free Movement of Goods and Services' in Adenas, Mads and Roth, Wulf-Henning (eds.), *Services and Free Movement in EU Law* (Oxford, Oxford University Press, 2002), pp. 67–139.

Snyder, Francis, 'The Effectiveness of European Community Law: Institutions, Processes, Tools and Techniques', (1993) 56 *Modern Law Review* 19–54.

Spätgens, Klaus, 'Irreführende Werbung – Verbraucherleitbild – Marktforschung', (2000) 46 *Wettbewerb in Recht und Praxis* 1023–1028.

Spaventa, Eleanor, 'From Gebhard to Carpenter: Towards a (Non-)Economic European Constitution', (2004) 41 *Common Market Law Review* 743–773.

Springer, Ralf, *Europäisches Gemeinschaftsrecht und die Auslegung des Irreführungsverbots gemäß § 3 UWG* (Baden-Baden, Nomos Verlagsgesellschaft, 1995).

Staudenmayer, Dirk, 'The Place of Consumer Contract Law Within the Process on European Contract Law', (2004) 27 *Journal of Consumer Policy* 269–287.

Stern, Klaus, *Das Staatsrecht der Bundesrepublik Deutschland, Band I: Grundbegriffe und Grundlagen des Staatsrechts – Strukturprinzipien der Verfassung* (2nd ed., München, C.H. Beck, 1984).

Straetmans, Gert, 'Note on Case C-124/97 *Markku Juhani Läärä et al. v Kihlakunnansyyttäjä (Jyväskylä) et al.* and Case C-67/98 *Questore di Verona v Diego Zenatti*', (2000) 37 *Common Market Law Review* 991–1005.

Straetmans, Gert, 'Note on Case C-6/01 *Anomar et al. v Estado português*, Case C-243/01 *Criminal proceedings against Piergiorgio Gambelli et al.*, and Case C-42/02 *Diana Elisabeth Lindman*', (2004) 41 *Common Market Law Review* 1409–1428.

Strassner, Stefan, *Verbraucherinformationsrecht: rechtliche Grundlagen und rechtsökonomische Aspekte* (Saarbrücken, ÖR-Verlag, 1992).

Stuyck, Jules, 'The legal control of unfair advertising in Belgium', in Balate, Eric (ed.), *Unfair advertising and comparative advertising – Publicité déloyale et publicité comparative*, (Brussels, Story-Scientia, 1988), pp. 111–133.

Stuyck, Jules, 'Observations: L'arrêt Keck et Mithouard (vente à perte) et ses conséquence sur la libre circulation des marchandises', (1994) 30 *Cahiers de droit européen* 431–458.

Stuyck, Jules, 'Gambling and Sales Promotion in the EU', in Micklitz, Hans-W. (ed.), *Rechtseinheit oder Rechtsvielfalt in Europa: Rolle des Verbraucherrechts in der EG und in den MOE-Staaten* (Baden-Baden, Nomos Verlagsgesellschaft, 1996), pp. 331–430.

Stuyck, Jules, 'Minimum harmonisation in the field of consumer law', in Krämer, Ludwig and Micklitz, Hans-W. and Tonner, Klaus (eds.), *Law and diffuse interests in the European legal order: Liber amicorum Norbert Reich* (Baden-Baden, Nomos Verlagsgesellschaft, 1997), pp. 279–289.

Stuyck, Jules, 'European consumer law after the Treaty of Amsterdam: Consumer Policy in or beyond the Internal Market?', (2000) 37 *Common Market Law Review* 367–400.

Stuyck, Jules, 'Gourmet : une nouvelle brèche dans la jurisprudence « Keck » ?', (2001) 37 *Cahiers de droit européen* 683–705.

Stuyck, Jules, 'The consumer and European competition policy in the past and in the next decade', (2002) 18 *Tijdschrift voor Consumentenrecht* 154–160.

Temple Lang, John, 'Legal Certainty and Legitimate Expectations as General Principles of Law', in Bernitz, Ulf and Nergelius (eds.), *General Principles of European Community Law* (The Hague, Kluwer Law International, 2000), pp. 163–184.

Tesauro, Giuseppe, 'The Community's Internal Market in the light of the Recent Case-law of the Court of Justice', (1995) 15 *Yearbook of European Law* 1–16.

Thünken, Alexander, 'Die EG-Richtlinie über den elektronischen Geschäftsverkehr und das internationale Privatrecht des unlauteren Wettbewerbs', (2001) *Praxis des Internationalen Privat- und Verfahrensrechts* 15–22.

Tinbergen, Jan, *International Economic Integration* (2nd ed., Amsterdam, Elsevier, 1965).

Tilleman, Bernard and Du Laing, Bart, 'Directives on Consumer Protection as a Suitable Means of Obtaining a (More) Unified European Contract Law?', in Grundmann, Stefan and Stuyck, Jules (eds.), *An Academic Green Paper on European Contract Law* (The Hague, Kluwer Law International, 2002), p. 81–102.

Tridimas, Takis, *The General Principles of EC Law* (Oxford, Oxford University Press, 1999).

Twigg-Flesner, Christian/Weatherill, Stephen/Willett Chris, 'Law, Information and Product Quality. Introductory Remarks by the Editors of the Special Issue', (2002) 25 *Journal of Consumer Policy* 291–297.

Tunney, James, 'The Neglected Tension Between Disclosure of Information in Consumer and Competition Law Contexts', (2002) 25 *Journal of Consumer Policy* 329–343.

Ulen, Thomas S., 'Information in the Market Economy – Cognitive Errors and Legal Correctives', in Grundmann, Stefan/Kerber, Wolfgang/Weatherill, Stephen (eds.), *Party Autonomy and the Role of Information in the Internal Market* (Berlin, de Gruyter, 2001), pp. 98–129.

Ulmer, Eugen, *Das Recht des unlauteren Wettbewerbs in den Mitgliedstaaten der Europäischen Wirtschaftsgemeinschaft: Gutachten erstattet im Auftrag der Kommission der Europäischen Wirtschaftsgemeinschaft vom Institut für Ausländisches und Internationales Patent-, Urheber- und Markenrecht der Universität München – Band I Vergleichende Darstellung mit Vorschlägen zur Rechtsangleichung* (München, C.H. Beck Verlag, 1965).

Usher, John Anthony, *General Principles of EC Law* (London, Longman, 1998).

Usher, John Anthony, 'Note on Case C-376/98 *Germany v Parliament and Council (Tobacco Advertising)*', (2001) 38 *Common Market Law Review* 1519–1543.

Usher, John Anthony, 'Disclosure Rules (Information) as a Primary Tool in the Doctrine on Measures Having an Equivalent Effect', in Grundmann, Stefan/Kerber, Wolfgang/Weatherill, Stephen (eds.), *Party Autonomy and the Role of Information in the Internal Market* (Berlin, de Gruyter, 2001), pp. 151–161.

Van Huffel, Michel, 'Commercialisation à distance des services financiers: derniers développements d'une – déjà – longue histoire...', (2001) *Revue européenne de droit de la consommation* 295–340.

Vedder, Hans Hermann Bernard, *Competition Law and Environmental Protection in Europe – Towards Sustainability* (Groningen, Europa Law Publishing, 2003).

Vogelaar, Floris O. W. and Stuyck, Jules and van Reeken, Bart L. P. (eds.), *Competition Law in the EU, its Member States and Switzerland* (The Hague, Kluwer Law international, 2000).

de Vrey, Rogier W., 'Eerlijk is eerlijk: de consument voorop? – Het richtlijnvoorstel 'oneerlijke handelspraktijken' nader bezien', (2004) 20 *Tijdschrift voor Consumentenrecht* 2–11.

Vriesendorp-van Seumeren, Rolanda Maria, 'Grenzen aan het opleggen van informatieverplic htingen', (2002) 8 *Nederlands tijdschrift voor Europees recht* 183–185.

Wagner, Gerhard, 'The Economics of Harmonisation: The Case of Contract Law', (2002) 39 *Common Market Law Review* 995–1023.

Weatherill, Stephen, 'The Role of the Informed Consumer in European Community Law and Policy', (1994) 2 *Consumer Law Journal* 49–69.

Weatherill, Stephen, *Law and Integration in the European Union* (Oxford, Clarendon Press, 1995).

Weatherill, Stephen, 'The Evolution of European Consumer Law and Policy: From Well-Informed Consumer to Confident Consumer?', in Micklitz, Hans-W. (ed.), *Rechtseinheit oder Rechtsvielfalt in Europa: Rolle des Verbraucherrechts in der EG und in den MOE-Staaten* (Baden-Baden, Nomos Verlagsgesellschaft, 1996), pp. 423–471.

Weatherill, Stephen, 'After *Keck*: Some Thoughts on how to Clarify the Clarification', (1996) 33 *Common Market Law Review* 885–906.

Weatherill, Stephen, *EC Consumer Law and Policy* (London, Longman, 1997).

Weatherill, Stephen, 'Consumer Policy', in Craig, Paul/de Búrca, Graínne (eds.), *The Evolution of EU Law*, (Oxford, Oxford University Press, 1999).

Weatherill, Stephen, 'Recent case law concerning the free movement of goods: mapping the frontiers of market deregulation', (1999) 36 *Common Market Law Review* 51–85.

Weatherill, Stephen, 'The European Commission's Green Paper on European Contract Law: Context, Content and Constitutionality', (2001) 24 *Journal of Consumer Policy* 339–399.

Weatherill, Stephen, 'Justifying Limits to Party Autonomy in the Internal Market – EC Legislation in the Field of Consumer Protection', in Grundmann, Stefan/Kerber, Wolfgang/ Weatherill, Stephen (eds.), *Party Autonomy and the Role of Information in the Internal Market* (Berlin, de Gruyter, 2001), pp. 171–196.

Weatherill, Stephen, 'The Commission's Options for Developing EC Consumer Protection and Contract Law: Assessing the Constitutional Basis', (2002) 13 *European Business Law Review* 497–515.

Weatherill, Stephen, 'Can There Be Common Interpretation of European Private Law?', (2002) 31 *Georgia Journal of International and Comparative Law* 139–166.

Weatherill, Stephen, *Cases and materials on EC law* (6th ed., Oxford, Oxford University Press, 2003).

Weatherill, Stephen, 'European Contract Law: Taking the Heat Out of Questions of Competence', (2004) 15 *European Business Law Review* 23–32.

Weatherill, Stephen, 'Why Object to the Harmonization of Private Law by the EC?', (2004) 8 *European Review of Private Law* 633–660.

Weatherill, Stephen and Beaumont, Paul, *EU Law* (3rd ed., London, Penguin Books, 1999).

Weinand, Armin, *Europarecht und Recht gegen den unlauteren Wettbewerb* (Baden-Baden, Nomos Verlagsgesellschaft, 1998).

Westphal, Dietrich, 'Media Pluralism and European Regulation', (2002) 13 *European Business Law Review* 459–487.

Weyer, Hartmut, *Freier Warenverkehr und nationale Regelungsgewalt in der Europäischen Union* (Berlin, de Gruyter, 1997).

White, Eric L., 'In Search of the Limits to Article 30 of the EEC Treaty', (1989) 26 *Common Market Law Review* 235–280.

Wiebe, Andreas, 'Die „guten Sitten" im Wettbewerb – eine europäische Regelungsaufgabe', (2002) 48 *Wettbewerb in Recht und Praxis* 283–293.

Wilhelmsson, Thomas, 'Questions for a Critical Contract Law – and a Contradictory Answer: Contract as a Social Cooperation', in Wilhelmsson, Thomas (ed.), *Perspectives of Critical Contract Law* (Aldershot, Dartmouth, 1993), p. 9–52.

Wilhelmsson, Thomas, 'Jack-in-the-box Theory of European Community Law', in Krämer, Ludwig and Micklitz, Hans-W. and Tonner, Klaus (eds.), *Law and diffuse interests in the European legal order: Liber amicorum Norbert Reich* (Baden-Baden, Nomos Verlagsgesellschaft, 1997), pp. 177–194.

Wilhelmsson, Thomas, 'Consumer Law and the Environment: From Consumer to Citizen', (1998) 21 *Journal of Consumer Policy* 45–70.

Wilhelmsson, Thomas, *Is There a European Consumer Law – and Should there Be One?* (Rome, Centro di studi e ricerche di diritto comparato e straniero, 2000).

Wilhelmsson, Thomas, 'The Consumer's Right to Knowledge and the Press', in Wilhelmsson, Thomas / Tuominen, Salla / Tuomola, Heli (eds.), *Consumer Law in the Information Society* (The Hague, Kluwer Law International, 2001), pp. 367–384.

Wilhelmsson, Thomas, 'Private Law Remedies against the Breach of Information Requirements of EC Law', in Schulze, Reiner/Ebers, Martin/Grigoleit, Hans Christoph (eds.), *Informationspflichten und Vertragsschluss im Acquis communautaire* (Tübingen, Mohr Siebeck, 2003), pp. 245–265.

Wilhelmsson, Thomas, 'The Abuse of the "Confident Consumer" as a Justification for EC Consumer Law', (2004) 27 *Journal of Consumer Policy* 317–337.

Wilhelmsson, Thomas, 'Contract Law Enforcement of Provisions on Marketing: The solution of the Consumer Sales Directive', in Collins, Hugh (ed.), *The Forthcoming EC Directive on Unfair Commercial Practices* (The Hague, Kluwer Law International, 2004), pp. 223–240.

Wissink, Mark Hendrik, *Richtlijnconforme interpretatie van burgerlijk recht* (Deventer, Kluwer, 2001).

Woods, Lorna and Scheuer, Alexander, 'Advertising Frequency and the Television Without Frontiers Directive', (2004) 29 *European Law Review* 366–384.

Wolf, Manfred, 'Party Autonomy and Information in the Unfair Contract Terms Directive', in Grundmann, Stefan/Kerber, Wolfgang/Weatherill, Stephen (eds.), *Party Autonomy and the Role of Information in the Internal Market* (Berlin, de Gruyter, 2001), pp. 313–330.

Wurmnest, Wolfgang, 'Common Core, Grundregeln, Kodifikationsentwürfe, Acquis-Grundsätze – Ansätze internationaler Wissenschaftlergruppen zur Privatrechtsvereinheitlic hung in Europa', (2003) 11 *Zeitschrift für Europäisches Privatrecht* 714–744.

Youngs, Raymond, *English, French and German Comparative Law* (London, Cavendish Publishing, 1998).

Zweigert, Konrad and Kötz, Hein, *Introduction to Comparative Law* (3th ed., Oxford, Oxford University Press, 1998).

Table of Cases

Court of Justice

Court of First Instance

High Court of England and Wales (Queen's Bench Division)